Zhuangzi and the Happy Fish

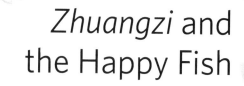

Zhuangzi and the Happy Fish

ROGER T. AMES
TAKAHIRO NAKAJIMA

UNIVERSITY OF HAWAI`I PRESS   *HONOLULU*

© 2015 University of Hawai`i Press
All rights reserved
Printed in the United States of America

20 19 18 17 16 15   6 5 4 3 2 1

Library of Congress Cataloging-in-Publication Data

Zhuangzi and the happy fish / edited by Roger T. Ames and Takahiro Nakajima.
        pages   cm
Includes index.
ISBN 978-0-8248-4683-1 (cloth)— ISBN 978-0-8248-4684-8 (alk. paper)
1. Zhuangzi.   2. Taoist philosophy.   3. Philosophy.   I. Ames, Roger T., editor.
II. Nakajima, Takahiro, editor.
BL1900.C576Z4945 2015
299.5'1482—dc23
2014033413

University of Hawai'i Press books are printed on
acid-free paper and meet the guidelines for permanence
and durability of the Council on Library Resources.

Designed by Milenda Nan Ok Lee

For two more happy fish:

Shinji Kajitani and Masato Ishida

Contents

Introduction

This book—like so many good things—began in a classroom. With the generous support of the Uehiro Foundation on Ethics and Education, we were able to convene the first meeting of the University of Tokyo–University of Hawaiʻi (UTUH) Residential Institute for Comparative Philosophy in August 2012 at the East-West Center on the University of Hawaiʻi campus. Our teaching team included five professors from UT and UH (Kobayashi Yasuo, Takahiro Nakajima, Kajitani Shinji, Ishida Masato, and Roger T. Ames), and the participants included some thirty graduate students from the two institutions with an additional ten international scholars. In addition to hosting a series of thematic lectures, our mission as faculty was to introduce our participants to a close reading of original texts in Chinese and Japanese philosophy, a skill that is deemed essential for every student in our comparative philosophy programs.

During the UTUH institute it became apparent that we needed to establish an interpretive historical and intellectual context in the reading of canonical texts. Specific Japanese, Confucian, and Daoist readings were used to demonstrate the argument that locating the discussion within such a context makes a profound difference in the possibilities available for interpretation and allows the reader to avoid a pernicious cultural reductionism at least to some degree. A further argument was that such an interpretive context is a concern not only for Western students of Asian culture but also for contemporary Chinese and Japanese students who in their studies have appropriated a philosophical lens heavily colored by Western theoretical and conceptual assumptions.

THE *ZHUANGZI*

Of course, in a close reading of classical Chinese texts, the *Zhuangzi* seems invariably to be the text of choice for students and at the same time one of the most challenging of the canons for their teachers. The *Zhuangzi* is traditionally coupled with the *Daodejing* (or *Laozi*) as one of the two most seminal texts associated with classical Daoist philosophy that is often referred to simply as the Lao-Zhuang lineage. Beyond these two seminal texts, we might also include the Han dynasty's syncretic *Huainanzi* (c. 140 BCE) and the *Liezi,* a text compiled into its present form around the fourth century CE, as constituting the traditional corpus of philosophical Daoism.

As a canonical text, the *Zhuangzi* for the most part addresses the project of personal realization and is only derivatively and incidentally concerned with social and political order. In many ways the *Zhuangzi* establishes a unique literary and philosophical genre of its own, and although clearly the work of many hands, it is still one of the finest pieces of literature in the classical Chinese corpus. It uses every trope and literary device available to set off rhetorically charged flashes of insight into the freest and most unrestrained way to live one's life without being constrained by often oppressive conventional values and judgments. And as the essays collected in this volume demonstrate all too well, the *Zhuangzi* as a text and as a philosophy is never one thing; indeed, as we will see, it always has been and continues to be many different things to many different people.

In keeping with the fact that the inspiration for this volume emerged from an international collaboration in comparative philosophy, the editors have consciously selected the essays to be included herein from the broadest possible compass of world scholarship on this seminal text. Many of the essays have been written especially for this volume and are being published for the first time. Some of the chapters have come to print before in other world languages—Chinese, Japanese, German, and Spanish— and have been translated specifically for this anthology. Moreover, several of them have been previously published in English-language forums over the past several decades and have been selected for the quality of their arguments as they have engaged each other in formulating their very different positions.

This volume of essays constitutes an attempt by a range of different scholars to provide their own exegesis of one of the most frequently rehearsed anecdotes of the *Zhuangzi* that appears at the end of the "Autumn Floods (*qiushui* 秋水)" chapter and that is often referred to as "the Happy Fish debate." Perhaps the first step in establishing an interpretive context for this text is to identify, to the extent possible, its dramatis personae: Zhuangzi, Huizi—and the fish as well.

WHO IS ZHUANG ZHOU 莊周 (369-286 BCE)?

The primary source of information we have about Zhuang Zhou is a series of anecdotes included in a book that bears his name, the *Zhuangzi*.[1] This text includes several vignettes found primarily in the "Outer" and "Miscellaneous Chapters," including a short bibliographical sketch in the curious and uncharacteristically judgmental chapter that closes this work, "All under the Heavens" (*tianxia* 天下). We might begin from the only source beyond the *Zhuangzi* itself: a brief account given in the *Records of the Grand Historian* by Sima Qian (145?–89? BCE), who, in compiling this unofficial history, typically drew on whatever sources were available in the court archives of the early Han dynasty:

> Zhuangzi was a man of the Meng district in the state of Song (modern Anhui or Henan province) and was named Zhou. He once served as a minor official in the Lacquer Garden in Meng and was a contemporary of King Hui of Liang (r. 370-319 BCE) and King Xuan of Qi (r. 319–301 BCE). In his scholarship he was broad and eclectic, though the roots of his teachings trace back to Laozi. Thus, in his oeuvre of over 100,000 words, he in large measure relied upon the metaphorical and the allegorical.[2] He wrote chapters such as "The Old Fisherman," "Robber Zhi," and "Rending Satchels" to satirize the followers of Confucius and to shed light on the teachings of Laozi.[3] Other chapters such as "Leigui Xu" [presumably "Xu Wugui"] and "Gengsangzi" are all fictitious and have no historical provenance. Zhuang Zhou was good at formulating his ideas in words and at rhetorical flare and was adroit at making connections and characterizing situations that he would then marshal in attacking and refuting the teaching of the Confucians and the Mohists. Not even the most distinguished and erudite scholars of the age could

defend themselves against his prowess. His torrents of language surged forth without constraint with no other purpose than to entertain himself; thus no one from the king and his high ministers on down were able to turn his words to their own account.

King Wei of Chu (r. 339–329 BCE) had heard that Zhuang Zhou was a person of high character and ability and sent an emissary with handsome gifts to invite him to his court, promising to make him his Prime Minister. Zhuang Zhou laughed out loud and said to the emissary from Chu: "A thousand weight of cash would be a substantial gain for me and the title of Prime Minister is certainly a high and much respected office. But have you not seen the ox used in the southern suburban sacrifice? It is groomed and fed for many years, clad richly with embroidered cloth, and then at last is led into the Grand Ancestral Hall. On reaching this moment, even if the ox would gladly change places with a stray piglet, how could it manage this? Be gone with you! Don't you get me dirty! I would rather wallow happily in a muddy ditch than be hogtied by some ruler. Happily doing as I please, I will never—to the end of my days—serve in office."[4]

This biographical notice makes much of perhaps the most salient characteristics of the *Zhuangzi* text: its authors' evident mastery of the written language and their power of expression, as well as the difficulty commentators have had in classifying the often metaphorical and allegorical stories that constitute this text as being committed to any one specific and identifiable philosophical position or outlook. The biography claims that Zhuang Zhou's philosophical position is rooted in the teachings of Laozi and that his text has to be read as a deliberate challenge to the doctrines of the Mohists and the Confucians, which were circulating at the time of its compilation.

Sima Qian's short account concludes with a version of one of the stories told in the *Zhuangzi* about its own ostensive author.[5] Indeed, it is from these same anecdotes that we can glean our clearest profile of a Zhuangzi persona. Still, we would do well to read the larger-than-life portrait we are able to piece together from these stories as a literary construct that conveys recommendations for a particular style of living rather than as an episodic account of the narrative and career of a historical figure.

The exaggerated caricature of Zhuangzi we can cobble together from these anecdotes is consistent with the story told in this biographical sketch, which portrays him as an impoverished yet highly educated and distinguished scholar who, by the considerable literary and philosophical talents that are evidenced in his extensive writings, becomes known to those in the highest seats of authority. Although these kings and princes would reward him handsomely for his services, he is unwilling to stoop so low as to accept high office and, rebuking them roundly, refuses to be compromised and co-opted by their promises of wealth and power. He instead chooses to continue his nomadic and philosophically promiscuous existence, which can perhaps be best captured in the much-repeated aspiration for a life of "carefree and easy wandering" (*xiaoyaoyou* 逍遙遊).

Another possible avenue for bringing the person of Zhuang Zhou into clearer focus would be to rely on the traditional assumption that the seven "Inner Chapters" of the text were by his own hand and then on that basis to lift out of these same pages a "philosophical" biography. We might be encouraged in this project by Steve Coutinho's report on the conventional understanding of the authorship of the *Zhuangzi* as a text:

> Despite frequent differences of opinion there is, surprisingly, a great deal of agreement with regard to the classification of major portions of the text. It is generally agreed for example that the historical Zhuangzi was in all probability the author of the first seven chapters, which have come to be known as the *Inner Chapters*, while the rest, divided into the *Outer* (8–22) and *Miscellaneous Chapters* (23–33), is taken to have been written by followers, and others, from the time of his death to at least the founding of the Qin empire.[6]

This traditional attribution of the Inner Chapters of the *Zhuangzi* to one author has recently been contested by David McCraw, who chooses to use quantitative methods and statistical measurements to analyze the structure of the text rather than an appeal to the more subjective and speculative method of assessing differences in ideas to argue that these Inner Chapters are themselves a patchwork from the ink of many different authors:

> We have demonstrated that most likely many hands took part in forming Zz; indeed, allowing for later passages tacked onto various chapters, probably more than a dozen hands took part in forming the Inner Chapters alone. Does this mean we have to abandon the notion of a coherent "Zhuangzian" philosophy? Not necessarily; notions of "family resemblance" and the labors

of Zz's editors will still allow those so inclined to perceive coherence among its parts.[7]

Again, Coutinho takes McCraw up on this challenge to find philosophical coherence and a pattern of "family resemblances" amid the putative linguistic dissonance in claiming the following:

> [R]egardless of who wrote them, the *Inner Chapters* and passages attributed to followers of the *Inner Chapters* express a distinctive worldview and approach to life. Moreover, while there may be problems of consistency, as in any philosophical text, half the pleasure of reading such texts is precisely to come up with a coherent interpretation that plausibly resolves the apparent inconsistencies.[8]

Indeed, it is precisely the delight one finds in this search for one's own sense of coherence that has motivated the authors of this volume to proffer their various interpretations of the Happy Fish debate.

In the bibliographical chapter titled "All under the Heavens" at the end of the *Zhuangzi* we encounter a description not of the person of Zhuangzi per se but again of the flamboyant and unconstrained language in which his ideas are expressed:

> Shadowy and vast, it is shapeless; transforming, it is without constant horizon. Is this life or death? Do I emerge together with the heavens and earth? Do I journey forth with the spirits and gods? Ever so hazy, where do I go? Ever so obscure, where have I arrived? Everything is laid out before me and there is nothing worth returning to.
>
> The ancient art of the way lies in such language, and when Zhuang Zhou got wind of these questions, he delighted in them. Expressing himself in strange and hyperbolic language, in wild and uncanny words, in indecipherable and unbounded phrases, he was always a free spirit and unbiased in his opinions and never saw things from just one particular point of view. Watching a world sinking in turbidity before him, he could not speak to it in solemn language. He used his "tipping goblet words" for the steady flow of his writings, canonical words for authenticity, and metaphorical words to give him broad compass. He alone came and went with what is quintessential in the heavens and earth and yet did not look with arrogance on other things. Refraining from being judgmental, he dwelt among the common lot.

Though his writings hang together circuitously like a string of jade, they are harmless enough. And though his language is erratic and unrestrained, his pretenses and simulations are worth a second look. The capaciousness and solidity of these teachings make them inexhaustible. Above he wandered freely with the maker of all things, below he kept company with those who stand outside of life and death and for whom there is neither beginning nor end. With respect to the root of all things, he opened it out in its breadth and expanse and was unbridled in surveying its penetrating depths. With respect to the ancestor of all things, he could be said to be in tune with it and accommodating of it, following it to new heights. Even so, in his responsiveness to the process of transformation and in his unraveling of things, his understanding of them was inexhaustible, and in his approach he could not be deterred. So abstruse and obscure, his writings are unfathomable.[9]

It would seem that these early commentators are more comfortable in treating Zhuangzi as the language of an unmanageable and obscure text rather than as a person, and for good reason. These early accounts are dealing with the same problem that we are left with today. The Outer and Miscellaneous Chapters appear to be the work of later students of the *Zhuangzi,* who, attracted to the text by its brilliance and its allusiveness and inspired by it to find their own exaggerated, allegorical language, proffered their diverse and sometimes conflicted commentaries based on discernable themes they might have drawn from selected portions of the text. And this same commentarial narrative continues today. As we will see, a happy gaggle of the best scholars of our generation continue to participate in the hermeneutical unfolding of this text in their own way to offer markedly different accounts of what, if anything, would constitute the philosophical coherence of the *Zhuangzi.*

WHO IS HUI SHI 惠施 (380–305 BCE)?

But first an earlier voice in this continuing Zhuangzian saga: Hui Shih.

A good example of how establishing an interpretive context makes a difference in our reading of the canonical texts is the recent work by an international group of sinologists and comparative philosophers who have taken on the challenge of reinstating the *Mozi* as integral to the intellectual debates that flourished in the pre-Qin period: A. C. Graham, Robin D. S. Yates, David B. Wong, Chad Hansen, Chris Fraser, James Behuniak,

Carine Defoort, Nicolas Standaert, Dan Robins, Hui-chieh Loy, Ben Wong, Ian Johnston, and many more.[10] Although it would serve these scholars poorly to assume that they have a univocal interpretation of the Mohist doctrines and a shared understanding of the responses these teachings elicited from contemporaneous philosophers, they would at least be in agreement on registering a strong Mohist current in the prevailing intellectual tide of the pre-Qin period and on the claim that this Mohist current provoked a sharp response from both Daoist and Confucian rivals alike.

Lisa Raphals makes the compelling argument that the portraits of Hui Shi as he appears in the classical corpus are several and conflicted, and we would do well to respect the disparities of these representations without overwriting them with some contrived uniform identity.[11] In so doing, the pervasive presence of the sophist Hui Shi wandering through the pages of the *Zhuangzi* adds another layer of complexity to the philosophical milieu from which it emerged.

Few scholars would describe Hui Shi (or Huizi 惠子) as a Mohist. For example, A. C. Graham would argue that although Hui Shi resembles "the Mohists in defending universal love and condemnation of aggressive war," he would more closely associate him with the earlier sophists and paradox-mongers such as Gongsun Long 公孫龍 who "practice disputation (*bian* 辯) for its own sake"[12] in arguing against the commonsensical. Nonetheless, Graham perceives some alignment of Huizi with the Mohists: "The loss of almost all the writings of the sophists makes it impossible to judge how much the Mohists owed to the founders of disputation in the 4th century."[13]

The image that we have of Hui Shi as he appears in the many anecdotes of the *Zhuangzi* as Zhuangzi's faithful foil is fairly consistent, with the exception of the decidedly negative description of him as a wasted talent and bombastic bore provided in the bibliographical chapter, "All under the Heavens," which seems to be tagged on at the end of the *Zhuangzi*:

> Hui Shi was a man of many ideas, and his writings filled five carts, but his doctrines were unconventional and strange, and his teachings fell wide of the mark. . . . Hui Shi thought his sophistries to be a grand advance in the world of thought, bringing real clarity to the art of disputation. And all of the world's debaters shared his enjoyment in them. . . . These debaters responded to him with just such sophistries that continued inexhaustibly throughout their lives.

Huan Tuan and Gongsun Long were followers of these disputers. They could dazzle the hearts and minds of people and alter their views. But the limitation of these disputers was that even though they could triumph over others verbally, they would still fail to win over their hearts and minds. Hui Shi would daily exercise his wits in debating with others and was especially admired as being exceptional among the other disputers in the world—this was all that he accomplished. And so he took himself to be rhetorically the cleverest among this crowd. "Who can best me in this world?" he would say. He was the cock of the walk, but had no art.

In the south there was a curious fellow named Huang Liao, who would ask: Why doesn't the sky fall? Why doesn't the earth collapse? And where do the wind, rain, thunder, and lightning come from? Hui Shi, undaunted, would take him on, babbling without thinking and leaving nothing out in his ramblings. Talking without end in a bottomless abundance, when it seemed as though he was at last running short of things to say, he would pile on more bizarre assertions. He took what was contrary to be true and looked to make a name for himself in winning the argument. This is why he did not get on with ordinary people. Thin on virtue and thick on acquisitiveness, his was a dark and devious path. If we take a look at Hui Shi's abilities in the big scheme of things, they were nothing more than the buzzing of a mosquito or gnat. What was he good for?

To master one thing is commendable, and it might be said that the more value there is to it, the closer it is to the proper way. But Hui Shi was incapable of settling for this and never tired of scattering himself over everything so that in the end he had a reputation for no more than being a good debater. What a pity—that the considerable talents of Hui Shi were wasted and came to naught. Chasing after everything without turning back, he was like the voice trying to get the better of its echo or the body trying to outrun its shadow. How sad indeed![14]

Angus Graham, who spent a lot of time with the later Mohist Canons, reads them as in degree being derivative of these earlier sophists. He thus offers us a very different assessment of the ancient Huizi. Allowing that the author of this "All under the Heavens" vignette is discussing what is taken here to be "the one school that is entirely worthless, Hui Shih and the Sophists," Graham would blame this author for failing to take Huizi's proper measure: "This passage deriding Hui Shih *because* he is an original thinker remains our main sources for the little we know about his thought."[15] Indeed, the seemingly conflicting accounts of Hui Shi that Raphals has registered are taken by Graham to reflect the enormous scope and originality of his ideas:

> The sparseness of the remains of Hui Shih [Shi] is perhaps the most regrettable of all the losses in ancient Chinese literature, for everything recorded of him suggests that he was unique among the early thinkers for his breadth of talents and interests, a true Renaissance man. . . . How did a sophist become chief minister of the state of Wei? And how is it that we keep meeting this most successful man of the world in the company of that disreputable layabout Chuang-tzu [Zhuangzi], who mocks his rigid logic but laments him after his death as his only truly stimulating opponent?[16]

As we will learn later, praise for the characters found in the *Zhuangzi* and the ostensive philosophical commitments of these characters are frequently a reflection of the interpreters' own philosophical proclivities, and Graham in this regard seems to be no exception. Graham takes what is clearly a condemnation of Hui Shi's boundless verbosity in the biographical vignette translated earlier (which in substance is consistent with Graham's fuller rendering of this chapter in his own translation of the *Zhuangzi*) to be descriptive of "a further dimension missing from almost all thinkers of the classical period, a genuine curiosity about the explanation of natural phenomena."[17] On this basis, Graham translates this same passage into what seems to me to be commendation (rather than condemnation) for what Graham takes to be philosophical and scientific skills that he himself most admires:

> There was a strange man of the south called Huang Liao, who asked why heaven did not collapse or earth subside, and the reasons (*ku* [*gu*] 故) for wind, rain, and thunder. Hui Shih answered without hesitation, replied without thinking, had explanations for all the myriad things, never stopped explaining, said more and more and still thought he hadn't said enough, had some marvel to add.[18]

Thus, the answer to the question "Who is Hui Shi?" seems to depend on who is asking it.

WHO ARE THE FISH?

And then there are the fish. In this particular Happy Fish debate, the character "fast" (*shu* 儵) is used in the text as a variant of its cognate, *tiao* 鯈, which describes a small fish, requiring the addition of the generic character for "fish" (*yu* 魚) to give "fast" its reference. The text here seems to privilege the quality of action—"a darting-about kind of fish"—over the semantic specificity that would in fact identify the species of fish.

This same character, *shu* 儵, occurs as the personal name of the inadvertently thoughtless Lord of the "South Sea" (an association with water) in the *Zhuangzi*'s account of the killing of Lord Hundun, again referencing the abruptness in this case of his untoward action in drilling orifices in the amorphous "Hundun" or "Spontaneity": "The Lord of the South Sea was 'Fast (*shu* 儵),' the Lord of the North Sea was 'Sudden,' and the Lord of the Central Kingdom was Hundun."[19]

Fortunately, beyond this technical textual note, we can rely on the Franklin Perkins essay in this same volume to provide us with a clearer understanding of the important role that fish play in the *Zhuangzi*. Perkins begins by noting that although a full parade of insects and animals migrates through the text, fish in particular are the most prominent among these creatures, occurring in more than thirty passages. In interpreting the prominent role played by the fish, Perkins observes the following:

> The immediate importance of fish lies in the assumption that fish have a world and that this world is radically different from our own. . . . At the same time, insofar as fish are thought to have a world or a perspective, they have a status equal to that of human beings, whose own world or perspective has no privileged place in nature. In this sense, fish represent an equality or evenness across the most radical difference.[20]

Indeed, it is this compelling conclusion—that the *Zhuangzi* gives no special privilege to the human world—that has required us to give equal notice to the fish as a member of the cast of characters in the Happy Fish debate.

PREVAILING INTERPRETATIONS OF COHERENCE IN THE *ZHUANGZI*

Having introduced the original dramatis personae in this particular vignette, we now turn to the more recent additional cast of characters who continue to play their own particular roles in this never-ending story of interpreting.

Piggybacking on Harold Roth in the *Stanford Encyclopedia of Philosophy*, we wish to review some of the positions offered by a generation of Western comparative philosophers who have engaged each other in a continuing debate over whether Zhuangzi and his text should be classified as a skepticism, a relativistism, a perspectivistism, or, indeed, something else.[21] A pioneer in this effort is Chad Hansen, who has a self-conscious affinity with the loquacious but resolutely rigorous Zhuangzi, offering himself personally as a clear example of Zhuangzi's perspectival relativism by announcing with high praise that "Chuang Tzu's [Zhuangzi's] familiarity with and confident handling of the technical language of ancient Chinese semantics make it probable that he had the ancient Chinese equivalent of analytic philosophical training."[22] Indeed, in Roth's account, Hansen uses this language of "perspectival relativism" to argue that all discrimination and classification are relative to some changeable context of judgment. Since relative judgments necessarily yield only relative, conditioned knowledge, there is no perspective from which the world can be known to be objectively true. In Hansen's own words:

> Lacking any theoretical limit on possible perspectives, guiding systems of naming, we lack any limit on schemes of practical knowledge. No matter how much we advance and promote a practical guide, a way of dealing with things, there are things we will be deficient at. To have any developed viewpoint is to leave something out. This, however, is not a reason to avoid language and a perspective; it is the simple result of the limitless knowledge and limited lives.[23]

David B. Wong's own qualified relativism reads the *Zhuangzi* as offering a continuing seesawing between the confidence one might have in having acquired a grasp on genuine knowledge and a productive skepticism that requires us to continue the search:

The dialectic includes a stage of skeptical questioning of whatever one's current beliefs are, but the aim is not merely to undermine but to reveal something about . . . the world that is occluded by one's current beliefs. However, one is not allowed to rest content with the new beliefs but is led to question their comprehensiveness and adequacy precisely because they are suspected of occluding still something else about the world.[24]

Janghee Lee again has his own interpretation, reading the *Zhuangzi* as a radical kind of "naturalism" that rejects all human artifice as an offense against nature and spontaneity:

Zhuangzi represents Daoist "naturalism" in the late Warring States period. Naturalism denotes a unique Chinese worldview; it is based on neither a mechanical, impersonal notion of nature, nor a shamanistic "animated" one. "Nature" or "*tian*" is what produces all of the myriad things, including human beings; it provides human beings with the model or norm to follow, as well as being the source of morality. . . . Zhuangzi is a very radical "naturalist" in his rejection of any human activity as "falsity or fake (*wei* 偽)."[25]

In addition, P. J. Ivanhoe argues that Zhuangzi should not be read as a relativist at all because he clearly recommends a certain way of being in the world. And with respect to skepticism, although Zhuangzi was neither a "sense skeptic" nor an "ethical skeptic," we can say that he was both an epistemological skeptic about intellectual (in contrast to intuitive) knowledge and a language skeptic who doubted distinctions between right and wrong and the capacity of words to give full expression to the *dao*.

Ivanhoe argues contra Lee that Zhuangzi's "Heavenly" perspective, although underscoring the inherent value of everything in the world, does not therefore exclude the human point of view. Instead, "These passages, in which Zhuangzi argues for the Heavenly point of view, are better read as a form of therapy, designed to curb our terrible tendency toward self-aggrandizement. They are to remind us that we are part of a greater pattern within which we are simply one small part."[26]

Lisa Raphals finds that, although Zhuangzi uses skeptical methods, he is not committed to skeptical doctrines and thus does not advocate a "true skepticism." Zhuangzi's distinction between ordinary "small knowledge" (*xiaozhi* 小知) and an extraordinary, greater form of knowledge that he calls "illumination" (*ming* 明) is a claim that we have access to a higher plane of knowledge. Raphals concludes the following:

> While Zhuangzi does state unambiguously that language is the source of the false distinctions of the Ruists and Mohists, that statement is not in itself a skeptical doctrine. . . . Zhuangzi and Plato each presents a hierarchy of knowing that contrasts a kind of superior knowing, which is never precisely defined, with inferior "knowledges" that are discussed at great length. . . . In the *Zhuangzi,* the superior knowledge is *dazhi* "great knowing" and is identified with *ming* and *dao.*[27]

We can add Paul Kjellberg to our list of positions as the attribution of a species of Pyrrhonian rather than epistemic skepticism to Zhuangzi that, like Ivanhoe's interpretation, is "therapeutic" rather than "conclusive." In answer to the question, why should skeptical arguments be made?, Kjellberg would argue that "Sextus says they should, because suspension of judgment gives rise to peace of mind. Zhuangzi agrees, but for the different reason that uncertainty leads to a skillful and natural life."[28]

In characterizing his own position, Roth joins Lee Yearley in allowing that, in addition to elements of skepticism and relativism, Zhuangzi was also a mystic. Whereas Yearley argues for an "intraworldly mysticism," in which the goal is not union with some unchanging monistic principle but instead full participation in the natural world, Roth sees a "bimodal" mystical experience in Zhuangzi. Roth argues that the higher kind of knowledge posited by Raphals and the acceptance of intuitive knowledge allowed by Ivanhoe derive from a firm grounding in a meditative practice attested to in both the *Zhuangzi* and other texts of early Daoism. Roth calls this apophatic practice an "inner cultivation" that involves sitting quietly and systematically circulating the breath until mind and body become tranquil and the contents of consciousness gradually empty, thus ultimately providing the adept with a direct experience of *dao*.

And Steve Coutinho rejects the categories of mysticism, relativism, and skepticism, arguing instead for a pragmatic and existential interpretation of the *Zhuangzi*:

> I see the Zhuangzian worldview and way of life as a nature-oriented form of pragmatism involving mind-body discipline and cultivation of tranquility; it

is existential in spirit and comparable, but not identifiable, with the way of life recommended by the ancient Stoics.[29]

Indeed, Coutinho would read Zhuangzi as a pragmatic fallibilism rather than as any kind of skepticism:

> Fallibilism is sometimes confused with scepticism, but the fallibilist does not challenge our claim to know things, as does the sceptic. The fallibilist merely challenges our claim to know things with finality and certainty.[30]

However, Deborah H. Soles and David E. Soles argue against the attribution of perspectivalism, relativism, or skepticism to Zhuangzi as being fundamentally mistaken, maintaining that Zhuangzi's attacks on the concepts of truth and knowledge are better seen as a species of epistemological nihilism that rejects the concepts of truth, reality, and knowledge as ultimately meaningless:

> The man of far-reaching vision has no use for categories. The point is that *all* attempts at categorisation fail. And if all attempts at categorisation fail, to categorize a judgment as true, even true from a perspective, is to attempt what cannot be done, and it is to miss the whole point of Zhuangzi's nihilism. . . . Any attempt to use language in a declarative or assertoric manner will fall into the trap of classifying and discriminating. But a paradoxical use of words may allow one to "see" past the parameters of one's perspective. To be sure, this "seeing" cannot be judgmental; its content cannot be conceptualised; it cannot be described. And to even speak of an "ineffable reality" is to inject more content, as an "object" of this "seeing," than Zhuangzi wants. That is the *point* of the *Tao*.[31]

And so these contemporary scholars continue their hermeneutical quest as they take their seats on the seemingly endless carousel of the well-argued and textually grounded interpretations that have come before.

AND THE MERRY-GO-ROUND KEEPS ON TURNING

The authors of the essays in this volume on the Happy Fish debate join ranks with and make their own unique contributions to this evolving commentarial tradition, demonstrating that even within the bounds circumscribed by this one single Zhuangzian anecdote of just a few lines, the scope of the available interpretations is as boundless and conflicted as Zhuangzi's rhetorical style is purported to be in the several biographical sketches cited earlier.

The introductory essay is a happy reminiscence by distinguished Nobel laureate Hideki Yukawa about how his early childhood reading of the *Zhuangzi* and other philosophical canons has been an inspiration to him in revisioning assumptions that have guided professional thinking in elementary particle physics. Indeed, in the *Zhuangzi*'s Happy Fish debate he is able to find the two extremes offered by science itself. The first attitude insists on accepting only what has been proven, whereas the second gives us carte blanche in our speculations. His conclusion, of course, is that good science needs both attitudes but can only be found somewhere in between them.

In his essay "*Yuzhile*: The Joy of Fishes, or, The Play on Words," for example, Hans Peter Hoffmann offers a new, literary approach to what has truly become one of the most famous stories in the entire *Zhuangzi*. On the basis of a new philological interpretation of the expression *yuzhile* 魚之樂, coupled with his close, self-consciously literary rather than philosophical reading of the text, Hoffmann is committed to providing a novel interpretation of this anecdote without introducing assumptions or generating contradictions that do not fit with the *Zhuangzi* text as a whole.

In his chapter, "The Relatively Happy Fish," Chad Hansen argues that Hui Shi and Zhuangzi are fellow relativists but with different foci and conclusions. Hui Shi typically pushes his relativism to absurdity—radical monism or subjectivism. He starts with a relativist analysis and then applies his conclusions to knowledge or meaning *univocally*. In this exchange, Hui Shi challenges Zhuangzi's simple assertion that the fish swimming "free and easy" below them are "at leisure" by insisting that such a judgment can be made only from the fish's point of view. Zhuangzi snares him on the absurdity of his challenge and then points out how the relativity of knowledge is assumed in both Hui Shi's initial challenge and in Zhuangzi's claim about the fish. We know things from the outside *here,* not from the inside *there.* Hansen concludes that this illustrates Zhuangzi's greater focus on indexicals as the basis of his relativism and his consistency in applying it to epistemic norms as well as semantics and other social mores. For Hansen, this short dialogue illustrates how Zhuangzi's philosophical parables work and serves to demonstrate how a focus on philosophy of language can inform our interpretation of these stories.

Eske Janus Møllgaard in "Zhuangzi's Notion of Transcendental Life" argues that a strong sense of transcendence is expressed in Zhuangzi's notion of transcendental life, or the life of Heaven (*tian* 天) as opposed to the life of human beings (*ren* 人). He further insists that Zhuangzi's central notion of "wandering" (*you* 遊) must be understood against the background of this notion of transcendental life. Since such wandering is the setting for this debate about the happy fish, this dialogue must be read by reference to Zhuangzi's notion of a transcendental plane of experience. Møllgaard concludes that such an interpretation of the dialogue shows that Zhuangzi does not, as is often claimed, fall into naturalism.

Sham Yat Shing in his essay "Knowledge and Happiness in the Debate over the Happiness of the Fish" rehearses and critiques two articles found in recent issues of the Taiwan philosophy journal *Ehu* by contemporary scholars Pan Boshi and Chen Guimiao. Each of these scholars comes to the debate with a very different interpretation and set of arguments. In important respects they reveal very different approaches. Sham is able, after careful deliberation, to come away with real insight from these two essays, especially Chen's article, but also attempts to offer his own more capacious reading of the anecdote. Indeed, in his analysis of these two contributions Sham offers up nothing less than a clinic in rigorous philosophical analysis by formalizing the arguments offered and following them to their logical conclusions. But he does not stop there. He suggests that one way of approaching his debate is with philosophical rigor and the adjudication of arguments, a path taken by several of the contributors to this volume. The second way of reading the text is through an appreciation of a Zhuangzian transcendentalism that is reminiscent of the interpretation offered by Eske Møllgaard in the essay that immediately precedes this one in this volume.

In "The Relatively Happy Fish Revisited," Norman Y. Teng engages the Hansen essay by employing the logic more familiar to early Chinese thinkers developed in the "Lesser Pick" (or "Lesser Selection") of the later Mohist Canons as a methodological device to analyze the dialogue between Zhuangzi and Hui Shi. He argues that the logical terms and patterns of discourse expounded in the Lesser Pick provide us with a way of modeling in a suitably historical perspective the intricate dialectic of the reasoning in the dialogue. It is thus that Zhuangzi's final statement, which is notoriously recondite when viewed through the modern inferential frameworks, becomes a natural conclusion for the dialogue.

Kuwako Toshio in "Knowing the Joy of Fish: The *Zhuangzi* and Analytic Philosophy" locates this Happy Fish anecdote within the "other minds" debate, which has been a central theme of analytic philosophy over the recent century, taking into account the "other species" concerns expressed in the more recent philosophical literature by Thomas Nagel and Peter Singer. He then extends his concerns to contemporary discussions about access to "other cultures." Kuwako argues for a singular experience beyond a subjective perceptual demonstrability available only to some and which is called "the joy of fish." Such an experience is to be had in a particular situation where in this case the "I" encounters the fish at the Hao River.

In his essay, "Of Fish and Knowledge: On the Validity of Cross-Cultural Understanding," Zhang Longxi uses Zhuangzi's "happy fish" episode as a model for the acquisition of knowledge. He argues for the validity of a cross-cultural understanding that takes us beyond relativism and universalism. For Zhang, Zhuangzi's perspective also informs a critical reexamination of the Chinese rites controversy and the relativist insistence on untranslatability and helps open up our horizon for understanding that transcends linguistic and cultural differences.

Takahiro Nakajima in "*Zhuangzi* and Theories of the Other" builds on the Kuwako essay and provides an argument in which he is able to recover what he takes to be two different logics from Huizi and Zhuangzi. The logic of Huizi is "tautology," which absorbs the other into the self as an isolated subjectivity. Contrary to this, the logic of Zhuangzi is the logic of "proximity" as "that place" shared by the "I" (not the self) and others. If we follow the logic of proximity, the "joy of fish" is not an experience of the isolated self as subjectivity but is one coestablished in a fundamental passivity of the "I" and others who are put into "proximity." This in turn provides us with a different attitude toward the "others" that constitute our context.

In "Of Fish and Men: Species Difference and the Strangeness of Being Human in the *Zhuangzi*," Franklin Perkins locates the "happy fish" within the broader role of fish stories in the *Zhuangzi*. According to Perkins, fish play such a prominent role in the text because they are taken as having a perspective or world, but one that is decidedly different from our own. In this way, fish illustrate the limits of any perspective and what it means to be at home in a perspective (for better or worse). Interactions between human beings and fish thus provide various models for addressing the problems of communication across different perspectives, with stories of fishing providing one model and the story of the "happy fish" another. Perkins argues that the ways in which the *Zhuangzi* presents human beings as like and unlike fish help to illuminate the inevitable strangeness of being human.

In "The Happy Fish of the Disputers" Han Xiaoqiang argues the happy fish story addresses the difficulty that arises when analyzing the dialogue in terms of familiar patterns of inference and provides a reasoned explanation for its apparent oddness. Indeed, Han suggests that the dialogue becomes perfectly intelligible if it is read against the backdrop of the disputations practiced in ancient China. His contention is that the real purpose of the dialogue is to expose the fundamental unreliability of the disputers' logic by means of the logic itself.

Peng Feng with his "Fact and Experience: A Look at the Root of Philosophy from the Happy Fish Debate" asks this question: in this Happy Fish debate are the fish really happy, or is Zhuangzi experiencing the happy fish? After carefully scrutinizing Zhuangzi's text and surveying representatives of its vast commentaries, he argues that the debate can only allow for Zhuangzi's experience of the happy fish and cannot state with certainty that the fish are happy. For Peng, a philosophy based on fact would be only a philosophy of discourse, whereas a philosophy based on experience could provide a philosophy as a way of life. This story in the *Zhuangzi* is a testimony to the claim that traditional Chinese philosophy prefers life to discourse.

Hans-Georg Moeller, in "Rambling without Destination: On Daoist 'You-ing' in the World," discusses the prominent notion of *you* 遊 (to roam, to ramble) in the *Zhuangzi*'s Daoism as nothing less than a technical philosophical term. Based on a careful analysis of the meanings of this term in the text, two interpretations of the "Happy Fish" story emerge, one more "poetic," one more "prosaic." In accordance with the "prosaic" interpretation of the Happy Fish debate, Moeller endorses "*you*-ing" or "rambling on" as an entirely defensible philosophical method.

In the final essay, " 'Knowing' as the 'Realizing of Happiness' Here, on the Bridge, over the River Hao," Roger Ames argues for the need to set an interpretive context in the reading of canonical texts such as the *Zhuangzi*. He then explores what might be taken to be some pervasive assumptions that ground a general Daoist cosmology, beginning from what he calls a commitment to process and to a radical contextuality. He then tries to locate the example of *Zhuangzi*'s "Happy Fish" story within this cosmology as it is contested by the Mohists to determine what if any difference such an effort to register its context might make for the substance of our own interpretation. Indeed, a capacious epistemology that embraces both the processual nature of experience and its radical contextuality transforms "knowing" into a realizing of the happiness that is to be found in learning to be fully situated.

While editing this volume, we—Ames and Nakajima—have had the occasion to recall the happy event that inspired it—the 2012 UTUH Institute for Comparative Philosophy. Indeed, indelible memories of a truly novel experiment in higher education have come flooding back. It was with enormous satisfaction that, at the closing dinner of the institute, the faculty from both of our institutions—the University of Tokyo and the University of Hawai'i—found a long moment seemingly outside of time to sit down quietly and enjoy a glass of wine together and to contemplate the animated and happy philosophical discussions taking place among our students sitting at their various tables. We were keenly aware that something had happened in the summer of 2012 that would make a profound difference in the professional and personal lives of these bright young people and that somehow or other they, too, had found their way to *you* 遊 together on the bridge over the river Hao.

Roger T. Ames
Takahiro Nakajima

NOTES

1. Joseph Needham, *Science and Civilisation in China,* vol. 2 (Cambridge: Cambridge University Press, 1956), 35.

2. The present *Zhuangzi* is only about sixty thousand characters, but the present thirty-three-chapter volume was edited down from an earlier fifty-two-chapter text by Guo Xiang 郭象 (died c. 312).

3. The first two of these chapters purport to be a record in which Confucius is sorely undone in a debate in which he attempts to defend his ideas. The third chapter invokes themes such as getting rid of erudition as a distraction from what is spontaneous—a repeated injunction in the *Laozi.*

4. Sima Qian 司馬遷, *Records of the Grand Historian* (*Shiji* 史記) (Peking: Zhonghua shuju, 1959), 2143–2145: 莊子者，蒙人也，名周。周嘗為蒙漆園吏，與梁惠王、齊宣王同時。其學無所不闚，然其要本歸於老子之言。故其著書十餘萬言，大抵率寓言也。作漁父、盜跖、胠篋，以詆訿孔子之徒，以明老子之術。畏累虛、亢桑子之屬，皆空語無事實。然善屬書離辭，指事類情，用剽剝儒、墨，雖當世宿學不能自解免也。其言洸洋自恣以適己，故自王公大人不能器之。 楚威王聞莊周賢，使使厚幣迎之，許以為相。莊周笑謂楚使者曰：「千金，重利；卿相，尊位也。子獨不見郊祭之犧牛乎？養食之數歲，衣以文繡，以入大廟。當是之時，雖欲為孤豚，豈可得乎？子亟去，無污我。我寧游戲污瀆之中自快，無為有國者所羈，終身不仕，以快吾志焉。」

5. *Zhuangzi* 17 has a parallel story with the exception that the "Autumn Floods" chapter describes the plight of a three-thousand-year-old sacred tortoise preserved in an ornamented chest rather than that of a sacrificial ox awaiting its doom—situations similar in that both of these objects of reverence would gladly be elsewhere.

6. Steve Coutinho, *Zhuangzi and Early Chinese Philosophy: Vagueness, Transformation, and Paradox* (Aldershot, Hants: Ashgate, 2004), 35.

7. David McCraw, *Stratifying* Zhuangzi: *Rhyme and Other Quantitative Evidence* (Taipei: Institute of Linguistics, Academia Sinica, 2010), 47.

8. Steve Coutinho, *An Introduction to Daoist Philosophies* (New York: Columbia University Press, 2013), 203 note 8.

9. *Zhuangzi* 33: 芴漠無形，變化無常，死與生與！天地並與！神明往與！芒乎何之？忽乎何適？萬物畢羅，莫足以歸，古之道術有在於是者。莊周聞其風而悅之。以謬悠之說，荒唐 之言，無端崖之辭，時恣縱而不儻，不以觭見之也。以天下為沈濁，不可與莊語；以卮言為曼衍，以重言為真，以寓言為廣。獨與天地精神往來，而不敖倪於萬物，不譴是非，以與世俗處。其書雖瑰瑋而連犿無傷也，其辭雖參差而諔詭可觀。彼其充實不可以已，上與造物者遊，而下與外死生、無終始者為友。其於本也，宏大而 辟，深閎而肆；其於宗也，可謂稠適而上遂矣。雖然，其應於化而解於物也，其理不竭，其來不蛻，芒乎昧乎，未之盡者。

10. For a recently published summary of the ongoing scholarly research on Mohism and its corpus, see Carine Defoort and Nicolas Standaert, eds., *The Mozi as an Evolving Text: Different Voices in Early Chinese Thought* (Leiden: Brill, 2013).

11. Lisa Raphals, "On Hui Shi," in *Wandering at Ease in the Zhuangzi*, ed. Roger T. Ames (Albany: State University of New York Press, 1998), 143–161.

12. A. C. Graham, *Later Mohist Logic, Ethics and Science* (Hong Kong: Chinese University Press and School of Oriental and African Studies, University of London, 1978), 19.

13. Ibid., 61.

14. *Zhuangzi* 33: 惠施多方，其書五車，其道舛駁，其言也不中。。。 惠施以此為大觀於天下而曉辯者，天下之辯者相與樂之。。。 辯者以此與惠施相應，終身無窮。 桓團、公孫龍辯者之徒，飾人之心，易人之意，能勝人之口，不能服人之心，辯者之囿也。惠施日以其知，與人之辯，特與天下之辯者為怪，此其柢也。 然惠施之口談，自以為最賢，曰：「天地其壯乎！」施存雄而無術。南方有倚人焉，曰黃繚，問天地所以不墜不陷，風雨雷霆之故。惠施不辭而應，不慮而對，遍為 萬物說：說而不休，多而無已，猶以為寡，益之以怪。以反人為實，而欲以勝人為名，是以與眾不適也。弱於德，強於物，其塗隩矣。由天地之道觀惠施之能，其猶一蚉一虻之勞者也，其於物也何庸！夫充一尚可，曰愈貴，道幾矣！惠施不能以此自寧，散於萬物而不厭，卒以善辯為名。惜乎！惠施之才，駘蕩而不得，逐萬物而不反，是窮響以聲，形與影競走也。悲夫！

15. Graham, *Later Mohist Logic, Ethics and Science,* 376.

16. A. C. Graham, *Disputers of the Tao: Philosophical Argument in Ancient China* (La Salle, IL: Open Court, 1989), 76.

17. Ibid., 77.

18. Ibid.

19. 南海之帝為鯈，北海之帝為忽，中央之帝為渾沌。

20. Franklin Perkins, "Of Fish and Men: Species Difference and the Strangeness of Being Human in the *Zhuangzi*," in this volume.

21. Harold Roth, "Zhuangzi," *The Stanford Encyclopedia of Philosophy* (Fall 2008 edition), ed. Edward N. Zalta, http://plato.stanford.edu/archives/fall2008/entries/zhuangzi/.

22. See Hansen's website at http://www.philosophy.hku.hk/ch/zhuang.htm.

23. Ibid.

24. David B. Wong, "Chinese Ethics," *The Stanford Encyclopedia of Philosophy* (Spring 2013 edition), ed. Edward N. Zalta, http://plato.stanford.edu/archives/spr2013/entries/ethics-chinese/.

25. Janghee Lee, *Xunzi and Early Chinese Naturalism* (Albany: State University of New York, 2005), 15.

26. P. J. Ivanhoe, "Was Zhuangzi a Relativist?" in *Essays on Skepticism, Relativism, and Ethics in the* Zhuangzi, ed. Paul Kjellberg and P. J. Ivanhoe (Albany: State University of New York Press, 1996), 200.

27. Lisa Raphals, "Skeptical Strategies in the *Zhuangzi* and *Theatetus*," in Kjellberg and Ivanhoe, *Essays on Skepticism, Relativism, and Ethics in the* Zhuangzi, 35, 41.

28. Paul Kjellberg, "Sextus Empiricus, Zhuangzi, and Xunzi on 'Why Be Skeptical?'" in Kjellberg and Ivanhoe, *Essays on Skepticism, Relativism, and Ethics in the* Zhuangzi, 21.

29. Coutinho, *Introduction to Daoist Philosophies,* 83.

30. Coutinho, *Zhuangzi and Early Chinese Philosophy,* 139–140.

31. Deborah H. Soles and David E. Soles, "Fish Traps and Rabbit Snares: Zhuangzi on Judgment, Truth and Knowledge," *Asian Philosophy* 8, no. 3 (1998): 162–163.

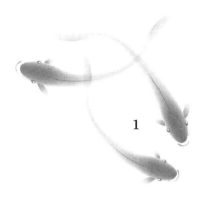

1

Zhuangzi

The Happy Fish

Hideki YUKAWA

Even before primary school, I had studied various Chinese classics. In practice, this means merely that I repeated aloud after my grandfather a version of the Chinese texts converted into Japanese. At first, of course, I had no idea what it meant. Yet, oddly enough, I gradually began to understand even without being told. Most of the works I studied were connected with Confucianism, but, with the exception of historical works such as *The Historical Records,* the Confucian classics held little interest for me. They dealt almost exclusively with moral matters, and I found them somehow patronizing.

Around the time I started middle school, I began to wonder whether the Chinese classics might not include other works that were more interesting, with a different way of thinking, and I searched my father's study with that in mind. I hauled out *Laozi* and *Zhuangzi* and began reading them and soon found that *The Book of Zhuangzi* in particular was interesting. I read it over and over again. I was only a middle-school boy, of course, and later I sometimes wondered whether I had really understood it and what exactly was so interesting to me.

Originally published in *Experimental Essays on Chuang-Tzu (Zhuangzi),* ed. Victor H. Mair (Honolulu: University of Hawai'i Press, 1983). Reprinted with permission. Romanization of Chinese terms was changed to the standard pinyin used throughout this anthology.

Four or five years ago, I was thinking one day about elementary particles when, quite suddenly, I recalled a passage from *Zhuangzi*. Freely translated, the passage in question, which occurs in the last section of the inner part of *Zhuangzi,* runs as follows:

> The Emperor of the South was called Shu, and the Emperor of the North, Hu. [Both characters mean "very fast," "to run swiftly," and the two characters together in Chinese signify something like "in a flash."] The Emperor of the Center was known as Hundun ("chaos"). One time, the emperors of the South and the North visited Hundun's territories, where they met with him. Hundun made them heartily welcome. Shu and Hu conferred together as to how they could show their gratitude. They said, "All men have seven apertures—the eyes, the ears, the mouth, and the nose—whereby they see, hear, eat, and breathe. Yet this Hundun, unlike other men, is quite smooth with no apertures at all. He must find it very awkward. As a sign of our gratitude, therefore, let us try making some holes for him." So each day they made one fresh hole, and on the seventh day Hundun died.

Why should I have recalled this fable? I have been doing research on elementary particles for many years, and by now more than thirty different types of such particles have been discovered, each of which presents something of a riddle. When this kind of thing happens, one is obliged to go one step further and consider what may lie beyond these particles. One wants to get at the most basic form of matter, but it is awkward if there prove to be more than thirty different forms of it; it is more likely that the most basic thing of all has no fixed form and corresponds to none of the elementary particles we know at present. It may be something that can be differentiated into all kinds of particles but has not yet done so in fact. Expressed in familiar terminology, this is probably a kind of "chaos." It was while I was thinking along these lines that I recalled the fable of *Zhuangzi*.

I am not the only one, of course, who is occupied with this question of a fundamental theory of elementary particles. Werner Karl Heisenberg in Germany, speculating on what lies beyond elementary particles, used the term *Urmaterie* (primordial matter). Whether one calls it "primordial matter" or "chaos" does not matter, but my ideas and Heisenberg's, although alike in some respects, also have their differences.

Recently I have found a renewed fascination with Zhuangzi's fable. I amuse myself by seeing Shu and Hu as something like the elementary particles. So long as they were rushing about freely nothing happened—until, advancing from south and north, they came together on the territory of Hundun, or chaos, where an event like the collision of elementary particles occurred. Looked at in this way, which implies a kind of dualism, the chaos of Hundun can be seen as the time and space in which the elementary particles are enfolded. Such an interpretation seems possible to me.

It may not make much sense, of course, to fiddle with the words of men of old in order to make them fit in with modern physics. Zhuangzi, who lived some twenty-three hundred years ago, almost certainly knew nothing of the atom. Even so, it is interesting and surprising that he should have had ideas that, in a sense, are very similar to those of people like me today.

Science developed mostly in Europe. Greek thought, it is often said, served in the broad sense as a basis from which all science was to develop. Erwin Schrödinger, who died in 1961, wrote that where there was no influence from Greek thought, science underwent no development. Historically speaking, this is probably correct. Even in the case of Japan since the Meiji Restoration, the direct influence of Greek thought may have been minor, yet indirectly at least it has provided a starting point for Japan's adoption of the science developed in Europe, and in this way we Japanese have inherited the Greek tradition.

Concerning what happened in the past I have nothing further to add. Yet when one considers the future, there is surely no reason for Greek thought to remain the only source for the development of scientific thought. The Orient produced all kinds of systems of thought. India is a good example, and the same is true of China. The ancient philosophies of China have not given birth to pure science. So far, this may have been true. But one cannot assume that it will remain so in the future as well. Today, just as in my middle-school days, Laozi and Zhuangzi are the two thinkers of ancient China for whom I feel the most interest and affection. In some ways Laozi's ideas are, I realize, more profound than those of Zhuangzi, but the precise meaning of what Laozi writes is far from easy to grasp. His use of words and phrasing is difficult, and even the commentaries often fail to elucidate the obscurities. What one gets, in the end, is only the framework of his thought. Zhuangzi, on the other hand, has all kinds of interesting fables; biting irony is balanced by a grand imagination. Under the surface exists a profound and consistent philosophy. Simply seen as prose, moreover, the work is incomparable. Many things in Zhuangzi,

I believe, stimulate the reader's mind and make it work better. The fable I quoted earlier was in itself almost certainly written not about a microcosm but about the great universe as a whole. Quite obviously, it deals neither with the infinitesimally small particles that form the basis of the natural world nor with the correspondingly small time and space in which they move. Yet in practice I have the feeling that in it one can dimly discern the microcosm that we have finally arrived at as a result of our studies of physics; one cannot dismiss the parallel as a coincidence. When one looks at things in this way, I believe that one cannot say that Greek thought is the only system of ideas that can serve as a basis for the development of science. The ideas of Laozi and Zhuangzi may appear to be essentially alien to Greek thought, yet they constitute a consistent, rationalistic outlook that holds much that is still worthy of respect today as a natural philosophy in its own right.

Where both Confucianism and the mainstream of Greek thought grant significance to the self-determined, voluntary actions of humankind, believing them to offer a valid prospect of realizing the ideals that we cherish, Laozi and Zhuangzi believe that the power of nature is overwhelmingly the greater, and that human beings, surrounded by forces beyond their control, are simply tossed now one way, now the other. During my middle-school days, I found this outlook extreme, yet was attracted to it. From my high-school days on, I began to find the idea of humanity's impotence intolerable, and for a long time I stayed away from the philosophy of Laozi and Zhuangzi. Yet all the while I cherished at the back of my mind a suspicion that, however unpalatable it might be for human beings, their ideas harbored an incontrovertible truth.

Laozi has a passage that runs as follows: "Heaven and Earth are without compassion; they see all things as straw dogs. The wise ruler is without compassion; he sees the common people as straw dogs." The brevity and the air of finality are typical of Laozi. Zhuangzi, on the other hand, prefers attractive metaphors such as the following:

A certain man was afraid of his own shadow and loathed his own footprints. So he started running, thinking to rid himself of them. But the oftener he raised his feet as he ran, the greater the number of his footprints became; and however fast he ran, still his shadow followed him. Telling himself that he was still not going fast enough, he ran faster and faster without stopping, until finally he exhausted his strength and dropped dead. Foolish man: if he had stayed in the shade, he would have had no shadow; if he had been still, there would have been no footprints.

The outlook expressed here is without doubt fatalistic—a mode of thinking usually described as "Oriental"—but it is far from irrational. Indeed, for us who, with the advance of scientific civilization, find ourselves, ironically enough, increasingly hard pressed by time, the story contains an uncomfortable home truth.

Half my mind revolts against this outlook, and half of it is attracted by it, which is precisely why it remains forever in my memory. Books make their appeal in many different ways, but I am particularly fond of the kind of work that creates a world of its own in which, if only for a short time, it succeeds in immersing the reader. *Zhuangzi* for me ranks as a typical example of that type of book.

People are constantly coming and asking me to write some words for them on the traditional strip of paper used for the purpose or to do a piece of calligraphy for them to frame. In the former case, I can usually get by with a poem of my own, but with a request for calligraphy—where some suitable short phrase from the classics is usual—I have trouble finding something suitable. In some cases recently, though, I have been writing the three Chinese characters that mean, literally, "know," "fish," and "pleasure." When I do so, I am invariably asked to explain the meaning. The phrase comes, in fact, from the seventeenth chapter, "The Autumn Floods," of *The Book of Zhuangzi*. The general meaning of the original passage is as follows:

One day, Zhuangzi was strolling beside the river with Huizi. Huizi, a man of erudition, was fond of arguing. They were just crossing a bridge when Zhuangzi said, "The fish have come up to the surface and are swimming about at their leisure. That is how fish enjoy themselves." Immediately Huizi countered this with: "You are not a fish. How can you tell what a fish enjoys?" "You are not me," said Zhuangzi. "How do you know that I can't tell what a fish enjoys?" "I am not you," said Huizi triumphantly. "So of course I cannot tell about you. In the same way, you are not a fish. So you cannot tell a fish's feelings. Well—is my logic not unanswerable?" "Wait, let us go back to the root of the argument," said Zhuangzi. "When you asked me how I knew what a fish enjoyed, you admitted that you knew already whether I knew or not. I knew, on the bridge, that the fish were enjoying themselves."

This conversation, which looks rather like a Zen question-and-answer session, is in fact very different. Zen always carries the argument to a point beyond the reach of science, but the exchange between Zhuangzi and Huizi can be seen as an indirect comment on the question of rationalism and empiricism in science. The logic of Huizi's manner of arguing seems to be far better throughout than Zhuangzi's, and the refusal to accept anything that is neither well defined nor verifiable, such as the fish's enjoyment, is, of course, closer to the traditional scientific attitude. Nevertheless, although I am a scientist myself, I am more in sympathy with what Zhuangzi wanted to imply.

Very generally speaking, scientists' ways of thinking lie somewhere between two extremes—between the outlook that will not believe anything that is not verified and the outlook that will discount nothing that was not verified not to exist or not to have happened. If all scientists had clung to either one of these extremes, science as we know it today could hardly have come into being. Even in the nineteenth century, much less in the time of Democritus, there was no direct proof of the existence of the atom. Despite this, the scientists who worked on the assumption that atoms existed achieved a far deeper and broader perception of the natural world than those who sought to understand it without such an idea. The history of science makes it absolutely clear that the attitude that will not accept anything that is not already proven is too stringent.

It is equally clear, on the other hand, that the attitude that refuses to discount anything that cannot be completely denied empirically or logically is too easygoing. In the processes of their thinking or experiments, scientists must carry out an inevitable task of selection. In other words, they must either discount or forget for the moment, consciously or unconsciously, the majority of all the possibilities they can conceive. In practice, there is no scientist who clings obstinately to either extreme of outlook; the question is, rather, to which of the two extremes one is closer.

The most puzzling thing for the physicist at the moment is the true nature of the so-called elementary particles. One thing that is certain is that they are far smaller even than the atom, but it seems likely that, viewed more closely, they will themselves prove to have their own structure. In practice, it is next to impossible to distinguish such detail directly by experimental means. If one wanted to take a good look at one elementary particle, one would have to find out how it reacted when another elementary particle was brought up very close to it. In practice, however, our experiments can give us knowledge of what happens before and after, but not of what happens at the actual moment of the reaction. In such a state of affairs, physicists tend to gravitate toward one or the other of the two extremes I have already described. Some of them maintain that scientists should confine their consideration to the situation when the two elementary particles are apart and assert that there is no point in speculating on the detailed structure of elementary particles. I myself believe, conversely, that it will be possible by some means or other to obtain a logical grasp of the structure of elementary particles, and I am constantly racking my brains for possible answers. The day will come, I believe, when we will know the heart of the elementary particle, even though that will not be achieved with the ease with which Zhuangzi knew the heart of the fish. To do so, however, we may well have to adopt some odd approach that will shatter accepted ways of thinking. One cannot exclude such a possibility from the outset.

In September 1965 an international conference on elementary particles was held in Kyoto to commemorate the thirtieth anniversary of the meson theory. It was a small gathering of some thirty scientists. At a dinner held during the course of the conference, I translated the exchange between Zhuangzi and Huizi into English for the benefit of the physicists from abroad. They seemed to find it interesting, and it amused me to imagine each of them considering which of the two philosophers, Zhuangzi or Huizi, he himself was closer to.

2

Yuzhile

The Joy of Fishes, or, The Play on Words

Hans Peter HOFFMANN

A PERSONAL HISTORY

Shadick: A First Course in Literary Chinese is an introduction that has for generations provided students (not only at German universities) with a first glimpse into the secrets of classical Chinese. In chapter 12 of the first volume we find a short story out of "Autumn Floods" from the book of *Zhuangzi*, which, as scholastic common property as well as an unsolved problem, demonstrates sinological consciousness like few others. This story is called "Yu zhi le," commonly translated as "The Joy of (the) Fishes."[1] Here is the story in a translation by Burton Watson:

> Chuang Tzu [Zhuangzi] and Hui Tzu [Huizi] were strolling along the dam of the Hao River when Chuang Tzu said, "See how the minnows [little fishes] come out and dart around where they please! That's what fish really enjoy!"
>
> Hui Tzu said, "You're not a fish—how do you know what fish enjoy?"
>
> Chuang Tzu said, "You're not I, so how do you know I don't know what fish enjoy?"
>
> Hui Tzu said, "I'm not you, so I certainly don't know what you know. On the other hand, you're certainly not a fish—so that still proves you don't know what fish enjoy!"

Chuang Tzu said, "Let's go back to your original question, please. You asked me *how* I know what fish enjoy—so you already knew it when you asked the question. I know it by standing here beside the Hao."[2]

The standard explanation normally given to beginners in Chinese studies, which structurally is also the only explanation for this little story, has always remained incomprehensible to me. I understood it very well, but I did not see it—and I have to confess that I still do not see it. But at the time, whenever I was with other students and we happened to go past a little lake or a pond, an aquarium, or a takeout fish-and-chips shop, we remembered this little story. And every time, every year we asked each other the same question: "Do you understand it now?" And every time this question was followed by a shaking of heads or a repetition of the standard explanation. But the meaning remained elusive. Every time we repeated the same counterarguments, which mostly just led to a shrug and a remark such as "That's the way the Chinese are" or "You're neither Zhuangzi nor a fish!"

All of a sudden this little story had become a symbol of the problems Westerners have with China or, in less self-critical instances, a symbol of the illogical eccentricity of Chinese thinking. Mostly it was the latter that was suggested by interpretations of the story found in books not only in the West. As it often happens, a real development did not take place until I changed the perspective, changed the objective, and changed my approach to the text. The story had always been treated as a "philosophical" text— and after years of translations and research in the field of modern Chinese literature, I suddenly began to look at it as a literary interpretation.

Exactly what this means we will see later, but first let me sum up the available interpretations of this little anecdote, which, without exception, are all based on the same interpretational decisions.

THE INTERPRETATIONS OF "YU ZHI LE"

An Unauthorized Change of the Paradigm: On the Common Structure of the Interpretations

The structural correspondence between the different interpretations has its roots in a strong tradition that begins with Guo Xiang (252–312), the first commentator of the *Zhuangzi*.

According to Guo Xiang, Zhuangzi reacts to Huizi's completely convincing argument that he is not Zhuangzi, but he clearly knows that Zhuangzi is not a fish by recapitulating Huizi's original statement and saying the following:

> He who himself is not a fish should not know anything about fishes. But not being me, you claim to know that I am not a fish and ask me how I know what the fishes enjoy. But if you really know that I am not a fish, then we know something about each other, and that means that one can know the other without being the other and that someone, without being a fish, can know something about fishes.
>
> So if you ask *how* [my italics] I know, you already know that I know. And if you ask me once again, then I know it because I am standing on the bridge over the Hao. Why should I first have to jump into the water![3]

With this argument by analogy Guo Xiang is not content—and he adds a further argument that refers to Zhuangzi's remark that he knows something about the joy of the fishes because he is standing on the bridge:

> Where these animals live cannot be changed by heaven and earth. No Yin and no Yang can take away from them what makes them happy. So if you start out from what satisfies beings living ashore, then you also know what satisfies beings living in the water. That is no big deal![4]

According to this structure Master Zhuang and Master Hui are standing on a bridge, and Zhuangzi makes a remark about the joy of fishes. The interpreters say that Huizi, as a consequent relativist and a philosophical thinker, is skeptical about Zhuangzi's ability to make statements about the joy of fishes since, in the end, Zhuangzi is no fish—a point of view that the book *Zhuangzi* vehemently supports. After that, Zhuangzi tries to defend himself by saying, "You are not me. So how do you know that I don't know what fish enjoy?" This is neither a very convincing nor a very intelligent argument, and, as the interpretations reveal, Zhuangzi is promptly checkmated by Huizi, who says, "I am not you, that is true, but I know for certain that you are not a fish!"

According to the commentaries, Zhuangzi is so bogged down that he has no other way out than to go back to the starting point of the dialogue, which he scotches with two mysterious statements: "Although you asked a challenging question—how I know the joy of fishes—you already knew that I know it. And I know it because I am standing on the bridge over the Hao."[5]

According to the interpretations, Huizi's question is taken by Zhuangzi as implicit approval. Why should this be so? And what kind of logic does Zhuangzi follow when he says that he knows the joy of fishes because he is standing on a bridge?

According to all of the interpretations I know, Huizi is simply stampeded by Zhuangzi. This conclusion is possible only because the interpretations allow themselves a logical leap: although Huizi is talking about fish and human beings as different species and states only in this sense that Zhuangzi is not a fish, Zhuangzi is said to come to the following conclusion:

> Whoever accepts that I am not a fish, that is to say, whoever knows what a fish is and what a human being is at the same time admits that we can know something about each other. And if we can know something about each other, then I can also know something about fish.[6]

But just at this point we have a logical leap. The categorizations "fish" and "human beings" are biological ones, whereas statements about grief or joy presuppose the knowledge of psychological features. Here the argumentation of Guo Xiang becomes skewed.

With the same common confusion of interpretation and text, Sham Yat Shing blames Zhuangzi for this change of the paradigm; bogged down as he is, Zhuangzi takes Huizi's statement and concludes that whoever knows what a fish is can also know whether it is happy:

> Zhuangzi apparently was not aware of the difference between these two meanings . . . and out of this unconscious confusion came the illusion that one could also reverse the statement, i.e., reverse "whoever knows the joy of fishes knows what a fish is" into "whoever knows what a fish is knows whether it is happy."[7]

Just as unconvincing is the argument by analogy that a living being would only have to be in its element—ashore or in the water—in order to be happy. After all, we cannot say that human beings are happy without exception just because they are ashore, and we cannot say that they are always unhappy being in the water.

On the Interpretations of the Story

While all of the structures of the common interpretations without exception follow Guo Xiang's analysis, the explanations themselves sometimes differ dramatically in the way they describe the content of the story and the notions framing it. Consider the following examples.

Chang Tsung-tung and Intuitionism

How far several interpreters are willing to go in order to support this in the end not really convincing structure can be demonstrated with the example of Chang Tsung-tung [Zhang Zongdong]. He states that he is "very impressed by the ready wit of Master Chuang [Zhuang], who embarrasses Master Hui in the end," and he states that "up to now the epistemological relevance of this amusing debate has been overlooked":[8]

> Master Chuang first of all explains his view—that the fishes he sees comfortably swimming feel happy and satisfied. Master Hui on the other side takes a radically relativistic standpoint and, like a severe behaviorist, fundamentally denies the possibility of knowing something about the inner feelings of other subjects; first Master Chuang tries to answer with the same argumentation but immediately realizes that then he would have to agree with his opponent's opinion. Therefore he quickly returns to his starting point and refers to the common intuition of human beings, which is already evident in the possibility of communication between him and Hui Shi. With this argument he states that Hui Shi's question is absurd.[9]

But even if we are willing to consider Huizi's question as absurd, can we really accept Chang's interpretation, which boils down to this conclusion: A living being is a living being, and if Zhuangzi is able to talk with Huizi, he is also able to talk with a fish?

In order to further back up his interpretation, Chang refers to the "evidence" of an intuition common to all human beings, proven by the ability to communicate and by "everyday experience":

> Master Chuang bases his knowledge of the joy and happiness of fishes on the well-known fact that human beings, in dealing with other human beings and with animals, have the ability to read their behavior and facial expressions. Maybe it is because of this that he did not see any need to waste any

further comment on it. And indeed, everyday experience teaches us that human beings very often have to, and normally can, believe in their intuition, that is to say, in their instinctive ability to grasp things in a direct way.[10]

Besides the fact that this may be true where dogs or horses are concerned but not if we try to read the facial expression of a goldfish in a goldfish bowl in order to find out whether it is happy, this traditional interpretation also shows that it is missing something. Something that is not made clear in the text has to be added. Otherwise the sentence "Maybe it is because of this that he did not see any need to waste any further comment on it" would not have been necessary.

Chang adds what he calls "intuitionism"[11] but not without the following reservation: "As far as their relevance to some real cognition is concerned, intuitions are limited by the visual, cultural, and pragmatic horizon of the recognizing subject."[12]

With this there is a return to the illogical nature of Chinese thinking—since, according to these interpretations and to Chang, what Zhuangzi is talking about is nothing else than a typical Chinese form of intuition, which cannot be understood by Westerners.

The Sophism: The Stupid Zhuangzi or: the Incompetent Epigones

After considering interpretations referring to a culturally limited intuition and this categorically subjective σύνοιδα εἰδώς, we gratefully read the judgment that Robert Allinson passes on our little story. He starts out from the same interpretational structure but ends up with a completely different conclusion in quoting Zhuangzi's last statement as

> a form of naïve, perceptual realism. He knows what fish enjoy by simple observation. He uses the testimony of others to buttress his knowing what fishes enjoy (Hui Tzu had assumed that Chuang Tzu knew what fish enjoyed by asking him *how* he knew rather than *if* he knew).[13]

Allinson here refers to Burton Watson, whose translation conforms completely to Guo Xiang's and emphasizes the little word 安 *an* (how) with italics in order to hint to the reader how this sophistic swerve should be read. According to the emphasis on the little word "how," Zhuangzi had said, "Well, okay, let's return to our starting point. You asked me *how* I know. So you already admitted *that* I know, and you only wanted to know *where* I got this knowledge."

Allinson now has the courage to give vent to his completely understandable displeasure with this understanding:

> The problem with this story is that it is hardly worthy of the stature of Chuang Tzu. First of all, Hui Tzu may not have really thought that Chuang Tzu did know what fish enjoyed. He simply may have left an ellipsis in his argument. What he may have meant to have said [*sic*] was, "If you know what fish enjoyed, how would you come to that knowledge?" . . . The ellipsis in Hui Tzu's statement is not sufficient to prove that he believed that Chuang Tzu did in fact know what fish enjoyed. To make this claim is to be guilty of a sophism which is not worthy of a philosopher of the caliber of Chuang Tzu.[14]

Second, Allinson comes out against the simple *evidence* of such insights as postulated by Chang, who considered "the evidence of our senses to be trustworthy."[15] Last but not least, even if we were willing to forgive Chuang Tzu for this cheap sophism, his answer still would be no more plausible. Allinson concludes: "Hence, I cannot find this to be a genuine example of the reasoning of Chuang Tzu."[16] But despite his courage, even Allinson would rather see the compilers of the book of Chuang Tzu as incompetent epigones and our little story as inauthentic than to say good-bye to the seemingly sacrosanct interpretational structure.

Chen Zhengrong more or less comes to the same understanding of our story. Only the question of who is guilty for this faux pas is answered differently. For him, and indeed for the entire discussion of the "Joy of the Fishes" in Taiwan, the question of who the "winner" is is central. And who is the loser? Huizi or Zhuangzi? The cheap sophistic trick he ascribes not to a compiler or an epigone but to Zhuangzi himself. Zhuangzi's sophism is not plausible to him, either, but this again does not make him doubt his premises but rather Zhuangzi's intellectual abilities and the loyalty of the compilers, who would have been better off not including this story in the book of Chuang Tzu:

> "The debate about the Joy of the Fishes between Zhuangzi and Huizi is part of the book of Zhuangzi. But the debate ends with the defeat of Zhuangzi, therefore the compilers of the book should not have included it."[17]

I could go on for quite a while and discuss all the different interpretations of our little story, but this would not be fruitful since all of the interpretations that I have found go back to Guo Xiang, whose premises have never been questioned. Thus, in order to establish a new interpretation, we will have to go back before Guo Xiang, and that means we have to go back to the text itself.

FISH AND "TROPE": THE PLAY ON WORDS

Interpretational Decisions in the Traditional Readings

In order to establish a new analysis we must first of all be aware of the interpretational decisions that explicitly or implicitly build the background of the traditional readings and investigate the soundness and plausibility of their logic.[18] Then we will be able to decide whether—and, if so, which—other approaches may allow a more constructive and more plausible reading of the text.

The following are the most important interpretational decisions of the traditional readings:

a. The story can be translated and understood only in the way it has been traditionally translated and understood. All grammatical possibilities are unambiguous and as such have been correctly understood.
b. The story is narrated in a realistic way and means what it appears to say. As such, it has to be read as a piece of philosophy and not, let us say, as a piece of literature, and that means it is a documentary report. Zhuangzi and Huizi are standing on a bridge discussing whether human beings are able to know something about the feelings of fishes. They are talking about this question alone and nothing else.
c. The story has no relationship to other parts of *Zhuangzi*. That means, for instance, that possible repetitions of words, notions, or images of the fish, of knowledge, of joy, of water, of bridges, of swimming, and of wandering have nothing in common with the same words, notions, or images in the rest of the book. This decision is especially remarkable since, above all, the image of the fish occurs conspicuously often and in very significant parts of the text.

In the following I investigate these interpretational decisions and analyze the text for other interpretational possibilities.

The Joy in Fishes: On the Grammatical Interpretation of "Yu zhi le 魚之樂"

As far as the grammatical or semantic analysis is concerned—in our case synonymous with the translations of our little text—none of the interpretations and translations seem to have taken into account the interpretational decisions made. This may be because the text seemingly had no grammatical ambiguities. Nevertheless, in each and every case such an interpretational decision *has* been made—even with regard to the central group of words: *yu zhi le* 魚之樂.

All of the translations understand the relationship established by the "subordinative [subordinating] conjunction"[19] *zhi* 之 between the noun *yu* (fish) and the noun *le* (joy, music) as something that in Latin grammar is called the "subjective genitive" (*genitivus subjectivus*). According to the *Duden* dictionary, the subjective genitive shows the genitive word as the "subject of an action," that is, the subject of an event to which the genitive word is referring. In our case, that is, "the joy of fishes," does this mean the "fishes are enjoying themselves"? For someone familiar with grammatical problems it seems quite natural for such a description to be followed by a logical question, that is, the question of whether this relation could be understood in another way, for example, as an "objective genitive" (*genitivus objectivus*). The objective genitive shows the genitive word as the "object of an action." In our case this means "the joy *in* fishes."

But before we can go on to the question of what such an interpretation would mean for our little anecdote, we first have to determine whether reading the text in such a way is really possible in classical Chinese. Under the headword "*zhi* as particle of the genitive," the old grammar by Georg von der Gabelentz gives two examples in which *zhi* can establish a relation between two words that he describes as "genitive of the passive object" and which is identical to our objective genitive: "Genitive of the passive object can occur and cause trouble."[20] For us, one of his examples may be sufficient since it comes very close to our formulation. It appears in the book *Mengzi* 6B7: 三王之罪人 *san wang zhi zui ren,* which in the context of the book can have only one meaning: crime *against* the three kings (and not the crime *of* the three kings).[21] Since the book *Mengzi* is normally considered to be older than the book *Zhuangzi*, this may be enough evidence for the historical and philological possibility of such a reading. Moreover, Shadick's book itself exemplifies such a possibility, too. In the exercises in volume one we find the following sentence: 善游者為不游者說山水之樂 *shan you zhe wei bu shan you zhe shuo shanshui zhi le*—clearly, those who travel a lot are not talking about the somehow abstract "joy of a landscape" but about "the joy they had" in seeing the landscape, that is, "the joy *in* the landscape." These are parallel cases. Furthermore, it would be helpful if we could find some formulations like this in the *Zhuangzi*, too, and it would be even better if the ambivalence of such a formulation were guaranteed by the debate, let us say, contained in some of the commentaries, one pointing in the direction of a subjective genitive, the other in the direction of an objective genitive. And indeed we have so many of these formulations in the *Zhuangzi* that it is impossible to list all of them here. There are also two commentaries pointing in the two grammatical directions we are looking for. We find, for example, the following sentence in chapter 2, the "Qiwulun" (Discussion on Making All Things Equal), a chapter that is considered to be one of the most authentic of the whole book:

是故滑疑之耀, 聖人之所圖 *shi gu hua yi zhi yao, sheng ren zhi suo tu*
The torch of chaos and doubt—this is what the sage steers by.[22]

Chen Guying sums up the different readings of this phrase:

[F]or these two sentences we have two opposite interpretations. The first says: "It is the inner light that matters to the sage." Accordingly, it says in the commentary by De Qing: "*Hua yi zhi yao* means to hide one's light under a bushel, not to make a show of oneself. To talk about the light without being in the light—that is what matters for the sage."

The other one says: "It is the dark light that causes trouble in the heart of man, and that the sage wants to be rid of." Accordingly, Jiang Xichang says: "The *shiwen* commentary [the commentary by Lu Deming of the Tang dynasty] quotes Sima by saying: "*Hua*, that means to get into trouble, into chaos." *Huayi* points in the direction of the different concurrent schools [the so-called one hundred schools of the Warring States period], which are enough to trouble a man's heart."[23]

In other words, once again we have two directions: on the one hand, the light is the light that illuminates the darkness of chaos and doubt (the light *in* chaos and doubt); on the other hand, the dark light of wrong meanings *is* chaos and doubt itself.

For our story this means that *yu zhi le* can grammatically mean both "the joy *of* fishes and the joy *in* fishes." (By the way, this ambiguity can be found in the English expression using "of" as well. In 1972 a scandalous little book with the title *The Joy of Sex* was published. And it is clear that this did not mean the joy that the sex enjoyed.) Moreover, for our story this would mean that Zhuangzi is talking about *his* joy at seeing the fishes swim, while Hui Shi misunderstands him and talks about how fishes enjoy themselves. Zhuangzi would talk in an objective genitive, whereas Huizi would discuss the matter with a subjective genitive. If we change the translation of our little anecdote so that this implicit misunderstanding is more obvious, it might sound like this:

THE JOY OF FISHES

Zhuangzi and Huizi were taking a walk over the bridge of the Hao River.

Zhuangzi said: Hey, the fishes are jumping out of the water! That is pure joy.

Huizi then said: Come on, you're not a fish. How do you know that that is pure joy?

Zhuangzi replied: You're not me, so how do you know that I don't know that that is pure joy?

Huizi: I'm not you, that's true. But you're obviously not a fish, and this makes it clear that you do not know anything about the joy of fishes.

Zhuangzi: Well, take it easy, and let's see how things started: You said, "You're not a fish. How do you know that this is pure joy?" But even though you asked me that, you knew that I knew that this is pure joy. And this I know from standing here on the bridge.

In short, Zhuangzi makes a fool of Huizi. When he becomes aware of the fact that Huizi misunderstands him, he plays a word game with him. They talk around each other, Zhuangzi consciously, Huizi unconsciously. This reading has the advantage that we do not have to insinuate into Zhuangzi's words such an unworthy sophistic swerve since, read like this, his last sentences make sense. Read in this way, he can say, "But even though you asked . . . , you knew that I knew that this is [for me] pure joy. And this I know from standing here on the bridge."

Well, this may be funny somehow and solve one of the problems of the traditional interpretations, but still there is this question: what the hell does that mean? Such a scene may be fit for a movie by the Marx brothers, who fool around with the misunderstanding provoked by the same pronunciation of "viaduct" and the question "Why a duck?" (in *The Cocoanuts* (1929))—but how does it fit into a book like the *Zhuangzi*?

Just at this point we run into a further unspoken decision made in the traditional interpretations: namely, we took this little scene as a part of a movie, as a part of a documentary movie. We took the whole of the story literally—fishes are fishes, a bridge is a bridge, and Zhuangzi and Huizi are discussing whether or not it is possible for human beings to know something about the feelings of fishes. But what happens if we understand the same scene as literature, as calculated and knowing all the tricks of speaking in tropes? What happens if we take the text not literally but somehow "metaphorically"? "Tropically"?

WORDFISHES AND FISHWORDS: TOWARD A TROPIC INTERPRETATION

In order to be able to relate the tropes of the whole book to our little text, it is first of all necessary to list the components of the scene—this is not difficult to do. As nouns we have the following: Zhuangzi, Huizi, fishes, the river, the bridge, and joy (knowledge). As verbs we have the following: taking a walk, swimming, coming out of something (*chu* 出), knowing, and enjoying. We also have more difficult words like the negation (*fei* 非), the turning back (*xun* 循), and the origin, the starting point (*ben* 本). There is much to say about all of these words, but to keep it short, let us concentrate on the word—or should I say "trope"?—that stands in the center of the story: the fish.

If we count the giant fish *kun* from the first lines of the first chapter among them, this trope occurs overall twelve times in the book *Zhuangzi*. Most interesting for us is one short, quite famous passage that, in relation to our not-too-amusing pun or play on words, gives it a meaning that is worthy of a philosopher of Zhuangzi's caliber:

> The fish trap exists because of the fish; once you've gotten the fish, you can forget the trap. The rabbit snare exists because of the rabbit; once you've gotten the rabbit, you can forget the snare. Words exist because of meaning; once you've gotten the meaning, you can forget the words. Where can I find a man who has forgotten words so I can have a word with him?[24]

What does that mean for our problem? The fishes could be read as an image of ideas or meanings, for example, the word *fish* for the trap. Zhuangzi expresses a meaning; Huizi only listens to the words—followed by the already well-known misunderstanding. In this sense, the "Joy of the Fishes" does no more and no less than put the just-quoted passage into a visual scene with the intention of expressing the fact that most human beings only listen to words themselves and do not attend to their meaning and that this phenomenon makes real understanding impossible.

But besides this surface meaning we can also observe a strange doubling of the image: we not only have a misunderstanding about a topic, for example, about fishes and pure joy. If we read our story through the lens of the little passage just quoted we also have the word "fish" in a double meaning: "fish" is a word, and as a word it is a fish trap. The fish trap of the word "fish" captures and conveys a meaning, and in this case this meaning is "fish." In other words, if we use the little passage about fish traps to understand our anecdote about the joy of the fishes, we find that the word "fish" here means both "word" and "meaning," "language," and "idea." And with that it also speaks about the problem of speaking, of language, of communication, of describing truth or knowledge in terms of language, and, last but not least, of the relationship between literal and literary meanings and readings. "Fish" in the "Joy of the Fishes" is "fish" as word and as meaning; thus "fish trap" and "fish" are signifier and signified at the same time.

With the expression "joy of the fishes" two things have been achieved: first of all, a misunderstanding is evolving because of the ambivalence of the expression and because of the dependency of its understanding on the reader's subjective point of view—a very important topic in one of the most famous and seemingly most authentic chapters of the *Zhuangzi,* chapter 2, "Qiwulun." Second, the possibility and maybe even the necessity of misunderstandings are shown as the typical "joy of language" (what the trope "fish" is standing for) as its mischievousness, as its humor, and maybe even as its absurdity. Being a cross between idea and word, content and form, it is the joy of language to withdraw from an unambiguous and absolute understanding through its self-offsetting (self-canceling) and iridescence between image and notion by means of a trope or talking in tropes.

This quality of language is the main topic of our little story. It is shown as a little scene of a play, and as such it is ironically mirroring the self-assurance with which human beings deceive themselves regarding the reality of their knowledge and recognition. The return to the origin, *xun qi ben* 循其本, which Zhuangzi postulates as a "going back to the starting point" of the dialogue, symbolizes the return to the origin in a philosophical sense, a return to ideal identity between language and reality, which, according to our little story, in terms of language can be shown only as a cycle of misunderstandings. This cycle is not a unique one—and here it becomes clear that our little passage is very well thought out and written with all the literary and philosophical refinement that other interpretations claim it is missing. The movement of the dialogue is not only returning to its starting point; in fact, the first sentence anticipates the whole story; the beginning of the text presupposes the result of the following events, which had led to the beginning of the story. In other words, the writer of the story knew its end. He had to know it, for only in having gone through the whole story could he start with the ambiguity that is inherent in the expression *yu zhi le* (this is the joy of fish). Only then is he able to tell a story that presupposes its own end and, in doing so, has no real beginning and no real end. This circling is not pausing in a static repetition but is developing a paradoxical dynamic, the repetitive development of which succeeds in withdrawing from any effort to interpret it in an absolute or unambiguous way.

The Jump [*chu* 出] of the Fishes, a Bridge, and
the Flight of the Bird Peng

But how is such a way of speaking possible? How is it to be understood? Is it a way of speaking that is constituted by a withdrawal, a way of speaking that wants to speak and at the same time wants to forget the words? Through this description we already know what it looks like: it must be a way of speaking that is no longer useful and can no longer be used as an argument in debates, as a weapon of discerning, as a means and—remembering that the text is from the horrific era of the Warring States—a legitimation of war; a way of speaking, however, that at the same time insists on the importance and the effectiveness of its ideas. This way of speaking is speaking in "goblet words,"[25] as described in chapter 26 of the *Zhuangzi*. It is a way of speaking that, according to Western traditions and together with Zhuangzi, could be called "speaking out of heaven, out of the water":

Maybe we have to express it this bizarrely because in both cases we are dealing with a way of speaking that does not belong to everyday language.

Whoever speaks in this "ouranophatic" or "oceanophatic" way is not speaking about heaven and sea but is speaking out of the wet element, out of the high sphere itself—and this in a way that the speaker does not lose the might of the womb, where he is dissolved, by his emerging and the raising of his voice.[26]

This is neither the time nor the place to go into an investigation of the problem of the "womb" or to go more deeply into an investigation of the Great Female, as Laozi puts it, or the motif of the door in the *Laozi* and the *Zhuangzi*, which would involve a further discussion of the ideas and images of death in the *Zhuangzi*. For us it may be enough now to state that the "emerging" of Master Zhuang and Master Hui and their appearance "on the bridge" (*hao shang* 濠上) are closely connected with the "emerging" (*chu* 出) of the fishes. This *chu*, in connection with a fish, occurs in another passage of the *Zhuangzi* in the myth that makes up the beginning of chapter 1 of the book and the Inner Chapters, which are central to Zhuangzi's philosophy as a whole. This myth is important for our interpretation of the "Joy of the Fishes" not only because of the parallelism of the tropes in this initial myth, the attitude of the saint, and the way the Dao is described and our little story is related to one of the most important ideas of the whole *Zhuangzi*. It starts with the following lines:

In the northern darkness there is a fish. Its name is Kun.

Kun is huge.
I don't know how many thousand li
It changes and becomes a bird
Its name is Peng.[27]

This bird is synonymous with his transformation, his metamorphosis:

Rises [*shang*]—ninety thousand miles
Breaks through the clouds
Shoulders the azure of heaven
On his way to the southern darkness

It is just this rising arch that is described as the fish that has become a bird, which is also symbolized by the *chu* of the fishes and the "on the bridge" of Zhuangzi and Huizi. It is this flight, this jump, this appearance of consciousness—or of language or a dialogue—between two darknesses that also appears through Zhuangzi's and Hui Shi's standing on the bridge. Right at this point, here, on the bridge, in this flight, the basic difference and the fundamental common ground between both become visible.

Huizi, with a kind of negative dialectics, posits his knowledge with a negation, with a *fei* 非, which, in a negative way, defines individuality: *fei yu* 非魚 (you are not a fish). The swimming, diving, flying "I" dissolves in its environment and becomes an armed individual who has cut off its relationship to the ten thousand things with a *fei* (no): the world is not me. Still, this individual has a kind of relationship to the "joy of the fishes" and "the fishes of joy," but it is far from a great insight: "If you parade your little theories and fish for the post of district magistrate, you will be far from the Great Understanding."[28]

According to my reading, Zhuangzi on the other hand recognizes this way of speaking as a bridge, as a jump, as a misunderstanding, and as something funny and absurd, something that cannot be proved logically, something that is condemned to fail. In this sense "fish" and "joy" mean the same thing and thus become tautological. In this joy Zhuangzi and Huizi meet. Their dialogue is their jump, their emergence, their flight, *and* the joy of the words/fishes that they are. The joy *of* the fishes and the joy *about/ in* the fishes become identical, and the dichotomy between object and subject is dissolved. But not, as Ralf Moritz[29] assumes, in the sphere of the subject but in the dynamic paradox of a never-ending shift, in other words, in goblet words.

Here Zhuangzi's strange statement can for the first time be embedded in the sense of the dialogue without break. Now he can say, "You asked me how I know the joy of the fishes, and you knew it [the answer] when you asked me the question." The stress must not be put on the word "how"— as traditional readings beginning with Guo Xiang do—but on the word "asked." In asking, Huizi becomes part of the happy flight, part of the passing illumination of language; the question as question, as linguistic utterance is identical to the linguistic statement by Zhuangzi.

On Joy, Music, and Knowledge

Finally, let me add another whirl[30] to that already described when establishing the typical goblet-word style of the *Zhuangzi*. In order to do so we have to look a little more closely at the conspicuous confrontation of the concept of *zhi* 知 (knowledge) and *le* 樂 (joy). In doing so, the whole story nearly dissolves into more and more ambiguities. On top of the ambiguity of whether the "joy" is the joy of the fish or the joy that Zhuangzi feels while observing fish, another ambiguity can be found in the words "knowledge" and "joy." In a short description of the particular goblet-word style of the *Zhuangzi*, A. C. Graham typically takes the word *zhi* for "knowledge" in order to illustrate this specific way of interpreting the *Zhuangzi*:

> Chuang-Tzu's regular mode is the language which spontaneously rights itself like the spilling vessel; he uses words *not like a philosopher but like a poet, sensitive to their richness, exploiting their ambiguities, letting conflicting meanings explode* against each other in apparent contradiction. Thus Chuang-Tzu and his school delight in using "know" in different senses in a single sentence. [my italics][31]

Chen Daqi describes a similar phenomenon in his attempt to explain the little story about the joy of the fishes. For him, two kinds of knowledge come into conflict here: the so-called inner knowledge (*neizhi* 內知), which can be attained through self-examination (*zixing* 自省), and the outside knowledge (*waizhi* 外知), which can be achieved through observation and investigation of the object of interest. In his eyes Zhuangzi is just talking about an outside observation that the fishes seem to be happy. Hui Shi understands this as an expression of inner knowledge, of inner conviction that he can have only as long as he himself is concerned.

Even if this approach does not help to solve the problems of the story, this suggestion is not unimportant as it confirms the value of a literary reading of the text even on the level of a single word. We have a whirl of ideas and arguments, a whirl that is the whirl of words—a whirl that we find yet again if we look more closely at the word *le* (joy). In a footnote to a passage in chapter 14, "Tianyun 天運," Burton Watson explains as follows:

> It should be noted that, because the words for "joy" and "music" are written with the same character, phrases translated here as "perfect music," "the music of Heaven," etc., can also be interpreted to refer to states of emotion. The phrase "perfect music" in fact appears later as the title of section 18, where I have rendered it as "perfect happiness."[32]

Here we find another completely different approach to interpreting our anecdote—as long as we allow it to be a piece of literature and do not force it to be philosophy, and that would also mean forcing it to be unambiguous. A literary text taken as a philosophical reading is seized by a characteristic and insurmountable horror; it is the horror of ambiguity, the horror of metaphor, the horror of the loss of the shelter of definition and notion. In short, it is the horror of language.[33] It is because of this horror that philosophical readings very often cannot deal with ambiguity. They try to transform metaphor into notion and always try to decide which meaning in an ambiguity is the right one. Normally it is impossible for philosophical interpretation of the text to take and accept a metaphor or an ambiguity as just that: a metaphor or an ambiguity. In other words, it is impossible for a philosophical interpretation of a text to take the different directions in which an ambiguity is pointing seriously as a statement, as maybe even the "real" meaning of a text. Not one direction but a variety of directions may be the answer—or, as in the *Zhuangzi,* the shifting sum of all of the various construals. In the *Zhuangzi* this is not only stated but also formed in a poetical or literary way. But this way of speaking or writing, again, is not just a quirk of the writer or the writers but is central to the philosophy of the *Zhuangzi.* This philosophy does not believe in fixed notions but tries to build up a literary language that is in motion and in the turn of a trope. Thus our little story could indeed be interpreted taking this reading of *le* as *yue* as another form of pun—Zhuangzi talks about what he *hears,* and Hui Shi takes him as talking about what he *knows.* Moreover, it may no longer astonish us that this contradiction, that between knowledge and joy/ music, is deeply rooted in classical Chinese thinking. In these two concepts we have the fundamental problem that the aforementioned hundred schools are struggling with: on one side, we have the discursive thinking of knowledge with its most important presuppositions: soberness and rationality; on the other side, we have a thinking of enthusiasm and joy that reaches its highest goals in a form of ecstasy (*chu*).

Starting from here we find that the basic presuppositions deepen the contradiction between joy and knowledge toward a general Daoist musicology that could be shown as an epistemological and social-ethical counterpart to the theories of knowledge and rites (*li* 禮). Suggestions in this direction, bringing political overtones into our little story, can be found everywhere:

Very early, the relationship between joy and music led some Chinese philosophers...toward the philosophy of language. Especially the confrontation by the Confucian thinker Hsun-Tzu [Xunzi] had a deep effect, a confrontation that can be traced back to *earlier approaches* [my italics]...He took music as the element of culture that unites people beyond all differences, whereas its no less important counterpart, the ritual (*li*), divides people into different classes.[34]

Finally, in this way it is possible to fully unfold the complex meaning of our, in the beginning so dubious, little story about the joy of fishes. It can be understood not only as a mischievous placement of Zhuangzi's linguistic and epistemological critic into a visual scene but also as a musicological thumbnail sketch of the great piping of heaven, where the most characteristic motifs of Daoist thinking are discernible. In the end it is a little story that, as far as its depth and its intellectual exploration are concerned, has no need to fear comparison with the so-called authentic parts of the *Zhuangzi*.

NOTES

1. A short list of Western translations of the passage:

Wing-tsit Chan, *A Source Book in Chinese Philosophy* (Princeton, NJ: Princeton University Press, 1963), 209f.

Tsung-tung Chang, "Subjektivität der Erkenntnis—vom Relativismus zum Intuitionismus," in *Metaphysik, Erkenntnis und praktische Philosophie im Chuang-Tzu* (Frankfurt: Vittorio Klostermann, 1982), 137f.

James Legge, trans., *The Texts of Taoism*, part 1, vol. 39 of *The Sacred Books of the East* (New York: Dover, 1962), 391f.

Ralf Moritz, *Die Philosophie im alten China* (Berlin: Detuscher Verlag der Wissenschaften, 1990), 127.

Hubert Schleichert, *Klassische chinesische Philosophie* (Frankfurt: Klostermann, 1980), 121f.

Arthur Waley, *Three Ways of Thought in Ancient China* (London: Allen and Unwin, 1939), 22.

Burton Watson, trans., *The Complete Works of Chuang-tzu* (New York: Columbia University Press, 1968), 188f.

Léon Wieger, *Les pères du système taoiste* (Paris: Cathasia, Les Belles Lettres, n.d.). In English translation by Derek Bryce, *Wisdom of the Daoist Masters* (Lampeter, Wales: Lanerch Enterprises, 1984), 196.

Richard Wilhelm, *Dschuang Dsi—das wahre Buch vom südlichen Blütenland* (Cologne: Diederichs Gelbe Reihe, 1969), 192.

2. Watson, *Complete Works of Chuang-tzu*, 188–189.

3. Guo Xiang, Commentary, in *Sibubeiyao*: 四部備要, vol. 342. *Zhuangzi,* juan 6, p. 15. Also see Guo Qingfan 郭庆藩, 庄子集解释, vol. 3 (Beijing: Zhonghua shuju 中華書局, 1993), 607f.

4. Guo Qingfan, Guo Xiang, 607f.

5. Tsung-tung Chang, "Subjektivität der Erkenntnis," 138.

6. Cen Yicheng 岑溢成, "The Debate on Fish Happiness: Knowing and Being Happy," in *Ehu* 鵝湖 29 (1977): 9.

7. Ibid.

8. Tsung-tung Chang, "Subjektivität der Erkenntnis," 138.

9. Ibid.

10. Ibid.

11. Ibid., 139.

12. Ibid.

13. Robert E. Allinson, *Chuang-Tzu for Spiritual Transformation* (New York: University of New York Press, 1989), 140.

14. Ibid.

15. Ibid.

16. Ibid.

17. Chen Zhenrong, "Further Discussion about the Zhuang-Hui Debate on the Happy Fish," in *Ehu* 鵝湖 3/4 (1976): 41.

18. Western notions are here used as "ladder notions," which, when placed in parentheses, allow us to talk about the topic without transferring Western ideas to Chinese texts.

19. Harold Shadick, *A First Course in Literary Chinese,* vol. 2 (Ithaca, NY: Cornell University Press, 1968), 222.

20. Georg von der Gabelentz, *Chinesische Grammatik* (Halle, Germany: Niemeyer, 1960), 184.

21. Ibid.

22. Watson, *Complete Works of Chuang-tzu,* 42.

23. Chen Guying 陈鼓应, *A New Commentary and Translation of Zhuangzi* 庄子今注今释, vol. 1 (Beijing: Zhonghua shuju 中華書局, 1983), 69f.

24. Watson, *Complete Works of Chuang-tzu,* Kap. *waiwu,* 302.

25. For a more detailed discussion of the topic see Hans Peter Hoffmann, *Die Welt als Wendung: Zu einer literarischen Lektüre des* Wahren Buches vom südlichen Blütenland (Zhuangzi) (Wiesbaden: Harrassowitz, 2001).

26. Peter Sloterdijk, "Uterodizee als Lehre von den letzten Dingen," in Peter Sloterdijk, *Weltfremdheit* (Frankfurt: Suhrkamp, 1993), 195.

27. Translation by Hans Peter Hoffmann.

28. Watson, *Complete Works of Chuang-tzu,* 296.

29. See Ralf Moritz, *Die Philosophie im alten China* (Berlin: Deutscher Verlag der Wissenschaften, 1990), 112–132.

30. For a more detailed discussion of this notion see Hoffmann, *Wendung.*

31. A. C. Graham, *Chuang-tzu: Textual Notes to a Partial Translation* (London: School of Oriental & African Studies, University of London, 1982), 26.

32. Watson, 158.

33. For a more detailed discussion of this question see Hoffmann, *Wendung.*

34. Wolfgang Bauer, *China und die Hoffnung auf Glück* (Munich: Suhrkamp, 1971), 32.

The Relatively Happy Fish

Chad HANSEN

ZHUANGZI: See the (?)fish swimming freely about—this is fish happiness.

HUI SHI: You're not a fish. How (whence) do you know fish happiness?

ZHUANGZI: You're not me; how (whence) do you know I don't know fish happiness?

HUI SHI: I'm not you, so I certainly don't know you. You're certainly not fish, and that's enough to say you don't know fish happiness.

ZHUANGZI: Let's go back to the beginning. When you said, "How (whence) do you know fish happiness?" it was asking me already knowing I knew it. I knew it above the river.

PUZZLES AND CHALLENGES

One might wonder why this simple exchange gets so much play and so little close analysis.[1] Few treat it as central to understanding Zhuangzi's philosophy.[2] We do not suspect that the conversation actually took place.[3] We do not even know if Zhuangzi and Hui Shi were actually friends.[4] It is not clear that anyone understands the point of the exchange.[5] Standard commentary consistently treats Zhuangzi as not seriously participating in the debate. His posture is described as "playful" or "dismissive" of Hui Shi's logic, as being smugly assured of his mystical knowledge, or even "sarcastic." Rather than crucially informing our view of Zhuangzi, we usually read the passage to "confirm" "what we already know" about both

Originally published in *Asian Philosophy* 13, no. 2–3 (September 2003). Reprinted with permission.

Zhuangzi and his fellow discussant, Hui Shi—the mystic versus the logician.[6]

We can explain the fascination with the passage from a different direction, however. Commentators often fondly recite this story of Zhuangzi's lament for Hui Shi:

> Chuang-tzu [Zhuangzi], among the mourners in a funeral procession, was passing by the grave of Hui Shih [Hui Shi]. He turned round and said to his attendants:
>
> "There was a man of Ying who, when he got a smear of plaster no thicker than a fly's wing on the tip of his nose, would make Carpenter Shih [Shi] slice it off. Carpenter Shih would raise the wind whirling his hatchet, wait for the moment, and slice it; every speck of the plaster would be gone without hurt to the nose, while the man of Ying stood there perfectly composed.
>
> Lord Yüan [Yuan] of Sung [Song] heard about it, summoned Carpenter Shih and said "Let me see you do it." "As for my side of the act," said Carpenter Shih, "I did use to be able to slice it off. However, my partner has been dead for a long time.
>
> "Since the Master died, I have had no one to use as a partner, no one with whom to talk about things."[7]

We understand the lament as the loss of a philosophical partnership, of two like-minded but disagreeing intellectual companions engaged in the joys of productive philosophical argument. The lament paints a poignant picture of mutual respect, constructive engagement, and what must have been a lot of common purpose and shared attitudes—albeit with a substantive pattern of disagreement. The disagreement should have been "fertile" for Zhuangzi's intellectual growth. Zhuangzi could reach the height of his craft only in shared conversation with Hui Shi. This picture fuels the Graham/Harbsmeier lament that we know too little about the writings and philosophy of Zhuangzi's great and prolific friend (and perhaps teacher).[8]

The fish story portrays this constructive debating relation. Arguably, it is the main one with an unequivocally "philosophical" content and style[9]—and a kind of philosophy even Westerners can recognize at first glimpse—epistemology![10]

Angus Graham proffers a related explanation of the distinctive value of the passage:

> This is the only instance of disputation with Hui Shih in the *Outer chapters* (interest in the Sophists was already failing), and is remarkable for a playfulness which in parodying logical debate is more faithful to the detail of its structure than anything else in *Chuang-tzŭ*. When Hui Shih defended the paradoxes listed without explanation in "Below in the Empire" . . . he must have been talking like this, as the Later Mohists do in the explanations of some of their *Canons;* what a pity we never hear what he had to say![11]

Graham's depiction here contains the main elements of the manifest image. The passage ridicules logic but also exhibits it in great detail. It is precisely the detail of this philosophical discussion that makes the passage difficult to interpret, however. Graham postulated a crucial clue when he suggested that the rather rare use of 安 *an*[where] in the question "From whence do you know . . .?" helps make sense of Zhuangzi's final comment. It also links Zhuangzi's position in the dialogue to the perspectivalism, which is one of the philosophical themes of the *Zhuangzi.* It is a particularly strong theme in chapter 17, "Autumn Floods," where we find this dialogue.

I accept and follow this Graham line.[12] That the conclusion Zhuangzi draws is a "positional" one is clearly implied by his concluding statement. Translations before Graham had seen this point, but few had linked it as closely to the language used as Graham's analysis did. His hypothesis about *an*[whence] distributes the perspectival point throughout the dialogue.[13] I do not rely heavily on this lexical claim but focus on the rest of the structure of the argument—which, I shall argue, fills out the perspectival analysis.

Graham's insight gives us a line on Zhuangzi's concluding remark but does not really solve the other philosophical puzzles posed by the dialogue.[14] How is the final remark a resolution or a plausible conclusion to the disagreement? What perspectival point is Zhuangzi's argument supposed to have made? Are there not internal contradictions in each discussant's position? Isn't Zhuangzi's penultimate riposte a non sequitur? Is Hui Shi right that Zhuangzi is forced by his own logic to acknowledge that he does not know fish happiness? And so forth. While accepting Graham's insight, I venture some answers to these remaining questions and attempt to do so in a way that illuminates the distinctive form of philosophical perspectivalism in epistemology exemplified in the *Zhuangzi* text.

While I do make Zhuangzi's point in this debate consistent with the perspectivalism of this chapter and with a theme of relativism/perspectivalism that runs through much of the rest of the *Zhuangzi,* I do not accept—as a condition on the adequacy of an interpretation—that a passage *must* be made consistent with an entire book.[15] It is surely possible to imagine that the correct interpretation of the passage would expose or illustrate an incoherence or a contradiction in another *Zhuangzi* position.[16] Despite the frequent appeal to whole text coherence as a standard of good interpretation, the coherence relevant to issues of meaning is the coherence of the entire community's discourse.

Coherence of a line of thought is not a bad thing, of course. While it is not semantically required, coherence with some larger theme in the *Zhuangzi* provides an answer to an *explanatory* question of textual origin or motivation—what is the reason for including this dialogue **here** in the text? There are other ways of answering the question besides expository coherence—political commentary, changing interests, animosity toward persons or groups, accident, and so on. However, an interpretation that makes the point of this exchange a way of clarifying or bolstering some position taken elsewhere in the text can give us a straightforward account of more of the detail of the passage.[17] As a way of explaining text inclusion, broad coherence has advantages over external explanations—for example, the decline in interest in logical matters, political developments, defection, and so on. External causes can partially explain some "tenor" of a passage, but the interpreter still tends to rely on coherence to explain inferentially articulated detail.[18] The more detail we consider, the harder it is to explain without appealing to inferential patterns among sentences.

Ironically, part of the historical difficulty in understanding this exchange may lie precisely in tying it too closely to **perceived** *author* coherence—coherence with the "manifest image" of the two speakers. The problem is not merely Zhuangzi's image as a mystic but includes Hui Shi's converse image as a logician. Neither image, I argue, helps us explain the detail of this exchange.

Rather than explaining the dispute, the manifest image tends to explain it **away**. It becomes a familiar **miscommunication** between a logician and a mystic. Preidentification of philosophical position prevents us from construing this dialogue as a productive philosophical discussion between cooperating intellects—the kind of discussion that would underlie Zhuangzi's lament about Hui Shi's passing.

I propose, instead, to flip the standard analysis on its head to explain the deep structure of the dialogue as manifest in its fine detail. Zhuangzi is the more skillful dialectician leading the intuitionist (Hui Shi) into a logical trap. The trap is a close relative of one that catches Hui Shi in other places, and the discussion reveals a common pattern of agreement and disagreement between these two ancient thinkers—they agree in their perspectival relativism and disagree on how to formulate its implications.

In the *Zhuangzi* as a whole, I believe Hui Shi *thematically* plays the role of sharing the relativist point of view (maybe even originating it) but of misstating the consequences of that shared position. He frequently lands in contradictions that Zhuangzi manages to avoid. Zhuangzi, the more logically consistent of the two, exposes these contradictions in their disputes and shows how more careful reasoning from their shared position should go. Arguably, this picture of their relationship better explains Zhuangzi's lament. He honed his insights into their position by these dialectic exchanges revealing Hui Shi's mistakes. The dialogues help him (Zhuangzi) think more carefully about what the valid conclusions of his relativism are.

Graham used his locative analysis of *an*[whence] to explain mainly Zhuangzi's closing remark—but rather than developing the perspectival theme in detail, he combined that insight with the common view that Zhuangzi is playfully dismissing "logic." Looking for the alternate picture, which is of the debate as a reductio of one of Hui Shi's illegitimate inferences from relativism, should more thoroughly explain the role of this locative way of asking "How do you know?"

The mystic versus logician theme does not make clear sense of the fond picture we have of *fertile* philosophical discussion between the two. If Zhuangzi tended to ignore, make fun of, and dismissively laugh off Hui Shi's logically sound arguments, in what sense could he have gained anything or *needed* stimulation from Hui Shi? The argumentative exchanges represented by that common picture would have been philosophically barren. The problem with the orthodox analysis of this particular discussion is that someone who is looking at the dialogue but knows nothing about the two participants would have a hard time telling which of the two was more committed to picky, analytic debating points.

If the first key to unraveling the exchange is to escape from the grip of the mystic versus logician image, the second is to note that Zhuangzi shifts the debate by semantic ascent to the epistemic principle to which Hui Shi is committed. The issue is not simply "does Zhuangzi know?" but "what is the appropriate standard of attributing knowledge?" We can view the discussion as an example of a productive philosophical exchange by tracing how Zhuangzi's questions lead Hui Shi to a reductio of his assumption that only one **perspective** (the subject's) counts as real knowing (for example, such things as pleasure and knowledge). Zhuangzi's rival view is that multiple standards for attributing knowledge (even of such things) are appropriate for different contexts and different kinds of knowledge claims.

What I do here, accordingly, is focus on steps in the discussion to explain the detail in ways that make the exchange "productive." The picture that will emerge is quite different one of a Zhuangzi who outthinks Hui Shi in his own terms—a Zhuangzi who, far from haughtily dismissing reasoning, accepts and meets a reasoned challenge by inferring a better result than that posed by his opponent. We have a passage that shows us how a Zhuangzi could possibly have honed and perfected his philosophical position from a real-life exchange of the sort abbreviated here.

This result, like the mystic-logician alternative, **does** fit the dialogue into a coherent (but alternative) picture of the philosophical relation between Zhuangzi and Hui Shi. They are fellow relativists who disagree about how correctly to formulate the consequences of their relativism. However, the result does not prove, against modern textual skeptics, that the two actually were friends or that the relationship pictured in the stories was a historically accurate one. It **can** be made into a more coherent exchange, and the advantages of that, again, are not that such is a condition of adequacy but that it accounts for more detail, explaining the inclusion of this dialogue in the collection. The same explanation of detail could equally explain the "invention" of the dialogue (if that is what it was). The invented detail is still motivated by inferential relations of the responses of the two personae—whether real or fictional.

For our own purposes in trying to understand Chinese thinking, this passage is one of a small cluster of examples of reasoning in ancient Chinese texts that sinologists recognize as having a surface resemblance to Western philosophy more than to the manifest image of Chinese thought. As usual, the greater value of such examples lies in careful analysis of them to identify and elaborate the deep conceptual differences behind the surface similarity. Difference usually stands out more starkly against the background of the familiar. The traditionalist identifies "Western-style reasoning" to justify skipping over it. From the point of view of any serious student of Chinese thought, these are precisely the cases that deserve the most careful analysis and scrutiny.

THE ANALYSIS

See the Fish Swimming at Leisure

Zhuangzi starts with a simple inference,[19] ostensibly the beginning of a conversation.[20] Translators worry about the correct way to translate the modifier Zhuangzi uses here of the fish.[21] I will not dwell on the issue here. He describes the fish using the phrase *chu*[comeout] *you*[swim:roam] *cong*[follow:from] *rong*[easy] (出遊從容 come out and swim freely and leisurely) and then says: "*Shi*[this] *yu*[fish] *le*[pleasure] *ye*[assertion]" (是魚樂也 this is fish happiness). The inferred consequent has two crucial ambiguities.

1) In classical Chinese, knowledge and other propositional contexts are usually rendered as complex noun phrases—using a possessive between subject and predicate. (See the discussion below in the section titled "How Do You Know?") Translators can choose to render Zhuangzi's conclusion in propositional form: "[The] fish are happy." As we will see, the ambiguous formulation may motivate the disagreement. Hui Shi's skeptical response reads Zhuangzi's statement "this is fish happiness" as entailing cognitive access to something like Nagel's[22] "what it is like for a fish to be happy." His skepticism is more clearly in order on that reading. In the alternate reading, it is a more familiar form of "other minds" skepticism—you cannot know that fish are happy (even if they were to laugh out loud).

2) The character 樂 *le*[pleasure:happy] need not be read in the strongly subjective way that Western philosophers normally assign to our concept of "pleasure" or "happiness." As Fingarette urged years ago, Chinese psychological terms seldom have such exclusively subjectivist meanings.[23] They evoke inner states by describing human embodiment in situations—as we so often see in Chinese poetry.[24] In other words, *le* could imply only that the fish are engaged in a pleasant *activity*—leisure or playful behavior. That insight makes the inferential gap between Zhuangzi's antecedent evidence and his conclusion seem much less precarious. Those fish swim at their leisure, play, or enjoyment (as opposed to searching for food). We could analyze Zhuangzi's position adverbially. "See the way of swimming—that is leisurely swimming for a fish. They are taking a stroll—as we are."

How Do You Know?

Hui Shi's first "move" in the "happy fish dialogue" illustrates an interesting parallel between ancient Chinese and modern Western language games.[25] When we assert P, someone may respond with "How do you know P?" While it may seem too obvious to comment on, the reliance on this norm of assertion will figure crucially later in the dialogue. Briefly, the "way" of assertion is one that is efficient for a community relying on transmission of information. Those who hear our assertions take them on our authority and may appropriately transmit them to others. We, in effect, implicitly license the hearer to repeat our claims to third parties. The hearers, accordingly, have a right (perhaps even a duty) to assure themselves that you know what you assert—that the license to repeat it is valid. So the conversational norm governing assertion is that you should be prepared to respond to a challenge to your right to claim knowledge of what you have said.[26]

When Zhuangzi asserts "That's fish happiness," the rules of ancient Chinese, like those of modern English, allow Hui Shi's challenge: "How do you know that?" Zhuangzi implicitly acknowledges the appropriateness of the challenge by responding (and implicitly relying on the principle himself). His response answers a question with a question, which some regard as impolite but is a common practice among philosophers. I discuss this further when I return to Zhuangzi's response below.

A second interesting parallel is that the challenge normally invites one to give your way of accessing the knowledge—"How do you know?" (as in most translations). The form is not merely "Do you know?" A hearer asks you to give your reasons so she can decide whether to acknowledge your claim to know what you are asserting. The interesting departure *in this dialogue* is that the natural and more familiar 何以知 he^{how} yi^{with} zhi^{know}? is replaced here by what Graham identified as the locative question form 安知 an^{whence} zhi^{know}? (Whence do you know?). The form of the challenge is perspectival. Implicitly, this form invites Zhuangzi to give a perspectival account of his point of view or route of access to the knowledge.

Hui Shi does not simply rely on the norm, allowing a "How do you know?" challenge. He also motivates it by an inference from 子非魚 $zi^{you/master}$ fei^{is-not} yu^{fish} (you are not (the/a) fish). We can fit Graham's hypothesis of the perspectival context of the discussion to this challenge. The *Zhuangzi* famously uses the perspective of different species and their different standards of beauty and comfort as an illustration of the complexity of the notion of different points of view.

Hui Shi, as a rule, takes relativism to entail something about a correct perspective. In this case, that for judging if a thing is in a state, the correct perspective is the thing's own. If a thing takes something to be beautiful, then it **is** beautiful. Zhuangzi does not know the happiness from the fish's perspective and, accordingly, should make no assertion about it.

Hui Shi's skeptical challenge, thus, implicitly commits him to there being a single correct **standard** for claiming knowledge of fish happiness—the self or subjective standard. That is the standard appropriate for both interpreting Zhuangzi's comment and for endorsing that Zhuangzi knows what he asserts. That the debate from this point shifts to discussion of Hui Shi's proposed standard is a crucial key to this interpretation.

Notice that Zhuangzi already preceded his claim with an inference. His implicit answer to "How do you know?" had already been given. Zhuangzi explicitly inferred it from their manner of swimming (under his interpretation of it). He didn't **originally** phrase this in a perspectival way. It was a simple inference from an (interpreted) observation.

Hui Shi's position that knowledge of such things can only be the direct, noninferential knowledge entails that we should reject Zhuangzi's implicit standard. Only an immediate, intuitive apprehension of the happiness itself counts as "knowing," not an inference from some observation. Thus his question not only poses a standard but also implicitly rejects the one already in play—the inferential, indirect, third-person standard that Zhuangzi explicitly relied on in his opening comment.

Hui Shi's challenge, like the original question, exploits the structural ambiguity of propositional contexts in ancient Chinese mentioned above. Common assertions *may* exhibit the ambiguity, but knowledge claims *almost always* do. Knowledge contexts are rarely explicitly propositional—as they would be in English.[27] In Indo-European languages, we would structure the challenge using the familiar grammatical pair: propositional belief versus knowledge. What we know (or merely believe) is normally expressed as a *that*-phrase. We know or believe that P—where P can be replaced by a whole grammatical sentence.

Chinese 知 *zhi*[know] typically takes a noun-phrase object. The noun phrase is formed by nominalizing the S-P sentence that occurs in the *that*-

clause of Western belief contexts: The "thing" known is S's P. What we know is a thing's property. I have argued in previous publications that this feature (together with the nonsentential features of counterparts of a *belief* structure in Chinese) explains a tendency, now common among interpreters of Chinese philosophy, to treat knowledge claims on the model of knowing *of* or knowing *how* rather than knowing *that*.[28] Hui Shi's implicit standard thus exploits the nominalized reading we noticed above. Again, it makes his skepticism more intuitively plausible. The correct standard for an assertion may depend on the form of the claim. The ambiguity here is a function of the ambiguity in the form of Hui Shi's challenge.

How Do You Know I Don't Know?

Simply to respond to the challenge, Zhuangzi would cite *some* means of access to what he (allegedly) knows. Here he does not. (As we saw, he had already stated his ground for the assertion.) Instead, he turns the discussion to the first-person standard presupposed in Hui Shi's challenge and its implied rejection of Zhuangzi's third-person standard. Zhuangzi's response is not **merely** the impolite evasion of answering a question with another question. It's a counterattack. Hui Shi committed himself to a privileged status for the first-person standard. Zhuangzi interprets this as the nonrelativist claim—that correctly to claim to know X's inner state, you must be X.

To assume Zhuangzi here responds directly to the challenge is to read it as a defense of a dogmatic or antiskeptical position. Thus commentators read it (as Beckwith complained in note 5, this chapter) as simply saying, "I know what I know," or, as Chinn (note 13) does, as antiskeptical. If it is merely that, then Zhuangzi's answer is also evasive and impolite—both conversationally wasteful responses. Zhuangzi's response can be viewed as both principled and appropriate and extremely efficient conversationally if we acknowledge the ascent to a philosophical issue.

Zhuangzi's response illustrates the "semantic ascent" typical of philosophy. He focuses on a "second level" or metaclaim. Zhuangzi does not reject the assumption that he should be accountable for warranting his claim to know what he asserts. Technically, that was not at issue in Hui Shi's challenge since Zhuangzi had prefaced his claim with his reason. The question was, "whence"—from what perspective—does he know it? Zhuangzi can fairly turn his attention to the interpretation Hui Shi places on his assertion in insisting on the first-person perspective. Hui Shi has read "this [is] fish happiness" as "I am in direct contact with fish happiness—the kind of contact a fish would have." For that reading, the presupposed standard "you must be a fish" is warranted.

Zhuangzi's pluralist position should commit him to there being multiple interpretations of his original assertion. Each would be governed by different standards of knowing. Hui Shi's insisting that only his "inner" or "subjective" standard is right implies only the matching interpretation of "this is fish happiness." Zhuangzi now leads Hui Shi into a reductio of his view that the "inner" is the only correct standard. The reductio here lacks the volubility of Plato's Socratic performances, so we must tease the steps out of the inferential details of the dialogue.

More ambiguities lurk in the ancient Chinese grammar that will be overspecified in almost any English translation. First, classical Chinese common and proper nouns work alike grammatically in this example. I argued years ago that the Chinese dialecticians were theoretically treating all nouns as logically singular terms.[29] Thus, Zhuangzi's shift from "fish" to "me" is not as jarring as the parallel inference would be in English. What Hui Shi presupposes is not classic "other-minds" skepticism. Technically, his implied standard is "being of the same species," not "being the very same individual subjectivity." Zhuangzi here extrapolates that standard, but he need not do it on the basis of a subjective analysis of (aspects of) consciousness. In effect, he is simply taking the grammatically *ambiguous* standard, "one must be X to know X's F"—where F can be replaced by either *le*[happiness] or *zhi*[knowledge]. In replacing 魚 *yu*[fish] with 我 *wo*[1] in the X position, Zhuangzi is replacing one singular term with another in the formula schemata.

Second, Zhuangzi's extrapolating the standard from knowing *le*[happiness] to knowing *zhi*[knowledge] would also be grating on its face if delivered in an English dialogue. Even if we take both to be internal states, we might still object.[30] One is cognitive and the other affective. We might think it easier to know other rational people's cognitive states than their affective states.

This cognitive-affective distinction was not as marked in ancient Chinese; witness the common translation of 心 *xin* as "heart-mind." *Zhi*[know] seems to have a wide range of uses, which, according to definitions in the Mohist Canon, includes something like "consciousness"[31] (e.g., Canon: A24 When you sleep, your *zhi*[know (consciousness)] does not *zhi*[know]). Further, if we take Hui Shi to be skeptical about whether Zhuangzi knows "what it is like to be a happy fish," then it is arguable that the state of knowledge in question **consists in** duplicating the inner state in one's own inner field. This should make Zhuangzi's extrapolation of the principle from le[happiness] to zhi[know] somewhat less objectionable. If that is what knowing is, then knowing one's knowing must involve the same difficulty. Ancient Chinese thinkers seldom seem to have operated with an implicit "true belief plus an account" concept of zhi[know].

Interestingly, however, Zhuangzi's counterquestion at this point is a relatively rare example of a fully propositional object of zhi[know]: 安知我不知魚之樂 an[whence] zhi[know] wo[I] bu[not] zhi[know] yu[fish] zhi's le[play:leisure]?[32] Presumably, Zhuangzi could have put his point in nominalized form, though it would have been a bit of fun saying it (安知我之不知魚之樂 an[whence] zhi[know] wo[I] zhi's bu[not] zhi[know] yu[fish] zhi's le[play:leisure]?). The change, however, could be significant. An explicit propositional form exploits the ambiguity of the "fish [are] happy" in a way that favors Zhuangzi's claim to knowledge. The question looks more like an ordinary other-minds question: can we know *that* X (Zhuangzi or the fish) is/are in state Y (happy or knowing)?

We might object, on Hui Shi's behalf, that he has not claimed to know that Zhuangzi does not know. He has only asked Zhuangzi to justify his cognitive "right" to the assertion. Hui Shi **might** have responded, "I don't know if you know or not—that's precisely what I was asking you." To take that position, Hui Shi would implicitly abandon his exclusive reliance on the subjective standard for attributing knowledge. He could be taken innocently and openly to have asked what other standard is involved.

In his next response, however, Hui Shi acknowledges the exclusivist reading of his challenge as implying that Zhuangzi does not know.[33] If we accept this interpretation of the challenge, then the norm of assertion we discussed at the beginning comes back into play. If he is committed to "Zhuangzi doesn't know . . . ," he, too, should be prepared to respond to a challenge: "how/whence do you know that Zhuangzi doesn't know?" If the only standard is his subjective standard, then Hui Shi should withdraw his implicit claim on the same grounds that he argues Zhuangzi should withdraw his original comment about the fish.

Hui Shi ignores another way he might avoid the trap Zhuangzi is setting for him. He might insist on the interpretation of his standard as species based, not as an individual or subjectivist standard. This would undermine the parallel Zhuangzi draws between the two knowledge commitments. He opts not to draw either of the distinctions that could extricate him from Zhuangzi's reductio.

Right! Not being You, I don't know You; You, not being Fish,
don't know Fish—That Is the Whole of it!

Hui Shi's next move takes Zhuangzi's bait. He clings to his subjective standard while he accepts:

(a) That in claiming something, one should know it
(b) That his subjective principle should be applied to different individuals as well as to species
(c) That the standard applies to $zhi^{knowledge}$ as it does to affective attitudes like $le^{pleasure}$
(d) That his challenge amounts to claiming that Zhuangzi does not know fish happiness

Hui Shi then draws two dangerous conclusions: "I don't know your knowledge state" and "you don't know the fish's $le^{pleasure}$ state." But the second contradicts the first when we combine it with (a) the norm of assertion. Hui Shi is committed to both that he knows and that he does not know what Zhuangzi knows.

In drawing the first conclusion, Hui Shi could have used his subjective standard in two ways: a direct and an inferential way. Being Hui Shi, he knows directly that he does not know what Zhuangzi knows. However, Hui Shi chose to formulate the conclusion inferentially. He recommitted himself to his standard and **inferred** from it that he does not know Zhuangzi's knowing. What he does conflicts with his commitment to the inner-perspective principle. If his principle is correct, he should not apply it. He has implicitly committed himself to two different standards—knowing (what it is like first person) and knowing by inference. Both commitments still lead to his conclusion that he does not know Zhuangzi's "knowing."

Then he uses his standard again in an **inference** to "Zhuangzi doesn't know the fish are happy." This time, however, his commitment and what he does with it lead to different results. He cannot claim to know what he asserts (that Zhuangzi does not know fish happiness) by using his inner-perspective method. The trap is closing. Not noticing his own predicament, he declares his case "complete." His triumphant tone of confidence attaches to the proposition known by violating his own principle. It is knowing from the outside, at a distance—not the subjective principle he champions. If he knows it—as the triumphal refrain signals, then his principle must not be the only way of knowing.

Zhuangzi is right—Hui Shi cannot consistently express his objection to Zhuangzi's knowing the fish while relying on his subjective standard for attributing knowledge. If he tries to express his skepticism, Hui Shi ends up committed both to knowing Zhuangzi's cognitive state and to not knowing it. The conflicting commitments come in different ways from his principle of privileging the inner perspective—but following the way of knowing he favors, he must conclude he does not know whether Zhuangzi knows fish happiness or not. If he accepts that the subjective principle is one of a plurality of correct tests of knowing, then he can escape the contradiction. However, that would allow Zhuangzi to return to the inference stated at the beginning of the dialogue.

Hui Shi is in a bind. He needs inference from the principle to justify his claim that Zhuangzi does not know, but his principle rules out knowledge by inference. His only escape is to say he does not know whether Zhuangzi knows or not—and to withdraw his assertion. He may continue to believe that Zhuangzi does not know what he asserted, but Hui Shi, relying on the principles he does, should not comment on Zhuangzi's assertion. If Zhuangzi were committed to Hui Shi's principles, he would have asserted nothing as well. One consequence of Hui Shi's "way" of knowing is the familiar antilanguage conclusion. Neither should have spoken.

Thus, this dialogue does not depict a rigorously logical Hui Shi trapping Zhuangzi, who escapes by mischievously refusing to acknowledge logic. It rather shows a Hui Shi trapped by his persistent tendency of slipping from relativistic premises to absolutist conclusions that conflict with his relativism. He starts by being perspectival about joy but slips into making an absolute claim about the standard of knowing it.

LET'S RETURN TO THE BEGINNING

The account dominated by the manifest image of Zhuangzi (humorous mystic) and Hui Shi (logician) would, at this point, treat Zhuangzi as cavalierly dismissing Hui Shi's thoroughly logical proof, changing the subject, and just verbally goofing around to display his disdain for logic. We no longer have to treat it this way. Hui Shi's original challenge allowed Zhuangzi to invoke philosophical ascent. Zhuangzi refocused the issue away from the question of whether Zhuangzi knows and instead addressed Hui Shi's consistency in using his subjective principle to question Zhuangzi's right to the assertion. Does that principle allow Hui Shi to dispute a claim to knowledge? He ends up trumpeting a conclusive claim to know that violates the principle. He must now acknowledge that we have other ways of knowing besides "from the inside."

This denouement is notoriously recondite. One tempting confusion stems from the common assumption that Zhuangzi is denying that Hui Shi knows what he knows. On the contrary, Zhuangzi's position is epistemic pluralism; a multiplicity of standards governs judgments of what counts as knowing in different situations. He can and should allow that Hui Shi *does* know what Zhuangzi knows.

This confusion may tempt us to misread Zhuangzi when he recommends following the discussion back to its beginning. Then it becomes easy to suspect, as I thought years ago, that Zhuangzi is about to resort to a silly and inconsistent sophistry. Ordinarily, in asking "how do you X?" we presuppose that you *have* done or can do X. "How do you make the yo-yo sleep?" Then the question seeks information about what method you used in (admittedly) actually doing X. The form of the "how" question *ordinarily* implies that one acknowledges the ability itself. Is Zhuangzi simply relying on this verbal trick? In asking " 'How do you know?' you presupposed that I knew."[34]

I was tempted to read Zhuangzi in this way in part because I was still caught up in the familiar view that Zhuangzi was trapped by Hui Shi's logic. That motivation largely disappears when we see that it is Hui Shi who is trapped. Zhuangzi has lured him into a reductio of his absolutist epistemic theory. Even then, the reading hardly comports with the rest of the standard view of a Zhuangzi dodging logic from his playful, mystical perspective. On this account, he evades it by using a verbal trick, a paradigm of philosophical sophistry. It is a sophistry because, in a challenge to knowledge, the phrase "How do you know?" normally has the opposite presupposition.[35] It yields a Zhuangzi behaving like a *bad analytic* thinker—not a mystic.

I now have three connected worries about reading Zhuangzi's penultimate sentence in this way.

- First, it is a weak sophistry—an almost textbook case of Wittgenstein's analytic philosopher's disease. We get caught in a puzzle because we impose a rigid interpretation on a **grammatical form** ("How do you . . . ?") and then carry it from its "home" use to a different "language game" (knowledge challenges), where it plays a different role.
- Second, Zhuangzi's own prior response clearly commits him to the opposite (and proper) reading of Hui Shi's challenge. His own challenge clearly interprets Hui Shi's prior question as entailing that he (Zhuangzi) does not know. Zhuangzi thus acknowledges that Hui Shi's "whence" implied doubt, not endorsement, of Zhuangzi's knowledge claim. The line of interpretation makes Zhuangzi dishonest as well as sophistic.
- Third, it is difficult to see how to fit this verbal trick into the flow of the dialogue. It neither picks up on the reductio of Hui Shi's use of his subjectivity principle nor leads effectively to the puzzling conclusion: "I knew it from above the Hao [River]." The verbal trickery neither illuminates nor develops the perspectival thrust of the discussion.

To develop an alternative way of understanding this passage, let's go back to some basics. First, we should focus on the implicit pragmatic theory of language in traditional Daoist texts—the core role of language is normative guidance, not factual representation. This is one key to seeing how Zhuangzi's theory fits with his version of perspectival skepticism. Commitments to different norms of term use (description) give rise to different directions of guidance. Second, if we regard Hui Shi's Ten relativist "theses" as an inspiration to Zhuangzi, then we need to identify how he thinks he improves on Hui Shi's position. My thesis is that Zhuangzi avoids incoherent derivation of absolutist (monist) conclusions. Hui Shi, like careless relativists everywhere, keeps being tempted to draw absolute conclusions from his relativist premises.

The first item helps make Zhuangzi seem refreshingly "modern." Naturalist pragmatism now portrays epistemology and semantics as being deeply normative, and modern developments in these fields are borrowing analyses developed in ethics, aesthetics, and political theory. In Zhuangzi's terms, we can think of daos of speaking, of interpreting, of inferring, and asserting, just as there are of acting and painting. It naturally becomes obvious that, as in ethics, the standards for these normative epistemic judgments are "relative" to the judging situations, in which different ends, values, purposes, roles, and so forth—in a word, with different contextual daos—are in play. The standard of what counts as "knowing" in responding to a Cartesian or twin-earth skeptic is different from the standard appropriate for more ordinary contexts of assertion. The standard of recognizing barns in "barn façade county" is not the same as it is in Montana.

This is a way to understand why the paradigm case arguments do not successfully defeat a Cartesian skeptic. While it is true that the "normal" standards for the use of "know" do not require certainty, when a skeptic points out a somewhat fantastic possibility of error, simply citing the "normal" use, does not effectively respond to the context of the argument. It can merely show why, in normal situations, we do not have to use "know" in the skeptic's way. The skeptic can escape by *recommending* a reform of normal usage. At that point, decisive rebuttal would have to show that the skeptic's recommendation is incoherent in some way.

Consider a related situation within sinology. Professor Ames and I both routinely deal with beginning students or interested nonsinologists who ask us what an inscription or a passage means. We look at the passage and simply "read it." We treat meaning in that context as "obvious" to someone who has learned Chinese. Our answers to these beginning students sound like observation sentences. We simply look at the passage and "see" the meaning. Given our training and the context of the question, neither of us needs any implicit inference from the evidence to answer the question.

Where we stand at this moment, however, the situation is different. We are at a sinology conference, surrounded by other "experts" in classical Chinese, debating the meaning of some familiar passage like the one before us. In this context, for either of us to react to the disagreement before us by something that sounds like a simple observation sentence of the type we used with our first-year students would be out of place. No one would take such an "observation" seriously as warranted in **this** context. Neither of us is **here** entitled to claim knowledge in that direct, perceptual way. The situation imposes a different standard on both of us. We have essentially similar training and mastery of Chinese, and we both "know what the other knows." Since we disagree, the question of which of us knows the meaning must now rely on a standard more appropriate to the context of the question. Merely claiming to "see the meaning" would be semantically "inappropriate." This is a twist on Hume's contrast of his views when he dines, plays backgammon, or converses with friends: he is not plagued by the doubts that come when he does philosophy.[36]

Zhuangzi's intriguing form of skepticism makes a similar point. He does it explicitly in the "Gaptooth" discussion about "knowing that you do not know." There his skeptical mood starts with doubts that we can know something simply because everyone agrees to it. Clearly, this philosophical doubt implies a higher standard of knowledge than we use for "ordinary" knowledge claims. Normally (that is, outside of philosophical discussions of skepticism) we accept the "authority" of others and of our own past beliefs. However, as soon as we formulate this normal attitude as an explicit rule, we reject it. It, in fact, creates a contradiction because one of the things everyone "knows" is that what everyone "knows" is often wrong.[37] As the skeptic Wang Ni continues to reject formulations of skepticism and ends with something like the Pyrrhonian conclusion that we do not know whether we know. But Wang Ni ultimately bases that conclusion on doubts about correct word use. "How do I know that what I call knowing is not ignorance? How do I know that what I call ignorance is not knowing?"[38]

Now let's return to Zhuangzi's troubling final remark for another look. We need to construe it slightly differently to make the discussion follow a coherent line. Hui Shi has been caught in a reductio because he tries to restrict knowledge to the norm appropriate for a first-person assertion—the (subjectivity) standard. Zhuangzi would presumably allow that there are two ways of knowing about affective states. The way I can know I am happy is different from the way you can know it. Hui Shi wants to "privilege" one of these ways of calling something "knowing." Only the inner should be so classified. Yet, he cannot avoid relying on a third-person standard (using inference rather than direct awareness) if he wants to use his privileged standard to draw any conclusions about knowing—in particular to conclude that Zhuangzi does not know fish happiness.

We can now view Zhuangzi's final comment as an explanation that will help Hui Shi with his perplexity. Hui Shi's enthusiastic confidence in his argument shows that he treats his conclusion about Zhuangzi's not knowing as firm, solid knowledge. So he uses and trusts the inferential, outside perspective, third-person standard. Zhuangzi has consistently relied on the same standard—and does so now in acknowledging that Hui Shi does know what he, Zhuangzi, knows. Zhuangzi knows the fish are happy, and Hui Shi knows what Zhuangzi knows—what his state of knowledge is and how/whence he got it. Allowing a third-person perspective removes any puzzle. Hui Shi **knew** at the beginning, and his challenge was formulated precisely because he did know how Zhuangzi knew and on what he relied. He knew Zhuangzi was not claiming to know "what it was like to be a happy fish." His problem came because he adopted a commitment to an unrealistic standard of knowing. His challenge was motivated by that standard and by **knowing that Zhuangzi knew in a way** that did not follow the inner-perspective way of knowing.

Hui Shi knew that the ground of Zhuangzi's assertion was the observed manner of swimming. Hui Shi, standing with Zhuangzi "above the Hao" saw exactly the same thing and knew precisely in which sense, how and whence, Zhuangzi knew about the fish.

In laying out this discussion in terms of standards for the use of "know," I have occasionally helped myself to concepts, distinctions, and tools of analysis to draw the attention of readers to relevant features of the argument. Some of these are terms that I have argued were not available to Zhuangzi and Hui Shi. Where we use sentential notions (e.g., "truth" and "inference," "subjective" and "objective"), ancient Chinese thinkers used different notions, built around things like "terms," "assertability," "way," and "dependency." So their focus would not be on inference or logic but on what approving or disapproving of the use of a term in a context depends or relies on. They would speak of a way rather than a norm, of outer versus inner perspective rather than subjective-objective, and so on. We should be able to go back and retrace all the steps in the reasoning in terms familiar in the *Zhuangzi* without losing the point. I have scattered such rephrasing throughout my account but not attempted to replace all of them. I leave that as an exercise to the interested reader.

The component of this orientation to discussion of theory of language (arguably contributed by Hui Shi) is the insight that what is appropriate to say depends on a perspective—which Zhuangzi broadened to include purposes (useful and useless), indexicals, and background assumptions or standards. So it is perfectly in character for this discussion to be shaped around the idea of what it is appropriate to say from various "points of view." Thus Graham's insight about the "whence" points to a crucial aspect of the character of philosophical discussion in ancient China.

Perhaps as important as the revised image of a careful and principled philosopher such as Zhuangzi is the linked revision in our picture of Hui Shi—his foil. For this exchange at least, Hui Shi's contribution shows no hint of sophistry. The closest anyone comes to a pure sophistry is the rejected interpretation of the final passage from Zhuangzi. Nor is there a trace of logic in Hui Shi's contribution. He is doing epistemology, but logical statements per se play no role in his contribution. Logic figures when it helps *us* notice that he is caught in a reductio. Nor do we find Hui Shi making or insisting on fine distinctions. On the contrary, he ignores crucial distinctions that might have saved him from Zhuangzi's trap. Hui Shi's standard is the direct standard characteristic of intuitionism as opposed to Zhuangzi's reliance on inference from evidence at a distance.

CONCLUSION

I have been experimenting with an alternative set of assumptions about the philosophical persona of Zhuangzi and Hui Shi in interpreting this widely cited dialogue. How much can we conclude from the enriched picture of this beloved story? Does it settle outstanding controversies about Zhuangzi? Abandoning the traditional view of Zhuangzi's intellectual heritage and character has independent motivation. A recent series of archeological discoveries has spawned some turmoil in textual theory of the *Laozi*. These discoveries have reinforced the scholarly doubt of the popular image of Laozi and Zhuangzi as prophet and follower. As recently as 1979, it was intellectually respectable to picture the *Zhuangzi*'s role, as Stuart Hackett did, as that of providing the reasoning, elaboration, exposition, and defense of *Laozi*'s aphoristic insights.[39] We still find that explanation of Zhuangzi in "capsule" encyclopedia presentations, but scholarship has been steadily chipping away at the traditional picture.

The alternate story, however, also has deep roots in the traditions of interpretation, starting with Guo Xiang's "individualistic" reading of the *Zhuangzi* and its contrasts with Wang Bi's take on the *Laozi* found in Wang Xianqian's hypothesis of a linguistic basis of Zhuangzi's thinking. As early as 1948, Fung Yu-lan focused more on the influence of Hui Shi than that of Laozi—though he still classifies Laozi and Zhuangzi as the second and third "phases" of Daoism.[40] Graham gave the new picture enormous momentum with his early insights into the "Qiwulun," his discovery of the technical theory of language insights scattered throughout the *Zhuangzi,* and his lovely aphorism "Zhuangzi never knew he was a Taoist." However, the image of Zhuangzi as a Laozi "development" persists as a background to interpretation despite the scholarly undermining of the story that originally grounded it.

This tour through the "fish happiness" passage adds to these historical and textual reasons for recasting our view of Zhuangzi. It adduces an interpretive advantage of the rival picture—its explanatory power. It illustrates the interpretive advantages of substituting a rival picture of a truly philosophical Zhuangzi who outdoes Hui Shi at a distinctively Chinese style of philosophical dialectic from a shared perspective of relativism in the philosophy of language. If we focus on the detailed inferential structure of the discussion, we can illuminate fine details that show Zhuangzi's argument to be principled and responsive. The "playful mystic" picture, by contrast, motivates a policy of dismissing inferential detail on the hypothesis that Zhuangzi is not merely ignoring Hui Shi's inferences but poking fun at them. We found instead a line of interpretation that portrays a Zhuangzi who conscientiously considers his rival's arguments and positions, shows how they lead to incoherence, and offers a more sound way to develop their shared perspectival insight. We exploit the picture of a Zhuangzi who "sharpens his skill" with another dialectician—a Zhuangzi who draws consistent conclusions from the perspectival analysis. Hui Shi, by contrast, shares the relativist starting point but mishandles its implications.

The form of Hui Shi's weakness relative to Zhuangzi is consistent throughout several philosophical issues. Hui Shi appears to draw metaphysical or absolute conclusions from relativist premises. An obvious form of the issue was first isolated (perhaps accidentally) by Graham, who argued that Hui Shi's theses led to logic discrediting itself.[41] If everything is relative, then there are no **real** distinctions.[42] The "all is one" mystic did, after all, draw the correct conclusion from relativism. The statement of Hui Shi's theses in chapter 33, "The Social World," indeed includes this conclusion—"The world is one body,"—as Graham also noticed. Graham saw that Zhuangzi rejects this conclusion in chapter 2, "Qiwulun" (Discourse on Equalizing Things). However, he did not put these insights together to revise his traditional view of Hui Shi as a logician and Zhuangzi as antilogic. I maintain that it is Hui Shi who is not simply a mystic but also, as illustrated here, an intuitionist. Hui Shi was never a logician or much of a sophist. He was simply a less consistent relativist than was Zhuangzi.

Careful reflection on this dialectical relation between the two thinkers should also help avoid common errors in expressing Zhuangzi's relativism—in confusing it with Hui Shi's. If interpreters make Hui Shi's mistake in thinking about relativism, they misconstrue Zhuangzi. For an example, consider Hui Shi's conclusion that we should "love all things equally." Standard interpretations would attribute something very close to Zhuangzi—the most common translation of his "Qiwulun" (chapter 2) is "A Discussion on Making Things Equal."

We should not take Zhuangzi to be committed to the claim that all views are (equally) correct or wrong. From Zhuangzi's relativist philosophy, no judgment about absolute value follows. The *Zhuangzi* takes its relativism to entail neither that all views are equally good nor that they are equally bad. "Error theory"—the conclusion that all views (or all "ordinary" views) are wrong is like "all views are right" or "all views are equal" in purporting to be absolute judgments, made from the absolute perspective of *nowhere.*

The *Zhuangzi* seems rather to deny that we can make sense of these purported judgments. The cosmos does not make judgments. The point of view of the cosmos (or any absolutist point of view—including the perfect man) is so irrelevant as to be unintelligible to us as we seek ways in this world.

Zhuangzi himself carefully stays within the relativist perspective—balancing the skeptical awareness that his is **a** point of view with his remaining within it. He consistently resists Hui Shi's invitations to state the "view from nowhere" on the world of perspectives. From his *actual* perspective, Zhuangzi makes all kinds of judgments. Things are not equal.

From **my** (relativist) point of view, for example, it is clear to me that the Christian (or Muslim or Hindu or Buddhist) fundamentalist is wrong—I might even say crazy, irrational, and stupid. Nothing in relativism requires me to stop either making these judgments from within my perspective or defending them and living by them. It only reminds me that there are other perspectives and that, had I grown up in another or remained in my own fundamentalist religious tradition, I would now *see things* quite differently. Perspectivalism, pluralism, or relativism fosters only a mild skepticism inducing greater tolerance but not the conclusion that I should abandon or refuse to express my natural, contextual judgments.

A relativist recognizes that hers is a point of view and that there are others. She is not, however, rationally committed to the normal expression of her position as "*just* a point of view." Her perspective has no work for the "just" to do. The "just" is not a part of the relativist insight—but belongs to the **absolutist's** restatement of it. The crux of the issue between

Zhuangzi and Hui Shi is how to state their relativism without being inconsistent.

What about other matters of textual history? This alternate image does little to dispel the skeptical hypothesis about Zhuangzi and Hui Shi. Was there really any relationship between these two alleged philosophical friends? The detailed examination hardly suggests that the passage is a verbatim recording of an actual conversation. Even if there were an actual discussion behind this section, the exchange is extremely unlikely to have been so brief and with the points so efficiently condensed. While it could be a précis of a more lengthy discussion that actually took place between two philosophers, it is certainly still plausible as a "staged" dialogue fictionally developing the supposed philosophical relationship. We can read the passage in the same way while assuming it contributes to the Zhuangzi persona rather than recording a history of the person.

The passage, accordingly, can do little to confirm the alternate story of "Zhuangzi's lineage." However, we need not surrender wholesale to historical skepticism. Like all skeptical arguments, skepticism of the Zhuangzi–Hui Shi friendship makes assumptions and presupposes intellectual motivations. One expressed motivation for the doubt is the dominant image of the philosophical postures of Zhuangzi and Hui Shi. That image, as we saw, makes a productive philosophical friendship and exchanges unlikely. Consequently, a more plausible account that reveals a productive pattern of philosophical discussion would undermine that motivation. Zhuangzi and Hui Shi can be seen as working in the same "school" of relativistic analysis—albeit with different ways of formulating their conclusions.

With that motivation removed, the skepticism may start to look slightly "metaphysical."[43] Given the commonplace observation that we know almost nothing about Zhuangzi personally beyond what we learn from the text, it seems that we can phrase the limit of skepticism this way: if we know **anything** about Zhuangzi, we access that knowledge via the channel that indicates he had a friendship with Hui Shi.[44] The stories of their exchanges do not suggest anything physically impossible, and they reflect the real-life phases a relationship might go through (death of a spouse, professional separation, jealousy, death of a friend, and so on).

A final point concerns whether the passage undermines or supports the view of Zhuangzi as a skeptic.[45] On the surface, Hui Shi raises a classic skeptical worry, and Zhuangzi dismisses it. However, we have seen that the issue is not simply Zhuangzi's knowing or not knowing; it is an issue of the standard of knowing (and the pragmatic or perspectival reasons for different standards in different contexts). The happy fish dialogue turns out to be a gloss on the *Zhuangzi* chapter 2 skeptical position: How do I know that what I call "knowledge" is not ignorance and what I call "ignorance" is not knowing?

NOTES

1. This study arose from an invitation from the Australasian Society for Asian and Comparative Philosophy to do an interpretive "duet" with Roger Ames. We selected this text as a theme to illustrate our differing views on interpretation of the *Zhuangzi* in the course of interpreting what this passage of the *Zhuangzi* says about interpretation. I extend my thanks to Professor Ames for his comments and stimulation. His analysis was published as Roger T. Ames, "Knowing in the *Zhuangzi*: 'From Here, on the Bridge, over the River Hao,' " in Roger T. Ames, ed., *Wandering at Ease in the* Zhuangzi (Albany: State University of New York Press, 1998), 219–230. I am obviously also heavily indebted to the many earlier studies that try to locate the "secret" of the exchange in obscure meanings of lexical items. I draw particularly on Graham's "positional" insight and share with many interpreters the feeling that the point of the exchange has something to do with our own interpretive activity—an indebtedness and feeling that Professor Ames and I clearly shared.

2. Yukawa's early piece almost suggests that mainly nonspecialists find the exchange interesting. See Hideki Yukawa, "Chuangtse: The Happy Fish," in Victor Mair, ed., *Experimental Essays on Chuang-tzu* (Honolulu: University of Hawai'i Press, 1983), pp. 56–62, reprinted in this volume.

3. The conversation is found in chapter 17, "Autumn Floods," which is traditionally included in the supposedly "less authentic" "outer chapters" of the *Zhuangzi*. One attribution is to a supposed "school of Zhuangzi." For an interesting discussion, see Liu Xiaogan, *Classifying the* Zhuangzi *Chapters* (Ann Arbor: University of Michigan Center for Chinese Studies, 1994).

4. See Bruce Brooks, Warring States Workshop e-mail communication #2808, May 2, 2001, for a statement of skepticism of the historicity of their friendship. Ames (1998) presents a defense of the traditional claim, as does Paul Kjellberg, quoted in Warring States Workshop e-mail communication #2808, May 2, 2001, via Bryan Van Norden. Brooks' skepticism arises because there is no documentary evidence of the friendship outside of the *Zhuangzi* stories themselves. The closest viable candidate would be the *Xunzi* account in chapter 22, which pairs Zhuangzi with Hui Shi.

5. Chris Beckwith's complaints are particularly forceful and clear. "I always wondered about Chuang Chou's philosophical point here. My feeling when I read that passage is he's saying he knows what he knows, and where does Huitzu get off saying C doesn't know it? How does H know, anyway? H keeps saying C is not a fish so he can't possibly know what fish like. So maybe C is saying he knows how fish feel (= empathy between species), but he's also saying H has no idea what C knows (= lack of contact

between different minds even of the same species), and of course H also believes this because he asks, 'How do you know?' " See Beckwith, Warring States Workshop e-mail communication #2147, October 3, 2000.

6. Lisa Raphals helpfully traces accounts and images of Hui Shi in "On Hui Shi," in Ames, *Wandering,* 143–162.

7. A. C. Graham, trans., *Chuang-tzu: The Inner Chapters* (London: Allen and Unwin, 1981), 124.

8. See Graham's comment below and in Graham, *Disputers of the Tao: Philosophical Argument in Ancient China* (Chicago: Open Court, 1989), 211.

9. The closest competitors were the discussions about the usefulness of the useless—but these are more examples of Zhuangzi lecturing or instructing Hui Shi than of a mutual philosophical exploration via argument.

10. Ames and I were using the debate as a metaphor for interpretation and as support for each of our respective methodologies of interpretation. Bruce Brooks agrees that it is about interpretation. Brooks, Warring States Workshop e-mail communication #2136, October 1, 2000. I will not be arguing at length for this broader implication of the debate—though on the whole I agree that the debate is relevant to interpretive issues—certainly as a helpful example (and an exercise) if not as a lesson in interpretive theory. Interpretation is intertwined with the epistemology throughout the argument, but it is never made an explicit target. So I am less confident that it could plausibly have been intended as a theory of interpretation.

11. Graham, *Inner Chapters,* 123.

12. Ames and I share our indebtedness to Graham on this point and agree that seeing the dialogue in this way is central to seeing it as relevant to interpretation.

13. Many translators now incorporate Graham's point into their rendering of the dialogue. See, for example, Ewing Y. Chinn, "Zhuangzi and Relativistic Scepticism," *Asian Philosophy* 7, no. 3 (1997): 207–221.

14. See Chris Beckwith's complaints in note 5, this chapter.

15. For a statement of this condition on adequate interpretation, see Brian V. Van Norden, "Competing Interpretations of the Inner Chapters of the *Zhuangzi,*" *Philosophy East and West* 46, no. 2 (1996): 247–269.

16. A famous example is the warring passages on "the use of uselessness." See the *Zhuangzi,* chapter 20. Interesting motivations and developments of this point may be found in Chris Fraser and Dan Robins, "Texts without Masters: On the Anonymity of the Warring States Classics" (1998), unpublished manuscript, staff seminar, Philosophy Department, University of Hong Kong, and a distinctively successful application to the *Xunzi* and the thesis that "human nature is evil" in Dan Robins, "The Warring States Debate about Human Nature," PhD diss., University of Hong Kong, 2001.

17. Notice that the explanatory advantage comes regardless of whether Zhuangzi was the author, whether the dialogue actually took place—even whether Zhuangzi and Hui Shi ever knew each other or were philosophical friends in the way the textual accounts of their exchanges suggest.

18. Consider an "external cause" extrapolated from Graham's explanation of the earlier passage. We may suppose the passage was either invented or selected from range of stories of exchanges between Hui Shi and Zhuangzi in order to discredit Hui Shi because of the "decline in interest in the school of names" or in order to distance Hui Shi and Zhuangzi. But that explanation leaves unanswered any questions we may have about the detail of the argument. Why this way of discrediting or distancing (let alone

whether the dialogue *does* effectively do this)? Why this discussion? This opening gambit? This response?

19. Some translators (e.g., Graham, Palmer, and Watson) do not treat this as an inference but as discrimination of method (Graham: "That's how fish are happy") or as the cause, not the evidence of their happiness (Watson and Palmer: "That's what fish really enjoy"). See Burton Watson, *The Complete Works of Chuang Tzu* (New York: Columbia University Press, 1968), and Martin Palmer with Elizabeth Breuilly, *The Book of Chuang Tzu* (New York: Penguin, 1996). I do not know the justification for either analysis. The earlier Legge and Lin Yutang translations treat it as a vague identification consistent with it being an inference. See James Legge, *The Texts of Taoism* (Oxford: Clarendon, 1891), and Lin Yutang, *The Wisdom of China* (London: Michael Joseph, 1954).

20. It could be a continuation of some philosophical discussion—say of the relativism of judgments to species or comparing the reaction of fish to philosophers and beautiful ladies at court. For our purposes, we can suppose it is just an innocent passing comment—a bit of "ordinary" language as opposed to a deliberately controversial philosophical thesis ("Hey, look at the fish playing around down there!").

21. A common translation is "minnows." For an interesting discussion of a current analysis of the term in question by Paul Kroll, see the brief report and discussion by Paul Radkin Goldin, Warring States Workshop e-mail communications #3939, March 28, 2002, and #3963, April 2, 2002. Some speculations concern whether a color of the fish might be a "signal" of their state of mind. I forgo any appeal to hidden meanings of this obscure character.

22. Thomas Nagel, "What Is It Like to Be a Bat?" *Philosophical Review* 83 (1974): 435–450.

23. Herbert Fingarette, *Confucius: The Secular as Sacred* (San Francisco: Harper and Row, 1972), chapter 3.

24. The character 樂 itself can also be read as *yue*[music], and it in turn is really a more general term for "concert" or even "concert complete with dancers and acrobats." (This insight helps explain Mozi's famous "opposition" to *yue*[music].) See my discussion in Chad Hansen, *A Daoist Theory of Chinese Thought* (New York: Oxford University Press, 1992), 136.

25. For a discussion on this point see Robert B. Brandom, *Making It Explicit* (Cambridge, MA: Harvard University Press, 1994), 200–202.

26. For more detail see Timothy Williamson, "Knowing and Asserting," *Philosophical Review* 105, no. 4 (1996): 489–523.

27. For a further discussion see Christoph Harbsmeier, "Conceptions of Knowledge in Ancient China," in H. Lenk and G. Paul, eds., *Epistemological Issues in Classical Chinese Philosophy* (Albany: State University of New York Press, 1993), 11–12. For an exception close by, see fn. 104.

28. Chad Hansen, *Language and Logic in Ancient China* (Ann Arbor: University of Michigan Press, 1983), 43–45.

29. See the explanation in Chad Hansen, "Term-Belief in Action: Sentences and Terms in Early Chinese Philosophy," in Lenk and Paul, *Epistemological Issues,* 45–58.

30. Knowing, of course, is not internal, though its component, belief, may be. Knowing has an objective component in Western true-belief-plus-justification accounts as well as in Chinese counterparts. *Zhi*[know] could not be translated as "know" unless it had this implicit "success" component.

31. Canon A3 defines 知 zhi^{know} as 才 $cai^{ability}$ and explains it as "that with which you know, and necessarily know [it?]." Furthermore, A6 explains knowledge as one's 知 zhi^{know}, postulating things and knowing them.

32. This is one of the few examples I know of in classical philosophy where the object of 知 zhi^{know} is a sentential proposition—although interestingly, the embedded knowledge claim is still nominalized in the usual way. We may speculate either that (a) it is explained by the embedding of a knowledge claim within a knowledge claim and the stylistic awkwardness of the double nominalization; or (b) that the nominalization is the counterpart of our "that" and what we see here is like the English propositional knowledge claim with "that" excluded. Either way, the example clearly shows that the expression of propositional knowledge is grammatically possible. Further, it is clear that other verbs take sentences as objects, for example 曰 yue^{say}, 見 $jian^{see}$, and so forth. A phrase structure grammar for ancient Chinese is almost sure to have some kind of rewrite rule like Term → Sentence. Arguably this makes it even more significant that zhi^{know} so rarely takes a grammatical sentence object.

33. As we will see in the section titled "Let's Return to the Beginning," it is important that Zhuangzi also takes the negative claim to be implicit in the challenge "how do you know?"

34. This interpretation seems to be reflected in most translations, for example, Lin Yutang's "Your very question shows . . . ," Palmer's "Therefore . . . ," Graham's "you asked me the question already knowing that I knew," And Watson's "so you already knew." Interestingly, Legge's seems not to, and Chinn, though he doubts that Zhuangzi is being skeptical, sees the point I endorse here—that Hui Shi knew not merely that but also *how* (and whence) Zhuangzi knew when he first asked the question. It is not that the form of the question entails it.

35. As Timothy Williamson in "Knowing and Asserting" points out, this "how" question need not always be a challenge. I may exclaim in delight to something my son says with "How do you know that?" In that use, I endorse his knowledge claim and ask where he learned it or how he figured it out. Similarly, in some uses outside of knowing, the "how do you" question may be an implicit challenge to the claim that you can.

36. David Hume, *A Treatise on Human Nature* (London: John Noon, 1739), section VII, "Conclusion."

37. Notice the parallel moved from the social to the individual level. For each belief I have, it is the case that I believe it is true. But, when I formulate the generalization "All my beliefs are true," I don't believe that.

38. *Zhuangzi,* chapter 2 (translation from Graham).

39. Stuart C. Hackett, *Oriental Philosophy: A Westerner's Guide to Eastern Thought* (Madison: University of Wisconsin Press, 1979), 56–57.

40. Fung Yu-lan, *A Short History of Chinese Philosophy: A Systematic Account of Chinese Philosophy from Earliest Times to the Present Day,* ed. Derk Bodde (New York: Macmillan, 1948), chapters 6, 9–10.

41. Perhaps accidentally because Graham typifies the sinologist's tendency to assume that this was the *correct* conclusion to draw from relativism. Zhuangzi *correctly* concluded that Hui Shi's "logic" destroyed itself. My view here is that it is exactly the opposite. Hui Shi draws the invalid conclusion (along with Graham) that "all is one." Zhuangzi (as Graham noted) criticizes the incoherence of that conclusion. See Graham, *Disputers,* 176–183.

42. Many opponents of perspectival readings of Zhuangzi base their arguments on taking Hui Shi's mistaken conclusions from relativist insights to be the *definition* of relativism. See Philip J. Ivanhoe, "Skepticism, Skill and the Ineffable Tao," *Journal of the American Academy of Religion* 61, no. 4 (1993): 639–654, and "Was Zhuangzi a Relativist?" in Paul Kjellberg and Philip J. Ivanhoe, eds., *Essays on Skepticism, Relativism and Ethics in the* Zhuangzi (Albany: State University of New York, 1996), 197–214; Van Norden, "Competing Interpretations"; and Ewing Y. Chinn, "Zhuangzi and Relativistic Scepticism" and "The Natural Equality of All Things," *Journal of Chinese Philosophy* 25, no. 4 (1998): 471–482.

43. What I mean by this is that the skepticism is fueled by a general caution about beliefs more than by an argument *against* the view in question. The only concern (as in classic external world skepticism) is absence of proof of some desired strength, not a positive argument against the possibility of its truth. For example, we could doubt that there ever was a Zhuangzi on that grounds that our main evidence for his existence is the book, which might have been forged. This is skepticism via the availability of alternative hypotheses. However, if the belief that Zhuangzi actually existed does not introduce any incoherence into our belief system, we would have no *positive* reason for doubting his existence.

44. That is not to say that if we know anything about Zhuangzi, we know that he was friends with Hui Shi. All we are saying is that the grounds for our personal conclusions about Zhuangzi, including his friendships, are the same grounds—the evidence in the text that bears his name.

45. See Chinn, "Zhuangzi and Relativistic Scepticism" and "Natural Equality." His grounds might be different from those I state here.

4

Zhuangzi's Notion of Transcendental Life

Eske Janus MØLLGAARD

It is a widely held opinion in the West that for the ancient Chinese the real is one homogeneous process, a continuity of being without ontologically different levels of being. In reading Western Zhuangzi scholarship one often gets the impression that Zhuangzi 莊子, who lived in China in the late fourth century BCE, must have been somewhat similar to the nice, pragmatic, and vaguely postmodern philosophy professor you had in college, who could reassure you that there is no absolute Truth, that metaphysical questions make no sense, and that claims of transcendence are mere pretense. My aim here is to break with this antimetaphysical tendency in recent Zhuangzi scholarship and give an account of the specific notion of transcendence we find in Zhuangzi, and in particular his notion of transcendental life.

I argue that we find in Zhuangzi an ontological difference and at least two distinct notions of transcendence. I first show that Zhuangzi's notions of the "Way" (*dao* 道) and "Heaven" (*tian* 天) clearly imply a notion of transcendence and that Zhuangzi posits an ontological difference between the realms of things and no-thing. Then I turn to Zhuangzi's notion of transcendental life, or the life of Heaven, as opposed to human

Originally published in *Asian Philosophy* 15, no. 1 (March 2005). Reprinted with permission.

life. In light of the discussion of Zhuangzi's notion of transcendental life, I explain Zhuangzi's unique notion of "wandering" (*you* 遊), and I show that Zhuangzi's thought does not, as it is often assumed, fall into naturalism.

THE WAY (*DAO*)

François Jullien argues that there is no ontological difference in Chinese thought. Jullien quotes Plotinus, who says that the divine One is not namable; it is an "unknowable darkness," absolute, undifferentiated, and formless. Like the "Way" (*dao*) in Zhuangzi, Plotinus' One is not "a thing among things."[1] This sounds Daoistic, but, says Jullien, this first impression is deceptive. For in the Chinese case "there is no difference of levels, such as between becoming and being, the sensible and the intelligible . . . instead of separating two levels of being, the difference introduced here within the real operates between two stages."[2] To be sure, the "Way" (*dao*) is invisible and escapes the senses, but, according to Jullien, in China the invisible

> does not constitute another level, such as another world . . . The invisible is indeed beyond the visible but as an extension of it; it is of the order of the evanescent and not the unintelligible (noeton). . . . This invisible is rather the diffuse basis of the visible[,] from which the latter ceaselessly actualizes itself. In short, this invisible lacks metaphysical consistency.[3]

Therefore, although the Chinese notion of the visible and the invisible constitute "an original dialectic that can be seen as parallel to Western ontology," it does not imply "an ontological rift."[4] In China, says Jullien, "there is no metaphysical rupture between the phenomenal and its foundation," and in reading Chinese texts "we quit Greek ontology for the Chinese conception of the process of the real," which instead of ontological levels operates with stages between the not yet actualized and the actualized.[5]

The *Zhuangzi*, however, explicitly says that the Way is beyond the dichotomies of "full" (*ying* 盈) and "empty" (*xu* 虛), "root" (*ben* 本) and "branch" (*mo* 末), "to accumulate" (*ji* 積) and "to disperse" (*san* 散), that is to say, beyond the continuum that, according to Jullien, constitutes the totality of the ancient Chinese philosophy of process.[6]

The *Zhuangzi* also explicitly says that the Way cannot be attained through "meditation" (*si* 思), "reflection" (lü 慮), or "knowing" (*zhi* 知)

or through some kind of practical know-how, such as "abiding" (*chu* 處), "submitting" (*fu* 服), or "following" (*cong* 從), or by any "method" (*dao* 道) in general (*Zhuangzi yinde* [Z], 22/5). Therefore, it is highly questionable whether in Zhuangzi, as Jullien says, the Way "is of the order of the evanescent and not the unintelligible." To be sure, when the *Zhuangzi* describes the Way as a "reality" (*qing* 情) beyond "form" (*xing* 形), "color" (*se* 色), "name" (*ming* 名), and "sound" (*sheng* 聲), then it is not thinking of a Platonic "form" (*eidos*) (Z, 13/67), but with these descriptions the *Zhuangzi* does, as Christoph Harbsmeier says, enter "a higher metaphysical realm," and it is unnecessary to insist with Jullien that Zhuangzi's conception of the Way "lacks metaphysical consistency."[7] There are, then, strong indications that Zhuangzi's notion of the Way does imply some kind of transcendence.

Zhuangzi's categorical distinction between the realm of things and the Way makes the transcendence of the Way especially clear. In Zhuangzi the realm of "things" (*wu* 物), including human beings (as things), is the totality of facts that make up *our* world as every thing we perceive, name, and use. All of these facts are relative, they are all a "this" (*shi* 是) as opposed to a "that" (*bi* 彼), and this opposition gives rises to disputes, strife, and general insecurity. Therefore, according to Zhuangzi, the highest attainment of the ancients was to realize that there is "a realm [or state] before there are things" (*weishi youwuzhe* 未始有物者) (Z, 2/40). The realm before there are things is the "Way" (*dao*), which "things things" (*wuwu* 物物) but is "not a thing" (*feiwu* 非物) and so, strictly speaking, "nothing" (*wu* 無) (Z, 22/75).

Zhuangzi says that the realm "before there are things," namely the Way, is posited at a different level from things, distinctions, and the ensuing value judgments (Z, 2/40–42). There is no continuity between these two realms. The *Zhuangzi* says, "what things things," the Way, "has no border with things" (*yuwu wuji* 與物无際), for "borders" (*ji* 際) are found only in the realm of things (Z, 22/50–51). Similarly, Zhuangzi says that the "outer" (*wai* 外), or the realm of things, and the "inner" (*nei* 內), or the realm of the Way, "do not touch upon each other" (*bu xiangji* 不相及) (Z, 6/66–67). Zhuangzi makes a categorical if not ontological distinction between the realm of things and the Way. Western Zhuangzi scholars generally disregard this crucial difference between the realm of things and the Way, but Chinese and Japanese scholars often treat it as central to Zhuangzi's thought. Ikeda Tomohisa, for instance, places early Daoist thought squarely in the fields of ontology and metaphysics, and he says that in Laozi and Zhuangzi there are two distinct realms: the realm of "things" (*wu*), which is under the constraint of time and space, and the realm of the "Way" (*dao*), which transcends beings and forms in time and space.[8]

HEAVEN (*TIAN*)

In Zhuangzi the notions of *tian* (Heaven) and *dao* (Way) are closely connected, and in many respects they are equivalent. The word *tian* is sometimes translated as "nature," but in Zhuangzi *tian* does not mean "nature" in our modern sense of a natural world, understood in terms of biological evolution, or in the seventeenth-century sense of matter extended in space and governed by a set of mechanical laws, or in the Christian medieval sense of God's creation subservient to his purpose. If we must translate *tian* as "nature," the word should be understood rather in the ancient Greek sense of an alive, intelligent, ceaseless movement of coming-into-being.[9] In this sense nature is not an outer object but rather an inner experience. Pierre Hadot writes that, according to ancient Greek and Roman philosophy, it is "*within ourselves* that we can experience the coming-into-being of reality and the presence of being." When we have this experience,

> the world then seems to come into being and be born before our eyes. We then perceive the world as a "nature" in the etymological sense of the word: *physis,* that movement of growth and birth by which things manifest themselves. We experience ourselves as a moment or instant of this movement; this immense event which reaches beyond us, is always already there before us, and is always beyond us. We are born along with the world.[10]

This experience of the "immense event which reaches beyond us" well describes Zhuangzi's experience of *tian* as the ceaseless "transformation" (*hua* 化) of things. It is important to note that this inner experience of *tian* should be distinguished from the common experience of *tiandi* 天地, "heaven and earth," that is to say, physical nature as it extends before us in space. In Zhuangzi the experience of *tian* is the experience of *the coming-into-being of things;* it is not the experience of things as things among things, not even the totality of such things. I will return to this crucial point shortly.

In Zhuangzi the word *tian* often means "sky" in the concrete sense of the sky above us. But since the vast blue sky above us seems infinite—Zhuangzi wonders: "Is the deep blue of the sky (*tian*) its true color? Or is it that it is so distant that it reaches no limit?" (*Z*, 1/4–5)—the word *tian* comes to represent "the infinite" (*wuqiong* 無窮), which equalizes the relative realm of things and the valuation human beings attach to things. In the realm of things *x* is bigger than *y* but smaller than *z*, but from the point of view of Heaven or the infinite there is neither big nor small.

In opposition to *tian* (Heaven) in this transcendental sense, the phrase *tianxia* 天下 (below heaven) refers to the world in general and to the world of human beings in particular. Zhuangzi's thought as a whole is determined by what A. C. Graham calls the "metaphysical crisis" in the fourth century BCE, when "Heaven" (*tian*) parts from "man" (*ren* 人), and in Zhuangzi the realm of "Heaven" (*tian*) is defined in categorical opposition to the realm of "man" (*ren*), understood as the realm of human "making" (*wei* 為).[11] According to Zhuangzi, to know the difference between Heaven and man is the highest perfection (*Z*, 6/1). The realm of man is the "outer" (*wai*), the "form" (*xing*), and everything that is produced through "artifice" (*wei* 偽), in particular the whole socioethical order. According to Zhuangzi, we should withdraw from this outer world (*Z*, 6/39). Heaven, on the other hand, is "inner" (*nei*); it has no form and knows no artifice.

Even if there is a categorical difference between the realm of Heaven and the realm of man, according to Zhuangzi, it is possible for human beings to experience Heaven. The perfected human being, says Zhuangzi, is "a follower of Heaven" (*yutian weitu* 與天為徒) (*Z*, 6/20), and as such the perfected human being "relies on Heaven's structuring" (*yihu tianli* 依乎天理) (*Z*, 3/6), draws on his or her "Heavenly Mechanism" (*tianji* 天機) (*Z*, 6/7), harmonizes the value judgments of man within "the bounds of Heaven" (*tianni* 天倪) (*Z*, 2/90), "rests in the potter's wheel of Heaven" (*xiuhu tianjun* 休乎天鈞) (*Z*, 2/39–40), and "illuminates things in the light of Heaven" (*zhaozi yutian* 照之於天) (*Z*, 2/29). It is even possible for the perfected person to "enter the unity of vast heaven" (*ru yu liaotian yi* 入於寥天一).[12] It is beyond the scope of this essay to explain each of these ideas. In the following I focus on what Zhuangzi means by "living a life engendered by Heaven" (*tianersheng* 天而生) (*Z*, 6/1). To understand this crucial notion in Zhuangzi we must first distinguish between two forms of transcendence.

TWO KINDS OF TRANSCENDENCE

On November 12, 1210, some followers of Amalric of Bena were burned at the stake because Amalric had interpreted the claim of the Apostle that "God is all in all" to mean that, as Giorgio Agamben writes, "God is in every thing as the place in which every thing is, or rather as the determination and the 'topia' of every entity."[13] Agamben adds that the consequence of this heretical view is that the transcendent "is not a supreme entity above all things; rather, *the pure transcendent is the taking-place of every thing.*"[14] Agamben then elaborates on this idea of transcendence:

> God or the good or the place does not take place, but is the taking-place of the entities, their innermost exteriority. The being-worm of the worm, the being-stone of the stone, is divine. That the world is, that something can appear and have a face, that there is exteriority and non-latency as the determination and the limit of every thing: this is the good. Thus precisely its being irreparably in the world is what transcends and exposes every worldly entity.[15]

We should, then, distinguish between two kinds of transcendence. In the first kind, which is dominant in the Western tradition from Plato's forms, through the Christian concept of God, to Descartes' cogito, transcendence means that there is a realm or an entity y that goes beyond and surpasses x. This beyond is conceived of as timeless and absolute. In the second kind of transcendence, it is the taking-place of x, the being-*such* of x, that goes beyond x as a thing or an object. Or, as Agamben says, it is the very "taking-place of the entities," their "being irreparably in the world," the very fact "[t]hat the world is, that something can appear" that is "the pure transcendent." This second kind of transcendence eludes the distinction between immanence and transcendence, and I suggest that this is the fundamental sense of transcendence in Zhuangzi.

Isabelle Robinet has perhaps best explained the kind of transcendence that is fundamental in Zhuangzi. Robinet says that Zhuangzi's essential experience is that "'there is' world" (*"il y a" du monde*).[16] Zhuangzi's thought, says Robinet, is entirely oriented toward the "coming of the world" (*l'avènement du monde*) and "coming into ex-istence" (*advenir à l'existence*) in general: the moment when something begins to emerge from "nothing" (*wu* 無) into "being" (*you* 有)—or, from "there is not" to "there is"—without as yet being a positive, differentiated, and identifiable thing.[17] This moment—Robinet calls it the "birth of beings" and the "origin of the world"—is ceaseless, but it is not a fact *in* the world, and therefore, in this sense, it is eternal and outside time. It is, writes Robinet, "a hole in time, an atemporal forgetfulness" (*un trou dans les temps, oubli atemporal*). When we experience this moment of emergence, we feel the force of the "spontaneously self-so" (*ziran* 自然), or the force of nature as self-emerging being.

According to Robinet, in Zhuangzi there is a *wu* ("nothing") more radical than the *wu* that is opposed to *you* ("something"). The *Zhuangzi* calls this radical nothing the "nonexistence of nothing" (*wuwu* 无无) (*Z*, 22/67), which Robinet renders with "the absence of absence" or "the non-being of non-being." Robinet says that this radical nothing, which is also the Way (*dao*), transcends the continuum of opposites, which defines an immanent process. For the radical nothing is the ontological precondition for "there is world," but it itself is never given as a fact in the world. There is, then, a genuine ontological difference at work in Zhuangzi between what appears (differentiated things) and appearance as such, which does not appear:

> In regard to the order to which the undifferentiated and the differentiated pertain, the difference is absolute. . . . This invisible [the radical nothing, the Way] manifests as invisible in the visible, as that which cannot appear and does not appear. The possibility of this double mode of being, invisible and yet visible (*invisible et par là visible*), is a sign of its irreducible immanence. That is to say that one should not confuse that which appears, the ontic content, with the event of appearing independent of this content (*le fait d'apparaître indépendant de ce contenu*).[18]

When Zhuangzi says, "that which gives birth to the living is not born" (*shengshengzhe busheng* 生生者不生) (*Z*, 6/42), Robinet adds an explanatory comment: "and so it does not appear, in the same way as appearance does not appear (*l'apparaître n'apparaît pas*)."[19] We have, then, an ontological difference between the event of appearing and that which appears. As Robinet points out, this ontological difference is not incompatible with immanence—but an immanence more radical, indeed more transcendent, than the transcendence of some *y* in relation to some *x*:

To insist, as does Jullien, on the immanence of the foundation of the world and not see that the nature of this immanence is to be irreducibly and forever invisible is to stop half-ways. That which is immanent can never become an object of knowing without losing its character of immanence.[20]

The essential form of transcendence in Zhuangzi is the pure appearance of things, which transcends things without being some-thing beyond the realm of things. And yet, Zhuangzi often mentions a "Creator of Things" (*zaowuzhe* 造物者) or a "Creator of Transformations" (*zaohuazhe* 造化者), and so he brings into play the other kind of transcendence, where there is a *y* (a Creator) that is beyond and causes *x* (things). One of the earliest accounts of Zhuangzi, which is found in the last chapter of the *Zhuangzi* itself (Z, 33/67–68), characterizes Zhuangzi as someone who "above wanders with the Creator of things, and below is friends with those who are beyond life and death and have no beginning and end." These friends of Zhuangzi are of course the fictional characters that Zhuangzi himself created. Like Zhuangzi, these friends "ascend to Heaven" and wander in the infinite "beyond the spatial world" and "beyond the dust and dirt of the mundane world," and they become "companions of the Creator of Things" (*yu zaowuzhe weiren* 與造物者為人).[21] Zhuangzi describes the "Creator of Transformations" (*zaohuazhe*) as a smith whose forge is "heaven and earth" (*tiandi*) (Z, 6/59–60). The Creator is a kind of Demiurge who fashions the material world. Similarly, Zhuangzi says that the Way and Heaven have no form but give forms to things (Z, 5/56). Like the Creator of Things, Heaven and the Way are creators of things, but they are not themselves things. The picture of Heaven as a transcendent creator is reinforced when Zhuangzi says that Heaven determines the destiny of things (Z, 5/10) and their life span (Z, 6/2) and that Heaven can punish human beings (Z, 5/31, 6/71).

The conception of Heaven and the Creator of things as anthropomorphic, transcendent causes of things seems incompatible with the idea of the Way and Heaven as the self-emergence and being-*such* of things. Why does Zhuangzi vacillate between these two notions of transcendence? One may venture a psychological explanation. It is perhaps natural that someone like Zhuangzi, whose essential experience is the awareness of pure coming-into-being—the astonishing fact *that* the world is—should sometimes retreat from this experience and contemplate *how* the world comes into being. For it is much easier to understand transcendence as some *y* that surpasses and causes *x* than to tarry with the notion of transcendence as the pure emergence and being-*such* of *x* as opposed to *x* as a thing. The difficulty is, on the one hand, not to let this form of transcendence collapse into a simple immanence and, on the other hand, not to objectify pure self-emergence into a principle or a force external to things themselves. Everything here depends on being able to think transcendence without a transcendent object or being. For it is *a split in the thing itself that constitutes transcendence,* namely, the split between the thing as being this or that thing, that is to say, inscribed in the relative realm of differences or the realm of "man" (*ren*), and the thing as being-*such as it is* and indifferent to differences, or the thing as engendered by Heaven.

One may also point out that the vacillation between seeing the ceaseless emergence of beings (nature) either as self-generated or as caused by some agent is a universal problematic. The Greeks, as we have noted, saw nature (*phusis*) as a ceaseless self-generating movement of coming-into-being. Plato relies on this notion of nature, but in Book 10 of the *Laws,* he argues that a movement that engenders itself can be ascribed only to the soul—the soul, which is "older than matter"—and that, therefore, the soul must be the first cause of all movement. For self-generating motion is "the source of all motion" and "infinitely superior to all other forms of motion." In other words, the self-engendering movement of nature is now seen as a first principle and a first cause.[22] There seems then to be a tendency for transcendence as the pure emergence and being-*so* of the thing to slip into transcendence as an agency and cause beyond the thing. At any rate, whatever form of transcendence Zhuangzi brings into play at a particular point in his discourse, it is always defined in opposition to human life.

HUMAN LIFE

It is a pervasive theme in the *Zhuangzi* that human life is a life of misery and a sad delusion. Human life, says Zhuangzi, is tied to our "form" (*xing*), that is to say, to our body and self insofar as they are visible in the "outer" (*wai*) realm. The body, obviously, is visible, but the self, too, is visible in "names" (*ming* 名) and "achievements" (*gong* 功). According to Zhuangzi, this visible body/self is the "counterpart" (*ou* 耦) to our true Self, which is not visible in the outer realm but a matter of inner experience, namely, the experience of being engendered by Heaven. When we lose or forget our "counterpart"—that is to say, that part of us that is visible to others and therefore caught in the self-other dichotomy—then we gain the experience of our true Self, which experiences itself as the pure emergence of self-generating life (Z, 2/1–9).

As long as we identify with our human life, then we exhaust ourselves in competition with others and in the pursuit of imaginary goals. Zhuangzi writes:

> Once we have received the completed physical form, we do not forget it while we wait for extinction. Cutting into and grinding together with things we rush on to the end like a galloping horse no one can stop. Is it not sad? All of our life we labor and do not see any results. We exhaust ourselves in tiresome labor and do not know where it comes to rest. Is it not lamentable (Z, 2/18–19)?

The human "heart and mind" (*xin* 心) has become mechanical, swift and deadly in its judgments, and human beings hold fast to and fight for their own point of view as if they had sworn a blood oath to defend it. According to Zhuangzi, judgment in terms of "right" (*shi* 是) and "wrong" (*fei* 非) is a technical achievement, like releasing arrows from a "crossbow trigger" (*jigua* 機栝). Such mechanical minds or hearts, says Zhuangzi, decline day by day until they can hardly be made to recover life (Z, 2/11–13). It is life itself that dries up in our ceaseless activity to maintain our self in the outer world.

In the view of Zhuangzi, human life is a dream. We think that we are awake and with "dense" or "stubborn" (*gu* 固) confidence we say: "Ah, there is a ruler! Oh, that is a shepherd!" (Z, 2/83). For we know our way around in *our* world, and we take it for real. But this absorption in the symbolic order is a defense against the "inevitable" (*budeyi* 不得已) course of life ending in death. Human life with its social and symbolic structures is essentially a defense against death, and Zhuangzi's remarkable acceptance of death, which A. C. Graham in particular has emphasized, is due to the fact that Zhuangzi transcends this defense mechanism.[23] Zhuangzi repeats again and again that we must give up our "love" (*yue* 悅) for and our "seeking" (*qi* 蘄) human life and that the perfected person does not value life more than death but views "death and life" (*sisheng* 死生) as one unity and therefore is not affected by the transformation of one into the other (Z, 2/73, 4/44, 5/5, 5/30, 6/1, 6/8, 6/24, and 6/69). As Zhuangzi sees it, the real *human* tragedy is that the very drive that tries to avoid death withdraws from life itself. Only a "great awakening" (*dajue* 大覺) that releases us from human life into transcendental life, the life beyond "life and death," will shatter this delusion. According to Zhuangzi, we must give up our attachment to things, even our attachment to human life (where we are things among things); we must transcend time in terms of past and present and "enter into [the realm of] no death no life" (*ru yu busi busheng* 入於不死不生). This is the realm where "that which kills the living does not die and that which gives birth to the living is not born" (Z, 6/41–42). In other words, it is the experience of transcendental life, the ceaseless, infinite life beyond the living and dying of particular living beings. When we experience transcendental life our whole perception of the world is transformed: we come to "see with the clarity of morning light" (*chaoche* 朝徹) and "envision uniqueness" (*jiandu* 見獨).[24]

Without the experience of transcendental life, human beings are like fish on dry land that blow moisture on each other to remain alive (Z, 6/22–23). And yet there is the possibility of transcending this miserable life. In a dialogue with his friend Hui Shi 惠施, Zhuangzi says that it is possible that "human beings do not harm themselves inside with [value judgments in terms of] good and bad but rather always follow the spontaneously self-so and not add to life" (Z, 5/57–58). Hui Shi is obviously shocked by Zhuangzi's suggestion that human beings should discard their most treasured ability to judge things right or wrong and simply "follow the spontaneously self-so" (*yinziran* 因自然) of self-emerging life and "not add to life" (*buyisheng* 不益生). "If human beings do not add to life," asks Hui Shi, "how can they even maintain themselves [as humans]?" (Z, 5/58). If nothing essentially human is added to life, how can there be *human* life at all?

Zhuangzi answers that the "appearance" (*mao* 貌) and "form" (*xing*) of human beings have been given us by the Way and by Heaven. It is our fate to have the form of a human being, but the form is merely something outer; it is not our true being. Unfortunately, we do not recognize this but get lost in appearances and entangled with things. Look at yourself, says Zhuangzi to his friend, you wear yourself out with your sophistic logic and disputation, and in the process you harm your "inner" (*nei*), you "push your spirit into the outer realm and wear out your essence" (Z, 5/58–60).

For Zhuangzi the problem is not the outer form as such. After all, it is on the basis of our appearance in the form of a human being that we have human "being-with" (*yu* 與) each other, or, as Graham translates, "the guise which is from man assimilates us to each other" (*renzhimao youyu ye* 人之貌有與也).[25] That is to say, because we have the outer form of a human being, we can assimilate to the social structures and the symbolic order of human society. But precisely because human life is based merely on appearances, or the outer forms, it cannot generate our true being. Human life produces difference but never the unique. In human life we may be the same as this one or different from that one, but we are never our true, "unique" (*du* 獨) being, which is not inscribed in the realm of human life but generated by transcendental life, or the life of Heaven. As Zhuangzi says, "the life of Heaven (*tianzhisheng* 天之生) causes things to be unique (*du*)" (Z, 3/13).

When human beings experience themselves as generated by Heaven, an uncanny transformation happens. The entire socioethical order is turned upside down: the mutilated outcast who lacks a foot becomes the spiritual exemplar, and the noble Confucian, who in accordance with the demand for "filial piety" (*xiao* 孝) anxiously preserves his outer form, becomes the villain. For, says Zhuangzi, "the freak (*jiren* 畸人) is a freak among men, but he is equal to Heaven. Therefore it is said: 'the vulgar in Heaven are the noble among men; the noble among men are the vulgar in Heaven.'" (Z, 6/74).

Because our true being cannot be generated by human life, Zhuangzi's sage does not identify with human life but "wanders" (*you*) beyond all of the states and activities that define human existence. The sage, says Zhuangzi, sees

> knowledge as a curse, social bonds as glue, virtue as making connections, and skill as peddling. The sage does not scheme, so what use does he have for knowledge? He does not split things up, so what use does he have for glue? He is deprived of nothing, so what use does he have for making connections? He has nothing to sell, so what use has he for peddling? (Z, 5/52-53)

But if the sage does not take part in the commerce of human life, how does the sage sustain him- or herself? The sage, says Zhuangzi, "receives food from Heaven, so what use does he have for man?" (Z, 5/53–54). The sage has the form of a human being, and so in the outer realm the sage "groups together with humans" (*qun yuren* 群與人) (Z, 5/54). But the sage does not have the "essence" (*qing* 情) of a human being, he does not issue value judgments in terms of right and wrong, and so he is not identified with the outer but has his center of gravity in the inner: "How tiny and small is that which categorizes him as a human being, how huge and great is the way he uniquely completes his Heaven (*ducheng qitian* 獨成其天)" (Z, 5/54–55). The life of the sage is nourished by self-emerging life itself, the life of Heaven, which generates each being in its own unique way.

We now see Zhuangzi's astonishing critique of the human condition. Even in exercising our highest and most treasured abilities, in particular our defining ability to issue value judgments, but also the exercise of virtue, skill, and even wisdom, we as human beings sell ourselves short: we do not live the life we could live, namely the life generated by self-emerging transcendental life itself, which strictly speaking is the only life there is. Zhuangzi calls it the "life of Heaven" (*tianzhisheng* 天之生) or "living a life engendered by Heaven" (*tianersheng* 天而生) (Z, 3/13, 6/1).

It may seem that Zhuangzi totally strips the subject of all that is human and that he, as the early Confucian Xunzi 荀子 said, should be criticized for being absorbed in Heaven and neglecting the human. Zhuangzi's aim, however, is not to denigrate human existence but to redeem it. Zhuangzi wants to liberate human existence from the false values and views we have imposed on it, and he wants us to see through the human *form* to the ceaseless emergence of life itself. Therefore Zhuangzi's negation of the human leads to an affirmation of humanity as being engendered by Heaven. Here Zhuangzi is in general accord with the mainstream of ancient philosophy in the West. In regard to the ancient Greek philosophers, Hadot writes:

> Doesn't "stripping off man" mean that the philosopher completely transforms his vision of the universe, transcending the limited viewpoint of what is human, all-too-human, in order to elevate himself to a superior point of view? Such a perspective is in a way inhuman; it reveals the nudity of existence, beyond the partial oppositions and false values which human beings add to it, in order, perhaps, to attain a state of simplicity prior to all distinctions. . . . This tendency to strip ourselves of "the human" is constant throughout the most diverse schools—from Pyrrho, who remarked on how hard it is to strip ourselves of the human, to Aristotle, for whom life according to the mind is super-human, and as far as Plotinus, who believed that in mystical experience we cease to be "human."[26]

THE LIFE OF HEAVEN

At the beginning of "On the Equality of Things" (Qiwulun 齊物論), the second chapter in the *Zhuangzi*, a certain Master Ziqi 子綦 enters into meditation and experiences the loss of his "counterpart" (*ou*), that is to say, he loses his outer bodily form and the outer self, which are inscribed in the self-other dichotomy. His body becomes like "withered wood" and his mind "like dead ashes." When his disciple asks for an explanation of the Master's meditative state, the Master in reply makes a distinction between three kinds of "pipes" as in musical wind instruments: "the pipes of man" (*renlai* 人籟), "the pipes of the Earth" (*dilai* 地籟), and "the pipes of Heaven" (*tianlai* 天籟). The pipes of man give voice to the differences in the realm of man. The wind that blows in the pipes of the Earth equalizes these differences. Finally, the pipes of Heaven articulate the self-emergence and the being-*so* of things beyond difference. Zhuangzi says that in the pipes of Heaven the wind "blows at all things in different ways," and so it "makes each be itself" (*shi qi ziyi* 使其自己), and each phenomenon "chooses for itself" (*ziqu* 自取) (Z, 2/8–9). In other words, after the differences of the realm of man (one is American, the other Chinese) are equalized from the point of view of the Earth (nature as a whole), the self-emerging life generated by Heaven emerges. This experience of self-emerging life generated by Heaven, the very fact that each thing is being-*such as it is*, is Zhuangzi's essential experience of transcendence. And yet Zhuangzi immediately asks whether there may not be an "agitator" (*nuzhe* 怒者) behind it all (Z, 2/8–9). Zhuangzi, as already explained, vacillates between these two kinds of transcendence, and he provides no answer to his own question.

As a counterpoint to Master Ziqi's experience of being engendered by Heaven, Zhuangzi immediately evokes the misery of human life as described earlier (Z, 2/9–13). In particular Zhuangzi focuses on the shifting human emotions. He writes: "Pleasure and anger, sorrow and happiness, worries and sighs, vacillation, sluggishness, frivolity, indulgence—they are like music that comes from empty spaces, like mushrooms that form from vapor. Day and night they alternate before us, and nobody knows from where they sprout" (Z, 2/13–14). We notice that Zhuangzi rhetorically draws a parallel between our shifting emotional states and the wind that blows through the pipes of Heaven. Like all other phenomena in nature our emotions self-emerge and change, and we do not know whether there is an "agitator" behind them. But in drawing this parallel Zhuangzi also suggests that our changing moods and emotions, the very drives and attachments that bind us to human life, are in fact generated by Heaven. Zhuangzi's crucial point is this: human life, which he describes as a life of conflict and delusion, is in fact also engendered by Heaven—it is only that it does not recognize itself as such. According to Zhuangzi, if we regard our moods and emotions with indifference (that is to say, from the point of view of the pipes of the Earth), then we will realize that they are in fact not our own doing but are engendered by Heaven. It is only when human beings appropriate the spontaneous self-emerging moods and emotions for their own ends—when they think that they are "in charge of right and wrong" (*si shifei* 司是非) and they solemnly "guard their victory" (*shousheng* 守勝) over the other—that life dries up and we become like fish on dry land gasping for life. For we forget the mysterious source of our being. From where does our being-*so* sprout? Lost in wonder at the mysterious self-emergence of moods and emotions—the pure appearance of phenomena—Zhuangzi exclaims: "Enough! Enough! It just happens unexpectedly like this. Perhaps *this* is that from which they arise (*sheng* 生)."[27]

According to Zhuangzi, our emotions arise just like the sounds elicited by the wind that blows through the pipes of Heaven. Furthermore, our very "self" (*wo* 我), which depends for its existence on the "other" (*bi* 彼), is ultimately caused by the "True Ruler" (*zhenjun* 真君), another name for the Creator of Things, Heaven, and the Way. Zhuangzi writes:

> If there is no "other," there is no "self"; if there is no "self," there is no "other" to be had. Surely this is quite true, and yet I do not know what acts as a cause for it [the self]. It seems that there is a True Ruler, but we just do not see its trace. That it can set [the self] in motion is certain, but we do not see its form. It has reality but no form. (*Z*, 2/14–16)

Our very self, which is constituted by the self-other dichotomy, is set in motion by the True Ruler (the Creator of Things, Heaven, the Way), who has no form but is "real" (*qing*)—and real precisely because it is no-thing. If we could only recognize this, then we would have the same experience of transcendental life as Master Ziqi: we would hear the pipes of Heaven and be redeemed from the realm of things. For once we recognize ourselves as things engendered by Heaven, then we are no longer mere things among things but our own unique being-*so*.

And how do we gain the recognition of our own being-*so*? Chapter 15 of the *Zhuangzi*, "Ingrained Opinions" (*keyi* 刻意) (Victor Mair's rendering of this chapter heading), consists of one single essay that indicates what kind of spiritual exercise could lead to this recognition. The chapter first criticizes various ways of self-cultivation. As one would expect, it rejects Confucian practices of "humanness and righteousness" (*renyi* 仁義) and "ritual" (*li* 禮) in the service of the state. But it also distances itself from forms of self-cultivation that we may consider Daoist, such as withdrawing from society and going into nature in order to practice "nonaction" (*wuwei* 無為), breathing exercises, and various other forms of psychophysical exercises (*Z*, 15/1–6). Instead of these forms of self-cultivation the chapter proposes that we "rest" (*xiuxiu* 休休) in a state of natural tranquility and clarity that "matches Heaven's integrity" (*he tiande* 合天德). The "symbol" (*xiang* 象) for this kind of rest is water, which is naturally placid when not disturbed (*Z*, 15/9–17). The sage is in this state of rest, which does not mean that he does not move at all but that his every movement is generated by Heaven: "The life of the sage is the movement of Heaven" (*shengren zhisheng ye tianxing* 聖人之生也天行), and "when [the sage] moves he is moved by Heaven" (*dong er yitian xing* 動而以天行) (*Z*, 15/10, 15/18). This is precisely the same idea that we found in "On the Equality of Things," where it is said that the self, including its moods and emotions, is set in motion by the True Ruler. In both cases the key point is that we can rest in released detachment from the realm of man and experience ourselves as engendered by Heaven. This experience, says the chapter titled "Ingrained Opinions," cannot be symbolized, but it may be called "being with God" (*tongdi* 同帝) (*Z*, 15/19).

Zhuangzi's own experience of "wandering" (*you*), which is his spiritual exercise par excellence, is very much like the experience of "being with God" as it is described in the chapter titled "Ingrained Opinions." For "wandering" does not depend on a particular way of self-cultivation; it is not a technique or a method but the simple release of the thing into its being-*so*, its pure coming-into-being, which is the inner experience of being engendered by the life of Heaven.

WANDERING (*YOU*)

Wandering is perhaps Zhuangzi's most important notion, and it is also one of the least understood. It is commonly thought that Zhuangzi's notion of wandering is all about going along with the flow of things. Even some of the best Zhuangzi scholars share this deficient understanding. Victor Mair says that " 'wandering' implies a 'laid-back' attitude towards life in which one takes things as they come and flows along with the Tao unconcernedly."[28] For his part, A. C. Graham says that Zhuangzi uses the term "wandering" like the word "tripping" was used in the psychedelic slang of the 1960s and 1970s.[29] Against these interpretations it should be pointed out that Zhuangzi uses the term *you*, or "wandering," in a very precise sense that can be understood only in the context of Zhuangzi's crucial distinction between "human life" (*renzhisheng*) and "the life of Heaven" (*tianzhisheng*), or what I call transcendental life.

Human life is generated by transcendental life, but usually we are so immersed in human life that we have no sense of being engendered by transcendental life. In the moment of "wandering," however, we experience ourselves as being generated by transcendental life. We experience freedom and joy that are not found within the confines of human life. Far from simply going along with the flow of things and events of human life, which are precisely what *prevent* us from experiencing transcendental life, the person who is wandering is liberated from things and unaffected by human life but is wholly engendered by transcendental life. This release into transcendental life can happen in everyday life, and it does not require any particular method of self-cultivation. This is exemplified in the well-known dialogue between Zhuangzi and Hui Shi as they cross the Hao River.

The two friends are "wandering" (*you*) across the Hao River, when Zhuangzi suddenly remarks, "The minnows have come out and are swimming around so at ease. That is the joy of fish!" The word "wandering" (*you*) can mean merely traveling or touring, or it can, as in Zhuangzi, refer to the surpassing ease in the articulation of one's own unique being, that is to say, one's being insofar as it is engendered by transcendental life. It is this authentic sense of wandering that Zhuangzi is alluding to when he says that the minnows are "swimmimg around so at ease." In fact, it is the same word *you* 遊 that is used both for Zhuangzi's "wandering" and for the "swimming around" of the fish. Zhuangzi's remark, then, is not simply a proposition with reference to the fish; it is rather an indirect, impromptu indication of the pure experience of "wandering" (*you*), entirely immersed in the flow of "life" (*sheng*). For when we "forget ourselves in life" (*xiangwang yisheng* 相忘以生), the transcendental life, which is "everlasting" (*wusuo zhongqiong* 无所終窮), then we are like fish that "forget themselves in rivers and lakes" (*xiangwang yu jianghu* 相忘與江湖) (Z, 6/62, 6/23). We attain *you,* or the carefree wandering of transcendental life.

When Zhuangzi says that the fish "come out" (*chu* 出), he is indicating pure coming-into-being, the very moment "just when" (*fang* 方) something emerges from "there is not" to "there is." As I have already mentioned, following Robinet, this moment of pure appearance is Zhuangzi's essential experience. This moment of coming-into-being is not yet a "thing" (*wu*), but it is also not the absence of things (as when things remain absorbed in a primordial unity). It is a moment of presence without objectification, a moment of uniqueness. It is awareness of the simple, almost banal fact that there is something rather than nothing. As Robinet says, it is the experience that "'there is' world" ("*il y a" du monde*); it is the moment when something begins to emerge from "nothing" (*wu*) into "being" (*you*), the "birth of beings." It is the experience of pure appearance, the very being-*so* of the thing that transcends the thing as thing. In Zhuangzi's terms, we have an ontological difference between *chu,* or the pure occurrence of coming out into appearance, and *wu,* the thing that appears. This experience of pure coming-into-being is the experience of "wandering" or of being engendered by transcendental life.

When Zhuangzi adds, "that is the joy of fish!" it is not a "protocol sentence" meant to record some fact of the matter; rather, the statement refers to Zhuangzi's own "joy" (*le* 樂), which is not his but belongs to everybody and nobody in that moment of crossing the river. Here again Zhuangzi formulates his own version of a universal theme in ancient philosophy. As already pointed out, the ancient Greeks experienced nature as *phusis,* or the ceaseless movement of the self-emergence and flourishing of all beings. Pierre Hadot explains that, for the ancients, joy, as opposed to pleasure and passion, is "to embrace this expansive movement [of *phusis*], and thus to go in the same direction as Nature, and to feel, as it were, the joy which she herself feels in her creative movement."[30] This is the joy the Stoics defined as "the good flowing of life" (*euroia biou*). According to ancient philosophy, writes Hadot, "[j]oy has its roots in that profound tendency of living beings which impels them to love that which makes them exist, and this means not only their own structure and unity, but the All, without which they would be nothing, and of which they are integral parts."[31]

Thus was the "joy" (*le*) of Zhuangzi as he wandered across the Hao River, and it was this joy Zhuangzi wanted to share with his friend, who at the moment, unfortunately, was unable to receive it. For Hui Shi breaks the enchantment of the moment and the word. He takes Zhuangzi's words as propositions that refer to some thing in the "outer" (*wai*) world. And then we hear the voice of the skeptic: "You are not a fish; how do you know the joy of fish?" The question is phrased as *anzhi* 安知, "how do you know?" and this idiom, as Graham points out, has the implicit sense of "whence do you know?" that is, from "what particular position do you know?"[32] This is, then, the question of perspectivism, around which Western philosophers who write on Zhuangzi endlessly circle: does Zhuangzi have access to some transcendent viewpoint from which he can adopt any or no perspective? Like many modern philosophers, Hui Shi is skeptical about this.

Zhuangzi, who for the moment plays by the rules of "disputation" (*bian* 辯), responds: "You are not me; how do you know that I do not know the joy of fish?" (*Z*, 17/89). But this argument is only too easy for the Sophist to refute: "I am not you, so certainly I do not know you. You surely are not a fish, so it holds that you do not know the joy of fish" (*Z*, 17/89–90). Hui Shi's argumentation is irrefutable: it "holds"; literally, it is "complete" or "whole" (*quan* 全). But precisely this desire for "complete" or "valid" discourse (*chengyan* 成言) prevents Hui Shi from acknowledging what actually took place in the flow of life as he crossed the Hao River with his friend.

Zhuangzi realizes this, and therefore he abruptly suspends the discourse of "disputation" (*bian*) and asks that they follow the dispute back to its "root" (*ben* 本). Zhuangzi takes up Hui Shi's initial proposition ("You are not a fish; how do you know the joy of fish?") and clearly *marks it as a proposition* (in the text it is marked with the quotation markers *yunzhe* 云者). Zhuangzi points out that Hui Shi's proposition, *as a proposition*, presupposes something, namely, the fact that Hui Shi already "knows" (*zhi* 知) that he, Zhuangzi, knows the joy of fish: "You asked me already knowing that I know it" (*Z*, 17/90). In other words, Hui Shi's question itself presupposes the knowledge it questions.

But what kind of knowing does Zhuangzi have in mind here? It cannot be propositional knowledge, for Zhuangzi claims *this* knowledge as the presupposition for all propositional knowledge. Zhuangzi's knowledge is the acknowledgement of pure appearance. Pure appearance can never be the object of propositional knowledge, for in order for there to be things in the outer world to which propositions can refer, these things must first appear. But pure appearance can be experienced as the coming-into-being of things, as the very self-emergence of life. This experience is indisputable, just like when we say, "I feel joy," for this expression is not a reference to some thing in the outer world but to the "self-so" (*ziran*) of life itself as it affects our being. In this sense Zhuangzi's impromptu words are the self-expression of life itself, and Zhuangzi wants Hui Shi to return to the very moment of enunciation, the moment when what was said was said and understood without immediately being "deemed" (*wei* 為) right or wrong. Therefore Zhuangzi says: "I know it from being here above the Hao River," and, furthermore, "you [Hui] asked me already knowing that I know it" (*Z,* 17/91). For Hui Shi *did* know it. His skeptical propositions are parasitic on this fundamental, original cognition, and in disavowing *that* knowledge Hui Shi only denies himself the unique articulation of his own being in authentic "wandering" (*you*), or the experience of transcendental life.

ON ZHUANGZI'S SUPPOSED NATURALISM

As we have seen, Zhuangzi uses the same word *you* for his own unique notion of "wandering" and for the "swimming around" of the fish. Is there then really a difference between Zhuangzi's transcendental "wandering" and the natural "swimming around" of the fish? Critics of Daoism tell us that there is no difference, that the highest perfection of the Daoist sage is a regression to an animal-like unity with nature, and that the ultimate wish of the Daoist is to be motivated by the same instinctive spontaneity that animals possess. One may be inclined to agree with these critics when one learns that in Zhuangzi it is the same "Heavenly Mechanism" (*tianji* 天機) that motivates animals and the perfected person.

In the *Zhuangzi* there is a story of a "unipede" that envies the millipede's control of its many feet.[33] The millipede in turn envies the snake, which is able to move along without any feet at all. But this envy is misplaced, for, and this is the point of the story, even if they have different forms, the snake and the millipede both ultimately rely on their "Heavenly Mechanism" (*tianji*) to move around as they do. In other words, there is an impulse beyond forms that sets the various forms in motion (*Z,* 17/53–60). In the course of a long description of the characteristics of the "True

Man" (*zhenren* 真人), Zhuangzi himself says that those who have deep-rooted desires have a shallow Heavenly Mechanism (*Z*, 6/7). Presumably the True Man is deeply rooted in his Heavenly Mechanism, perhaps as a result of the deep breathing he is said to practice. Our question can then be reformulated as follows: Is the Heavenly Mechanism that moves the perfected person the same as the Heavenly Mechanism that moves the millipede and the snake? If it is, then the highest human perfection is essentially the same as the animal's natural unity with nature, and we should criticize Zhuangzi for his regressive naturalism. Furthermore, we should ask why human beings have to exercise (do breathing exercises, for instance) in order to attain a naturalness that animals have naturally.

The answer is, first, that insofar as they are "things" (*wu*), human beings and animals are motivated by the same Heavenly Mechanism, or the Way, which "things things" (*wuwu*) but is not itself a thing (*Z*, 22/75). The crucial difference is that human beings can become aware that they are moved by the Way, and this awareness *is* their freedom. In this freedom, which Zhuangzi calls "wandering" (*you*), human beings are no longer mere things but companions of that no-thing that things things, namely the Way or the ceaseless self-emergence of life. Animals, on the other hand, are not aware that they are moved by the Way; they do not experience transcendental life; and therefore animals cannot "wander" (*you*). Undoubtedly, fish are happy when they "swim around" (*you*) in their element. But Zhuangzi's *experience* of the joy of the fish as *he* is "wandering" (*you*), which is really the experience of the joy of *his own* existence as it is generated by transcendental life, is something qualitatively different. It is not the experience of natural well-being, which animals, too, surely experience, but the experience of that which makes all natural being possible, namely, transcendental life. This experience has nothing to do with the animal's unity with nature, and Zhuangzi does not suggest that human beings must exercise in order to attain a natural spontaneity that animals already possess.

Conversely, we could also ask the Daoist: is not our "mechanical mind" (*jixin*), the mind that issues value judgments in terms of "right" (*shi*) and "wrong" (*fei*) and has a marvelous ability to maintain human beings in their world, just as natural as the feet of the millipede? Does not the mechanical mind also get its motivation from the Heavenly Mechanism? Again, the initial answer is yes; the mechanical mind, insofar as it is a thing, gets its motivation from the Heavenly Mechanism, or the Way. Graham correctly points out that, according to Zhuangzi, "[i]n the last resort not only the spontaneous in man, but the deliberate actions for which he takes credit, derive from Heaven," and, as pointed out earlier, according to Zhuangzi, even our shifting emotions and moods are generated by Heaven.[34] But just as the fish are not aware that Heaven motivates their swimming around, so the mechanical mind is not aware that Heaven motivates its deliberations. The mechanical mind is mechanical precisely because it does not have that awareness, and it was that awareness that Hui Shi denied himself as he began to dispute Zhuangzi's remark about the joy of fish. Like the fish, Hui Shi is unable to "wander" (*you*), and the answer to Hui's skeptical question, "you are not a fish; how do you know the joy of fish?" is really this: it is precisely because I am not a fish (a thing) that I know the joy of fish; and furthermore, it is precisely because you, Hui, are really no different from a fish (a thing) that you do not know the joy of fish.

We should then distinguish among three different kinds of motivation in Zhuangzi. First, there is the thoroughly technical and mechanical motivation characteristic of the "mechanical mind" (*jixin*). Zhuangzi likens this motivation to a crossbow trigger, from which value judgments in terms of right and wrong issue and ensure human dominance of their world. This is the motivation behind Hui Shi's disputation. Second, there is the inherently natural motivation of a natural being to maintain itself and express itself as the natural being it is. This motivation is exemplified by the swimming around of the fish. These two kinds of motivation are essentially the same, for they are both inscribed in the realm of things. Third, there is the transcendental motivation that comes from the experience of transcendental life, or the pure coming-into-being of beings. This motivation is transcendental because it springs neither from technical deliberation nor from natural inclination but from transcendental life itself. This is the motivation behind Zhuangzi's "wandering" (*you*) and his impromptu words about the joy of fish.

Lee H. Yearley identifies three "drives" in Zhuangzi: (1) dispositional drives, whereby certain stimuli in our biological nature or social world trigger a specific response; (2) reflective drives, which reflect on and transform dispositional drives; and (3) transcendental drives, which come into play when the self has been fundamentally transformed by reflective drives.[35] I agree with Yearley that it is important to posit a transcendental drive as the highest motivating force for Zhuangzi; otherwise, we will see

Zhuangzi falling back on natural, instinctive drives. Yearley's approach is, however, too Aristotelian. For Zhuangzi the transcendental drive—the life engendered by Heaven, or what I call transcendental life—is not the result of human reflection transforming human dispositions; it is rather, if we have to stay with the Western vocabulary, an act of pure grace. To be released into transcendental life is a second birth. As the *Zhuangzi* says, once we have left human life behind and are no longer entangled in its misery, then we become "born again" (*gengsheng* 更生).[36] We cannot give birth to ourselves—no matter how much we reflect. Our first birth was into human life; our second birth will be into transcendental life.

NOTES

1. François Jullien, *Detour and Access,* trans. Sophie Hawkes (New York: Zone Books, 2000), 276.

2. Ibid., 280; translation modified.

3. Ibid., 290–291.

4. Ibid.

5. Ibid., 280–281.

6. *Zhuangzi yinde,* Harvard–Yenching Institute Sinological Index Series, suppl. 20 (Peking: Harvard-Yenching Institute, 1947), 22/51–52. Hereafter cited as Z in the text.

7. Christoph Harbsmeier, *Language and Logic in Traditional China,* in Joseph Needham, *Science and Civilisation in China,* vol. 7, part 1 (Cambridge: Cambridge University Press, 1998), 236.

8. Ikeda Tomohisa, *Rō Sō shisō* (Tokyo: Hoso Daigaku Kyoiku Shinkokai, 1996), 143–152.

9. R. G. Collingwood, *The Idea of Nature* (Oxford: Oxford University Press, 1960), 3–13.

10. Pierre Hadot, "The Sage and the World," in *Philosophy as a Way of Life,* trans. Michael Chase (Oxford: Basil Blackwell, 1995), 260.

11. A. C. Graham, *Disputers of the Tao: Philosophical Argument in Ancient China* (La Salle: Open Court, 1989), 107f.

12. *Zhuangzi yinde*, 6/82; Victor H. Mair, trans., *Wandering on the Way: Early Taoist Tales and Parables of Chuang Tzu* (New York: Bantam, 1994), 62.

13. Giorgio Agamben, *The Coming Community,* trans. Michael Hardt (Minneapolis: University of Minnesota Press, 1993), 13.

14. Ibid., 14.

15. Ibid.

16. Isabelle Robinet, "Une lecture du *Zhuangzi*," *Études chinoises* 15, no. 1–2 (Spring–Autumn 1996): 115.

17. Ibid., 115–116.

18. Robinet, "Lecture," 125.

19. Robinet, "Lecture," 141.

20. Ibid., 125n27.

21. *Zhuangzi yinde*, 6/60–71; Mair, *Wandering*, 59–61.

22. Trevor J. Saunders' translation of the *Laws* is pp. 1318–1616 in J. M. Cooper and D. S. Hutchinson, eds., *Plato: Complete Works* (Indianapolis: Hackett, 1997), 889e–899d; Pierre Hadot, *What Is Ancient Philosophy?* (Cambridge, MA: Belknap, 2002), 11.

23. A. C. Graham, trans., *Chuang-tzu: The Inner Chapters* (London: Allen and Unwin, 1981), 23–24.

24. *Zhuangzi yinde*, 6/41; Mair, *Wandering*, 57.

25. *Zhuangzi yinde*, 3/13; Graham, *Chuang-tzu*, 64.

26. Hadot, *Ancient Philosophy*, 113 and 211.

27. *Zhuangzi yinde*, 2/14; cf. Wang Shumin, *Zhuangzi jiaoquan* (Taipei: Zhongyang yanjiuyuan lishi yuyan yanjiusuo, 1988), 52.

28. Mair, *Wandering*, 385.

29. Graham, *Chuang-tzu*, 8.

30. Hadot, *Ancient Philosophy*, 240–241.

31. Ibid., 242.

32. Graham, *Chuang-tzu*, 123.

33. Mair, *Wandering*, 159.

34. Graham, *Chuang-tzu*, 168.

35. Lee H. Yearley, "Zhuangzi's Understanding of Skillfulness and the Ultimate Spiritual State," in Paul Kjellberg and Philip J. Ivanhoe, eds., *Essays on Skepticism, Relativism, and Ethics in the* Zhuangzi (Albany: State University of New York Press, 1995), 153–155.

36. *Zhuangzi yinde*, 19/5; Mair, *Wandering*, 175.

5

Knowledge and Happiness in the Debate over the Happiness of the Fish

SHAM Yat Shing

莊子與惠子遊於濠梁之上。

(I)　莊子曰:「儵魚出遊從容,是魚樂也。」
(II)　惠子曰:「子非魚,安知魚之樂?」
(III)　莊子曰:「子非我,安知我不知魚之樂?」
(IV)　惠子曰:「我非子,固不知子矣;子固非魚也,子之不知魚之樂全矣。」
(V)　莊子曰:「請循其本。子曰『汝安知魚樂』云者,既已知吾知之而 問我,我知之濠上也。」

One day Zhuangzi and Huizi were strolling across the bridge on the Hao River.

(I)　Zhuangzi said, "Look how these fish are swimming about with great ease. These fish are happy."

(II)　Huizi responded, "You are not a fish, so how do you know the happiness of the fish?"

(III)　Zhuangzi said, "You are not me, so how do you know that I don't know the happiness of the fish?"

Originally published in *Ehu Journal* 29 (1977): 2–12. Translated and reprinted with permission.

(IV)   Huizi said, "I am not you; therefore I do not know you. By the same logic you do not know the fish. So it is impossible for you to know the happiness of the fish."

(V)   Zhuangzi replied, "Please return to the beginning. When you asked me, 'How do you know the happiness of the fish?' you already knew that I knew, and therefore you asked me. My knowing happens over the Hao River."

REASONS BEHIND THE WRITING OF THIS CHAPTER

In *Ehu Journal* 27 (1977), it was quite unexpected to find two separate articles dealing with the Happy Fish debate between Zhuangzi and Hui Shi [aka Huizi] in the "Autumn Floods" chapter of the *Zhuangzi*. One article was by Pan Boshi, titled "Zhuangzi and Hui Shi's 'Happy Fish' Debate" (hereafter referred to as "Pan's essay"; see pp. 50–51 of the aforementioned journal). The other article was by Chen Guimiao and was titled "Huizi's Academic Career" (hereafter "Chen's essay"; see pp. 17–24 of the aforementioned journal). The major purpose of the present essay is to provide a holistic analysis of Hui Shi's thought and to take the measure of his place in the history of Chinese thought. A subsection of Chen's essay deals specifically with the Happy Fish debate (see pp. 19–20).

I truly believe that the publication of both of these essays in the same journal is a most auspicious coincidence. However, in this coincidental encounter both scholars come at the debate with a completely different interpretation and set of arguments. In several important respects they reveal very different approaches. After deep reflection and careful thought I have gleaned many lofty insights from these two essays, particularly from Chen's. However, on many points further deliberation is needed. Thus the goal of this essay is to investigate and evaluate precisely these points. It is my hope that this essay can provide a fuller, more accurate, and more reasonable account of this famous debate. Since in what follows I often refer to the debate in the original *Zhuangzi* text, I have at the beginning of this essay divided the text into passages with corresponding Roman numerals to make for easy reference.

A SUMMARY OF THE MAJOR POINTS
OF THE TWO ESSAYS

With respect to the question of who actually wins and who loses this debate, history is full of competing claims, and it is impossible to find any consensus. Some take it that it is inappropriate to apply "right" and "wrong" (*shifei* 是非) to this debate. Others hold that Huizi wins or that Zhuangzi is the victor. But Professor Pan certainly thinks that Huizi loses and that Zhuangzi is victorious. He takes these first two opinions to be "inconsistent with the original text" while claiming to take a "reasoned approach to the debate, with the assumption that if rigorous thinking prevails, clear conclusions will emerge from the encounter." According to Pan's argument, the crux of Huizi's position is that he opposes Zhuangzi by asserting that "You are not a fish." And with "You are not a fish" as his reason he argues for the certainty that there exist two separate and independent individual entities, and, as such, mutual knowledge is impossible. In other words, Huizi overlooks, if not denies, the power that language and symbols have in our interactions.

And when he employs the proposition "You are not a fish, so how can you know the happiness of the fish?" to attack Zhuangzi, this proves immediately that two independent entities can have knowledge of each other through language and symbolic reference. So even before Zhuangzi has put forth "When you asked me, 'How do you know the happiness of the fish?'" he had already indicated Huizi's reliance upon the capacity of language and symbols to know a separately existing entity. Only upon such a basis can he say, "How do you know the happiness of the fish?"

Therefore, through "free and easy wandering"—which Pan takes to be a matter of semiotics—Zhuangzi is able to know the happiness of the fish. Thus, by affirming the interactive power of symbolic language, Zhuangzi comes out victorious in this debate. But is Huizi's position ultimately one of acquiescence? Chen thinks not. He insists that "if we assess the argument merely from the standpoint of its logical form, then Huizi comes out on top. But if we assess the arguments on the basis of their content, it is not an easy matter to decide who is right and who is wrong."

Chen separates the logical form from the actual content of the arguments and assesses Zhuangzi's and Huizi's respective positions accordingly. First of all, he affirms that in the course of this debate both Huizi and Zhuangzi employ the logical method of "adducing" (*yuan* 援) as articulated in the "Lesser Selections" of the Mohist Canons. They both adduce implied premises from their opponent's stated premises in order to undermine their opponent's position. In the whole process they each employ one "adduction." In order to facilitate understanding, Chen takes the Happy Fish debate and divides it into three moments. The first moment is when Huizi attempts to dispute Zhuangzi's assertion by asking, "You are not a fish, so how could you know the happiness of the fish?" Here Zhuangzi uses the method of "adducing" to refute Huizi. This tactic works because, if Huizi's "You are not the fish, so how could you know the happiness of the fish?" is a valid question, then Zhuangzi's response, "You are not me, so how could you know I don't know the happiness of the fish?" is also a valid question. Thus it can be said that the victory of this moment goes to Zhuangzi. But this does not mean that Zhuangzi achieves a final victory. Rather, it leads to his ultimate defeat. In the second moment, Huizi similarly uses the method of "adducing" to get the upper hand.

Huizi's rhetorical device is to take Zhuangzi's question "You are not me, so how could you know that I don't know the fish are happy?" as valid and then to take as certain that Zhuangzi cannot possibly know the happiness of the fish. Huizi claims that just as he may not know (from experience) that Zhuangzi does or does not know the happiness of the fish, (from logical adduction) he can be sure that "You [Zhuangzi] are certainly not a fish; therefore your not knowing the happiness of the fish also follows necessarily [from our shared method of adduction]." When it comes to the third moment, it is simply a matter of Zhuangzi's subterfuge that he appears to get the upper hand, but in fact no victory is achieved. This is because Zhuangzi takes the "how can you know" (*anzhi* 安知) in Huizi's "You are not a fish, so how can you know the happiness of the fish" in an erroneous way [Trans.: Chen's contention is that Huizi's "how" should refer to "how is it *possible?*" not "how is it *actualized?*"]. Thus Zhuangzi fails to address the previous victory, which Huizi achieved in the second moment of the argument, and therefore Huizi is the ultimate victor.

In terms of the content of the argument, Chen thinks that before we can decide who is right and who is wrong, we must first answer two further questions: "Do nonhuman animals have the level of self-consciousness necessary for happiness? And if they do, are humans capable of knowing this happiness?" If the response to both of these questions is in the affirmative, then Zhuangzi is correct. If the response to either question is negative, then Huizi comes out on top. And if it is the case that neither question can have a determinate conclusion, then the Happy Fish debate between Zhuangzi and Huizi cannot be resolved.

AN ANALYSIS OF THE TWO ESSAYS

The arguments of the two essays are consistent, subtle, and revealing. However, if we want to decide the merits and faults of the two interpretations in our efforts to understand the debate, it is precisely the disparities between the two essays that can help us grasp their respective arguments and conclusions. This comparison and assessment will illuminate the debate. In my own interpretation of the Happy Fish encounter, the line that I take, the method that I employ, the attitude I hold, and the focus that I attain can all be reflected in a comparison between these two essays.

The Meaning of the Debate

A debate is a formal discussion between two or more people who take up different or opposing positions on a common topic. The intention in a debate is to use language to overturn an opponent's position and to prove that one's own position is correct. Therefore, any meaningful debate must meet at least the following six criteria: (1) There must be two or more participants in the debate (2) on a common topic (3) who have different positions and (4) with each participant having the intention of winning; and (5) arguments are exchanged, and (6) language is used in a univocal fashion. The first four criteria are the initial necessary conditions for a meaningful debate. If any one of these criteria is absent, a debate cannot even get off the ground. The latter two criteria are necessary conditions that arise in the process of the debate. After a debate begins, we need to focus on whether or not these two criteria are met.

The negotiating of positions in a debate requires that the participants actually interact with each other. Whether it is a matter of forming an opposite, or dialectically opposed, position, if the participants focus only on their own standpoint without paying any heed to the other's stance, then we do not have a debate. For this would produce nothing more than monologues by the participants. However, at times during the negotiating of their positions, the participants appear to be establishing opposite standpoints, but further analysis reveals this not to be the case. For example, two people debating the merits of a newly published book may come to the apparently competing view that it is either "very good" or "bad." One person may hold that the book is "bad" (on the basis of its lacking substantial content), whereas another person may hold the same book to be "very good" (on the basis of its technical information). If they continue to debate on the level of "bad" and "very good" without clarifying what they mean by "good" and "bad," then such a "debate" is meaningless. This is what is covered by the sixth criterion—the necessity of having univocity of language, which does not require the participants to use an identical natural or artificial language because different languages can be translated. However, it does entail that the participants share the same *meaning* of the words and phrases they are employing. Without this shared meaning, any interchange of positions or even the sharing of a common topic and the convergence or divergence of standpoints becomes impossible. Without being grounded in univocity, such a "debate" would occur in name only.

Using these six criteria we can then ask, is the Happy Fish debate between Zhuangzi and Huizi a proper debate or not? On the surface it would seem to be one, and in Chen's and Pan's treatments of the debate in their attempts to determine who wins and who loses, they accept it as such. So they certainly share the hypothesis that it is a meaningful debate. But is this a justifiable hypothesis? From a cursory glance at the original text of the debate, it would seem that all six of the criteria are present. Zhuangzi and Huizi are the participants, and they both have the intention of winning; these two criteria are obvious. Moreover, the remaining four criteria all seem to be present. A common topic is shared: "Does Zhuangzi know the happiness of the fish or not?" They take up opposing positions—Zhuangzi affirms his knowing, whereas Huizi denies Zhuangzi's knowing the happiness of the fish. They converge on a central problem: "Is it or is it not the case that nonfish can know the happiness of fish?" And they employ language univocally—the words employed by each are quite simple, and there are no obvious divergences of meaning.

Under these conditions, both Zhuangzi and Huizi believe that their debate is meaningful. But we should not forget that of these latter four criteria, three depend upon the final criterion to be fulfilled. Thus, if we simply take the debaters to be using words in a univocal fashion without further analysis, this would be rather rash. Zhuangzi and Huizi are the authorities in this debate, and we can forgive authorities who make a mistake; however, if we, as bystanders, make the same mistake, there must be some form of censure. From this standpoint, we must admit that both the Chen and Pan essays have neglected to consider the issue of univocity. Indeed, this issue is central to my analysis.

The Method of the Debate

When people participate in a debate, their ultimate goal is to overturn the position of their opponent and establish their own standpoint. On many occasions, such a goal can be reached through only one of two types of procedures. But if the participants of the debate have exactly opposite positions, one needs to carry out only one procedure. This is because under such conditions, to overthrow the opposition is to simultaneously establish one's own (dialectically opposed) position. This is the best way to establish one's own point of view. And there are many ways to attack an opponent's position. Among the myriad ways of overturning an opponent's position, the method most preferred by thinkers throughout the ages has been the reductio ad absurdum.

The so-called reductio ad absurdum, or simply reductio, for the purposes of refuting one's opponent, involves temporarily taking the assumptions of one's opponent's argument as true and then, by using the laws of logic, deducing from these assumptions a contradiction. I have already shown that both Huizi and Zhuangzi take their debate to be meaningful. Thus, their respective positions—whether or not one can *know* the *happiness* of the fish—are antithetically opposed. Under such conditions, reductio is the most useful strategy. And actually, both Huizi and Zhuangzi do employ this method of argument. Since both of them use this methodology, in assessing their respective positions, I use the reductio method as my guiding thread. But before I employ this interpretive methodology I first have to clarify the distinction between logical inference and substantial content.

Chen's essay focuses on this distinction. Indeed, even though Chen's interpretation rests on this distinction, his essay offers no explicit explanation of it. Perhaps it was just a matter of space and editing, but here I would like to elaborate where Chen is silent. I am sure that anyone with some knowledge of logic will not disagree. Whether or not the inferential steps are legitimate and whether or not the topical content is compatible with objective fact or truth are completely unrelated when assessing an argument. The former belongs to the realm of logical inference, and the latter, the level of factual content. These two levels are completely separate. For one cannot use logical inference to decide whether the content of an argument is factual, and conversely, one cannot use factual evidence to decide whether the logic of an argument is valid. For example, if we first establish two premises—"All humans are immortal" and "Some X is a human"—we can infer the conclusion that "X is immortal." According to the rules of logical inference, this is perfectly valid, but, according to factual content, "All humans are immortal" is clearly absurd, so the conclusion is also false. From this we can see that this distinction is quite important. However, in assessing Huizi and Zhuangzi's debate, is this distinction useful or even necessary?

The Chen essay does not address this question. The reason for this is that his description of Huizi's and Zhuangzi's methods of argument—relying as he does on the "Lesser Selection" of the Mohist Canon and its account of "adducing"—is not thorough enough. Chen writes, "Looking at their respective methods of argument, both Zhuangzi and Huizi use the method of adducing problematic conclusions from their opponent's premises. This is the method found in the Mohist 'Lesser Selections' called *yuan*. *Yuan* is like the using of a person's spear to attack his own shield—that is, one attempts to display a fundamental contradiction in the method of argumentation." How is it like "using a spear to attack a shield?" How does it fall into the trap of logical contradiction? On this point Chen is not very clear. Under such conditions we need to return to the method of reductio—a method that ensures that Huizi and Zhuangzi, "under the hypothesis that the premises of one's opponent are true, derive a contradiction using nothing but the rules of logical inference." In other words, we do not have to go outside of the debate itself to empirically determine whether or not the factual content of the participant's premises are true. Therefore, in deciding whether Huizi or Zhuangzi comes out on top in the debate, we can rely solely on the rules of logical inference. Operating thus, the need to distinguish between logical form and factual content becomes most evident.

Chen focuses on this distinction and consistently employs it in his analysis. In his treatment of the Happy Fish debate, he initially distinguishes these two levels and for each level offers a different analysis of their respective arguments. In this regard, Pan's essay is far inferior to Chen's because Pan never comes close to making this distinction. Thus Pan is only able to clarify Huizi's argument and claim that it fails. Is this failure a result of the argument's logical form or the factual content of the premises? This Pan never addresses. Thus, we can see that Pan never realizes the importance of this distinction. But if we were to apply this distinction to Pan's analysis, we would find that Zhuangzi's victory is a matter of the factual content of the premises (and not the logical form alone).

I have already made clear the distinction between logical inference and factual content. For the Happy Fish debate this is very important. And when we attempt to decide who won or lost this debate, we should really stay on the level of logical inference alone. On the other hand, if we do not heed this distinction, then we are more likely to reach Chen's conclusion: "Do animals have consciousness of happiness? If so, do humans have the ability to know their happiness?" The way Chen approaches this debate is settled in this way: "According to the logical form of their respective arguments, we can decide who is right and who is wrong, but according to the factual content, we cannot ever reach a definitive conclusion." This follows because in the process of this debate, we have no way to step outside for an empirical verification of either of the necessary premises. Thus, in our treatment of the debate we should focus solely on investigating the logical form. Now let us return to Pan's standpoint that Zhuangzi won the debate. Pan relies mainly on section V of the original text.

Pan first of all affirms Huizi's "You [Zhuangzi] are not a fish" and from this derives the claim that "two independent entities have no way of knowing each other." Then he deduces from section V that Huizi actually affirms the symbolic power of language to know an independently existing entity—namely, Zhuangzi himself. So Zhuangzi should be able to use the "symbolic language" of these fish—that is to say, their free and easy swimming—to know their happiness. Thus, Zhuangzi is able to overturn Huizi's position and achieve victory in the debate. From this analysis, what Zhuangzi purportedly overturns is the principle that "two independent entities have no way of knowing each other." In other words, Pan has already implicitly used this premise to replace Huizi's "You are not a fish. How could you know the happiness of the fish?" as his central point. (This replacement is actually illegitimate, as I will explain later.)

When it comes to the standpoint Zhuangzi takes up in the argument, this for Pan is clearly the "use of language and symbols." But this is affirmed only on the level of factual content. Actually, for Pan the distinction that Chen makes between logical form and factual content is already presupposed, and at a subconscious level Pan answers Chen's two necessary questions in the affirmative: "Does an animal have consciousness of its happiness? If so, can humans know this happiness?" However, how can Pan possibly answer these two questions relying on nothing but Huizi and Zhuangzi's abstract debate? How can we take "You are not a fish. Therefore how can you know the happiness of the fish?" and transform it into "Two independently existing entities cannot know each other"? Is this transformation or replacement what underlies Huizi's position? With regard to these questions, aside from "taking something for granted," it is difficult for Pan to offer any reasonable answers. We can use Professor Pan's own words to describe his interpretive methodology: "Don't rely on the original text or the sequence of the argument," he says and suggests instead that we "follow the line of thought implicit in the text and add some desirable conclusions." From this quote alone we have good reason to be suspicious of much of Pan's interpretation.

The Hermeneutics of Statements V and I

Although the substance of Pan's essay does not merit any further consideration, it has offered something worth our attention. This is his focus on proposition V. His entire essay is constructed around this very proposition. And this is precisely the proposition that Chen overlooks. Chen takes this to be nothing more than Zhuangzian rhetoric because Zhuangzi states here that "When you asked me, 'How do you know the happiness of the fish?' you already knew that I knew, and therefore you asked me. My knowing happens over the Hao River." However, the question "How do you know the happiness of the fish?" does not imply "You already know that I [Zhuangzi] have such knowledge." In order to win a conclusive argument in the debate, Zhuangzi will take Huizi's question "You are not a fish, so *how do you know (anzhi* 安知) the happiness of fish?" and distort Huizi's "How do you know" (安知) to mean "How have you come to know" as opposed to the intended "How can you possibly know?" Chen takes Zhuangzi's reply to Huizi's "*anzhi* 安知" to be a distortion because if one were to interpret the question as "*How can you possibly know* the fish are happy?" it would not imply that the questioner already knows that the questioner's interlocutor has such knowledge. But if we take the *anzhi* to mean "How do you know?" (that is, "What method do you employ?"), then such an implication would be allowed. When we ask about someone's method of knowing, we clearly presuppose that that person already possesses the knowledge in question. Broadly speaking, Chen's interpretation has two characteristics: First of all, it takes the *an* 安 of *anzhi* to be ambiguous and thus avoids a simplistic interpretation; second, through this kind of hermeneutical approach, statement V becomes disconnected from its context. In other words, statement V stands independently of the entirety of those statements that give it context. Moreover, without deciding whether or not the *an* 安 is ambiguous, can we even offer an interpretation of statement V? Without setting the structure of this statement in the broader context of the Happy Fish debate, is it even possible to provide an adequate hermeneutical approach? Pan's essay here provides some key insights.

The Pan essay has its own special characteristics. For example, in laying out the import of statement V regarding Huizi's "You are not a fish," Pan maintains that Zhuangzi ultimately gets the upper hand in this debate. For Pan, it could be said that statement V is the most important element in this entire debate. This position follows in a long line of commentary dating back to the *Xiang-Guo Commentary* on the *Zhuangzi* (hereafter, the *XGZ*).[1] In fact, I believe that Pan was deeply influenced by this traditional commentary. So, before I move on with my analysis, it will be helpful to see how the *XGZ* deals with statement V:

> In exploring the original statement of Huizi we have: "Not being a fish there is no potential to know a fish's experience." But now you are not me, but you ask me how I know the happiness of the fish, and you know that I am not a fish. But if you know that I am not a fish, then it is possible for "this" to know "that" [Trans.: that is, for two different sites of experience to have knowledge of each other]. So one doesn't have to be a fish to know a fish. So to return to your question, "How do I know?" this question already shows that you know that I know, so you want to ask how. I know precisely over the river Hao. One has to jump into the water!

Zhuangzi offers statement V in order to return to Huizi's original question, "You are not a fish, so how can you know the happiness of the fish?" Because Huizi is able to refute part III, the response of IV is rather convincing. Chen claims here that Huizi wins in terms of logical argument;

actually not only Chen thinks this, but even Zhuangzi himself believes he has lost, so he has to return to the beginning of the debate to readdress Huizi's challenge. According to the *XGZ*, what Zhuangzi wants to accomplish in part V is to prove that in Huizi's affirmation that Zhuangzi is not a fish and then in asking, "How can you know the happiness of the fish?" Huizi is already making a judgment about Zhuangzi. This means that Huizi at least acknowledges the possibility that Zhuangzi might know the happiness of the fish.

The reason that Zhuangzi makes statement V is that he wants to return to Huizi's original question: "You are not a fish, so how can you know the happiness of the fish?" ("Please let us return to the beginning"). Because Huizi's refutation of statement III is rather convincing, Chen's essay maintains that Huizi wins the debate based on this refutation and Huizi's formal logic. Actually, not only does Chen think this, but even Zhuangzi accepts that he has lost. So he has no choice but to return to the original problem and start the debate afresh. According to the *XGZ*, Zhuangzi in statement V wants to put his interpretive focus on Huizi's claim that "You are not a fish, so how could you know the happiness of the fish?" According to the *XGZ*, Zhuangzi wants to show that as soon as Huizi says that Zhuangzi is not a fish, he is already making a judgment about him and therefore has committed himself to the possibility of knowing another person's experience. According to this hermeneutic, Zhuangzi returns to the method that Huizi used in statement IV and produces the following argument: "When you say that I do not know the happiness of the fish, you have already affirmed that I am not a fish. Thus you reveal that you are capable of having knowledge of me. But if you are capable of having knowledge of me, then I am certainly capable of having knowledge of the fish. And if I can have knowledge of the fish, then it necessarily follows that I can know the happiness of the fish." In carefully examining this line of reasoning it is not hard to discover that Zhuangzi is simply following Huizi's assumptions and using logical deduction to derive a contradiction in Huizi's position. And he does this without having to deal at all with the factual content of the premises.

If we follow Zhuangzi and Huizi (or even the Chen-Pan debate), accepting that it is indeed a meaningful debate, and if we employ the hermeneutical method of the *XGZ*, then we can see that Zhuangzi is successful because of his use of the reductio. In other words, this particular argument operates solely on the level of logic.

So if we take up the *XGZ* hermeneutical approach, then Zhuangzi certainly proves to be the winner in this interchange. In deciding whether this is a meaningful debate (especially with regard to proposition V), what we need to do now then is to determine how to choose between the approach of *XGZ* and that found in Chen's essay.

Actually, the language Zhuangzi uses in this key passage is ambiguous. If one takes the passage literally, it is not easy to see a single true meaning. From "How do you know the happiness of the fish?" how can one possibly derive the conclusion "You already know what I know?" This is the key to Zhuangzi's whole argument. For any interpretation, if it cannot give an adequate response to this question, then it fails as a hermeneutically viable approach to this key passage.

However, Zhuangzi himself does not deal with the ambiguities in this passage. Thus a wide hermeneutical space has been opened up for a lively tradition of *Zhuangzi* interpretations. Because of this ambiguity, actually both Chen's essay and the *XGZ* interpretive stances can be said to work. However, regardless of this interpretive flexibility, we can still speak of better and worse, or the lofty and the base, in adjudicating between various interpretations.

As I have already mentioned, if we follow Chen's interpretation, then passage V is "surgically" removed from its preceding context. In terms of bringing some clarity to the debate between Huizi and Zhuangzi, this is most unfortunate. The *XGZ*, on the other hand, does not have this fault because it does not insist on taking Zhuangzi's response to Huizi's question "How do you know?" as a misunderstanding. Instead, it takes passage V to be a direct response to passage II and thus incorporates the passage in its overall context. For these reasons, in interpreting the debate between Zhuangzi and Huizi, we should opt for the *XGZ* stance. Moreover, *Zhuangzi* is a book that expresses the thought of Zhuangzi himself and often takes the form of debates between Zhuangzi and an interlocutor wherein Zhuangzi comes out on top. So in choosing an interpretive stance that most appropriately fits with the spirit of the text, we should choose one that conforms most closely to its overall content. Thus, since we have already chosen to go with the *XGZ* stance, we should make some fresh distinctions in the ordering of the happy fish passage. We can separate the text into two sections: the first section incorporates passages II, III, and IV, while the second section comprises passages II and V. In the first section we can say that Huizi comes out victorious, and even Zhuangzi admits as much. In the second section Zhuangzi emerges the winner. So in interpreting this passage we must keep in mind the distinction between these two sections of the text.

Except for passage V, Chen's interpretations of II and IV are for the most part astute and comprehensive readings. But this marks a sharp contrast with his misreading of I. Let us not forget that the origins of the Happy Fish debate lie in the dialogue of I and II. In understanding the origins of this debate, one cannot rely solely on II. No doubt II is an important source, but it comes in the context of how Huizi responds to what transpired in I. In other words, passage II relies on passage I. Moreover, starting from passage II, we cannot forget the importance of I; otherwise, we run the risk of taking "I [Zhuangzi] know the happiness of the fish" as equivalent to I. However, it is far from evident that passage I and "I know the happiness of the fish" are identical statements. Are the semantic implications of passage I and those of "I know the happiness of the fish" really interchangeable? The answer to this question is obviously a negative response. "I know the happiness of the fish" can express only "The fish are happy," but before this statement, do we not have to observe "how these fish are swimming about with great ease"? Thus, if we set aside passage I and start directly at II in the process of attempting to interpret the whole debate, we would be putting the cart before the horse. However, this overlooking of passage I is for the most part not the fault of interpreters but lies with Zhuangzi himself. This is because after producing statement I, Zhuangzi goes on to follow Huizi's conundrum—passage II—and only when concluding the debate does he return to I. This is a negative side effect of Zhuangzi's employment of the reductio and is one of the main reasons many interpreters stumble over the passage.

In this respect we find the only point wherein Pan's essay is valuable. Pan clearly sees that "I know the happiness of the fish" is not equivalent to statement I. Thus he attempts to interpret the meaning of "swimming at ease" as being part of the "linguistic symbolism of the fish." Although this interpretation is obviously not worth following, at least Pan recognizes that passage I is very important in attempting to provide an adequate interpretation of the entire debate.

Generally speaking, passage I in the Happy Fish debate holds a unique position and cannot be excluded or reduced to another passage. Therefore, seeking the meaning of this passage is our most important task.

INTERPRETING THE HAPPY FISH DEBATE

Examining the Continuity of Language

Before formally beginning an interpretation, I first need to summarize the preceding analysis. In the process of carrying out their exchange, both Huizi and Zhuangzi felt that it was indeed a meaningful debate. And the method they used to attempt to overcome their opponent was reductio ad absurdum. These features form a basic hypothesis for both Zhuangzi and Huizi. Under this hypothesis we need to separate the Happy Fish debate into two segments: statements II, III, and IV form the first segment, wherein Huizi is the winner, while II and V form the second segment, wherein Zhuangzi is victorious. We can now employ a kind of reductio by temporarily assuming the premises of Zhuangzi's and Huizi's shared hypothesis and then see whether or not the happy fish story is indeed a meaningful debate. Let us begin with the first segment.

The first segment begins and ends with statements emerging from Huizi's mouth. The first statement is II: "You are not a fish, so how can you know the happiness of the fish?" If we carefully analyze this statement, we discover that "Zhuangzi is not a fish" implies that Zhuangzi cannot know the happiness of fish. But since we already know Zhuangzi is not a fish, then it necessarily follows that he does not know the happiness of fish. The last statement, IV, is as follows: "I am not you; therefore I do not know you. By the same logic you do not know the fish. So it is impossible for you to know the happiness of the fish." Analyzed carefully, this statement implies that the statement "Huizi is not Zhuangzi and therefore cannot know Zhuangzi's happiness" is true. Thus the statement "Zhuangzi is not a fish; therefore he cannot know the happiness of fish" is also true. But we already know Zhuangzi is not a fish, so he cannot possibly know their happiness. In order to bring more clarity to this first segment let us use the notation of symbolic logic to express these arguments:

> Let "Zhuangzi" be represented by C, "Huizi" by W, "Fish" by F, "Happiness" by P, and the "happy fish" by FP (also, "Zhuangzi's happiness" is CP), while "knowledge/knowing" is K ("not knowing" is ~K), and, finally, "to be" is B (and "not to be" is ~B).

Statement II

1) (C) ~B (F) → (C) ~K(FP) *Assumption*
2) (C) ~B(F) *Already known*
3) ∴ (C) ~K(FP) *Modus ponens (MP)*

Statement IV

1) If (W) ~B(C) → (W)~K(CP)
2) Then (C) ~B(F) → (C) ~K(FP)
3) (C)~B(F) *Given*
4) ∴ (C) ~K(FP) MP

According to the hypothesis stated earlier, this is a meaningful debate, and both Huizi and Zhuangzi are using reductio ad absurdum as a method of argument. Therefore, statement III should follow from statement II and should logically entail statement IV. Thus as long as we know that statements II and III are posited as hypotheses, then we can be sure that III follows as a conclusion. According to II and IV, statement II should be considered a hypothetical proposition, and only then can we have a legitimate, logical argument.

Hypothetical proposition II

(a) If (C)~B(F) → (C)~K(FP)
(b) Then (W)~B(C) → (W)~K(CP) *Same principle as (a)*
(c) (W)~B(C)   *Given*
(d) ∴ (W)~K(CP)   *MP*

According to hypothetical proposition III, the legitimate conclusion is (W)~K(CP). But comparing this conclusion with premise 4 in the earlier argument formalized from statement IV, the latter does not hold up as a legitimate logical inference. The inference is illegitimate because (W)~K(CP) and (W)~K[C]~K(CP)] are clearly not semantically equivalent. In order to facilitate understanding, let us take these two propositions and translate them into ordinary language. Hypothetical proposition III means the following: "If 'Zhuangzi is not a fish implies that Zhuangzi does not know the happiness of the fish' is true, then 'Huizi is not Zhuangzi' implies that 'Huizi does not know Zhuangzi's happiness' is also true. But we already know that 'Zhuangzi is not a fish'; therefore 'Huizi does not know Zhuangzi's happiness' {(W)~K[(C)~ K(CP)]}." Statement III can be read as "If 'Zhuangzi is not a fish' implies that 'Zhuangzi does not know the happiness of fish' is true, then 'Huizi is not Zhuangzi' implies that 'Huizi does not know Zhuangzi's happiness' is also true. But we already know 'Huizi is not Zhuangzi'; therefore 'Huizi does not know that Zhuangzi does not know the happiness of fish' {(W)~K[(C)~ K(CP)]}." It is obvious that "not knowing Zhuangzi's happiness" is clearly not semantically equivalent to "not knowing Zhuangzi's not knowing the happiness of fish."

Thus when Zhuangzi makes the jump from "not knowing his [Zhuangzi's] happiness" to "not knowing whether or not he knows the happiness of the fish," he produces an illegitimate logical argument. So he cannot connect statement II with IV in terms of logical entailment. Therefore, in the first segment of the argument Zhuangzi cannot truly be said to be properly using reductio ad absurdum. This is because he cannot secure linguistic continuity with Huizi. Without linguistic univocity the first segment of the debate becomes meaningless. And in any meaningless argument, how can we possibly speak of victory or defeat? So we can be certain that Chen's essay, which uses mere logical form to show that Huizi is victorious, is a mistaken approach.

Having gone through a careful analysis of the first segment of the Happy Fish debate, we can see that if "Zhuangzi is not a fish" truly implies that "Zhuangzi cannot know the happiness of fish," then propositions (II) and (IV) are both sound logical moves in the argument. For example, if between "Zhuangzi is not a fish" and "Zhuangzi does not know the happiness of fish," we have the implication that either both are true or both are false, then Huizi's style of argument leads to an absolute truth, so there is no point in debating. Zhuangzi himself in the second segment of the argument realizes this point. So when he asks to start the debate afresh, he changes his point of attack, trying to show that the relationship between these two propositions is not one of logical entailment. What he needs to prove is that "Zhuangzi is not a fish" in no way implies that "Zhuangzi does not know the happiness of the fish"; if he can do so, then Huizi's argument cannot even get off the ground. So now, building upon what we've already covered, we can begin to interpret the second segment of the argument.

The second segment has two propositions—statement II has already been discussed, and we can rely upon *XGZ* to interpret statement V as follows:

Assume that statement II (C)~B(F) → (C)~K(FP) is true.

 Then it follows that (W)~B(C) → (W)~K(CP) is also true. (*same principle*)

 (1) Relying on the definition of "→"[2]
 (2) If (W)~B(C) is true
 (3) Then (W)~K(CP) is necessarily true. *MP*
 (4) Relying again on proposition II, Huizi takes (C)~B(F) as already given.
 (5) ∴ (W)K[(C)~B(F)] is true
 (6) And K[(C)~B(F)] = K(CP)[3]   *Assumption*
 (7) ∴ (W)K[(C)~B(F)] = (W)K(CP)   *From 6*
 (8) ∴ (W)K(CP) is true   *From 5, 7*
 (9) ∴ (W)~K(CP) is false   *From 8*
(10) Now (W)~B(C) is true   *Already given*
   ∴ (W)~B(C) → (W)~K(CP) is false *From 1, 9, 10*

If this argument stands, then Huizi's argument has been overturned. But is this in fact a series of valid inferences? A key component of this argument is whether or not the assumption made in 6 can withstand scrutiny. If we use ordinary language to translate 6, then we have Zhuangzi making the following assumption: "Knowing Zhuangzi is not a fish" is conceptually and semantically equivalent to "knowing the happiness of the fish." But it should be immediately obvious that this is not a sound assumption. How could it be possible that these two propositions are conceptually identical? It is equivocation that leads to the unsoundness of this assumption. And if this assumption cannot be made, then the entire argument does not get off the ground. Then this argument does not follow from statement II; in fact, segment two of the argument is also a meaningless debate. So the *XGZ* and Pan's interpretation that Zhuangzi is victorious in this segment of the debate are also groundless.

The Known and the Dissension of Knowledge

In the first segment of the debate, I pointed out that "knowing the happiness of the fish" and "knowing whether or not Zhuangzi knows the happiness of the fish" are not conceptually equivalent. Moreover, in the second segment of the debate, "knowing that Zhuangzi is not a fish" and "knowing the happiness of the fish" are obviously not equivalent, but Zhuangzi confuses them in his logical inferences. This cannot but count as a very strange phenomenon. Seeking the origins of this phenomenon is our task. Luckily statement V gives us an important thread to follow. Following the interpretation of *XGZ*, the crux of Zhuangzi's argument is as follows: "If you know that I'm not a fish, then by knowing this we can be said to know that even though I'm not a fish, I can potentially still know the happiness of the fish." From this we can see that Zhuangzi's whole argument can be separated into a series of steps. First of all, he takes the propositions "Huizi knows Zhuangzi is not a fish" and "Zhuangzi knows the happiness of fish" and turns them into "Huizi has some knowledge of Zhuangzi" and "Zhuangzi has some knowledge of the fish." The second step goes from "Huizi is not Zhuangzi, yet he still has some knowledge of Zhuangzi," to infer that "Zhuangzi is not a fish, but he still has some knowledge of the fish." The last step is to take "Zhuangzi has some knowledge of the fish" and replace it with "Zhuangzi knows the happiness of the fish." With these three steps his argument is complete. Prima facie this argument appears to be without flaw. However, it actually rests upon two errors. First, Zhuangzi conflates "Huizi knows Zhuangzi is not a fish" and "Huizi has some knowledge of Zhuangzi." And he conflates "Zhuangzi knows the happiness of fish" and "Zhuangzi has some knowledge of the fish." Finally, in the last step of his argument, he thinks he has proven that "Zhuangzi has some knowledge of the fish" and "Zhuangzi knows the happiness of the fish" are equivalent. Here we can see how the fallacious reasoning has emerged. It would seem that Zhuangzi failed to fully understand *shi* 是. In ordinary language people use *shi* in two senses: one is a "relationship of equivalence," and the other is a "relationship of belonging" to a class of objects. For example, "Qin Shihuang is (*shi* 是) the emperor" is an example of the relationship of equivalence, whereas "An apple is (*shi*) a fruit" is a case of the relationship of belonging.

According to Aristotelian logic, in a sentence expressing universality, besides the universal subject, what we have are minor accidents within the class of objects that the universal concept points out. It is evident that "knowing the happiness of the fish" is, in relation to "having some knowledge of the fish," a case similar to apples belonging to the class "fruit." Now, this is a case of a part and whole, or species and genus, relation. It is perfectly natural that a part is smaller than the class it belongs to. Thus, "knowing the happiness of the fish is having some knowledge of the fish" is an example of such a class of objects being picked out from a larger class. This is clearly a "relationship of belonging" and not one of "equivalence." Therefore, the two statements cannot be used interchangeably. I have already shown that Pan's essay is mistaken in replacing "two independently existent things cannot have mutual knowledge" for "two individual existent things cannot know the other's happiness." "You are not a fish, so how can you know the happiness of fish?"—this question is also grounded in this mistake. Perhaps thinking that "knowing the happiness of the fish" is equivalent to "having some knowledge of the fish" is too common a phenomenon. Even Zhuangzi did not realize that *shi* 是 has two senses. He simply took this statement as indicating a relationship of equivalence and thus mistakenly took the two propositions as interchangeable. This can be seen in Zhuangzi's appealing to the fact that Huizi is not Zhuangzi, yet he claims to have some knowledge of Zhuangzi (i.e., that Zhuangzi does not know the happiness of the fish) in order to refute Huizi's claim that since he is not a fish, he cannot know the happiness of the fish.

The first mistake is basically present in Zhuangzi's argument in the first and last sections, while the second mistake is present mainly in the second section. Let us put down for the moment an analysis of the first kind of mistake and focus on whether the second section of the argument can stand. In ordinary language some words have a very broad application and range of meaning, so it is not uncommon to see the same word varying widely in meaning depending on its context. The more fecund the range of use, the more dissension of meaning will occur. Moreover, when the applications vary widely, the more likely people will be to notice them. "Knowledge" is just such a word. In everyday speech it can vary quite widely in meaning. When a young child says, "I know that cars have four wheels," this is a kind of empirical knowledge. When a person experiencing regret says, "I know I was wrong," this is a kind of reflective knowledge. When a severely sick or injured person says, "I only know pain, but I do not know where it is painful," this is a kind of affective-perceptive knowledge. When a youth full of hope says, "I know next year I will achieve my ambitions," this knowledge is a kind of faith. From these examples we can see that the meaning of "know" changes greatly depending on context. So in attempting to determine what sense of "know" is active in any given statement that claims that someone either possesses or does not possess knowledge, we cannot simply look at the word indicating knowledge, but we must look at what is being claimed to be known in order to determine the context. In carrying out his argument Zhuangzi did not grasp the relationship between knowing and what is being known. The first part of the argument reveals that Zhuangzi realized that from "knowing Zhuangzi is not a fish" one cannot directly deduce anything about knowing the happiness of the fish. But this only reveals that he recognized that "Huizi knows Zhuangzi is not a fish" and "Zhuangzi knows the fish are happy" are not the same. With regard to the two different uses of "know" in the aforementioned propositions, Zhuangzi takes them to be identical.

Actually, if he were to recognize two different senses of "know" in the first part of the argument, the second part of his argument would not be able to proceed. This is because from "Huizi is not Zhuangzi, but Huizi has some knowledge of Zhuangzi" one cannot deduce "Zhuangzi is not a fish, but Zhuangzi has some knowledge of the fish." However, Zhuangzi clearly knows that "knowing that Zhuangzi is not a fish" and "knowing the happiness of the fish" are not the same. So when he treats having knowledge that Zhuangzi is not a fish and having some knowledge of the fish as having identical conceptions of knowledge, we can see his eagerness to win the argument. We cannot but be careful here. Unfortunately, Zhuangzi's line of argument rests on a mistake.

When Zhuangzi takes the two uses of "knowledge" to have the same meaning, he has already shown that he has separated the knower from the known in determining the context of knowledge. This is obviously an invalid method of argument because it fails to distinguish between the different senses of "knowledge" and leads to a fundamental ambiguity in the concept. What we need to do is put the two instances of using "knowledge" back into their contexts in order to clearly understand their respective meanings. In doing this we discover that "having knowledge of Zhuangzi" should be understood as "knowing Zhuangzi is not a fish," and "having some knowledge of the fish" should be understood as "knowing the happiness of the fish." The former is clearly a case of empirical knowledge, for one can know only by experience that the individual existent Zhuangzi is not a fish. In the latter case we have to look at statement II to get clear about the meaning of "know" being employed here. In statement II Huizi says, "You are not a fish, so how can you know the happiness of the fish?" This is the same as saying, "'If you want to know the happiness of some thing, then you have to be that thing." But this kind of knowledge would be a case of private subjective knowledge, which it is impossible for any other entity to share. Thus, unless this knowledge is like first drinking water and only then knowing whether it is hot or cold, it can only be like the case of the person who is experiencing extreme pain but is unable to pinpoint it. Otherwise, this statement cannot be understood. From here we can see that this knowledge can only be a case of affective-perceptive knowledge.[4] This also explains why Zhuangzi's second argument cannot get off the ground because saying that Huizi cannot have experiential knowledge of Zhuangzi due to the fact that Huizi and Zhuangzi are two separate entities is not the same as saying that Zhuangzi cannot have subjective affective-perceptive knowledge of the happiness of the fish. In sum, because of the inferential steps made in V—namely, the assumption made in step 6—statements II and V cannot stand as parts of a meaningful argument. This assumption rests on this failure to differentiate between two different types of knowledge and the resultant fallacious response to statement II.

This failure to differentiate types of knowledge is also the reason that statement III is a non sequitur to statement II. The use of "know" in statements II and IV involves cases of affective-perceptive knowledge, while in statement III the "know" in "Zhuangzi does not know the happiness of the fish" indicates a kind of metaknowledge of the affective-perceptive knowledge of the happy fish—*if* we maintain the distinction between object language and metalanguage.[5] In any event, because the senses of "know" are confused, the entire first segment of the Happy Fish debate is a meaningless debate.

In order to facilitate easier understanding of the complexities of the assumptions being made by Zhuangzi and Huizi in their exchange, it will be helpful to translate the debate into colloquial language to better assess the strengths and weaknesses of their respective positions:

(II) HUIZI: You [Zhuangzi] are not a fish, so how can you perceive the subjective happiness of the fish?

(III) ZHUANGZI: You [Huizi] are not me, so how can you have any metaknowledge of my not having subjective affective-perceptive knowledge of the fish's subjective happiness?

(IV) HUIZI: I am not you, so, of course, I cannot sense your subjective sensations.[6] But you also aren't a fish, so isn't it the case that you cannot possibly perceive the subjective sensation of the fish's happiness?

(V) ZHUANGZI: In what has been said so far you win. But we should return to the beginning [statement II], and start our debate afresh. Actually, when you claimed that I cannot possibly perceive the fish's subjective feeling of happiness, you already established that I am not a fish. But asserting that I'm not a fish implies that you have some empirical knowledge of me. You are not me, but you can have some empirical knowledge of me. So, although I am not a fish, I also can have affective-perceptive knowledge of the fish's subjective happiness. In this situation you asked me how it is that I perceive the subjective happiness of the fish. My answer is that my affective-perceptive knowledge of the subjective happiness of the fish happens on this bridge over the river Hao.

THE "HAPPINESS" OF THE FISH

The Happy Fish debate began when Zhuangzi said, "Look how these fish are swimming about with great ease. These fish are happy." And Huizi responded, "You are not a fish, so how do you know the happiness of the fish?" As we have seen, Zhuangzi proceeds to take Huizi's presuppositions as true and then carry out a reductio ad absurdum of Huizi's argument. But as I have shown, the two key words in Huizi's statement II, "knowledge" and "happiness," are taken to imply a type of sensation of one's subjective state of happiness or an epistemic awareness of one's sensation of one's own sensations. Only as an independently existing entity can one have this kind of knowledge by definition, so Huizi uses this point to challenge Zhuangzi. As long as Zhuangzi accepts on the empirical level that he is not a fish, statement II is a necessary truth. First, one needs to take a premise from an opponent's argument and show how it leads necessarily to a contradiction, thereby overturning the whole argument. Zhuangzi's carelessness in carrying out this method correctly not only indicates confusion over the subtleties of logical argument, but, even more egregiously, it reveals that the whole Happy Fish debate is meaningless.

If Zhuangzi had considered whether Huizi's argument had anything to do with his own statement I, he might have avoided this fundamental confusion. In other words, if we made the crux of the argument to be showing whether or not the usage of "knowledge" and "happiness" in statement I are logically equivalent to the same words in statement II, then we could quickly decide whether the argument should proceed at all. Of course, in our case this will not only bring about a meaningful debate but will also allow for a hypothetical dialectical discussion to occur. In any event, this interchange between Zhuangzi and Huizi would be provided with a greater degree of clarity.

In statement I Zhuangzi actually never mentions "knowledge" directly. But we can assume that since Zhuangzi asserts that "these fish are happy," he must also believe that he "knows" they are happy. This "know" is certainly not what Huizi meant by "'know," however. In statement V the closing lines of "My knowing happens over the Hao River" already shows that Zhuangzi's use of "know" is not some purely subjective affective-perceptive grasp of one's own inner experience as an independently existing entity.

The character "happiness" does show up in statement I. And since it is the case, as I have shown, that the knower cannot be understood with the known (that is, we have to take context into account when adjudicating subjective knowledge claims), "happiness" will have to be examined carefully as it is precisely the object that is known. Unfortunately, in statements II and V Zhuangzi just follows along unreflectively with Huizi's use of his terms, and in statement I it seems that Zhuangzi has no means of communicating exactly what he means by "happiness." Although there are no resources in statement I to help us determine the logical form and conceptual content of "happiness," it will always be an acceptable move to interpret this passage in light of the whole text of the *Zhuangzi*.

In common speech "sadness" and "happiness" are separated at the empirical level as particular psychological phenomena experienced as subjective sensations. The "happiness" Huizi speaks of in statement II is also a case of this relative happiness. But it is precisely this kind of "sadness" and "happiness" that Zhuangzi wants to transcend. In the *Zhuangzi*, in "The Secret of Caring for Life" (*yangshengzhu* 養生主) chapter, we find the following:

> When Lao Tan [Lao Dan] died, Ch'in Shih [Qin Shi] went to mourn for him; but after giving three cries, he left the room.
>
> "Weren't you a friend of the Master?" asked Lao Tzu's [Laozi's] disciples.
>
> "Yes."
>
> "And you think it's all right to mourn him this way?"
>
> "Yes," said Ch'in Shih. "At first I took him for a real man, but now I know he wasn't. A little while ago, when I went in to mourn, I found old men

weeping for him as though they were weeping for a son, and young men weeping for him as though they were weeping for a mother. To have gathered a group like *that,* he must have done something to make them talk about him, though he didn't ask them to talk, or make them weep for him, though he didn't ask them to weep. This is to hide from Heaven, turn your back on the true state of affairs, and forget what you were born with. In the old days, this was called the crime of hiding from Heaven. Your master happened to come because it was his time, and he happened to leave because things follow along. If you are content with the time and willing to follow along, then grief and joy have no way to enter in. In the old days, this was called being freed from the bonds of God.[7]

From here we can see that Zhuangzi holds that all human beings in the world—in their body and mind—are either following life or death. When life is perceived, there is happiness; when death is perceived, there is sadness. Unless one can see through the endless cycles of life and death as relative phenomena constantly in dialectical flux, then one is stuck perpetually in fluctuating patterns of alternation between gain and loss, happiness and sadness. Inasmuch as most people are stuck in such patterns, they embody what Zhuangzi means in saying "to hide from Heaven, turn your back on the true state of affairs, and forget what you were born with. In the old days, this was called the crime of hiding from Heaven." Such habitual patterns are the "bonds of God." The only way out is to "dwell in the moment and abide in ease" (*anshi er chushun* 安時而處順). This is because if one can "dwell in the moment and abide in ease, then sadness and happiness cannot enter in." The *XGZ* and Lin Yunming's *Essence of Zhuangzi* (*Zhuangzi Yin*《莊子因》) both provide compelling interpretations of this passage. The *XGZ* has the following: "Sadness and happiness are born of gain and loss, but now there are those adept sages who harmonize with transformation and who are at no time ill at ease, never miss an expedient path to be taken, and intuitively become one with cosmic creative transformation. Since everything is part of myself, what is there to gain or lose? Who is it that lives or dies? Thus if one affirms what one encounters, then happiness and sadness have no place to enter their experience." Lin Yunming has the following: "If people dwell peacefully in what is 'spontaneously so' (*ziran* 自然) and get life, this should not be considered happiness. And abiding in what is spontaneously so and receiving death, one should not count this as sadness." Although both of these interpretations are quite accurate, we still need to examine the original meaning of Zhuangzi's thought, for only then can we clearly grasp what it is we need to understand.

In terms of Zhuangzi's thinking, one phrase can capture its essence. This phrase is the "learning of the genuine person" (*zhenrenxue* 真人學). What precisely is a "genuine person"? How does one become a "genuine person"? What kind of realm have genuine persons reached? What are the heavens, earth, and the myriad things in the heart of the genuine person? And another important question is this: does the genuine person have happiness? If so, then what is the "happiness of a genuine person" like? These are all basic questions of the "learning of the genuine person." We can roughly say that the genuine person uses "fasting of the heartmind" and "sitting and forgetting" as methods of self-cultivation to overcome the relative values of the profane world and to achieve a realm of effortless action (*wuwei* 無為) and nonattachment (*juedai* 絕待). This way life and death, right and wrong, gain and loss, and all forms of common human evaluation become, on the whole, empty distinctions. In this realm the "knowledge" of the genuine person can never again be relative knowledge or knowledge gained through an empirical verification process. Rather, it is a transcendent kind of knowledge, an enlightened wisdom. This kind of enlightened wisdom is what allows the genuine person to embody the realm from which the statement "heaven and earth emerge with me, and the myriad things are one with me" is spoken. It is what allows the genuine person to "flow as one with *dao*." And everything in the cosmos, whether sentient or not, is caught up in the transformations of *dao*.

But this *dao* cannot be fully named or described. If we were forced to, we could say that it is "effortless action and spontaneity" (*wuwei ziran* 無為自然). Thus every thing in the cosmos has this effortless action and spontaneity as its very essence. The true world is just this "effortless action and spontaneity." And a true human life is just this "effortless action and spontaneity." Moreover, those who can harmonize with this effortless action and spontaneity are genuine persons. This is the kind of realm that both the *XGZ* and *The Essence of Zhuangzi* describe. But since the genuine person has no space in which sadness and happiness can enter, can we still speak of the "happiness" of a genuine person?

The common relative, subjective happiness is definitely not what the genuine person possesses. However, the genuine person does have "supreme happiness" (*zhile* 至樂). What is "supreme happiness"? It is "effortless action and authentic happiness" (*wuweichengleyi* 無為誠樂矣), and "supreme happiness is no happiness" (*zhile wule* 至樂無樂).[8] This is "effortless action," and it is supreme, or true, happiness. This supreme or true happiness is not something that the empirical or psychological concept of "happiness" can grasp. Furthermore, it is not any independently existing thing as a subjective experience of the empirical world. Supreme happiness is of a transcendent order. In order to grasp this happiness one must use the enlightened wisdom of the genuine person. In the realm of enlightened wisdom every person and every thing is an activity of the *dao*'s "effortless action and spontaneity." In other words, the expression of *dao* is supreme happiness. The meaning of statement I of the Happy Fish debate is revealed here. The activity of swimming about in great ease is the very expression of "effortless action and spontaneity," so the fish are supremely happy.[9]

From the perspective of Zhuangzi's thought, the identification of supreme happiness and *dao*-action is a necessary truth. Thus it can be said that statement I is a reflection of the core of Zhuangzi's thinking. Only in this way can we break the hermeneutical link between statements II and I by showing their fundamental logical incompatibility. The "knowledge" and "happiness" of II both fall in the empirical realm. But what Zhuangzi speaks of in statement I is a transcendent order. As such, it should be evident that the problem of conceptual content raised in Chen's essay is also a result of the two debate participants failing to see this slippage in meaning and thereby falling into a meaningless debate.

In investigating the Happy Fish debate we can either see it as a pure debate or approach it as a reflection of Zhuangzi's thinking. Between these two options, which one gains? Which one loses? Who succeeds and who fails? Those in the know will be able to judge.

NOTES

Translated by Joseph Harroff.

1. Although this commentary has both Guo Xiang and Xiang Xiu as authors, many recent scholars have questioned whether Guo Xiang provided much in the way of creative interpretation. The idea that he appropriated (or even plagiarized) from Xiang Xiu is rather plausible. But since we cannot prove this with any certainty, I simply refer to the text as the *Xiang-Guo Commentary*.

2. This "implication relationship" is defined as follows: if A implies B, then unless B is false and A is true, this implication is always true; otherwise, we have an invalid deduction.

3. The sign of equivalence here refers to conceptual equivalence and not logical equivalence. How Zhuangzi arrives at this assumption in the second segment of the debate is a topic for careful analysis.

4. This kind of affective-perceptive knowledge is moreover limited to the case in which one feels or perceives one's own subjective sensations.

5. When a statement directly indicates an object, we have an "object language," and when a statement indicates not an object but only the name of an object, we have a case of "metalanguage."

6. The original text has "Therefore I don't know you" (固不知子矣). But this can only be interpreted as "I cannot subjectively feel your sensations." For more on this see note 4.

7. Translation here from Burton Watson's *Chuang Tzu: Basic Writings* (New York: Columbia University Press, 1964), 48 - 49.

8. Both of these passages are from the "Supreme Happiness" (*zhilepian* 《至樂篇》) chapter. The outer chapters of the *Zhuangzi* are full of conflicting sayings of questionable quality, so in selecting passages one must be sensitive to the overall thrust of Zhuangzi's thinking.

9. The "Great Ancestral Teacher" chapter has the following passage, which is useful in comparison: "Fish interact in the water, humans interact in *dao*. Interacting in water a deep pond gives support. In interacting in *dao*, with no worries life is secured. Thus it is said: 'Fish forget each other in the rivers and lakes, and humans forget each other in the techniques of *dao*.'"

6

The Relatively Happy Fish Revisited

Norman Y. TENG

1

> Zhuangzi and Hui Shi were strolling along the bridge over the Hao River. "Out swim the minnows, so free and easy," said Zhuangzi. "This is fish happiness."
>
> "You are not a fish; whence do you know fish happiness?"
>
> "You are not me; whence do you know that I don't know fish happiness?"
>
> "I am not you, so I don't know you. You are not a fish, so you don't know fish happiness. That is the whole of it."
>
> "Let us go back to the root from which we have branched out into this conversation. When you said, 'Whence do you know fish happiness?' it was asking me, already knowing I knew it. I knew it from above the Hao."

This dialogue is found in the closing passage in the *Zhuangzi*, chapter 17, "Autumn Floods." My translation is basically a combined version of Graham's and Hansen's respective translations, with one exception: I foreground the metaphorical usage of 本 *ben*[root] in "Let us go back to the root," which was rendered as "the beginning" in Hansen's translation and "where we started" in Graham's.[1] My intent to render it this way will become clear in the following discussion.

Originally published in *Asian Philosophy* 16, no. 1 (March 2006). Reprinted with permission.

As Chad Hansen points out, "[T]his passage is one of a small cluster of examples of reasoning in ancient Chinese texts that Sinologists recognize as having a surface resemblance to Western philosophy more than to the manifest image of Chinese thought."[2] Let me add that this passage also provides an excellent opportunity for exploring ways of productive philosophical exchanges between the East and the West. The present study examines Hansen's analysis of it in this spirit.

Built on Graham's insight that 安 an[whence] in the question "Whence do you know . . . ?" marks an exchange of perspectives, Hansen proposes that we take this dialogue as exemplifying a distinctive form of philosophical perspectivalism in epistemology.[3] He argues for an inferential analysis to solve philosophical puzzles:

> How is the final remark a resolution or a plausible conclusion to the disagreement? What perspectival point is Zhuangzi's argument supposed to have made? Are there not internal contradictions in each discussant's position? Is not Zhuangzi's penultimate riposte a non sequitur? Is Hui Shi right that Zhuangzi is forced by his own logic to acknowledge he does not know fish happiness?[4]

Asking those questions is already a step toward dispelling the standard notion of Zhuangzi as not seriously participating in the debate and playfully dismissing Hui Shi's logic. Hansen goes on to turn the standard notion on its head and explain the deep structure of the dialogue, in which Zhuangzi is the more skillful dialectician, leading Hui Shi into a logical trap. According to Hansen, Hui Shi's opening question, when unpacked, presumes (1) an acceptance of the norm of assertion that in claiming something one should know it, and (2) a commitment to the privileged status for the first-person standard of knowledge. Zhuangzi plays along, answering Hui Shi's question with a question, which is in fact a trap. In his next move, Hui Shi takes Zhuangzi's bait: "I am not you, so I don't know you. You are not a fish, so you don't know fish happiness." The second sentence contradicts the first, given Hui Shi's acceptance of the norm of assertion and his commitment to the privileged status for the first-person standard of knowledge. Hansen concludes, "Hui Shi is committed to both that he knows and that he does not know what Zhuangzi knows."[5]

As to Zhuangzi's final statement, it seems that Zhuangzi simply relies on a verbal trick. Normally, when one takes part in debates, asking questions of the form "how (or whence) do you know X?" the debater is either questioning one's claim that one knows X or denying that one knows X. Zhuangzi acknowledges this point in his response to Hui Shi's opening question. Yet, his final statement reconstrues Hui Shi's question as a presupposition that he, Zhuangzi, already knows. From this perspective, Zhuangzi's final statement is a clear case of weak sophistry, or dishonesty. To develop an alternative way of understanding Zhuangzi's final remark, Hansen suggests that we focus on the implicit pragmatic theory of language in traditional daoist texts, that is, that its core role is to provide guidance rather than to manufacture factual representations.[6] Hui Shi has been caught in a logical trap because, in addition to the acceptance of the norm of assertion, he tries to restrict knowledge to the confines of the first-person perspective, which leads him into a contradiction that would otherwise force him to give up the norm of assertion. Zhuangzi's final remark is to guide Hui Shi to a broader view that there are different ways of knowing about affective states, and the way I can know I am happy (from the first-person perspective) is different from the way you can know it (from a third-person perspective). Relinquishing the unrealistic, first-person standard of knowing, Hui Shi should be able to see that the basis of Zhuangzi's initial assertion has been known to him all along simply because he, standing with Zhuangzi above the river, "saw exactly the same thing and knew precisely in which sense, how and whence, Zhuangzi knew about the fish."[7]

Hansen is certainly aware that, in laying out his discussion on the dialogue between Zhuangzi and Hui Shi, he has imposed an inferential framework alien to ancient Chinese thinkers, particularly regarding standards for the use of 知 *zhi*[know], "their focus would not be on inference or logic, but on what approving or disapproving of the use of a term in a context depends or relies on."[8] He believes, nonetheless, that it should be fairly easy to rephrase his argument in terms familiar to ancient Chinese thinkers without losing the point. I will argue that the dialogue takes on a shape different from the one Hansen has painted once one starts reanalyzing the dialogue in terms familiar to ancient Chinese thinkers.

2

I agree with Hansen that the dialogue between Zhuangzi and Hui Shi calls for a perspectival analysis. I also agree that the standard notion of Zhuangzi as not seriously participating in the debate is false. But I disagree with his inferential articulation of the dialogue, particularly his portrayal of Hui Shi's logical maneuvering as an inept handling of philosophical dialectic and Zhuangzi's response to Hui Shi's question as a contrived, logical trap. To do justice to both Hui Shi and Zhuangzi, I propose that we apply the logic (or patterns of discourse that guide our distinction between activity and disputation) developed in the later Mohist text, the "Lesser Pick" (*xiaoqu* 小取), to an analysis of the dialogue. Let me first quote a relevant passage from the Lesser Pick and then proceed with the analysis. When that is done, I will explain, albeit briefly, why applying the logic in this case is pertinent.

> What is present in one's own case is not to be rejected in the other man's, what is absent from one's own case is not to be demanded of the other man.... (A) "Illustrating" is referring to other things in order to clarify one's case. (B) "Parallelising" is comparing propositions and letting all "proceed." (C) "Adducing" is saying: "If it is so in your case, why may it not be so in mine too?" (D) "Inferring" is using what is the same in that which he refuses to accept and that which he does accept in order to propose the former.[9]

It is worth mentioning that here Graham translates 辭 ci^{phrase} as "proposition." According to Hansen, this translation can be misleading: "The ancient Chinese concept of 辭 ci^{phrase} ranges across any linguistic strings that we intentionally structure. It includes what we would call a compound word, a noun or verb phrase, duplicated verbs, whole sentences, and even pairs or groups of related sentences (couplets)."[10] I concur, but the following discussion does not rely on this lexical claim, and Graham's translation as it stands would do no harm in the present context.

Consider now Hui Shi's opening question and Zhuangzi's response to it.

Hui Shi: You are not a fish; whence do you know fish happiness?
Zhuangzi: You are not me; whence do you know that I don't know fish happiness?

Notice that Zhuangzi is parallelizing in this exchange to support his case. It is also an adducement, that is, a move in which one asks one's opponent to see that a parallel pattern is being established. From this perspective, if the opponent approves of his own case, he should approve of your case. It follows that Hui Shi should then take Zhuangzi's question to be as legitimate as his own. This move is a combined exercise of parallelizing and adducing rather than a contrived, logical trap.

Consider next Hui Shi's response:

> I am not you, so I don't know you.
> You are not a fish, so you don't know fish happiness.

Notice, again, that there is a parallel pattern in these two sentences. Hui Shi is using parallelizing in his response. It is also a move of inferring, that is, a move of forcing the opponent in the debate to approve of the second sentence, for there is a parallel pattern in what the opponent approves of (the first sentence) and what he rejects (the second sentence). It is a combined exercise of parallelizing and inferring rather than a mishandling of the dialectic.

Now, even if Hui Shi handles the dialectic adroitly, we can still ask whether or not he falls into the logical trap Hansen describes. This depends on whether Hui Shi approves of the norm of assertion that, in claiming something, one should know it and whether he commits himself to a privileged status for the first-person standard of knowledge. I will bypass questions concerning the norm of assertion, for it seems fairly clear that Hui Shi is making an assertion and is willing to abide by the norm of assertion. As to the first-person standard of knowledge, Hansen's textual evidence for Hui Shi's endorsement of it is meager. It seems that Hansen argues his case only on the basis of his inferential analysis of the dialogue. Indeed, we know so little about Hui Shi that any substantive claim about him should be hedged with conditions and caveats. That leaves us with the question of whether or not Hansen's analysis is a fair treatment of Hui Shi's line of reasoning in the dialogue. Here I think it is appropriate to draw attention to a guiding principle of debating as it is framed in the Lesser Pick: "What is present in one's own case is not to be rejected in the other man's; what is absent from one's own case is not to be demanded of the other man's."[11] From this perspective, debating is a joint enterprise. It entails an exchange of the debaters' views and demands that those who are engaging in a debate consistently align what they themselves approve or disapprove of with what is to be demanded of the others. Let us now see how we may read the dialogue from this perspective. Hui Shi's opening question, "You are not a fish; whence do you know fish happiness?" carries the message that Zhuangzi is not in a position to know or to make a knowledge claim about fish happiness. Notice that this is not an act of privileging the first-person perspective. Rather, it is about how members of one species come to know the affective states of members of other species. Zhuangzi's reply, "You are not me; whence do you know that I don't know fish happiness?" carries the message that Hui Shi is not in a position to know whether or not Zhuangzi knows fish happiness. This reply marks something of a turning point in the dialogue; it directs debaters' attention from species-specific perspectives to the first-person perspective. Zhuangzi is counting on Hui Shi's willingness to reorient himself with this shift in perspective by paralleling their respective questions. Hui Shi indeed follows and responds with this statement: "I am not you, so I don't know you. You are not a fish, so you don't know fish happiness." This line carries the message that if the switch from the species-specific perspectives to the first-person perspective is to be approved of, so is the reverse switch. Therefore, Zhuangzi should approve of the reverse switch and accept that he is not in a position to know or to make a knowledge claim about fish happiness. Again, this is not an inadequate act of privileging the first-person perspective. On the contrary, Hui Shi's response is both elegant and powerful from an ancient Chinese dialectical viewpoint.

The alignment of Zhuangzi's and Hui Shi's questions and responses crucially hinges on the parallel patterns dynamically established in the dialogue, which can be formulated as follows:

(P1) X is not Y; whence does X know the state Y is in?
(P2) X is not Y, so X does not know the state Y is in.

Both (P1) and (P2) can be indefinitely reapplied in a debating situation as long as one finds suitable candidates to fill in X, Y, and Z. I venture that Zhuangzi understands this possibility very well; he may choose to employ (P2) and rejoin, "You [Hui Shi] are not me, so you don't know that I don't know fish happiness." If Zhuangzi chooses to do so, the debate would end in deadlock or go on indefinitely. Zhuangzi foresees this, and presumably Hui Shi does, too. Neither would come out on top of this debating game. Instead of reapplying (P2), Zhuangzi invites Hui Shi to go back to the root, from which they have branched out into this situation, and answers, "When you said, 'Whence do you know fish happiness?' it was asking me, already knowing I knew it. I knew it from above the Hao." And the dialogue ends. I return to this final remark and probe its significance in the next section. Here let me quote again from the Lesser Pick:

(A) Of things in general, if there are respects in which they are the same, it does not follow that they are altogether the same. (B) The parallelism of propositions is valid only as far as it reaches. (C) If something is so of them there are reasons why it is so; but though its being so of them is the same, the reasons why it is so are not necessarily the same. (D) If we accept a claim, we have reasons for accepting it; but though we are the same in accepting it, the reasons why we accept it are not necessarily the same. *Therefore propositions which illustrate, parallelise, adduce and infer become different as they "proceed," become dangerous when they change direction, fail when carried too far, become detached from their base when we let them drift, so that we must on no account be careless with them, and must not use them too rigidly.* Hence saying has many methods, separate kinds, different reasons, which must not be looked at only from one side.[12]

The dialogue between Zhuangzi and Hui Shi ends at the point where the Lesser Pick warns debaters that further moves would become dangerous, detached from their base, or fail. Both Zhuangzi and Hui Shi turn out to be worthy dialecticians measured in terms of the patterns of discourse expounded in the Lesser Pick. The Lesser Pick is arguably the final word on logic in ancient China and also summarizes, I venture to say, the best patterns of disputation known to ancient Chinese thinkers.[13] That, I believe, makes it useful as an analytic tool to probe and measure the qualities and dialectical turns of debates like the one exemplified in the dialogue between Zhuangzi and Hui Shi. The foregoing analysis, if correct, neatly illustrates how the Lesser Pick is useful in this respect and particularly in explaining how participants in a debating game act on and contribute to the parallel patterns dynamically established in the ongoing discourse. (If readers have a different interpretation of the passages from the Lesser Pick, I hope that the analysis proposed here is still philosophically appealing and thus may at least serve as a thought experiment for them to explore different ways of interpreting these passages.) Indeed, we can go one better if we use tools of analysis afforded by the Lesser Pick to tackle Zhuangzi's final remark, which is notoriously recondite or confusing.

3

The puzzle about Zhuangzi's final statement lies in the aforementioned verbal trick: "When you said, 'Whence do you know fish happiness?' it was asking me, already knowing I knew it." The verbal trickery is glaringly unmistakable to an analytic mind. To Hansen, it is neither a piece of playful sarcasm nor a weak sophistry nor a dishonest move. It, however, neither picks up on Hui Shi's response nor effectively unravels Zhuangzi's puzzling conclusion, "I knew it from above the Hao." Hansen declares his diagnosis, "The verbal trickery neither illuminates nor develops the perspectival thrust of the discussion," and offers his inferential articulation as a solution, which is found wanting.[14] I propose that we confront the verbal trick at face value and see how it may play a part in the dialogue based on the viewpoint expounded in the Lesser Pick.

"Let us go back to the root" signals to Hui Shi that Zhuangzi is about to end the disputation, which they both know would otherwise end in deadlock or go on indefinitely, and instead engages Hui Shi in discussion from a different angle. His statement "When you said 'Whence do you know fish happiness?' it was asking me, already knowing I knew it" indeed is a verbal trick. The trick is used as a device for reorienting oneself to a different viewpoint and asking oneself whether one knew it all along. Zhuangzi then bets on Hui Shi's talents, acting on behalf of his beloved philosophical partner but answering the trick from his own perspective, "I knew it from above the Hao." That answer invites Hui Shi to turn back to where they started and be aware of the situation they have been in, that is, that they have been strolling on the bridge over the Hao River and sharing all along the experience of witnessing the fish swimming easily and smoothly. That, I submit, is a more sensible way to read Zhuangzi's concluding statement in the dialogue. According to this reading, Zhuangzi is playful, Hui Shi is his equal in the debating game, and the intricate dialectic of the dialogue is manifestly appealing. Moreover, it accords with the patterns of discourse known to ancient Chinese thinkers as they are expounded in the Lesser Pick.

We may conclude this analysis with a speculation that I think is fair to both Zhuangzi and Hui Shi, as they are portrayed in the *Zhuangzi*. Zhuangzi's initial response to the scene he and Hui Shi walked into carried a metaphorical message for Hui Shi: Do not exert yourself unnecessarily; let go of your personal interests and fears; as we witness the fish swimming easily and smoothly, we should be in the same state, be happy, and move easily and smoothly.[15] Let me digress a bit to explain a difference between Hansen's rendering of Zhuangzi's initial statement and mine. I purposely phrase Zhuangzi's initial statement as a simple response to the scene he and Hui Shi walked into instead of treating it exclusively as an assertion about the emotional state of the fish. I believe Hansen's inferential analysis forces him to take Zhuangzi's initial statement as an assertion, which causes him to overlook the possibility of interpreting Zhuangzi's final statement in the way proposed here.

It is worth noting that the interpretation proposed here is in agreement with Roger Ames' observation of the dialogue, which, I think, helps illuminate the tone of how the story unfolds. He writes:

> [F]or Zhuangzi, knowledge is performative, a function of fruitful correlations. Thus, it is something done—a qualitative achievement. Knowing a situation is the "realizing" of it in the sense of "making it real." Knowing is also perlocutionary in the sense of setting the affective tone of the experience. The knower and the known, the enjoyer and the enjoyment, are inseparable aspects of this same event.... One and one's posture or perspective is [sic] thus integral to and constitutive of what is known and contributes immediately to the quality of the experience.[16]

Joining Ames' observation to the analysis proposed here, it is safe to say that the metaphorical usage of "root" in Zhuangzi's final statement alludes to the qualitative experience he and Hui Shi jointly achieved as they walked into the scene. Zhuangzi was using an illustration in his initial response and rounded it off with a verbal trick in his final statement. This speculation gains plausibility if we insert into the foregoing interpretation of the dialogue a comment made in the *Zhuangzi* about Hui Shi:

> Hui Shih was incapable of satisfying himself with this, he never tired of scattering all over the myriad things, and ended with no more than a reputation for being good at disputation. What a pity that Hui Shih's talents were wasted and never came to anything, that he would not turn back from chasing the myriad things! He had as much chance of making his voice outlast its echo, his body outrun its shadow. Sad, wasn't it? (*Zhuangzi*, chapter 33, in Graham, trans., *Chuang-tzǔ*, 285)

Here Hui Shi is portrayed as one who was gifted with a sharp sense of debating games but prone to a weakness for pointless argumentation. Another passage, which comes just before the anecdote about Zhuangzi and Hui Shi ambling along the bridge over the Hao River, may reinforce the foregoing speculation:

> When Hui Shih was chief minister of Liang, Chuang-tzǔ went to visit him. Someone told Hui Shih
>
> "Chuang-tzǔ is coming, he wants your place as chief minister."
>
> At this Hui Shih was frightened and searched throughout the state for three days and nights.
>
> Chuang-Tzǔ did go to visit him.
>
> "In the South there is a bird," he said, "its name is the phoenix, do you know of it? The phoenix came up from the South Sea to fly to the North Sea; it would rest on no tree but the sterculia, would eat nothing but the seeds of the bamboo, would drink only from the sweetest springs. Just then an owl had found a rotting mouse. As the phoenix flew over, it looked up and glared at it, 'Shoo!' Now am I to take it that for the sake of that Liang country of yours you want to shoo at me?" (*Zhuangzi,* chapter 17, in Graham, trans., *Chuang-tzǔ,* 122–123)

Here Hui Shi is portrayed as one who could not let go of his personal interests and fears. Combined with the previous comment, this story may very well be interpreted as the background which leads to Zhuangzi's initiation of the conversation with Hui Shi on the bridge over the Hao River.

To sum up: my analysis shows that the dialogue begins with Zhuangzi's using an illustration in his initial response in the scene he and Hui Shi walked into. This is followed by Hui Shi's opening question, then by Zhuangzi's combined exercise of parallelizing and adducing in answering Hui Shi's question with a question, and later by Hui Shi's combined exercise of parallelizing and inferring. It ends with Zhuangzi's playful use of a verbal trick, which invites Hui Shi to go back to where they started and be aware of the setting in which they have been situated all along. Overall, Zhuangzi is playful; Hui Shi is his equal in their debating game but is prone to a weakness for pointless argumentation. The intricate dialectic of the dialogue leading to Zhuangzi's final statement accords with the patterns of discourse known to ancient Chinese thinkers as they are expounded in the Lesser Pick.

NOTES

1. See A. C. Graham, trans., *Chuang-tzŭ: The Seven Inner Chapters and Other Writings from the Book Chuang-tzŭ* (London: Allen and Unwin, 1981), 123; and Chad Hansen, "The Relatively Happy Fish," *Asian Philosophy* 13 (2003): 145.

2. Hansen, "Relatively Happy Fish," 149.

3. Graham, *Seven Inner Chapters*, 123.

4. Hansen, "Relatively Happy Fish," 147.

5. Ibid., 153.

6. Chad Hansen, *A Daoist Theory of Chinese Thought: A Philosophical Interpretation* (Oxford: Oxford University Press, 1992), chapters 6, 8.

7. Hansen, "Relatively Happy Fish," 157.

8. Ibid.

9. A. C. Graham, trans., *Later Mohist Logic, Ethics and Science* (repr., Hong Kong: Chinese University of Hong Kong, 2003), 483.

10. Hansen, *Daoist Theory*, 45.

11. Graham, *Later Mohist Logic*, 483.

12. Ibid., 483–484; my emphasis.

13. Chad Hansen, *Language and Logic in Ancient China* (Ann Arbor: University of Michigan Press, 1983), 139.

14. Hansen, "Relatively Happy Fish," 155.

15. For an account of metaphor that fits the present discussion, see N. Y. Teng, "生活處境中的隱喻 Shenghuo chujing zhong de yinyu" (An Embodied and Environmentally Embedded Perspective on Metaphor), *EurAmerica* 35 (2005): 97–140; and "Metaphor and Coupling: An Embodied, Action-Oriented Perspective," *Metaphor and Symbol* 21, no. 2 (2006): 67–85.

16. Roger T. Ames, "Knowing in the *Zhuangzi*: From Here, on the Bridge, over the River Hao," in Roger T. Ames, ed., *Wandering at Ease in the Zhuangzi* (Albany: State University of New York Press, 1998), 220.

7

Knowing the Joy of Fish

The Zhuangzi *and Analytic Philosophy*

KUWAKO Toshio

KNOWING THE JOY OF FISH

There is a chapter in the Outer Chapters of the Zhuangzi called "Autumn Floods" (Qiushui).[1] I would like to introduce the discussion of Zhuang Zhou and Hui Shi from the end of this chapter. As he watched the fish from the banks of a river called Hao, Zhuang Zhou remarked, "The minnows are swimming free and easy. Such indeed is the joy of fish, isn't it?" Hearing this, Zhuang Zhou's friend, the logician Hui Shi, asked him, "How is it that you understand the joy of fish, not being a fish yourself?" With that, Zhuang Zhou replied, "How is it that you have come to understand that I don't understand the joy of fish, not being me yourself?" Hui Shi responded, "Of course, because I am not you, I cannot understand you. Because you are not a fish, you do not understand the fish. Hence it is completely certain that you do not understand the joy of fish." Then Zhuang Zhou spoke as follows: "Shall we try to return to the beginning of the thing? When you asked me how I understood the joy of fish, you had already understood that I knew it. So then, it was on the banks of the Hao that I understood the joy of fish."

Contained within this dialogue are problems related to knowing the minds and mental states of others, including nonhuman animals. This problem of knowing the minds of others extends in several directions. To begin, there is the so-called problem of other minds, that is, the problem of the possibility of knowing the minds of other individual human beings. The problem of other minds has been one of the major topics developed in analytic philosophy since the beginning of the twentieth century.

The problem of knowing other minds also has applications in what is called the problem of multicultural understanding. This is the problem of whether or not the members of one group can understand the minds of members of another group. For example, a Japanese scholar might say, "On the whole, Western scholars are unable to understand the Japanese spirit," and others might claim that "Having started a war of aggression, Japanese living their lives of postwar prosperity cannot understand the minds of the people of Asia" or "The suffering of the Jews in the Holocaust is beyond our imagination." On top of this, people say things like "There's no way for a man to understand a woman's feelings."

However, the discussion of Zhuang Zhou and Hui Shi goes even beyond this, that is, to the problem of interspecies understanding of minds. To begin with, there is certainly a problem knowing the mind of another living thing as a separate individual, but in addition, there is also a problem with knowing the mind of another living thing at the level of a species. For example, research into the intelligence of dolphins rests on the presupposition that we can understand their minds. Moreover, the problem of interspecies knowledge has even come to be debated as a topic within environmental ethics. It presents us with the question of whether to recognize a right to life in other living things. Some people claim that animals capable of feeling pleasure and pain have a right to life but those incapable of such feelings do not have rights. Peter Singer takes this view. So, for example, dogs and cats or whales and dolphins and so on would have rights, but shrimp, crabs, and mollusks would not. On the other hand, because Zhuang Zhou claims to be able to understand the joy of fish, we would have to recognize the rights of fish as well (primarily, their right to life), and on top of that we should recognize their personhood.[2]

It is fair to say that these sorts of modern philosophical concerns are contained within this short discussion by Zhuang Zhou and Hui Shi. On the basis of the extent of the problems, I would like to take a look at a work by a modern philosopher who comes close to the perspective of Hui Shi—Thomas Nagel in "What Is It Like to Be a Bat?"—and try to see what sort of response Zhuang Zhou might give to the perspective of analytic philosophy.

"WE DO NOT UNDERSTAND THE MIND OF A BAT"

In "What Is It Like to Be a Bat?" Thomas Nagel claims that no matter how we intellectually analyze a bat, we will be unable to grasp the lived experience of being a bat.[3] According to Nagel, conscious experience arises at various levels of life, but the meaning that lies in saying that a life form has conscious experience is something that has already placed fundamental restrictions on our asking what it is like to be that life form.

For Nagel, though we cannot doubt that bats possess lived experience, we have nothing in our perception that resembles a bat's sonar in spite of its being a form of sensation. We have no basis on which to suppose that anything in our own experience or within our imaginative abilities subjectively resembles the lived experience of a bat. Because of this, it is difficult to think about what it is like to be a bat. The most that we can imagine is forming an understanding of what it would be like for us to behave like a bat. However, that is not the question. The thing I want to know is what it is like for a bat to be a bat. That is, unless the fundamental structure of my experience were changed, it would not be something resembling a bat's experience even if my appearance and behavior resembled those of a bat.

Nagel might ask how we could talk about what it is like to swim around playfully in the Hao if knowing the joy of fish means imagining becoming a fish. Since, however, Zhuang Zhou is not a fish, he must be unable to say what it is like for a fish to swim around in the Hao. This is because the sensory organs of humans and fish are very different. So, for example, even if fish have pleasures, the human Zhuang Zhou would not know what they are like. And yet, just because it is impossible to describe or comprehend lived experience, that is no reason to try to deny its actuality or logical meaningfulness. After all, we are able to believe in the existence of the seemingly eternally impossible fact of expression and comprehension between human beings.

What Nagel is problematizing here is not the mental privacy that only the possessor of the lived experience is able to know. According to Nagel, it is possible for one human being to know and to speak about what sorts of qualities another human being's lived experiences have. Nevertheless, there remains a subjectivity to lived experience. The basis for Nagel's claim is a related mind-body problem. This subjectivity is the basis of the difficulty implicit in reducing the psychological to the physical. The process of reduction increases objectivity, but this comes about through a decrease in the degree of reliance on any viewpoint particular to an individual or a species. In other words, a decreased degree of reliance on the viewpoint of human beings brings about an increased objectivity in a description. In the end, movement in the direction of greater objectivity is, if anything, a distancing from the nature of phenomena. We are, in the end, completely unable to think about the subjective character of lived experience apart from relying on our imaginative power, in other words, apart from trying to take the perspective of a subject with lived experience.

In this way, Nagel would probably reply to Zhuang Zhou that because we have our lived experiences using sense organs that are totally different from those of fish, we cannot know the joy of fish apart from imagination based on our own lived experiences. In other words, we cannot know what it is like to be a fish or what it is like for a fish to feel joy. Were Zhuang Zhou to understand the joy of fish, it would, at best, be through his imagination of what sorts of joys he might have if he were to become a fish.

KNOWING ON THE BANKS OF THE HAO

Well then, how might Zhuang Zhou respond to Nagel's arguments? Wherein does the true significance of his understanding of fish lie? The important point is that it was on the banks of the Hao that Zhuang Zhou knew the joy of the fish swimming there and not that he obtained universal knowledge about the psychology of fish. The importance of Zhuang Zhou's final words comes from their meaning just this. His cognition reveals the body as something standing in a particular relation in time and space with a relational schema to the fish that in turn has a certain relationship to his body. The establishment of this relationship between a body and its environment could take place only on the banks of the Hao. From the universal proposition that "there is no established relation of understanding of feelings between all humans and all fish," Hui Shi concludes that "Zhuang Zhou does not understand the feelings of fish." To this, Zhuang Zhou replies that one cannot infer from this sort of universal proposition whether or not one understands the feelings of fish. The importance of having this knowledge on the banks of the Hao is that knowing the joy of fish means something that occurs within the particular lived experience of a body schema. Zhuang Zhou's response is not to offer a concrete instance as a counterexample to a universal proposition. Rather, he is criticizing the very act of thinking about "knowing" within a framework of universal knowledge.

Zhuang Zhou shares his environment with the fish. His body has a relational schema within the environment. From the banks of the Hao, he sees the river and watches the swimming of the fish. The swimming of the fish is within Zhuang Zhou's environment. The agreeableness of swimming is surely not a lived experience occurring only within the mind. This lived experience is born within the environment. The agreeableness of swimming occurs within the totality of the swimmers' bodies, the Hao as the environment that surrounds the swimmers, and the mental states born within those bodies. Modern objectivity has come to take the emotion called "agreeableness" as an internal, passively subjective lived experience, but the agreeableness of swimming is an event first arising from the relationship between the embodied subject, which feels the agreeableness, and the outside world, which brings about the pleasure. One cannot reduce this to just the mind's internal lived experience.

Even more important, "the agreeableness of swimming" is not a relationship established only between a swimming subject and its environment. The establishment of the other swimming within the environment in which Zhuang Zhou is present is the establishment of "joy" as the totality of the mental states born within the body of the other, within the environment, and within Zhuang Zhou's body schema. It is the joy of the other born within Zhuang Zhou's embodied relationship of presence with the other in the environment. To be present in that place is to have a body schema.[4]

I think that we must not interpret the meaning of "the joy of fish" here as "the joy that humans believe arises in fish as well." It is really the joy of the fish in the Hao, the joy of the fish that Zhuang Zhou perceived. The error originates from the assumption that words like "joy" or "suffering" are always human terms or extrapolations from human joy and suffering. We are not extrapolating the meaning of the word "swimming" from our lived experience to the lived experience of the other. Rather, it is the opposite. For example, one knows the use of the word "swimming" and what sort of thing swimming is in seeing a fish or a person swimming, though not in swimming oneself. The framing of the problem as "the problem that, since joy and suffering are first of all human joy and suffering, how far can they be extrapolated?" is itself an error.

The cognition established by what I am here calling "body schema" is of course not something that can be asserted universality. Many human beings would not understand the joy of fish even standing at the Hao, and far more human beings, lost in the joy of fishing, would fail to understand the suffering of the fish caught when fishing. Even so, these counterexamples cannot be counted as universally refuting the possibility of cognizing the fish.

It may seem that "understanding the joy of fish from the banks of the Hao" holds great significance for the problem of what knowledge of the other is. For example, one important topic in the mind-body problem is whether or not mental states are identical to the processes occurring within the brain, but within this topic knowing the mind would be a question of logical or epistemic (psychological) concern.[5] Taking such an approach is natural for a standpoint that makes universality the archetype of knowledge. However, Zhuang Zhou's remarks take as their problem whether or not when located at a particular place and toward something with a particular state, knowing its joy is possible. It is the problem of knowledge of a kind that first makes its inquiry within a certain state. In establishing this knowledge, the connection of world and world through body schema and the other is indispensable. The problem of this sort of knowledge is, in other words, the problem of "what it is like to be" or "what it is like to live" for the knower within the world.[6]

The dialogue on the Hao was placed at the end of the "Autumn Floods" chapter. The central subject of "Autumn Floods" is the dialogue between the River God and Ruo of the North Sea, and in it, the essence of human beings is investigated along with the nature of knowledge. When asked by the River God what a human being is, Ruo of the North Sea replies that they are "the ones who pierce the snouts of oxen." This response points toward control, manipulation, and artificial enframing of nature as essential characteristics of humanity. These characteristics apply in the case of human "knowledge" as well. When we human beings seek to cognize the world, we enframe that cognition in order to limit the range over which it extends in relation to a domain that goes beyond the means of that cognition, then take pride in achieving total knowledge within that framework. Whatever goes beyond it is called unknowable or ineffable. Within this kind of framework of individuated lived experience, Zhuang Zhou's cognition of the joy of fish is totally excluded as outside the frame. In order to criticize this humanistic way of being itself, Zhuang Zhou employs a cognition that is established by a body schema.

Even though Peter Singer says we should recognize the rights and personhood of horses and dogs because they can feel pleasure and pain, he does not extend this recognition to shrimp or mollusks. What is suspicious about this debate is its deep connection to the dubiousness of the arbitrarily contrived enframement of human knowledge and, what is more, its connection to the ambiguous boundary of cognition around scientific cognition and experiential, active cognition. Zhuang Zhou is able to try to point out to us the dubiousness of this enframing.

Take, for example, the problem of whether we can understand the suffering of those sent to the gas chamber. It is not possible to debate this on the same level as the question of whether human beings can feel the pain of the other at all. Similarly, the question of whether Japanese people can know the suffering of the Asian people who were invaded cannot be reduced to a question about universal cognition. Establishing a framework for universal knowledge puts a ring in our snouts and leads us by the nose to make these questions impossible. Spending night and day analyzing the logical meaning of this nose ring and neglecting the problem itself in front of one's nose—such may be thought to be the background in which analytic philosophy lost its power at the close of the twentieth century.

NOTES

Translated by Carl M. Johnson.

1. "Autumn Floods" is a chapter located in the "Outer Chapters" of the *Zhuangzi*. The chapter is taken to be the work not of the actual Zhuang Zhou but of someone who inherited the thought of the *Zhuangzi*. Herein I use "Zhuang Zhou" to refer not to the historical Zhuang Zhou but to the Zhuang Zhou of "Autumn Floods."

2. Peter Singer states: "The basis of my belief that animals can feel pain is similar to the basis of my belief that my daughter can feel pain." See *Practical Ethics* (Cambridge: Cambridge University Press, 1993), 69.

3. Thomas Nagel, "What Is It Like to Be a Bat?" *Philosophical Review* 83, no. 4 (October 1974): 435–450.

4. Fukunaga Mitsuji's interpretation of this passage—"The whole of the truth cannot be grasped in the separated knowledge and speech of human beings but must be felt in the bodily experience of a state transcending argument" (Sōshi 荘子, *Asahi Shinbun* (1978): 216–219)—does not emphasize the importance of the body schema on the banks of the Hao. The problem is that how we comprehend "a state transcending argument" is not something that "cannot be grasped in the separated knowledge and speech of human beings." To generalize the Hao River into a "canalway" is of course to miss

Zhuang Zhou's intent (see Sōshi 莊子 by Endō Tetsuo, Ichikawa Yasushi, and Ishikawa Yasunari, *Meiji-Shoin* 8: 485–487). The sense of body schema I am getting at may seem closest to Nakajima Takahiro's concepts of "body" and "experience" ("Speaking of 'The Joy of Fish' Once More: Thoughts on Zhuangzi's 'Autumn Floods,'" *Research in Chinese Philosophy* 中國哲學研究, no. 2, 1990).

5. Although it is in relation to the mind-body problem that Nagel raises the question of what it is like to be a bat, he himself took a critical stance toward physicalism and the standpoint of the reductionists. See Thomas Nagel, "Physicalism," *Philosophical Review* 74, no. 3 (July 1965): 339–356. In comparison, Zhuang Zhou advocated the equality of all things and *qi*-monism. On the question of how *qi* philosophy relates to attitudes toward the mind-body problem, see my "Environment and Body: Observations from Neo-Confucianism" in *Contemporary Meaning of Virtue Ethics* edited by The Japanese Society for Ethics (Tokyo: Keio University Press, 1994), 95–111, and "Thinking about the Mutual Relation of Environments and Human Beings" in *The Annual of Comparative Culture*, edited by The Association of Comparative Culture. Vol.6. (Tokyo: Tokyo Institute of Technology, 1995), 37–50. For more on "Autumn Floods," refer to "The Ones who Pierce the Snouts of Oxen: The Philosophy of the Environment and Human Beings" in *Source Book for the Research of Life, Environment, and Science Technology*, edited by Fujimura Shinji et al. (Chiba: Chiba University Press, 1995).

6. In this sense, the problem of knowing the joy of fish in "Autumn Floods" is the problem of whether it is only a logical or psychological problem or perhaps an ethical problem—in a way that goes beyond the framework of European ethics. If ethics is limited to the conduct of beings that have personhood, then Zhuang Zhou's answer could not possess any ethical implications. To the contrary, however, Zhuang Zhou's answer shows that ethical problems include behavior toward the environment and all living things. On this point, I have my doubts about the so-called American interpretation of environmental ethics, in which ethics is understood as the extension of the concept of "personhood" to the nonhuman.

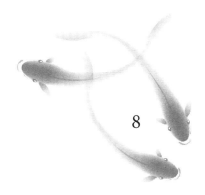

8

Of Fish and Knowledge

On the Validity of Cross-Cultural Understanding

ZHANG Longxi

"Que sais-je?" says the skeptic Michel de Montaigne. If the validity of knowledge is a basic question one may ask about self-understanding, that question is bound to appear far more importunate when we try to understand things in languages and cultures that are set apart and form very different identities, traditions, and histories. For cross-cultural understanding, therefore, China may serve as a useful test case because the mere distance between China and the West, in geographical as well as in cultural terms, makes it especially important to examine first of all the possibility of knowing, the grounds on which one can claim to comprehend things, to make legitimate use of a set of terms and concepts, and to acquire knowledge cross-culturally. Here we may encounter a skepticism that goes deeper than Montaigne's—a skepticism that does not ask "What do I know?" but, more fundamentally, "How do I know?" or "How *can* I know?" The question challenges not just the content but also the very possibility of knowing, and it raises doubts about the validity of cross-cultural understanding, the viability of intersubjective transference of consciousness and sensibility.

This essay undertakes to answer the challenging questions as to what and how one knows about different cultures, to inquire into the condition

Originally published in *Allegoresis: Reading Canonical Literature East and West*, by Zhang Longxi, 1–20. Copyright 2005 by Cornell University. Reprinted with permission.

of knowledge that one may acquire beyond one's own linguistic and cultural parameters, and to establish a theoretical ground for the viability of East-West studies. Although discussion of such issues may cover a wide range of topics, the focus will remain on the question of the viability of cross-cultural understanding. That is why Montaigne's question seems so appropriate for our endeavor. It is that question on the level of different cultures that we are concerned with here, and it is to answer that question that I investigate texts and interpretations across linguistic and cultural differences, above the real and imaginary distances between China and the West.

THE TRANSLATABILITY OF TERMS

Before we look into the matter of cross-cultural knowledge more closely, let us first contemplate the following debate, formulated as a delightfully witty conversation between two ancient Chinese philosophers, Zhuangzi (369?–286? BCE) and his rival, the captious but invariably outwitted Huizi, for their interesting debate on the validity of knowledge will illuminate the situation of knowing and the known and thus help us focus on the theoretical assumptions in our own effort at cross-cultural understanding:

> Zhuangzi and Huizi are strolling on the bridge over the Hao River. "Out there a shoal of white minnows are swimming freely and leisurely," says Zhuangzi. "That's what the fish's happiness is." "Well, you are not a fish, how do you know about a fish's happiness?" Huizi contends. "You are not me, how do you know that I do not know about a fish's happiness?" retorts Zhuangzi. "I am not you, so I certainly do not know about you," Huizi replies. "But you are certainly not a fish, and that makes the case complete that you do not know what a fish's happiness is." "Shall we go back to where we started?" says Zhuangzi. "When you said, 'how do you know about a fish's happiness?' you asked me because you already knew that I knew it. I knew it above the Hao River."[1]

The last statement, that Zhuangzi knew a fish's happiness "above the Hao River," as A. C. Graham observes, asserts the relative validity of knowledge, that "all knowing is relative to viewpoint," namely, acquired at a particular locale in one's lived world, related to the circumscribed whole of one's "concrete situation."[2] The emphasis here on the situatedness or circumstantiality is rather significant as it puts knowledge in a real, specific, and historical context and thereby differentiates it from the abstract notion of all-inclusive, transcendental knowledge based on pure reason. Here Zhuangzi appears to have articulated a concept of knowledge completely embedded in historicity and aided by a sort of empathetic imagination, with its claim to truth based on the specific ways in which the knowing subject and the known object are interconnected rather than on the abstract universality of mental faculties. Perhaps this is the kind of knowledge that reminds us of Aristotle's notion of practical knowledge in his distinction between *phronēsis* and *epistēmē,* or practical and theoretical knowledge, a distinction "which cannot be reduced," as Hans-Georg Gadamer remarks, "to that between the true and the probable. Practical knowledge, phronesis, is another kind of knowledge."[3] Thus, against the challenge of skepticism, Zhuangzi insists on the cognitive value of his situated knowledge as valid knowledge even though he may fully admit his all-too-human finitude and fallibility. But when we speak of Zhuangzi's situated knowledge as *phronēsis,* we are inviting the same skeptic challenge; we put ourselves in the same position as Zhuangzi occupied, where, from the skeptic's point of view, the very possibility of knowing becomes highly questionable. It is indeed the same question with which we began, the question or doubt about cross-cultural understanding: Can we speak of Zhuangzi and Aristotle in the same context? Is Zhuangzi advocating knowledge as a kind of *phronēsis*? Can such terms and concepts be translated at all? These are the most basic questions we must address before we can claim to attain any knowledge at all across the gaps of languages and cultures.

Like the other similar anecdotal arguments in the *Zhuangzi,* the disputation "above the Hao River" purports to illustrate Zhuangzi's philosophy and present it as superior to its rival positions. What is remarkable about this particular anecdote, as Graham notes, is its playfulness, which, "in parodying logical debate is more faithful to the detail of its structure than anything else in *Chuang-tzŭ.*"[4] Graham, however, seems to fall short of our expectation to bring out the full force of Zhuangzi's argument when he remarks that the philosopher in this passage is "making fun of [Huizi] for being too logical" and that Zhuangzi can offer "no answer to 'How do you know?' except a clarification of the viewpoint from which you know."[5] But insofar as practical or moral knowledge is concerned, the viewpoint from which one knows is the only perspective available in human understanding; that is to say, human knowledge is very often situated and conditioned, and its truth very often finite and relative.

Zhuangzi's knowledge of fish is not absolute in the sense that he cannot know fish as only a fish can, but hardly any knowledge worth having is absolute in that sense. Zhuangzi suggests that one does not have to *be* a fish to *know about* fish, for one's knowledge always has something of one's own in it. In Zhuangzi's claim to knowledge, there is surely a sense of playfulness and empathetic enjoyment, a vicarious pleasure that expresses his own happiness in seeing the free and graceful movement of the minnows, which Huizi completely missed or neglected in questioning the logical validity of Zhuangzi's claim. But the crucial point Zhuangzi makes in this passage, as I understand it, is not to counter Huizi's dry logic with a loose and slippery sophism but to pursue that logic vigorously to its very end (or, more precisely in this case, to its starting point), where it turns into its own negation. To be thoroughly skeptic about knowledge, Zhuangzi suggests, one must either give up the possibility of asking any question at all insofar as questioning already presumes the certainty of knowing something amiss, or—which comes to the same thing—one must admit that presumed certainty of one's negative knowledge. That is to say, by pushing Huizi's argument ad absurdum, Zhuangzi shows that his contender is not logical enough, that the skepticism of knowledge already presupposes, ironically but necessarily, knowledge of a certain kind, and that the answer to "How do you know?" is already implicit in the question, if only because it is asking about something already assumed to be known.

Skepticism and knowledge are thus revealed to be mutually implicated in a dialectical relationship. Notice that for all his doubts about Zhuangzi's knowledge, Huizi never has a moment of doubt about what he knows, namely, that Zhuangzi is not a fish; ergo, he does not know a fish's happiness. Throughout the conversation, Huizi's negative knowledge, his conviction that there is a difference between Zhuangzi and a fish, between "you" and "I," is stated most positively and assuredly. His skeptic attitude toward knowledge thus rests on his unreflective confidence in his own negative knowledge of the difference of things. For Zhuangzi, however, differentiation is arbitrary, and the difference between man and fish is by no means a fact established a priori; thus in positing difference as an unquestioned, known fact, Huizi already asserts the possibility of knowledge despite himself. It is Zhuangzi who proves to be truly radical in questioning the very logicality of differentiation, whereas Huizi never reaches that level of questioning. But if Huizi can have knowledge of Zhuangzi across the gap of intersubjective difference (between "you" and "I"), we must also grant Zhuangzi the knowledge of fish across another gap of intersubjectivity (between "man" and "fish"). And that, in fact, is how Chinese commentators have traditionally read this passage.[6] However counterintuitive it may appear, such a reading follows a stringent logic that refuses to take for granted any conventional notion of difference.

One may protest that the difference between man and fish is of a different kind from that between Zhuangzi and the rival philosopher and that the former is a greater and more obvious difference than the latter, but in that case we are arguing, like Huizi, on the basis of our conventional notions of difference. Instead of doubting the possibility of knowing, we implicitly assert, again like Huizi, differences of various kinds and degrees as given facts already known intuitively. Zhuangzi, however, is far too philosophical to honor such conventional notions. If everything is either a "this" (shi 是) or a "that" (bi 彼), he wonders whether there is any real distinction between the two categories except when viewed from a certain perspective. The deictic function of all words and categories is predicated on a certain point of view, a certain center of consciousness from which the rest of the world is seen as differentiated, fragmented, and knowable. But "every *this* is also a *that;* every *that* is also a *this*," says Zhuangzi. "*That* has its sense of right and wrong, and *this* also has its sense of right and wrong. Are there really *this* and *that*? Or are there no such things as *this* and *that*?"[7] Such truly skeptic and relativist reasoning is typical of Zhuangzi, but it serves to destabilize the fixation on difference as the basis of some absolute knowledge.

In his great "synthesising vision" of the universe, Zhuangzi tends to see all things as equal to one another in their primordial, natural, undifferentiated condition and to regard all differentiation as arbitrarily made to facilitate human understanding.[8] The equality or nondifferentiation of things constitutes the central theme of the second chapter of the *Zhuangzi,* and at the end of that chapter, where he recounts a fascinating dream of his, the philosopher claims that he is never sure whether he is dreaming or awake, whether he is a man dreaming of being a butterfly or a butterfly dreaming of being Zhuangzi the philosopher.[9] He is not, however, perversely denying all differences or their usefulness, but he does refuse to attach any special value to difference or the negative knowledge based on it. By revealing the undeclared assumptions of Huizi's argument, he shows that all knowledge, negative as well as positive, has only relative validity and that the negative moment necessarily contains and depends on a prior moment of the positive knowledge of differentiation. Ultimately, therefore, Graham is right to see the whole debate between Zhuangzi and Huizi as an argument for the relativity of knowledge. From that perspective, then, it would be untenable to insist on either the absolute validity of knowledge or its absolute impossibility, and to make a truth claim based on negative knowledge would appear just as pretentious as a dogmatic statement of truth.

RELATIVISM, UNIVERSALISM, AND THE RITES CONTROVERSY

The question of the validity of knowledge, of how to "establish and transmit understanding across the boundaries of language, geography, culture, and time," says David D. Buck, "lies at the very heart of Asian studies" or, one might say, cross-cultural studies in general.[10] Buck identifies cultural relativism and evaluative universalism as the two most commonly used paradigms in Asian studies and succinctly describes the core of relativist thinking as a skeptic's attitude toward "the issue of whether any conceptual tools exist to understand and interpret human behavior and meaning in ways that are intersubjectively valid."[11] But to speak of *human* behavior at all is already to have acknowledged the possibility of intersubjective understanding; otherwise, one can describe only one's own behavior empirically, without ever going beyond the strictly personal and subjective and comparing it with anyone else's to gain knowledge that pertains to the human, that is, intersubjective, condition. Buck's observation, however, concerns understanding across the gap of languages and cultures, which is presumably a much wider gap than that of mere intersubjectivity and in which the cultural differences involved are assumed to be much greater than differences within the same culture. It is for cross-cultural studies that Buck raises the question of whether conceptual tools are available across the gaps of fundamental differences.

In recognizing the importance of linguistic, national, ethnic, and other differences and in questioning the viability of using conceptual tools that are intersubjectively valid, Buck's relativist seems to bear some resemblance to Huizi, whose objection to Zhuangzi, as we have seen, is predicated on the recognition of fundamental differences. Zhuangzi, on the other hand, may resemble the universalist in assuming a shared sensibility and common knowledge beyond difference or differentiation. As Buck describes it, however, the universalist position is not really universal but culturally specific, for it is a position related to Western colonialism and imperialism, the ethnocentric position adopted by those Europeans and North Americans who "chauvinistically held that their civilization was superior to others."[12] Here we may see the influence of a predominant relativist paradigm in studying alien cultures and societies, a paradigm that has increasingly gained ground since the 1960s, when Western philosophers and cultural anthropologists began to argue for the internal coherence of cultural values and beliefs, the necessity of abandoning narrow and ethnocentric Western views and of not imposing them on non-Western cultures. This seems to be a morally commendable gesture of cultural critique, by means of which Western scholars genuinely try to dissociate themselves from the racism and cultural hegemony of an embarrassing and erroneous past of Western colonialism.

The change of paradigms in cultural studies, however, proves to be much more complicated than the mere denunciation of colonialism. As Richard Bernstein argues, in the entire range of human and social sciences in recent times, we have seen a "movement from confidence to skepticism about foundations, methods, and rational criteria of evaluation," and as a result the relativist paradigm reigns everywhere. "There seems to be almost a rush to embrace various forms of relativism. Whether we reflect on the nature of science, or alien societies, or different historical epochs, or sacred and literary texts, we hear voices telling us that there are no hard 'facts of the matter' and that almost 'anything goes.'"[13] Once the old positivistic dogmas concerning reality, objectivity, rationality, and truth are exposed as prejudices and illusions, and once a rigid objectivism or metaphysical realism collapses, nothing seems able to check the swing of the pendulum in the paradigmatic change from objectivism to relativism.

In this respect, the controversy around Peter Winch's works is quite significant. Drawing on Ludwig Wittgenstein's concept of language games and arguing against the positivistic notion of objective truth, Winch maintains that knowledge or truth does not coincide with any reality outside the language in which that knowledge or truth is expressed and that different cultures may understand reality differently and may have distinct rules for playing their language games. "Reality is not what gives language sense," says Winch in one of his most controversial essays. "What is real

and what is unreal shows itself *in* the sense that language has."[14] If different cultures are all different forms of life engaged in different language
games, and if there is nothing outside the various languages to provide
an independent basis for description and evaluation, this type of thinking would lead inevitably to a sweeping cultural relativism that sees various cultures as totally incommensurable, intelligible only to those already
living within the limits of a specific cultural system. Winch's argument
tends to lead precisely to such relativism even though he himself maintains that "men's ideas and beliefs must be checkable by reference to something independent—some reality," and he explicitly rejects "an extreme
Protagorean relativism."[15] Bernstein tries to disentangle Winch's argument
from the very relativism Winch disclaims, but in his own critique, he also
points out the controversial aspect of Winch's works, which does seem
"to entail a new, sophisticated form of relativism."[16] In facing an alien society, says Winch, the social scientist must become a participant in a language game different from his own, and his "reflective understanding must
necessarily presuppose, if it is to count as genuine understanding at all,
the participant's unreflective understanding."[17] That is to say, sociologists
or anthropologists must suspend their own views and must think, feel,
and act like natives of the alien society in order to understand it "unreflectively," from the native's point of view.

It is not at all clear, however, how anyone can achieve "unreflective understanding" in thinking about a different culture. If "unreflective" means
completely assimilated and internalized to the point of being unaware of
the very rules of the language game, one may wonder how anyone can enter and participate in a different game in the first place. It would be nearly
as impossible as knowing a fish's happiness as a fish does. The desire to
escape from one's own prejudice and to assume an alien point of view, as
Bernstein notes, simply reenacts "a parallel move in nineteenth-century
hermeneutics and historiography, where it was thought that we can somehow jump out of our skins, concepts, and prejudgments and grasp or know
the phenomenon as it is in itself."[18] Georgia Warnke also sees a connection between Winch and romantic hermeneutics. "Does Winch suppose,
as Dilthey does," Warnke asks, "that social scientists can simply leave their
native languages behind them in learning a new one? Or, as in Gadamer's hermeneutics, are the two languages or sets of prejudices brought into
relationship with one another and, if so, how?"[19] These are of course crucial hermeneutic questions that Winch's argument prompts us to consider,

questions that are particularly relevant to the concept of cross-cultural understanding. It is perhaps to this relevance that Gerald Bruns alludes when he characterizes Winch's works as "deeply involved with the subject of hermeneutics, that is, with its *Sache*—what hermeneutics is *about*."[20] Winch constantly calls our attention to the differences between cultures and languages, but the important hermeneutic question is, How does one achieve understanding beyond and in spite of those differences? His advice to assume a participant's "unreflective understanding," however, does not seem to offer a particularly helpful answer.

In his discussion of understanding alien societies, Winch is "mainly, though not exclusively, concerned about the nature of one man's understanding, in moral terms, of the lives and actions of *others*."[21] In his controversial essay "Understanding a Primitive Society," he explicitly states that he is trying "to suggest that the concept of *learning from* which is involved in the study of other cultures is closely linked with the concept of *wisdom*."[22] Here questions of hermeneutics become ethical questions as well, as one tries to understand an alien society in order to learn something from it, to expand one's vision, to get rid of one's ethnocentric prejudices, and to acquire moral knowledge of both the self and others. But understanding an alien society already presupposes a certain shared humanity rather than the insistence on difference, and adequate understanding does not entail abandoning one's own cultural values in order to become totally "unreflective" in one's own thinking. Understanding proves to be essential for the project of *Bildung,* or self-cultivation, but such learning and self-cultivation can neither be a projection of the self onto the Other nor a complete self-effacement to become the Other: it can be only a moment of mutual illumination and enrichment in what Gadamer calls the fusion of horizons. And that, as I have argued elsewhere, is the only way to learn from different cultures and societies.[23]

The openness to the challenge of others and the fusion of horizons will establish understanding and moral knowledge beyond skepticism and relativism without claiming absolute truth. In fact, it is often the cultural relativist that shows "a deep attachment to metaphysical realism itself" because the relativist argument usually proceeds in a specious line of all-or-nothing: "First, an impossible demand is made, say, for unmediated presentness to reality as it is in itself or for an actual universal agreement about matters of value. Next, it is claimed that this demand cannot be met. Then, without any further ado," as Martha Nussbaum shows in a cogent analysis, the relativist "concludes that everything is up for grabs and there are no norms to give us guidance in matters of evaluation."[24] What Nussbaum proposes as an alternative, or what she calls Aristotelian essentialism, is a list of basic human functioning capabilities that constitute the basis of a notion of goodness in human life without pretending to be either absolute or exhaustively universal. That is also essentially Bernstein's point in arguing for the necessity of breaking away from the dichotomy of either/or thinking and moving beyond objectivism and relativism.

Insofar as ethics is concerned, one may wonder whether the recognition of both cultural difference and its corollary relativist attitude is necessarily tied to a morally superior position, where one becomes a better person with more sympathy for others and greater respect for cultural heterogeneity. Conversely, one may wonder whether beliefs in any type of universal rights and values are necessarily related to ethnocentrism and cultural imperialism. If we go back to my earlier suggestion that Zhuangzi seems to resemble the universalist in assuming the possibility of common knowledge beyond fundamental differences, his universalism certainly has nothing to do with the universalism tainted by Western colonialism or imperialism since Zhuangzi's argument for the commonality of knowledge is based on an egalitarian rather than a supremacist point of view. Indeed, from the perspective informed by Zhuangzi's insights, I argue that the belief in the possibility of common knowledge and cross-cultural understanding and in the availability of conceptual tools for the interpretation of human behavior across the boundaries of language, geography, culture, and time can indeed come from a genuine appreciation of the *equal capabilities* of different individuals, peoples, and nations. In other words, a universalist position, like the one grounded in the belief—like Zhuangzi's—in the fundamental equality of things, is not tied to colonialism or ethnocentrism. On the other hand, it is entirely possible and perfectly logical for cultural supremacists to take a relativist position in order precisely to emphasize cultural difference and to insist on the superiority and correctness of their own values in preference to those of others.

We can find an illuminating example in the so-called Chinese rites controversy, which marked an early cultural conflict between the East and the West in the seventeenth century and the first half of the eighteenth and in which the Catholic Church, its popes and missionaries, the monarchs of Europe, the emperors of China, as well as some leading philosophers of the time, notably Voltaire and Gottfried Wilhelm Leibniz, were all involved. The rites controversy, as George Minamiki reminds us, has two related aspects: one has to do with "the problem of how Western man was to translate into the Chinese language the concepts of the divinity and other spiritual realities," that is, the issue of terminology, and the other concerns the problem of "how he was to judge, on a moral basis, the ceremonies performed by the Chinese in honor of Confucius and their ancestors," that is, the issue of rites proper, and the controversy brings to the fore a range of problems in "the whole field of cross-cultural understanding and missionary accommodation."[25]

Insofar as the terminology issue was concerned, the debate arose among the missionaries from a profound difference in opinion with regard to the nature of the Chinese language and thinking. Matteo Ricci (1552–1610), the famous Jesuit missionary and head of the China mission, learned the Chinese language and spread the idea that "traces of Christianity" existed in Chinese culture and customs, including "evidences of the cross among the Chinese."[26] He found in ancient Chinese writing the ideas of *tian* 天 (Heaven), *zhu* 主 (Lord), and *shangdi* 上帝 (Sovereign on High) and made use of these terms to translate the Christian God. Of the word *tianzhu* 天主 (Lord of Heaven) for translating "God," Ricci says that the missionaries "could hardly have chosen a more appropriate expression."[27] Obviously he had no doubt about the possibility of translating concepts and terms of Christianity into Chinese, and in *Tianzhu shiyi* 天主實義 (The True Meaning of the Lord of Heaven), his treatise on the Christian doctrine, written in Chinese and published in 1604, Ricci tried to present the Western religious content in Chinese garb as elegantly as possible. The book "consisted entirely of arguments drawn from the natural light of reason, rather than such as are based upon the authority of Holy Scripture," and it "contained citations serving its purpose and taken from the ancient Chinese writers; passages which were not merely ornamental, but served to promote the acceptance of this work by the inquiring readers of other Chinese books."[28] Here we see Ricci playing the language game according to its rules, but he is by no means unreflective in using an alien language to serve his own purpose, for he does so in order to win over some high officials at the court of the Chinese emperor and to work toward the eventual Christian conversion of China.

"Ricci's plan for the conversion of the Chinese," as Haun Saussy comments, "involved appropriating the language of the canonical books and official Confucianism to give Catholicism the vocabulary, and incidentally the prestige, it lacked. Converting the Chinese required, as a first step, converting the Classics."[29] For that conversion, linguistic and cultural differences were not of primary interest except as obstacles to be overcome, for Ricci was much more intent on seeing the Chinese as potential fellow Christians and the Chinese language and culture as somehow compatible with the Christian doctrine. His strategy to appropriate the Chinese classics was to argue that they contain the divine revelation of natural religion, which had prepared the Chinese to receive the light of revealed religion.[30] In reading the Confucian classics as compatible with Christianity, the Jesuit fathers gave the Chinese canonical texts a typological interpretation that separated them from their native context and presented them as shadows and prefigurations of the spiritual reality of Christ and his teachings. Lionel Jensen argues that "Confucius" is not a simple translation of the name of the great Chinese philosopher but a Jesuit invention, "a spiritual confrere who alone among the Chinese had preached an ancient gospel of monotheism now forgotten." Such appropriation of Confucianism and the Chinese classics enabled the missionaries to overcome the cultural strangeness they encountered in late Ming China and, more significantly, "to represent themselves to the natives as the orthodox bearers of the native Chinese tradition, *ru*."[31]

Filtered through Jesuit interpretation, Confucian moral and political philosophy had a notable impact on the European imagination, and the idea that the Chinese had achieved perfection in natural religion became especially appealing to many philosophers. By the end of the seventeenth century, as Arthur Lovejoy remarks, "it had come to be widely accepted that the Chinese—by the light of nature alone—had surpassed Christian Europe both in the art of government and in ethics."[32] In his enthusiastic desire for Europe and China to learn from each other, Leibniz held that "it would appear almost necessary that Chinese missionaries should be sent to us to teach us the use and practice of natural religion (*theologia naturalis*), just as we send missionaries to them to teach them revealed religion."[33] Voltaire's admiration of Confucius was boundless, and, in the words of Adolf Reichwein, this Chinese philosopher "became the patron saint of eighteenth-century Enlightenment."[34] Such widespread enthusiasm for a pagan culture, however, was bound to alarm the doctrinal purists in the Catholic Church. Ricci's belief in a common understanding of the concept of the divinity, the idea of the true God shared by peoples in China and the West, soon became the target of severe criticism after his death; it was contested by his opponents as the focus of the rites controversy and finally condemned in the official decrees issued by several popes from Clement XI in 1704 to Benedict XIV in 1742.

The cultural conflict between the East and the West came to a head in the rites controversy, in which the Catholic Church reasserted the spiritual exclusiveness of the Christian faith and the fundamental cultural difference between Christianity and the pagan Chinese culture. Whether the Chinese and the Europeans could possibly have the same idea of God and other spiritual realities across linguistic and cultural differences can be recast as the basic question of translatability, and it is the doctrinal purist's position in the church that the Chinese language, as a language of matter and mundane concerns, cannot possibly express the spiritual concepts and values of Christianity. The use of the Chinese expression of *shangdi* (Sovereign on High) to mean "God" and the word *tian* to refer to "Heaven" were officially condemned by Clement XI in 1704 and again in 1715. Of course, the problem of terminology bewildered not only the Catholic missionaries in their effort to convey Christian ideas in Chinese but also the Buddhist monks, who had encountered a similar problem earlier in history in translating their sutras from Sanskrit into Chinese, and the Protestant missionaries, who were again to face this question when they tried to put out their Chinese version of the Bible. The dilemma in translation, as Arthur F. Wright puts it, is a difficult and undesirable choice:

> Select, as equivalents for key terms, native terms which already enjoyed great prestige, and in so doing risk the obliteration of the distinctive meaning of the original concept; or select as equivalents terms which, when used in an explained technical sense, more adequately translate the meaning of the original, but at the cost of familiarity and prestige and at the risk of uncouthness.[35]

It seems that to translate is always to negotiate between such undesirable choices in an attempt to find conceptual and linguistic equivalents that are, unfortunately, never quite the same, never completely identical. The translation of terms turns out to be nothing more than a compromise reached at the end of this negotiating process, and it is consequently a makeshift, and unacceptable to the staunch purist, who demands nothing less than the unadulterated essence of the original. The frequent complaint is that the Chinese language, which is allegedly too concrete and this-worldly, cannot express the spiritual meanings of the religious concepts of Christianity. "Is there any convenient method of stating the doctrine of the Trinity, which does not imply the grossest materialism?" asked one Protestant priest in despair. "Who has been fortunate enough to discover a name for sin which does not dash us on the Scylla of civil crime or engulph [sic] us in the Charybdis of retribution for the faults of a former life?"[36]

According to the purist argument, linguistic and cultural differences are so unbridgeable that foreign ideas, especially those of Western religious thinking that have been molded in a long history from the Hebrews and the Greeks to the modern Europeans, are all untranslatable. Not only that, they are simply inconceivable in the Chinese mind and unavailable to the Chinese language. That is roughly the argument Ricci's opponents advanced against his assimilation of Chinese views and terms in propagating Christianity through cultural accommodation. They complained that the Chinese men of letters converted by Ricci remained as Confucian as ever and had no real understanding of Christianity and that "where they appear to speak of our God and his Angels," as the Franciscan father Antonio de Caballero remarks with obvious impatience and scorn, "they are merely aping the Truth."[37] Caballero's remark takes cultural difference as a matter of right or wrong, truth or deception, and his simian metaphor serves to expose the Chinese converts as fake Christians or inadequate imitators.[38] This should remind us of the ominous implications of the relativist position, the fact that when the cultural supremacists mark the fundamental difference and emphasize that they are different from the non-Western Other, they are in effect saying that they are better and superior and that they are the original model distorted by inadequate imitations.

Judging from Confucianism's tenacious grip on the Chinese mind in late imperial China and the negligible number of Chinese converts whom the missionaries succeeded in proselytizing, no one can overlook the enormous gap between Chinese and Western cultural traditions. In fact, the Jesuit approach of cultural accommodation was itself the outcome of a clear recognition of cultural differences, the realization that China was so far away and so different from Europe and had such a long history of its own civilization that it would be impossible to change the millions of Chinese into Portuguese or Italians. According to Bonnie Oh, the policy of cultural accommodation that Ricci implemented in China "took into consideration the high level of civilization in the Asian countries, recognized the futility of trying to make Westerners out of Asians, and demonstrated a willingness to accommodate to the native culture."[39] The policy dictated that the Jesuit missionaries "speak, read, and write the native languages; become an integral part of a particular civilization and behave like the natives of the country," in short, as Joseph Sebes puts it pointedly, "Become Chinese to win China for Christ."[40] The last clause makes it clear that the Jesuit policy of cultural accommodation was ultimately dictated by their religious agenda of the Christian conversion of China, but that does not change the fact that accommodation was based on the recognition of cultural difference, nor does it rule out the possibility that the Jesuit acculturation might have had consequences detrimental to their original agenda or motivation, as the Vatican seemed to believe.

If their accommodation to Chinese culture and customs was the result of a clear sense of cultural difference, then Ricci and his supporters should perhaps be characterized, in the sense Buck has defined, as relativist rather than universalist, but such a characterization would contradict Ricci's belief in the translatability of Western concepts and ideas into Chinese, the possibility of a shared understanding of the notion of God and other spiritual realities across the boundaries of language, geography, culture, and time. Such a contradiction does not so much reveal a problem with Jesuit accommodation as show the limitation and inadequacy of terms like "relativism" and "universalism" in cross-cultural studies, especially when certain values are attached to these terms. Relativism, the emphasis on cultural differences between the West and the non-West, may indeed suggest an open-minded acceptance of the values of an alien culture, the willingness to see the positive in what is different from one's own tradition. There is, however, nothing inherently benign about a relativist attitude; moreover, as the purist argument in the Chinese rites controversy shows, it is just as possible that the relativist emphasis on difference may serve to legitimize a position of cultural supremacy.

For a doctrinaire like Caballero, cultural difference, the difference between true faith and its poor imitation, is as categorical as the difference between humans and apes, and his metaphor recalls Huizi's assurance of the distinction between man and fish. In this connection, then, we may put the same question to the relativist as Zhuangzi did: "How do you know that I do not know about a fish's happiness?" To put it in a way more relevant to our concerns: How do you know that I do not know about another culture and its concepts? On what basis can you claim to have knowledge about me but at the same time deny me the possibility of knowing? Put in such terms, the question may help us realize that the purist or the skeptic, far from being a humble and unassuming relativist with a great deal of respect for the alien and the culturally different, assumes a great deal of knowledge about both the self and others despite the relativist claim that it is impossible to know the others. "Skepticism," as Saussy argues, "requires making even stronger epistemic claims than does naïveté. It requires that the naïve claims be testable and that it itself be capable of doing the testing."[41] Implicit in such skepticism is an unmistakable sense of superiority, even arrogance, a sense that only the skeptic knows both the East and the West and knows them to be fundamentally different and incommensurate.

To recast the question again in terms of translatability, the problem is not whether a particular translation is adequate or not but whether translation can be accomplished at all. Even if Ricci's use of *tianzhu* or *shangdi* as equivalent Chinese terms for "God" were bad translations, does that mean that the very idea of God or divinity is inconceivable in the Chinese mind and inexpressible in the Chinese language? Here I am concerned not with vindicating Ricci's choice of terms but with the implications of the question of translatability. With all sorts of associated connotations embedded in the nexus of Chinese words, *tianzhu, shangdi,* or *shen* 神 (spirit, deity, divinity) cannot be strictly *identical* to the word "God," but if we are talking about cross-cultural understanding at all, we are talking about the *equivalent,* not the identical. What is identical, anyway? If one cannot step into the same river twice, as the ancient Greeks knew, if we realize that all things exist in a state of flux in temporal as well as in spatial terms, can we still speak of a river as the same river, that is, identical to itself? Obviously not, and yet we speak of the "same river" in the sense of close equivalence or what Saussure calls "synchronic identity" as opposed to real identity.[42] Linguistic and cultural differences between China and the West are obvious, that is, in the etymological sense of "standing in the way" (*ob viam*) like obstacles, and it is the task of translation to clear the way for understanding and communication by discovering equivalent formulations underneath the changing surface of differences. If we insist on complete and absolute identity, then nothing can be translated, and the demand for an unadulterated original essence would preclude translation. From the purist and dogmatic point of view, the only language capable of expressing Christian ideas, insofar as the expression of spiritual meaning is concerned, is a Western language.

But what about the difference among the various Western languages themselves? Is the English word "God" always exactly identical to the Latin "Deus"? And do these words always precisely translate the Hebrew word *elohim*? If we go on asking, the question of translatability becomes more complicated and the answer less certain. The translation of the Bible into every modern language has never gone unchallenged for all sorts of reasons. William Tyndale had to defend his English translation in the early sixteenth century, and throughout the second half of that century, the Catholic polemicists repeatedly accused Protestant translators of "including deliberately heretical mistranslations in their versions."[43] Pushing its logic to the extreme, the purist position would do away with language altogether in order to preserve the concept of God as pure spirit. For a spiritualist theologian, even the biblical Hebrew may appear too concrete, too bound up with the literal sense of the physical world, and filled with too much anthropomorphism to express the pure idea of an abstract God.[44]

As Antoine Berman observes, resistance to translation was first of all "of a religious and cultural order" and "ordered around *untranslatability as a value*." Just as in the Jewish tradition it is believed that the oral Torah should not be translated into the written language, likewise "the sacred text should not be translated into other languages, lest it lose its 'sacred' character." This has tremendous influence on our thinking about secular literature as well because the rejection of translation, Berman goes on to say, "traverses the whole history of the West, with the dogma, never made explicit and continually refuted practically, of the untranslatability of poetry, without mentioning the famous 'prejudicial objection' against translation in general."[45] This seems to show that the prejudice against translation in the West has always been related to a religious and cultural notion of abstract concepts and transcendental values, the purist notion of untranslatable spiritual essence. One can well imagine how much greater the resistance would be to a translation that attempts to bridge the cultural gaps between the East and the West and how much more difficult it would be to answer the following question with any assurance: Can the Chinese language express abstract, spiritual notions?

The answer to this question can of course come from all directions, and a negative answer does not necessarily indicate a supremacist attitude. As a sinologist, Wright recognizes translation as always a compromise and finds the purist view impractical, but in his discussion of the difficulties of translation, he finally agrees with those grumbling missionaries in seeing Western concepts as impossible to translate into Chinese because "the Chinese [language] was relatively poor in resources for expressing abstractions and general classes or qualities. 'Truth' tended to develop into 'something that is true.' 'Man' tended to be understood as 'the people'—general but not abstract. 'Hope' was difficult to abstract from a series of expectations directed toward specific objects."[46] Here the cultural difference between the Chinese and the Western is formulated as fundamentally distinct ways of thinking and speaking, such as the ability, or lack of it, to express abstract ideas.

Jacques Gernet even more straightforwardly endorsed the Catholic purist view, especially that of Longobardi, whose work he considers to be "most interesting for the history of Chinese reactions to Christian theses."[47] In his discussion of the conflict between Christianity and Chinese culture, Gernet traces all the difficulties the missionaries encountered in China to a fundamental difference, "not only of different intellectual traditions but also of different mental categories and modes of thought."[48] In Chinese, he declares, it is "so difficult to express how the abstract and the general differ fundamentally, and not just occasionally, from the concrete and the particular. This was an embarrassment for all those who had, in the course of history, attempted to translate into Chinese concepts formed in inflected languages such as Greek, Latin, or Sanskrit. Thus, linguistic structures inevitably pose the question of modes of thought."[49] This statement flies in the face of all Chinese translations of Buddhist sutras in the past and of Western works in more recent times, but for Gernet probably all Chinese translations are nothing more than embarrassing corruptions of the original Indo-European ideas. With the assurance of an expert, Gernet asserts that the Chinese language "has the peculiar, distinctive feature of possessing no grammatical categories systematically differentiated by morphology. . . . Furthermore, there was no word to denote existence in Chinese, nothing to convey the concept of being or essence, which in Greek is so conveniently expressed by the noun *ousia* or the neuter *to on*. Consequently, the notion of being, in the sense of an eternal and constant reality, above and beyond that which is phenomenal, was perhaps more difficult to conceive, for a Chinese."[50] In such a formulation, the Chinese language appears to be a language of concrete things and specific objects, a language bogged down in matter and unable to rise above the ground of materiality and literality toward any spiritual height. The judgment is thus not on Chinese translation of particular foreign words and concepts but on the very nature and ability of the Chinese language as a whole. Given the fact that the relativist views, as Buck observes, are "advanced with much more frequency among Asianists" than universalist ones, it is not surprising that such a view of a concrete and material Chinese language has gained some currency in the circle of sinological studies.[51] A great deal of emphasis has been placed on the cultural difference between China and the West, and the formulation of that difference in terms of a contrast between the concrete and the abstract finds an elaborate counterpart in the study of Chinese literature.

NOTES

1. Guo Qingfan 郭慶藩 (1844–1895?), *Zhuangzi jishi* 莊子集釋, xvii, in vol. 3 of *Zhuzi jicheng* 諸子集成 (Beijing: Zhonghua, 1954), 267–268. Hereafter abbreviated as *Zhuangzi.*

2. A. C. Graham, *Disputers of the Tao: Philosophical Arguments in Ancient China* (La Salle, IL: Open Court, 1989), 81.

3. Hans-Georg Gadamer, *Truth and Method,* English translation revised by Joel Weinsheimer and Donald G. Marshall, 2nd rev. ed. (New York: Crossroad, 1989), 21. For *phronēsis,* see Aristotle, *Nicomachean Ethics,* VI, 8, 1142a: "That practical wisdom is not scientific knowledge is evident; for it is, as has been said, concerned with the ultimate particular fact, since the thing to be done is of this nature," in *The Basic Works of Aristotle,* ed. Richard McKeon (New York: Random House, 1941), 1030.

4. A. C. Graham, *Chuang-tzŭ: The Inner Chapters* (London: Allen and Unwin, 1981), 123.

5. Graham, *Disputers,* 80, 81.

6. In his exegesis of this passage, Cheng Xuanying (fl. 637–655) thus rephrases Zhuangzi's retort to Huizi: "If you argue that I am not a fish and therefore cannot know about fish, then how can you, who are not me, know about me? If you are not me and yet can know about me, then, I, though not a fish, can know about fish" (*Zhuangzi,* xvii, 268).

7. *Zhuangzi,* ii, 32.

8. The term "synthesising vision" is Graham's. The theme of the second chapter of the *Zhuangzi,* Graham maintains, is "the defence of a synthesising vision against Confucians, Mohists and Sophists, who analyse, distinguish alternatives and debate which is right or wrong" (Graham, *Chuang-tzŭ,* 48).

9. See *Zhuangzi,* ii, 53–54. Though less radical in doubting the difference of identities, Montaigne in a different context also asks: "When I play with my cat, who knows if I am not a pastime to her more than she is to me?" in Michel Eyqeum de Montaigne, "Apology for Raymond Sebond," *The Complete Essays of Montaigne,* trans. Donald M. Frame (Stanford, CA: Stanford University Press, 1958), II:12, 331.

10. David Buck, "Forum on Universalism and Relativism in Asian Studies, Editor's Introduction," *Journal of Asian Studies* 50 (February 1991): 29.

11. Ibid., 30.

12. Ibid.

13. Richard J. Bernstein, *Beyond Objectivism and Relativism: Science, Hermeneutics, and Praxis* (Philadelphia: University of Pennsylvania Press, 1983), 3.

14. Peter Winch, "Understanding a Primitive Society," *Ethics and Action* (London: Routledge and Kegan Paul, 1972), 12.

15. Ibid., 11.

16. Bernstein, *Beyond Objectivism and Relativism,* 27.

17. Peter Winch, *The Idea of a Social Science and Its Relation to Philosophy* (London: Routledge and Kegan Paul, 1958), 89.

18. Bernstein, *Beyond Objectivism and Relativism,* 104.

19. Georgia Warnke, *Gadamer: Hermeneutics, Tradition and Reason* (Stanford: Stanford University Press, 1987), 110.

20. Gerald L. Bruns, *Hermeneutics Ancient and Modern* (New Haven, CT: Yale University Press, 1992), 8.

21. Winch, *Ethics and Action,* 2.

22. Ibid., 42.

23. See Zhang Longxi, "The Myth of the Other: China in the Eyes of the West," *Critical Inquiry* 15 (Autumn 1988): 108–131. An expanded version appears as chapter 1 of my book *Mighty Opposites: From Dichotomies to Differences in the Comparative Study of China* (Stanford: Stanford University Press, 1998).

24. Martha Nussbaum, "Human Functioning and Social Justice: In Defense of Aristotelian Essentialism," *Political Theory* 20 (May 1992): 213, 209.

25. George Minamiki, *The Chinese Rites Controversy from Its Beginning to Modern Times* (Chicago: Loyola University Press, 1985), ix. For a study of the rites controversy that includes detailed discussion of many Chinese documents, see Li Tiangang 李天綱, *Zhongguo liyi zhi zheng: Lishi, wenxian he yiyi* 中國禮儀之爭：歷史，文獻和意義 (The Chinese Rites Controversy: History, Documents, and Meaning) (Shanghai: Shanghai Guji Press, 1998).

26. Matteo Ricci, *China in the Sixteenth Century: The Journals of Matthew Ricci: 1583–1610,* trans. Louis J. Gallagher (New York: Random House, 1953), 110, 111.

27. Ibid., 154.

28. Ibid., 448.

29. Haun Saussy, *The Problem of a Chinese Aesthetic* (Stanford: Stanford University Press, 1993), 36.

30. This view is well reflected in Nicola Trigault's "To the Reader," written in 1615, when he translated Ricci's diary from Italian into Latin and published it in Rome. If he could go back to China and have enough time, says Trigault, he would write about the Chinese and compose "the Code of Chinese Ethics, so that one may understand how well adapted is the spirit of this people for the reception of the Christian faith, seeing that they argue so aptly on questions of morality" (Ricci, *Journals of Matthew Ricci,* xv).

31. Lionel M. Jensen, "The Invention of 'Confucius' and His Chinese Other, 'Kong Fuzi,'" *Positions* 1 (Fall 1993): 415. The argument is fully developed in Jensen, *Manufacturing Confucianism: Chinese Traditions and Universal Civilization* (Durham: Duke University Press, 1997).

32. Arthur O. Lovejoy, "The Chinese Origin of a Romanticism," *Essays in the History of Ideas* (Baltimore: John Hopkins University Press, 1948), 105.

33. Gottfried Wilhelm Leibniz, *Novissima sinica* (1699), preface; quoted in Lovejoy, ibid., 106.

34. Adolf Reichwein, *China and Europe: Intellectual and Artistic Contacts in the Eighteenth Century,* trans. J. C. Powell (New York: Knopf, 1925), 77.

35. Arthur F. Wright, "The Chinese Language and Foreign Ideas," in Wright, ed., *Studies in Chinese Thought* (Chicago: University of Chicago Press, 1953), and in *American Anthropologist* 55, no. 5, pt. 2, memoir no. 75 (December 1953): 289.

36. C. W. Mateer, "Lessons Learned in Translating the Bible into Mandarin," *Chinese Recorder* (November 1908): 608, quoted in Wright, ibid., 291.

37. Caballero, alias Sainte-Marie, *Traité sur quelques points importants de la mission de Chine* (Paris, 1701), 105; quoted in Jacques Gernet, *China and the Christian Impact: A Conflict of Cultures,* trans. Janet Lloyd (Cambridge: Cambridge University Press, 1985), 33.

38. According to Ernst Robert Curtius, the core of the metaphorical use of *simia* is the idea of bad imitation or pretentiousness. The ape metaphor "can be applied not only to persons but also to abstractions and artifacts which assume the appearance of being something they are not," in Ernst Robert Curtius, *European Literature and the Latin Middle Ages,* trans. Willard R. Trask (Princeton, NJ: Princeton University Press, 1973), 539.

39. Bonnie B. C. Oh, Introduction to Charles E. Ronan and Bonnie B. C. Oh, eds., *East Meets West: The Jesuits in China* (Chicago: Loyola University Press, 1988), xix–xx.

40. Joseph Sebes, "The Precursors of Ricci," in Ronan and Oh, *East Meets West,* 23.

41. Saussy, *Chinese Aesthetic,* 10.

42. Saussure's notion of "synchronic identity" is in effect "equi-valence," that is, equal values to satisfy certain requirements. These are Saussure's examples: "we speak of the identity of two '8:25 p.m. Geneva-to-Paris' trains that leave at twenty-four-hour intervals. We feel that it is the same train each day, yet everything—the locomotive, coaches, personnel—is probably different. Or if a street is demolished, then rebuilt, we say that it is the same street even though in a material sense, perhaps nothing of the old one remains" (Ferdinand de Saussure, *Course in General Linguistics,* trans. Wade Baskin [New York: Philosophical Library, 1959], 108).

43. Gerald Hammond, "English Translations of the Bible," in Robert Alter and Frank Kermode, eds., *The Literary Guide to the Bible* (Cambridge, MA: Harvard University Press, 1987), 651.

44. See ibid., 647.

45. Antoine Berman, *The Experience of the Foreign: Culture and Translation in Romantic Germany,* trans. S. Heyvaert (Albany: State University of New York Press, 1992), 187.

46. Wright, "Chinese Language and Foreign Ideas," 287.

47. Gernet, *China and the Christian Impact,* 9.

48. Ibid., 3.

49. Ibid., 239.

50. Ibid., 241.

51. Buck, "Forum on Universalism and Relativism," 32. For works that present views more or less similar to Wright's, see Chad Hansen, *Language and Logic in Ancient China* (Ann Arbor: University of Michigan Press, 1983); David L. Hall and Roger T. Ames, *Thinking through Confucius* (Albany: State University of New York Press, 1987); and a number of other works. For a critique and a different view of the Chinese language, see Graham, "The Relation of Chinese Thought to the Chinese Language," appendix 2 to *Disputers of the Tao,* 389–428.

9

Zhuangzi and Theories of the Other

Takahiro NAKAJIMA

TAUTOLOGY AND THE DISTINCTIVENESS OF THE SELF'S EXPERIENCE: HUIZI AND ZHUANGZI'S DEBATE

I would like to begin my essay by reviewing the relevant passage of the *Zhuangzi*:

> Zhuangzi and Huizi were rambling on the banks of the Hao River.
>
> Zhuangzi remarked: "The minnows are darting and play at ease; this is the joy of fish."
>
> Huizi inquired: "How is it that you are not a fish, but you can know the joy of fish?"
>
> "How is it that you are not me, but you can know that I don't know the joy of fish?" asked Zhuangzi.
>
> Huizi responded: "Since I am not you, of course I cannot understand you. Since you of course are not a fish, so, too, it is that you cannot know the joy of fish, either."
>
> Zhuangzi replied: "Let's return to the beginning. When you posed the question: 'How do you know the joy of fish?' you asked this because you al-

Originally published as "*Soshi to tasharon: Sakana no tanoshimi no kozon*," in Takahiro Nakajima, *Soshi: Tori to natte toki o tsugeyo* (Tokyo: Iwanami Shoten, 2009), 163–180. Reprinted with permission.

ready knew that I knew it. I know it from on top of the bridge over the Hao River." (*Zhuangzi*, "Autumn Floods" *Qiushui* 秋水)

This argument is constructed from two logics. The first is the logic of Huizi, which asserts conclusively that "one cannot know the experiences of the other." What can be known is just the experience of the self, which possesses an isolated uniqueness, and so we cannot guess about the other. Thus, I would like to consider this a "tautology" (the logic of self-sameness, *tautos logos*).

That said, it is not so easy to carry out this logic thoroughly. After all, since it is a logos it is always open to communication with the other because this logic itself is something that the other ought to be able to know. Moreover, even if we assume "self-sameness" here, its status is unstable. It is difficult to decide whether what this assumes is the solitariness of each of the great multiplicity of selves in this world or the irreplaceable centrality of the self, which constructs this world and none other. On top of this, there is a problem in what gives the unique experiences of the self their uniqueness. That is, is the "blueness of the sky" that I perceive a special content in the sense that my perceptual contents are very different from those of other persons? Or, because it is a universal possibility as "blueness," is it unique to the degree that it can be exchanged? Questions of this sort keep cropping up.

Well then, where and in what manner does Zhuangzi rebut this? We are entering the second logic of the argument. The interesting thing is that Zhuangzi first attempts to refute Huizi's tautology by repeating it. At that point he asks, "How is it that you are not me, but you can know that I don't know the joy of fish?" That is, the possibility of the other, known as Zhuangzi, repeating the proposition that "one cannot know the experiences of the other" shows that this tautology is fundamentally not something that can be merely contained within the self. Zhuangzi attempts to bankrupt the tautology by repeating it.

Yet ironically, in so doing, Zhuangzi has instead reinforced the tautology. In other words, he demonstrates the power of this logic to be sustained and to survive in the other. What does this mean? Let's look at Huizi's response. Huizi says, "Since I am not you, of course I cannot understand you. Since you of course are not a fish, so, too, it is that you cannot know the joy of fish, either." His reply is an additional repetition. This shows that this tautology is not something only for himself but is something that can be agreed upon by the other as well. In this way, the tautology has crossed beyond the self and been extended.

That said, the other, who supports this expanded tautology, is not the other as an other but rather is one more of the self. Zhuangzi attempts to present himself as the other, who has been eliminated by the proposition "one cannot know the experiences of the other," but Huizi tailors this Zhuangzi into just one more of the self, who accepts the principle of "one cannot know the experiences of the other." In short, we may say that the dialogue that seems to be established between Zhuangzi and Huizi has erased the other twice.

What is erased at this time is not just the other. The expansion of the self as "self-sameness" also erases the self as singularity (let's call this the "I") as well. What we have to think through here is the *uniqueness* of the experience of the self. As Huizi supposes, the uniqueness of experience is not based just on the differences in the general structure of experience between two species, fish and human beings. There is also a personal and private uniqueness based on differences in experiential content, which is established even among individuals who, like Zhuangzi and Huizi, are thought to share a certain degree of structure in experience as members of the same human species. That is, because of differences in the general structure of experience, that one is not able to know the other means not only that, as a human, one cannot know the experiences of beings that are nonhuman but also that one cannot know the contents of the experience of others as individuals.

For this reason, Huizi's argument is all the more powerful. After all, it connects the universal and the particular by simultaneously placing on the same level the debate about the uniqueness of experience, the difference of general structures of experience, and the different experiential contents of individuals. Though the experience of the self is something personal and private, which someone else cannot guess at, at the same time the structure of this personal and private uniqueness would be something shared by everyone and everything universally.

However, the "I" is not something that can completely collapse all of the personal and private uniqueness of its experiences into this sort of self. The refutation that Zhuangzi carries out in the final portions of the text is an attempt to slip something out of the snare of the tautology, which has claimed total dominion over the uniqueness of the experiences of the self. Zhuangzi comes to elaborate his logic as the logic of proximity.

THE LOGIC OF PROXIMITY AND THE DEMONSTRABILITY OF THE SENSES: ZHUANGZI'S LOGIC

Let's take another look at the final portion of the exchange between Zhuangzi and Huizi.

Zhuangzi replied: "Let's return to the beginning. When you posed the question: 'How do you know the joy of fish?' you asked this because you already knew that I knew it. I know it from on top of the bridge over the Hao River." What Zhuangzi performs here is a reversal in which the self's uniqueness of experience is not born of personal privacy, which someone else cannot guess at, but of the proximity of the other. Said more strongly, its uniqueness must be established in the proximity of I and the other rather than in personal privacy.

Zhuangzi begins by problematizing the structure of experience itself. To establish experience as experience, it must be open to what is not itself. No matter how much one attempts to construct the experience of the self in isolation from the other, just because it is experience, it must in principle have been exposed to the nonself other. What is more, in this case, since Zhuangzi and Huizi have set about establishing something like a conversation, both are sure to have formally understood the openness of their experience to the other. And this will hold even if, for example, Huizi does not achieve a full understanding of the content of the other's experiences.

Zhuangzi reinforces this point about the contents of the other's experiences when he says, "I know it from on top of the bridge over the Hao River." In other words, by entering into some sort of relationship of proximity with the fish at that concrete place called the Hao River, "I" perceived "the joy of fish," and it was for me something so concrete and direct that it cannot be doubted. Nevertheless, we should not interpret this as something "self-evident," "natural," or "simple" that, as Ikeda Tomohisa says, is "understood in a simple sensation."[1]

To be sure, in the moment the self perceives something present to it here and now, the demonstrability of this knowledge would be backed up by the simultaneity of perception that leaves basically no scope for refutation. For example, should a perception be mistaken, the thing mistakenly perceived is itself demonstrative, and we are able to say only that it is mistaken from a separate perception anyway. So then, should "the joy of fish" be explained by such a rule of perceptual demonstrability, in other words, by a privileging of perceptual presentness? No, that is not it. If "the joy of fish" were demonstrable by the "then and there" of the Hao River as a transfigured "here and now," then for the self, which retains its self-identity over time, it would be only this experience that was doubtlessly, demonstrably guaranteed. That would be a return to the tautology that completely reinforces it. Instead, the pronouncement of "the joy of fish" is a way of being that overturns this kind of perceptual evidentiality.

KUWAKO TOSHIO: LIVED EXPERIENCE WITH A BODY SCHEMA

In relation to this, Kuwako Toshio has developed some extremely suggestive arguments. Kuwako starts by summoning a modern Huizi, Thomas Nagel:

> In this way, Nagel would probably reply to Zhuang Zhou that because we have our lived experiences using sense organs that are totally different from those of fish, we cannot know the joy of fish apart from imagination based on our own lived experiences. In other words, we cannot know what it is like to be a fish or what it is like for a fish to feel joy. Were Zhuang Zhou to understand the joy of fish, it would, at best, be through his imagination of what sorts of joys he might have if he were to become a fish.[2]

To this, Kuwako replies as a modern Zhuangzi. (This is a bit long, but since it is the most crucial part of the argument, I quote it without omission.)

> Well then, how might Zhuang Zhou respond to Nagel's arguments? Wherein does the true significance of his understanding of fish lie? The important point is that it was on the banks of the Hao that Zhuang Zhou knew the joy of the fish swimming there and not that he obtained universal knowledge about the psychology of fish. The importance of Zhuang Zhou's final words comes from their meaning just this. His cognition reveals the body as something standing in a particular relation in time and space with a relational schema to the fish that in turn has a certain relationship to his body. The establishment of this relationship between a body and its environment could take place only on the banks of the Hao. From the universal proposition that "there is no established relation of understanding of feelings between all humans and all fish," Hui Shi concludes that "Zhuang Zhou does not understand the feelings of fish." To this, Zhuang Zhou replies that one cannot infer from this sort of universal proposition whether or not one un-

derstands the feelings of fish. The importance of having this knowledge on the banks of the Hao is that knowing the joy of fish means something that occurs within the particular lived experience of a body schema. Zhuang Zhou's response is not to offer a concrete instance as a counterexample to a universal proposition. Rather, he is criticizing the very act of thinking about "knowing" within a framework of universal knowledge.

Zhuang Zhou shares his environment with the fish. His body has a relational schema within the environment. From the banks of the Hao, he sees the river and watches the swimming of the fish. The swimming of the fish is within Zhuang Zhou's environment. The agreeableness of swimming is surely not a lived experience occurring only within the mind. This lived experience is born within the environment. The agreeableness of swimming occurs within the totality of the swimmers' bodies, the Hao as the environment that surrounds the swimmers, and the mental states born within those bodies. Modern objectivity has come to take the emotion called "agreeableness" as an internal, passively subjective lived experience, but the agreeableness of swimming is an event first arising from the relationship between the embodied subject, which feels the agreeableness and the outside world, which brings about the pleasure. One cannot reduce this to just the mind's internal lived experience.

Even more important, "the agreeableness of swimming" is not a relationship established only between a swimming subject and its environment. The establishment of the other swimming within the environment in which Zhuang Zhou is present is the establishment of "joy" as the totality of the mental states born within the body of the other, within the environment, and within Zhuang Zhou's body schema. It is the joy of the other born within Zhuang Zhou's embodied relationship of presence with the other in the environment. To be present in that place is to have a body schema.[3]

The "agreeableness of swimming" is something that occurs within "a lived experience with a body schema" and is not an isolated mental phenomenon. We must not, like Nagel, rest in the understanding of "the joy of fish" as something that imaginatively transfigures the "subjective" joy of a human being or the self. Kuwako attempts to grasp "the joy of fish" as "the totality of the mental states born within the body of the other, within the environment, and within Zhuang Zhou's body schema." It is none other than "the joy of the other" which is grasped through Zhuangzi's "lived experience with a body schema."

If this is so, may we understand the pronouncement of "the joy of fish" as a different event from perceptual demonstrability? Because perceptual demonstrability is no more than "subjective" evidentiality, it can prove that Zhuangzi subjectively perceives the seriousness of his experience by his vivid perception of "the joy of fish" at a particular time and place. But this line of inquiry presumes the existence of a "subject" or "self" called Zhuangzi. It is not that there is a preexisting "self" that constructs a certain relationship with its own body and the fish and thereby demonstrably knows "the joy of fish." Rather, the singular experience called "the joy of fish" is established in the situation where the "I" encounters the fish at the Hao River. Though this experience is the experience of the "I" (through its being deeply rooted in the body), at the same time it is an experience that goes beyond the "I" (since it is an entirely passive experience for the "I").

No one can say whether or not such an experience will be born for an "I." Kuwako writes the following:

> The cognition established by what I am here calling "body schema" is of course not something that can assert universality. Many human beings would not understand the joy of fish even standing at the Hao, and far more human beings, lost in the joy of fishing, would fail to understand the suffering of the fish caught when fishing. Even so, these counterexamples cannot be counted as universally refuting the possibility of cognizing the fish.[4]

In all likelihood, it often occurs that though one sees the fish in the Hao, they pass right by one's eyes without triggering a reaction, or one just thinks of them as objects for fishing without even a passing thought about "the joy of fish." It follows that experiencing "the joy of fish" is a singular affair. It is not a cognition of the uniqueness of the experiences of the "self" but the establishment of the "I" as a singular "I" in an encounter of "the joy of fish" as "the joy of the other" in a certain circumstance. What we have is an experience of fundamental passivity. The "I" itself is established by the passive triggering of "the joy of the other."

Put differently, what the experience of "the joy of fish" shows is that the "I" and the fish enter into a relationship of proximity (neighboring) at the Hao River. It is not the active demonstrability of perceptual presencing "here and now" but a kind of "secret" originating beforehand. It is a "secret" that belongs to a certain *this world* in which I, together with the fish, have felt "the joy of fish." The demonstrability of perception becomes possible only after *this world*, in which one can catch a glimpse of passivity, is established.

THE JOY OF DEATH

I would like next to closely examine Kuwako's proposition that "to be present in that place is to have a body schema." It is not the case that just anyone who sees the fish swimming in the Hao River would be able to enter into an experience of "the joy of fish." "To be present in that place" does not mean merely being in "that place" but also accepting the particular time and space one is put into as "that place," which is impossible without the acceptance of passivity. To deepen our interpretation, let's take a look at an example beyond "the joy of fish." This is a situation we might well call "the joy of death":

> When Zhuangzi's wife died, Huizi came to pay his respects. Zhuangzi sat with his legs spread out, beating a drum, and singing a song.
> Huizi remarked: "When someone with whom you lived, raised children, and passed the years has died, it is one thing not to shed your tears, but is it not terrible to go on beating a drum and singing a song?"
> Zhuangzi replied: "This is not so. You have misunderstood. When my wife died, I too felt the enormity of the loss. However, I sought to return to the root of things. Doing so, first there was a time prior to her birth. Not only prior to her birth, but even prior to her form. Not only prior to her form, but even prior to her *qi*. In the hazy midst of things, where everything was mixed together, something changed, and her *qi* was born. In that *qi*, something changed, and her form was born. In that form, something changed, and her life was born. And now, there has been another change: one toward her death. In just this way, things move together through the four seasons of spring, summer, autumn, and winter. When my wife was lying asleep in a big room, there was nothing for me to do but cry, but when I realized this was because I had not seen the natural imperative (*ming* 命) through, I stopped my crying.[5]

This account is located in the chapter immediately following "Autumn Floods," which contains "the joy of fish" anecdote. Just as its title, "Perfection of Joy," suggests, this chapter treats the utmost extremes of joy. And this story also involves an exchange with Huizi. Huizi expects Zhuangzi to be weeping because he is predeceased by his wife. But rather than

Zhuangzi shedding tears by the casket, he is immensely enjoying beating a drum and singing a song. For Zhuangzi, this is a kind of memorial service (*kuyō* 供養). In other words, "being present in that place" does not lead Zhuangzi to the conventional grieving and shedding of tears but to enjoy "the joy of death" together with his dead wife.

When it comes to "the joy of fish," many authors concern themselves with the question of whether one is able as an animal to share "joy" between humans and fish. It seems, however, that we should probably concern ourselves with the larger question of whether one is able to share "joy" between living things and dead things, which appear to lack a mind altogether. However, this situation is thought to be unsuitable for an inquiry. This is because it is not about "the joy of fish," "the joy of death," or the "problem of knowing the other" between subject and subject as criticized in the Kuwako essay. Rather, what Zhuangzi is describing is the experience of "proximity" upon which "the joy of fish," "the joy of death," and so on come to stand. Though his dead wife cannot perceive "the joy of death" as subject, "the joy of death" is established in the proximity of Zhuangzi and his wife. Such circumstances are deserving of further consideration.

What I would like to draw attention to here is the necessity of accepting passivity in order to "be present in that place." One cannot accept "that place" in "proximity" with just a "simple" and "natural" attitude. What then is the condition of such acceptance? A knowledge of "seeing the natural imperative through." At first, Zhuangzi was grieving his wife's death by shedding tears, as Huizi wished. But, as it says, when he became aware that he had not "seen the natural imperative through," he ceased his weeping and immersed himself in "the joy of death." In other words, to know "the joy of death," it is necessary to "see the natural imperative through." Zhuangzi explains the content of that knowledge as "first there was a time prior to her birth. Not only prior to her birth, but even prior to her form. Not only prior to her form, but even prior to her *qi*. In the hazy midst of things, where everything was mixed together, something changed, and her *qi* was born. In that *qi*, something changed, and her form was born. In that form, something changed, and her life was born. And now, there has been another change: one toward her death. In just this way, things move together through the four seasons of spring, summer, autumn, and winter."

Without such a knowledge of "seeing the natural imperative through," it would have been difficult to meet with "the joy of death." By "being present" next to his wife's casket, the crying Zhuangzi was able to share in "the joy of death" when that knowledge had an effect. But what sort of thing is this "being present"? I would like to conclude by reflecting on the meaning of the word *kuyō* 供養 (memorial service).

THE DHARMA OF *KUYŌ*

The word *kuyō* is a bit of Buddhist terminology that has become well known in Japanese, but here I would like to examine some of its etymological resonances. *Kuyō* was used as a translation of the Sanskrit words *pūjā,* which had the old meaning of "offering, reverence, or veneration," or *upa-√sthā,* which means "closely" plus "continuing existence" or "reliance." While both carry the unavoidable connotation of a body schema, *upa-√sthā* especially has the literal sense of putting one's body close to the other, or existing by attending to and preparing for the other. Besides *kuyō, upa-√sthā* was also translated into classical Chinese using characters meaning "steadfast dwelling," "deportment," "close affinity," "origination," and "bona fide practice." In any case, this word shows that, when the other and I are "present in that place," a proximity is established, and a singular sort of experience is brought about.

But there is a tautology lurking within *upa-√sthā.* In other words, there is a danger that, when the "I" becomes a "self," the "other" will be assimilated into just one more of the self: *upa-√sthā* as a "steadfast dwelling" that never turns away from *kuyō.* It truly appears to be a condition where *upa* (the surrounding) is cast aside; that is, the condition of *sthāna. Sthāna* has meanings like "a reserve (of wealth), perfect tranquility, position, status, or rank" and was also translated into classical Chinese with the characters *fa* 法 (dharma, law, method) and *yi* 義 (appropriateness, rightness, morality).

To expand the discussion, I would like to take up a term related to *upa-√sthā: upa√ās.* This word is a compound of *upa* and *ās* (sit, stay, dwell) and has implications of "sitting nearby, respecting, or blessing" and, like *upa-√sthā,* is usually interpreted as "sitting nearby." The reason for the adoption of this word was not just that it resembles *upa-√sthā* in its construction and meaning but also because it was thought important on the basis of the "social" way of being in *upa-√sthā.* This is the way of being behind the more familiar words *upāsaka* (attendant [of the Buddha], masculine) and *upāsikā* (feminine). These followers of the Buddha made offerings and carried out *kuyō* as lay believers with a peripheral rank and had a vague, liminal existence, separate from the *bhikṣu* (monastics), who were pure members. According to the *Dictionary of Buddhism,* they "kept religious precepts and economically supported the organization."[6]

Concretely speaking, in order to take care of the monastics' basics needs, for the sake of "the other," they had to prepare food, obtain clothing, and provide shelter in place of "the other." For this reason they had to take pleasure in food, find satisfaction in warm clothing, and live in homes. Above everything else they (who were also known as "good men and women") were beings of pleasure and self-sufficiency and thereby were able to tear the food out of their own mouths. We would do well not to write off the "goodness" of such a way of being as a mere anachronism.

Let's return to Zhuangzi. Speaking in Buddhist fashion, one might say that Zhuangzi positioned himself near his wife and held a memorial service (*kuyō*) by drumming and singing and thereby enjoyed "the joy of death." This is something different from the social notion of conducting a funeral service, where the attendees are awash in tears due to their sorrow. This latter approach opens up a world that, in terms of Zhuangzi's relationship to his wife, is a "distant" world. In this case, for Zhuangzi, the wife is no more than a dead person for whom a funeral is being held. His wife's death is, like other deaths, a death with a position in society and something to be overcome. However, the relationship of *kuyō,* which is "present in that place," opens up a completely different "proximity." His wife's death appears meaningful and can be enjoyed as "the joy of death" from within Zhuangzi's body schema. Death is not an isolated phenomenon but appears as a shared meaning in the "proximity" of Zhuangzi and his wife.

This is the "secret" that Zhuangzi was trying to get across: "the joy of fish," "the joy of death," the deep relationship between the "I" and the other—an experience one first catches a glimpse of by enjoying immersion in a single *this* world. It is at the same time the protosociality that exists beforehand in any sociality and the condition for the possibility of being able to alter any sociality. It is not a lived experience obtained through the active perception of the subject. It is preceded by the other, but the other is in the shadows. Whether one becomes aware of the other in the shadows must not be decided in advance. But when one is aware to a degree, "proximity" has an effect, the "I" precipitates out, and "the joy of fish," "the joy of death," and so on appear as an experience of passivity.

At that time, just what will come to be between the "I" and the other? In enjoying "the joy of fish" or "the joy of death," an entirely different world is born for the "I." The "I" can give birth to a world where the fish are feeling good swimming, or it can give birth to a world where one's wife has passed away.

NOTES

Translated by Carl M. Johnson.

1. Ikeda Tomohisa, *Sōshi,* vol. 2 (Tokyo: Gakushu Kenkyusha. 1986), 486.
2. Kuwako Toshio, "Knowing the Joy of Fish: The *Zhuangzi* and Analytic Philosophy," this volume.
3. Ibid., 144–145.
4. Ibid., 146.
5. *Zhuangzi,* "The Perfection of Joy," *Zhile* 至樂.
6. *Iwanami Bukkyō Jiten,* 2nd ed. Edited by Nakamura Hajime, Fukunaga Mitsuji, Tamura Yoshirō, Konno Tōru, and Sueki Fumihiko (Tokyo: Iwanami Shoten. 2002), 74.

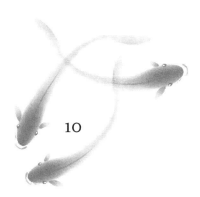

10

Of Fish and Men

Species Difference and the Strangeness
of Being Human in the Zhuangzi

Franklin PERKINS

> Many things are wonderful-terrible, but none is more wonderful-terrible than
> human beings.
> SOPHOCLES, *ANTIGONE*

> Heaven generates the hundreds of things, and human beings are most
> precious.
> *COLLECTED SAYINGS I*

> At first there is good, there is order, and there is no chaos. When there are
> people, there is what is not good. Chaos comes out from people.
> *CONSTANCY FIRST*

Human beings are strange. Although this observation has been elaborated
on and theorized about in as many different ways as there are different
cultures and times, there is no getting around this basic fact: we are peculiar animals. Our very diversity attests to it. The opening lines of the
first choral ode of the *Antigone*, cited in the first epigraph to this essay,
express this strangeness in its ambiguity—to say that human beings are

Originally published in *Harvard Review of Philosophy* 17 (Fall 2010). Reprinted with permission. (The essay in
this volume has been slightly revised.)

the most *deinon* is to say that we are most wondrous or awesome, but the wonder or awe of *deinon* arises not only from what is great but also what is monstrous, strange, or terrifying.[1] That this sense of our terrible strangeness is not just Greek but also human is suggested by the other two epigraphs at the beginning of this essay, both taken from bamboo strips buried around 300 BCE and discovered in China in the 1990s. The first most likely is Confucian (*ru* 儒). The preciousness of human beings lies in our explicit attachment to familial and social life, as well as our ability to make distinctions and organize the world.[2] The second line is more daoist.[3] Nature spontaneously follows a sustainable order of growth, change, and alternation. Only human beings disrupt this, through the imposition of categories and names and the production of artificial desires. Together, these two passages contain the same ambiguity as the *Antigone,* that human beings are wondrously great and wondrously terrible.

Across cultures, our strangeness often appears as a sense of alienation from the world around us. Neither god nor beast, we live *in* nature but are not fully *of* it. Heidegger brings out this sense of alienation in discussing *deinon* as *unheimlich,* (uncanny), playing on the sense of "*heim*" as "home" to indicate a feeling of being not-at-home while in one's home.[4] This common sense of being not entirely at home in the world is best illustrated by myths that link the origins of human beings or human culture to the divine. One of the more beautiful philosophical expressions of such myths is Plato's *Phaedrus,* where Socrates explains the "divine madness" of love and philosophy as following from our vague recollections of the divine, which our immortal soul glimpsed before losing its wings and dropping down to settle into an earthly body.[5] Nietzsche puts a more specific and pessimistic twist on this intuition:

> The best and highest in which humanity can participate is obtained through sacrilege, and its consequences must be taken up—the whole flood of sufferings and sorrows which the offended heavens visit upon that upwardly striving noble race of mankind.

He calls this conflict, in which human beings take and suffer from the divine, a problem that stands "like a boulder at the gate of every culture."[6]

Such myths are remarkably absent in classical Chinese thought, where the originators of human civilization are exceptionally talented human beings, the sages.[7] This contrast already shows that, although there may be something transcultural about our feeling of strangeness, it can be theorized in ways so different as to appear incommensurable and even mutually unrecognizable. On a general level useful for orientation, we can say that if the strangeness of human beings lies in our appearing both natural and supernatural, European and Chinese philosophers split on which side they take as fundamental. The tendency of European philosophers to take other-worldly difference as their basis appears already in the *Phaedrus* and is heightened under Christian influence. Human actions follow from a free will, radically different from the causal laws determining everything else in nature. Because we have souls that are not of this world, human beings are immortal, whereas everything else in nature changes and decays. Human beings have reason, which grants us unique access to eternal and necessary truths. The list could go on, but the root is that human beings are made in the image of a radically transcendent God. With such a view, the uniqueness of human beings is just what we would expect; the problems come in explaining our place in nature. Topics on that side of human experience—embodiment, emotion, human fragility, even family—tend to be ignored. The most profound philosophical problems lie in reconciling two kinds of reality—free will and natural causality, mind and body, reason and emotion, creation and evolution.

Such *problems of reconciliation* do not arise in classical Chinese philosophy, where human strangeness is theorized through an assumed continuity with nature. Although the divine, *tian* 天, customarily translated as "heaven," exhibits anthropomorphic characteristics in some texts, it is never outside the world, and over time it becomes more and more identified with the basic order of nature itself. All things and events take shape within broad patterns of change, mostly cyclical, and all are composed of the same stuff, *qi* 氣 (vital force or energy). Human beings may be the most valuable or the most problematic, but they are just part of nature, one of the "ten thousand things" (*wanwu* 萬物). As we might expect, Chinese philosophers emphasize those very aspects of our naturalness that are neglected in Europe—embodiment, emotion, human fragility, family. They take for granted that human actions and human history are explained in the same way as any other natural change. The difficulties—more often blind spots rather than explicit problems—lie in explaining how we differ from other things, the fact that we use words, act deliberately, go against the sustainable natural order, generate massive wars, and so on, issues that have been quite easy for European philosophers to explain.

This general contrast suggests an easy model for cultural exchange or comparative philosophy, in which we take the strengths of one tradition to fill in the gaps of the other. In particular, it seems fitting to turn to Chinese philosophy now, as global warming and mass species extinctions have prompted the European tradition to take our place in nature more seriously. Leibniz projects a similar model for the exchange of complementary strengths, calling it a "commerce of light" to go along with the "commerce of goods" then growing between Europe and China.[8] The result, he says, will be "as if a European steeple were placed on a pyramid of Egypt."[9] The absurdity of Leibniz's image reveals the limits of such an approach, which misses the ways in which concepts and theories are embedded in contexts, systems, and lines of problematization. One can rarely break off a piece here and insert it over there, putting the steeple on top of the pyramid. More dangerously, such an orientation tends to simplify Chinese philosophy in two ways, making Chinese thought merely the reverse image of European thought and taking Chinese philosophy as overly harmonious and coherent, as if philosophy in China were somehow not constructed primarily around *problems*. These words of caution are not meant to devalue comparative philosophy. The goal of this essay is to use a comparative approach to illuminate blind spots on both sides, but rather than seek Chinese answers to European problems, it seeks to clarify the problems by showing how they take form when approached from an opposite direction. More specifically, the focus of this essay is on the complexities that arise when one attempts to think through human strangeness from the fundamental assumption that human beings are part of nature. To avoid overgeneralizing, this essay focuses on one text, the classical daoist text known as the *Zhuangzi*.[10]

The *Zhuangzi* is one of the earliest and most thorough attempts to think through human beings as just another of the ten thousand things. This deflation of human importance is meant to disrupt our commitments to rigid and narrow perspectives and labels, allowing us to liberate our experience so as to reach *xiaoyaoyou* 逍遙遊 (carefree wandering, wandering far and unfettered, going rambling without a destination).[11] Among the strategies the *Zhuangzi* uses to introduce this flexibility is the equalizing of human beings and other animals, as in a famous dialogue that concludes as follows:

Monkeys like gibbons as partners, bucks exchange with does, loaches play [*you* 游] with fish. Mao Qiang and Lady Li are what people consider beautiful, but if fish saw them they would enter the depths, if birds saw them they would fly high, and if deer saw them they would dash away. Of these four, which knows the world's correct beauty?[12]

The *Zhuangzi* uses dozens of species, from ducks to cranes, butterflies to praying mantises, millipedes to the mythical unipedes, but in these comparisons, fish are the most prominent, appearing in around thirty passages.[13] This essay examines three ways in which fish are discussed in the *Zhuangzi*: first, how fish illuminate the limitations of any perspective; second, how fish illustrate (positively and negatively) what it means to be at home in a setting; and third, how the relationship between fish and humans addresses the possibility and challenges of communication across different perspectives. The role of fish will provide a concrete thread leading through the broader question of how the *Zhuangzi* presents human beings as both like and unlike other animals.

First, why fish? On one level, fish stand out because of their association with water, which commonly represented the *dao* 道 (the way).[14] The *Daodejing* says:

The highest good is like Water. Water is good at benefiting the ten thousand things and it does not contend, residing in what the masses of people dislike. Thus it is close to the way.[15]

Water has generative powers, like the way. It works without struggle and by going toward what is low and obscure; it is weak and soft, but "nothing is better at overcoming what is hard and strong."[16] This association with water is built into key concepts, such as the terms for pure (*qing* 清), deep (*shen* 深), profound (*yuan* 淵), and the overflowing power (*fan* 氾) of the *dao;* all are metaphorical extensions of qualities of water (reflected in their use of the water radical: 氵). One tradition, like Thales, took water as the basic material of the universe, as in another excavated text called "The Great Oneness Gives Birth to Water" (*Taiyi Sheng Shui* 太一生水), in which the "Great Oneness" generates water, which then assists it in generating heaven and earth.[17] The importance of water runs through Confucian texts as well. Mengzi praises the great sage Yu for enacting flood control not by imposing his will but by following "the way of the water" and doing what required "no work" (*wushi* 無事); in another passage, Mengzi describes the immense power of his vital energy (*qi*) as "floodlike" (*haoran* 浩然).[18] Given these associations, the profound relationship between fish and water naturally suggests itself as a metaphor for our relationship to the way. Even so, in the *Zhuangzi*, this connection between fish and water remains largely in the background. The immediate importance of fish lies in the assumption that fish have a world and that this world is radically different from our own. In one sense, fish become symbols of radical alterity: "Fish residing in water live but human beings residing in water die."[19] When we say that someone is "swimming with the fishes," we mean they are dead. At the same time, insofar as fish are thought to have a world or a perspective, they have a status equal to that of human beings, whose own world or perspective has no privileged place in nature. In this sense, fish represent an equality or evenness across the most radical difference.

We can now turn to the particular ways in which the *Zhuangzi* uses fish. Most fundamentally, appeals to fish illuminate the constraints of our worldview in contrast to nature (*tian*) itself. Just as fish forget water, we forget the air we breathe, taking our orientation and values as absolute. Pointing out that fish do the same thing, but in an inverted world, draws our attention to the limits of perspectives.[20] This function appears clearly enough in the earlier quotation on standards of beauty, which occurs in a dialogue between "Gaptooth" and Wang Ni. The dialogue begins with a series of skeptical claims in which Wang Ni denies knowing what all things affirm in common, denies knowing that he does not know, and then denies knowing that nothing can be known. He then describes disagreements between different animals, beginning with what it means to be at home (monkeys live in trees, fish in the water), moving to different tastes, and then to erotic beauty. The passage concludes with a more radical point:

> From where I see it, the sprouts of benevolence and rightness and the pathways of right and wrong are all mixed up and chaotic. How could I know their distinctions?[21]

The use of *duan* 端 (sprout, beginning) echoes the language of Mengzi, who lists four natural and spontaneous emotions as the "sprouts" of the virtues; one of those sprouts is the tendency to label things as so or not-so, *shi* 是 or *fei* 非, here translated as "right or wrong," but with a broad sense of affirmation and negation. When Wang Ni is then asked if sagely people at least know the standards of benefit (*li* 利) and harm (*hai* 害), two key terms for the Mohists, he scoffs that sagely people are not even concerned about life and death. This conclusion reveals the dialogue's deeper purpose: to show that human standards, particularly the ethical standards of the Confucians and the Mohists, are mere impositions on nature with no objective status and no privilege over the standards of other animals.[22]

The limitations of perspective appear in a different way in the fish story that begins the following text:

> The North Sea has a fish, whose name is "Minnow." Minnow is large, no one knows how many thousands of miles. It transforms and becomes a bird, whose name is Peng. Peng's back, no one knows how many thousands of miles it is. It rouses itself and flies up, its wings like clouds on the sides of the heavens. . . . The cicada and the fledgling dove laugh at it, saying. "With determination we rise up and fly, stopping when we land in an elm or a sandalwood tree. Sometimes we don't reach it and just tumble back to the ground. What is this using ninety thousand miles and going south?"[23]

Different things have different needs and conditions, and our perspectives and judgments always reflect these limits. From the little perspective of the cicada and the dove, the giant Peng looks ridiculous. The implication is that our judgments of others are similarly flawed, and the cicada is explicitly compared to people who brag about their political influence. It is worth noting that the cicada and the dove make fun of the giant creature only after it transforms into a bird and flies through their world. Its initial condition as a fish represents a more radical alterity, utterly inaccessible, a point suggested by naming this giant fish "Minnow" (*kun* 鯤).[24]

While these passages emphasize difference, they work on the assumption that fish have perspectives, desires, and homes just as we do. This point is crucial because one could easily take the radical otherness of fish to indicate that they have no world at all, reinforcing rather than undermining human superiority. The analogy between fish and human beings underlies the second way that fish are used in the *Zhuangzi*, which is to illustrate what it means to be at home in a perspective or an environment. One passage begins as follows:

When the springs dry up, the fish reside together on land, spitting to moisten each other, but that is not as good as their forgetting each other in rivers and lakes. Praising Yao and condemning Jie is not as good as forgetting both and transforming in the way.[25]

Confucius explains as follows:

Fish go together in water, people go together in the way. For those who go together in water, dig a pond and they will be nourished. For those who go together in the way, have no work and life will stabilize. Thus it is said, fish forget each other in rivers and lakes, people forget each other in the arts of the way.[26]

The natural ease and the forgetting of fish are held up as a model for human beings. Efforts to moralize the world by praising the sage Yao and condemning the evil Jie violate this natural ease and destabilize life. The *Daodejing* presents similar critiques of morality:

Thus when the great way is abandoned, there is benevolence and rightness. When the six relations are not in harmony, there is filial piety and kindness. When the state is in chaos, there are correct ministers.[27]

At best, such moralizing efforts are signs of a disordered age, the actions of landed fish desperately spitting on each other to stay alive. At worst, this moralizing itself causes disorder by rejecting our natural being in the world in favor of rigid categories of right and wrong, almost always enforced through violence and coercion.

This contrast between fish as natural and human beings as disruptive sometimes appears in practical advice for individuals, as one passage says that, if put on land, a fish as large as a boat can be tormented by the smallest of ants because it has lost its place. People who enter the human world of political struggle bring harm on themselves in similar fashion.[28] The same practical orientation appears on a grander scale as well:

When there is much knowledge of hooks, baits, nets, and traps, the fish are disrupted in the waters. . . . When there is much knowing deception and subtle poisoning, slipperiness of "hard" and "white" and breaking up of "same" and "different," then customs are confused by disputation.[29]

Human beings disrupt their own environment in just the same way as they disrupt the environments of fish and other animals. The passage goes on to describe the systematic dislocation of the sustainable natural order:

> Thus, they rebel against the illuminating brightness of the sun and moon above, scorch the refined essence of the mountains and rivers below, and overturn the orderly progression of the four seasons in between. From little wriggling insects and the tiniest flying creatures, there are none that do not lose their natures. Deep, indeed, is the chaos brought to the world by the love of knowing![30]

While it probably sounded far-fetched in the third century BCE, the disruption of the seasons eerily points toward global warming, just as animals losing their natures (*xing* 性) points to genetic manipulation.

In these passages, the natural life of fish contrasts with the friction caused by the deliberate struggles of the greedy and the moralizing. The imperative is to *be like the fish,* pointing toward an ideal of smoothness and ease modeled on the spontaneity of nature. But the fact that this is an imperative, an *ought* rather than an *is,* already reveals the strangeness of human beings and explains why the *Constancy First* passage cited at the beginning of the essay would lament that "Chaos comes out from people." In the *Zhuangzi* passage cited earlier, the cause of this disruption is the "love of knowing" (*haozhi* 好知), which here could mean only the love of some set of categories and labels. Our exceptional ability to cause destruction and disorder lies in our ability to know and thus to construct a world of deliberate striving and artificial desires. As the *Daodejing* says,

> Do not honor the worthy and the people will not contend; do not value goods that are difficult to obtain and the people will not become robbers; do not exhibit the desirable and the hearts of the people will not be in chaos.[31]

Our deliberateness, artificiality, and striving—which would be easily explained by free will or original sin—raise profound difficulties in the more naturalistic context of daoist thought.

A view of human distinctiveness as simply bad dominates the *Daodejing* and related chapters of the *Zhuangzi*.[32] Other chapters of the *Zhuangzi,* though, present a more radical view of human potential. Thus in some passages, fish illustrate the dangers of being at home in any limited perspective or element, best shown by the desperation of fish out of water. In these cases, fish are analogous to most human beings but different from sagely people, who develop a flexibility that allows for free and easy wandering. Sometimes the text points out practical advantages of flexibility. One passage notes that fish are afraid of pelicans but not afraid of nets. The point is that if we remain absorbed in a single view or become too confident in our knowledge, we miss dangers from unexpected directions.[33] For the most part, though, the *Zhuangzi* makes a more radical claim about the ability to wander freely. This point has already appeared implicitly in the passage criticizing moralizing appeals to Yao that says that fish forget themselves in *water* but that human beings forget themselves in the *way*. This difference is expanded in another passage on being at home in water, which uses water bugs rather than fish:

> Grass-eating animals are not distressed by a change in pasture; bugs that live in water are not distressed by changing the water. They go through small changes but do not lose the greater constancy, so pleasure and anger, sorrow and joy do not enter into their breasts. Now the world is what makes the myriad things one. Attain that which makes them one and unite with it, and then the four limbs and hundred bones become like dust and dirt, and life and death, beginning and end, become like night and day so that none can cause disruption.[34]

In distinguishing small changes from greater constancy, the passage divides what animals accept and what must cause distress. Applied to us, we would expect to hear that human beings are not troubled by moves within their element, perhaps small villages (for the *Daodejing)* or family (for the Confucians). Instead, human beings can take the world itself as their element, remaining undisturbed wherever they go. Guo Xiang puts it simply: "Death and life also are small changes."[35] But other animals do *not* take life and death as small changes, as we see in the fish that spit on each other to stay alive. Thus while fish (and almost all human beings) are limited to a proper environment, sages can become at home anywhere: even death may be a return to a long-forgotten home, as Zhuangzi points out.[36] While the animal struggle to stay alive could be described as spontaneous and natural, sagely people take up a different relationship to nature.[37] They "take heaven and earth as their palace and the ten-thousand things as their treasury." Unlike the fisherman who tries to hold onto his boat by hiding it in a gully, sagely people become invulnerable to loss because they "hide the world in the world."[38]

A full explanation of how such flexibility is possible would go too far into the *Zhuangzi*'s accounts of language, knowledge, and the heart (*xin* 心, heartmind), but it is rooted in three points. First, emotions and desires are inseparable from labels. It is only when we label something as valuable that we are saddened by its loss, which is why the *Daodejing* warns against elevating the worthy and valuing things that are hard to get. The most generic of these labels are *shi* and *fei,* so and not-so or right and wrong. Second, human beings view the world in a wide variety of ways. In fact, differences between species often stand for differences among human beings. That is the fuller context for the claim that fish live in water whereas human beings die:

> Fish in water live but human beings in water die. Those that differ from each other have loves and hates that are different. Thus the first sages did not take abilities as one and did not make duties the same.[39]

Aside from differences in customs and practices, the *Zhuangzi* presents various odd characters to show that almost any perspective is possible, such as the sage Wang Tai, who saw losing his foot as like shaking off some dust.[40] Finally, perspectives change and form through experience. The formation of a fixed perspective is discussed in terms of a "completed" or "formed" heart (*chengxin* 成心):

> If we follow a completed heart and take it as our authority, who alone is without an authority? How would it be only those who know the alternations and whose hearts affirm themselves that have them? The foolish would also have them. Not yet completed in the heart but having right and wrong—this is like leaving for Yue today and arriving there yesterday.[41]

The term *cheng* 成 usually has the positive sense of forming or completing something successfully, but the *Zhuangzi* emphasizes that any formation or completion also brings a loss of potentiality. This use of *cheng* has two aspects: it emphasizes the contingency involved in how the heart (or a path) takes form, and it shows that once such a form has been taken, creativity, flexibility, and potentiality are lost. According to this passage, the labels of right and wrong, which structure our desires and emotions and lead us into contention, follow only once a heart has been "completed," locked into some fixed point of view.[42] Sagely people avoid or undo this fixation of the heart and thus can go along with whatever happens. This process is called the "fasting of the heart" (*xinzhai* 心齋).[43]

We can now turn to the third way in which fish are used in the *Zhuangzi,* which is to address the problem of understanding across perspectives. Several passages suggest that perspectives would be incommensurable and mutually unintelligible. The cicada and the little dove have no chance of understanding the giant bird Peng because their realm of experience is so much more limited. The best they could do would be to not judge. A passage in the chapter on "evening things out" explains the problem, claiming that if you and I argue, there is no one who can settle the dispute because they would have to do so from a certain perspective. If their perspective is the same as yours, they will agree with you; if the same as mine, they will agree with me; if different from us both, they will disagree with both. This problem is rooted in the fact that even when we are together (*ju* 俱), we cannot know or understand each other (*xiangzhi* 相知).[44] The *Zhuangzi* may assume that those with differently completed hearts cannot really understand each other, but the possibility of overcoming the limits of perspective suggests this is not the whole story. The very concept of incommensurability depends on having a fixed scale for measuring, but sagely people have the ability to shift scales in order to fit different circumstances.

The interaction between fish and humans takes two forms, pointing toward two ways of addressing the problem of communication. The most prominent is fishing. In a famous passage, the king of the powerful state of Chu sends two messengers to request that Zhuangzi take over his government.[45] They find Zhuangzi fishing, and he tells them of a sacred turtle whose shell has been revered in the courts for millennia. Would that turtle rather be honored like that or alive dragging its tail in the mud? Of course it would rather be alive in the mud, and Zhuangzi responds that he also would prefer to remain in the mud. While fishing may simply represent leisure, Zhuangzi is presented in a liminal position.[46] He literally turns his back on the human world, refusing to look up at the messengers, and instead faces something other, dangling a hook and hoping for a response. Fishing as openness to something other appears elsewhere as well, as in a passage that describes a fisherman who stood on a mountain by the sea, using a giant hook with twenty oxen as bait. He waited day after day for a year until finally he caught a fish so large it fed the world. The passage comments that if he had shuffled off to a drainage ditch, he would have caught only carp. While this passage points out the practical advantages of "thinking big," the person fishing in the ditch is compared to those who take themselves seriously because of their political involvements.[47] Turning toward the vast ocean and waiting for a giant fish symbolizes openness to what is outside the categories of the human world, even if it is motivated by the ultimate goal of benefiting humanity. One passage explicitly connects fishing to communication:

> A fish-trap is for fish; once you get the fish you forget the trap. A snare is for rabbits; once you get the rabbit you forget the snare. Words are for intentions; once you get the intention you forget the words. Where can I get a person who forgets words, so that I can have a word with him?[48]

The use of fishing as a metaphor for communication across perspectives or worlds shows a profound awareness of the difficulty of the problem. On the one hand, we can do no more than remain open and wait for some response, for a bite. We cannot coerce someone into communication; we must lure them in. On the other hand, that waiting still takes a particular form from out of our own concerns—the hook or trap. If so, then there is an unavoidable tension between our genuine desire for openness and the fact that this openness must project from our perspective in some specific form. One possibility is that we do our best to forget the trap as soon as we make that initial connection, as Zhuangzi suggests. A more radical possibility appears in another passage, where the greatest fisherman is said to not even use a hook:

> As one who did not insist his fishing have a hook, he was always fishing.[49]

King Wen recognized this fisherman as a sage and put him in charge of the state. Because he did nothing, factions and struggles eventually ceased, and everyone came to form one community. When King Wen began speaking of conquering the world, though, the fisherman wandered away.

A different approach appears in a dialogue between Zhuangzi and his friend Huizi, a philosopher of the time famous for his paradoxes:

Zhuangzi and Huizi wandered (*you* 遊) on the bridge above the River Hao. Zhuangzi said, "The minnows come out and swim (*you* 遊) freely—this is the joy of fish." Huizi said, "You are not a fish. How do you know the joy of fish?" Zhuangzi said. "You are not me. How do you know I do not know the joy of fish?" Huizi said, "I am not you, so I surely do not know you. You surely are not a fish, so you do not know the joy of fish. That is the whole thing!" Zhuangzi said, "Please follow it back to the beginning. You said, 'How do you know the joy of fish?' and so on. So you already knew I knew it and then asked me. I know it above the Hao River."[50]

Zhuangzi takes the gap between human beings and fish to be the same in kind as the gap between himself and his best friend, Huizi. Thus either some understanding between human beings and fish is possible, or there is no understanding at all. In fact, Huizi's claim that since he is not Zhuangzi he does not know (*buzhi* 不知) him echoes the claim that disputes cannot be settled because we cannot know each other (*buneng xiangzhi* 不能相知). Thus Huizi affirms the position of incommensurability. Zhuangzi, though, does not back away from his claim that the fish are joyful. The difficulty is in how this understanding is possible. Zhuangzi's response, that he knows it by his location on the bridge, seems to be simply a clever play on the fact that the Chinese for "how," *an* 安, can also mean "where," but one clue to the basis for Zhuangzi's knowledge lies in the way the passage plays on another term, *you* 遊, translated as "wandering" in the ideal of "free and easy wandering" but extending to a sense of ease and play, as in a passage in which "Cloud General" comes across a sage named "Vast Ignorance," who is "slapping his butt and hopping like a bird."[51] When asked what he is doing, Vast Ignorance replies: *you*. The term *you* 遊 is nearly identical to the term for swimming, *you* 游. The first has the "walk" (辶) radical, and the second has the radical for water (氵), but in practice, the two were often interchangeable.[52] In the happy fish passage, Zhuangzi and Huizi are said to *you* 遊: to wander (or swim or play) onto the bridge, just as the fish below are said to *you* 遊: to wander (or swim or play) in the water. On one level, then, Zhuangzi might be saying that although we can never see the world as a fish or even as our best friend does, we can know when something is at ease in its environment, swimming, wandering, or playing, just as one does not need to be a fish in order to recognize their distress out of water.

On another level, Zhuangzi may see communication as possible because he, Huizi, and the fish all "wander," "play," or "swim" together in the same situation. This is why he knows it by virtue of being *there*, above the river.[53] For such communication, though, persons must give up the limits of their narrow perspectives. Otherwise, we end up like the dove, laughing at Peng, or the philosophers, arguing endlessly from different perspectives. This connection between swimming and wandering comes up in a passage that violates the basic alterity between fish and humans—the fact that in water human beings die. The passage begins with Confucius contemplating a river with rapids so violent that even fish cannot enter. He sees a man go into the water and rushes to rescue him, but the man emerges on his own, singing happily. Confucius asks in awe whether the swimmer has a way, a *dao*, that allows him to tread the water like this. The swimmer responds as follows:

> No, I have no *dao*. I begin in what is originary, grow in my nature, and take form by the conditions. I go in together with the center of the whirlpools and come out as companion to the surging torrent. I follow along with the way of the water and do not impose my own interests on it. This is how I do my treading.[54]

The passage uses two terms emphasizing togetherness and companionship, *ju* 俱 and *xie* 偕, respectively. The term translated as "companion to," *xie*, appears in an ancient poem from the *Books of Odes*, "The Wife Says the Rooster Crows":

> When they are ready, we will drink,
>   And I will grow old together (*xie*) with you.
>   With your lute in hand,
>   All will be quiet and good.[55]

The term *ju* has a similar meaning and has appeared earlier, in the passage which says that if you, I, and another person are together (*ju*), we still cannot settle a dispute because we cannot know each other. The swimmer does not attempt to dispute or convey his ideas. On the contrary, he is able to achieve this community or communion with the rushing water because he gives up any personal imposition (*si* 私). He has no way of his own, so he can follow along with the way of the water. This is what allows him to be at home in the most foreign environment. Ironically, the verb used to describe the man in the water is literally to "tread" or "step" (*dao* 蹈), a character containing the symbol for a foot (足), while it is only once the man emerges from the water that he is then said to *you* 游, to swim (or wander or play) along its bank. Although the issue of communication is not raised explicitly, one who has broken free of constraining views is able to wander or swim in anyone's world, even one as radically different as that of a fish.

The contrast between fishing and wandering in companionship as models of communication may be addressed on a more technical level by the idea of the fasting of the heart, which appears in the following advice:

> Make your resolve one. Do not listen with your ears but listen with your heart. Do not listen with your heart but listen with *qi* (氣, vital force). Hearing stops at the ears, the heart stops at symbols (fu 符). *Qi* is empty and awaits things. Only the way gathers emptiness. Emptiness is the fasting of the heart![56]

The origin of *fu* 符 (symbols or tallies) is in a system for guaranteeing the authenticity of commands. It refers to a piece of bamboo that would be split into two and then given to two parties; the authenticity of a command from one party could then be recognized if the two pieces fit together. Saying that the heart is limited to *fu*, then, is saying that what we can recognize is always limited by our own preconceptions and wishes.[57] The limits of *fu* resemble the limits of the hook or trap, the concrete expectation or goal that provides limits no matter how open we seek to be. The alternative is to become empty of expectations, labels, or goals and simply respond to the moment, here conceptualized as relying on the movements of *qi*, the energy or vital force animating all things. This reliance on emptiness and *qi* may sound like mysticism at best and nonsense at worst; in either case, it hardly satisfies as a philosophical answer to the problem of communication across perspectives. To see what the *Zhuangzi* is getting at, though, we must set aside any concept of communication as transferring ideas from one mind to another and instead focus on something more like cooperation or community. Consider the "communication" involved when two people dance or play together on a sports team. These require an attunement and subtlety of response that could never be captured on a conceptual or linguistic level—consider the limits of explaining to someone how they should move to pass the ball through two defenders or to spin gracefully. This kind of communication or communing is impossible if one acts only when one thinks or if one imposes one's own interest on another person. It requires something much like what the swimmer describes: giving up one's own way and following the way of the other so as to become the other's companion. Thus although seeing the world like a fish is as implausible as seeing the world like a bat, cooperation through engagement in a common situation is less implausible. Certainly many people claim to achieve this kind of understanding with their pets—and with their friends.

I began by noting that the *Zhuangzi* is one of the most consistent attempts to think through human beings as just another animal. Ironically, this attempt ends up revealing human beings as quite different. This emergence of human uniqueness should not be surprising if my initial claim about the strangeness of human beings is correct, but what is striking is the form this uniqueness takes, particularly when contrasted with its common forms in European philosophy. In Europe, the exceptional nature of human beings lies in some combination of the status of our moral principles and our knowledge. At a minimum, we are unique in recognizing and being subject to morality; frequently, our morality is seen as an objective part of the universe itself. Similarly, we human beings are exceptional in our ability to attain abstract, universal, or necessary truths; other animals at best have a kind of empirical know-how and, more often, have no knowledge at all. These marks of human uniqueness appear not just where we would expect, in highly anthropocentric thinkers like Augustine or Kant, but also in philosophers who, like Zhuangzi, emphasize our position as parts of nature. For example, Spinoza launches a devastating attack on the conception of human beings in nature as "a dominion within a dominion (*imperium in imperio*)," rejecting those who would explain human actions as something "outside of nature," but ultimately only human beings have the possibility of achieving adequate knowledge, which in turn enables us "to live from the leadership of reason" (*ex ducto rationis vivunt*) and even to attain a kind of immortality.[58] For a more contemporary example, although Peter Singer argues against radically distinguishing human beings from other animals *in terms of value*, he also claims that human beings are uniquely subject to morality, which follows from our greater capacity to know.[59]

In the more naturalistic context of early Chinese philosophy, the status of human knowledge and ethics is reversed. First, the ways in which fish respond to the world and seek their own survival are seen as the same in kind as what human beings consider knowledge and ethics. This assumption is common among other classical Chinese philosophers, for example, Mengzi, who argues that human beings must have a distinct nature (*xing* 性) precisely because every species has a distinct nature. Thus Mengzi claims that organic order (*li* 理) and rightness (*yi* 義) please our hearts in the same way that roasted meats please our mouths and that what pleases the mouth varies by species.[60] Even though our concerned relationships in the world are more complex and self-aware (and thus for the Confucians, we are more precious), all animals have them in their own way. Here again we see the priority of continuity with nature. For Zhuangzi, what makes human beings exceptional is that we can recognize that our knowledge and ethics have no more validity than those of any other species. One immediate result is that human uniqueness does not entail claims that human beings are more valuable.

This recognition naturally lessens our sense of self-importance and our attachments to the world. More radically, the awareness and flexibility of human beings empties the human of any fixed content.[61] One passage makes this point explicitly in claiming that sagely people no longer have fixed human emotions:

> Since they receive food from heaven, what use are humans! They have human form but do not have essential human feelings (*qing* 情). Having human form, they flock with humans. Not having essential human feelings, judgments of right and wrong do not reach to their selves.

Zhuangzi's friend Huizi then challenges him:

> Huizi said, "Since you call them human, how can they not have *qing*?" Zhuangzi said, "'Right' and 'wrong' are what I call *qing*. What I call having no *qing* refers to people not letting loves and hates inside to harm their persons, constantly relying on spontaneity and not adding to life."[62]

The term *qing* 情 in general means the essential or genuine reactions of a thing; in human beings, it refers to emotions. *Qing* is closely connected to the term for human nature, *xing*, where *xing* represents characteristic ways of reacting and *qing* are the reactions themselves. Thus the claim that sagely people lack human *qing* is really a claim that human beings need not be constrained by a fixed nature. In this, we stand in contrast to other animals. The flexibility of human emotions and desires follows from the flexibility in how we label things, how we apply *shi* and *fei* (right and wrong, or so and not-so). This flexibility usually has bad results, as it allows us to label trivial things as valuable, thus making them a source of contention and discontent. The same flexibility, though, allows sagely people to affirm whatever happens, becoming free of negative emotions. This is not letting likes and dislikes harm us, and it results in spontaneity, not adding to life, and wandering free and easy.

Paradoxically, what makes human beings exceptional is our freedom from being human: We can have human form without essential human emotions. This context explains why the Confucian philosopher Xunzi would say that Zhuangzi knew heaven but did not know the human since, for Zhuangzi, being human entails no fixed limits. Xunzi says that this blindness toward the human led Zhuangzi to emphasize only going along with things (*yin* 因).[63] This emptying the human of any fixed content—this "fasting of the heart"—does not lead to exiting the concrete world for some mystical unity with a transcendent heaven. Rather, awareness of nature/heaven provides a pivot within our singular experience, allowing shifts in how we label the concrete world around us. Ultimately, this flexibility allows us to affirm nature, not as the abstract oneness of all things but in its singularity in any moment.[64] The passage that best illustrates this flexibility is the famous story of Zhuangzi's reaction to the death of his wife. In that situation, he first feels sorrow, a kind of *qing* or feeling, then considers the broader context of nature, and finally ends up feeling joy, singing and banging on a tub.[65] In the possibility of such a shift, one sees a kind of freedom that may be uniquely human, but far from placing any ethical burden upon us, this freedom is a freedom from fixed ethical imperatives, claims of knowledge, or even set desires. In the *Zhuangzi,* this freedom not only allows us to recognize our insignificance in the world but also to accept it. Ironically, the possibility of accepting our status as merely another animal in nature may be what makes us most human—and most exceptional.[66]

NOTES

Epigraph. Sophocles, *Antigone.* Stanzas 332–334, in Peter Meineck and Paul Woodruff, trans., *Sophocles: Theban Plays* (Indianapolis: Hackett, 2003), 62. The translation is slightly modified from the word-for-word translation they give in the footnote.

Epigraph. Collected Sayings I. Liu Zhao 劉釗, ed., *Guodian Chujian Jiaoshi* 郭店楚簡校釋 (Fuzhou: Fujian Renmin Chubanshe, 2003), strip 18.

Epigraph. Constancy First. Cao Feng 曹峰, *Shanghai chujian sixiang yanjiu* 上海楚簡想研究 (Taipei: Wanjuanlou, 2006), strip 8.

1. Martha Nussbaum writes of the term *deinon* as follows: "Most generally, it is used of that which inspires awe or wonder. But in different contexts it can be used of the dazzling brilliance of the human intellect, of the monstrousness of an evil, of the terrible power of fate. That which is *deinon* is somehow strange, out of place; its strangeness and its capacity to inspire awe are intimately connected." Martha Nussbaum, *The Fragility of Goodness: Luck and Ethics in Greek Tragedy and Philosophy* (Cambridge: Cambridge University Press, 1986), 52. This complex sense of *deinon* usually forces translators to use more than one word. The more literary translation of Meineck and Woodruff is "Many wonders, many terrors, / But none more wonderful than the human race / Or more dangerous" (*Sophocles,* 16). Similarly, Robert Fagle translates *deinon* as "numberless wonders, terrible wonders." Robert Fagle, *Sophocles: The Three Theban Plays* (New York: Penguin, 1984), 76.

2. *Mengzi* 3A4 says that people were like animals until they were taught proper social relationships. All references to *Mengzi* are to Jiao Xun 焦循, *Mengzi zhengyi* 孟子正義, 2 vols. (Beijing: Zhonghua Shuju Chubanshe, 1987), cited by chapter, part A or B, and passage. In *Xunzi* 5.9, human beings are said to be distinct from (and able to eat) other bipeds because we can make distinctions, but the following passage explains social roles as the main kind of distinction. References to *Xunzi* are to Li Disheng 李滌生, *Xunzi jishi* 荀子集釋 (Taipei: Xuesheng Shuju, 1979), but are cited according to the divisions in John Knoblock, trans.. *Xunzi: A Translation and Study of the Complete Works,* 3 vols. (Stanford, CA: Stanford University Press, 1988, 1990, 1994).

3. The emphasis on distinct "schools" in Warring States China is misleading, and the category of "daoism" arose only later. The texts excavated from the end of the fourth century further blur the lines, and neither of the texts referenced here can be easily categorized. See the discussion of these issues in Mark Csikszentmihalyi, *Material Virtue: Ethics and the Body in Early China* (Leiden: Brill, 2001), 10, 15–32, and Edward Slingerland, "The Problem of Moral Spontaneity in the Guodian Corpus," in *Dao: A Journal of Comparative Philosophy* 7, no. 3 (2008): 239–240. Nonetheless, the claim that human beings are most precious is typical of the Confucians, and the view of human beings as most disruptive appears more in texts labeled as daoist.

4. Heidegger explains: "It is only for this reason that the un-homely [*das Unheimische*] can, as a consequence, also be 'uncanny' ['*unheimlich*'] in the sense of something that has an alienating or "frightening" effect that gives rise to anxiety." Martin Heidegger, *Hölderlin's Hymn "The Ister,"* trans. William McNeill and Julia Davis (Bloomington: Indiana University Press, 1996), 71, 63–64.

5. The theme runs throughout Socrates' "Second Speech" in the *Phaedrus.* Alexander Nehamas and Paul Woodruff, trans., *Phaedrus* (Indianapolis: Hackett, 1995).

6. Both quotations are from section 9 of *The Birth of Tragedy*, in Friedrich Nietzsche, *Werke in Drei Bänden* (Munich: Hanser, 1954), 59.

7. The divine is not absent, as *tian* 天 or *Shang Di* 上帝 were thought to reward virtue and thus explain the success of the sages. There may have been early origin myths involving gods, but even if so, it is striking that they had no significance for the philosophers of the classical period.

8. Leibniz uses the phrase "commerce of light" in a letter from 1697 to the Jesuit Antoine Verjus, who was a supervisor of the Jesuit mission in China. Rita Widmaier, ed., *Leibniz korrespondiert mit China* (Frankfurt: Klostermann, 1990), 55. For the claim that China and Europe have complementary strengths, see Leibniz's "Preface to the *Novissima Sinica*," also written in 1697. Daniel Cook and Henry Rosemont Jr., eds. and trans., *Writings on China* (Chicago: Open Court, 1994).

9. "Preface to the *Novissima Sinica*," section 7, 49. The phrase describes the Chinese emperor Kangxi's combination of Chinese and European knowledge. For an analysis of Leibniz's views of China and approach to comparative philosophy, see Franklin Perkins, *Leibniz and China: A Commerce of Light* (Cambridge: Cambridge University Press, 2004).

10. Everyone agrees that the *Zhuangzi* is an anthology, but it is common to take the first seven "inner" chapters as representing a coherent view identified with the historical Zhuangzi, who lived in the fourth century BCE. There is little evidence for this position, though, and the inner chapters clearly present multiple positions, some more radical than others. Here, I simply pursue one of the more radical lines without insisting it is the only one in the inner chapters. In short, I follow Lee Yearley's hope to avoid the problem of authorship by talking about "tendencies or motifs or strands in the *Zhuangzi*." Lee Yearley, "The Perfected Person in the Radical Chuang-tzu [Zhuangzi]," in *Experimental Essays on Chuang-Tzu*, ed. Victor Mair (Honolulu: University of Hawai'i Press, 1983), 125. When referring to "Zhuangzi" as a person, I mean only the character of that name who occasionally appears in the text. The same applies to "Confucius" and "Hui Shi," who should be taken as characters in the *Zhuangzi*.

11. The phrase is the title of the first chapter. The first translation is from Victor Mair, trans., *Wandering on the Way: Early Taoist Tales and Parable of Chuang Tzu* (Honolulu: University of Hawai'i Press, 1994); the second from Brook Ziporyn, trans., *Zhuangzi: The Essential Writings, with Selections from Traditional Commentaries* (Indianapolis: Hackett, 2009); the third from Angus C. Graham, trans., *Chuang-Tzu: The Inner Chapters* (Indianapolis: Hackett, 2001).

12. *Zhuangzi*, ch. 2; cf. Mair, *Wandering on the Way*, 20–21. References to the *Zhuangzi* are based on the text in Guo Qingfan 郭慶藩, *Zhuangzi jishi* 莊子集釋 (Beijing: Zhonghua Shuju, 1978). All translations are my own, but for reference, I have also cited the page numbers in Mair's translation.

13. In addition, there are a number of references to fishermen. For a study of these, see Kirill Ole Thompson, "What Is the Reason of Failure or Success? The Fisherman's Song Goes Deep into the River: Fishermen in the *Zhuangzi*," in Roger T. Ames, ed., *Wandering at Ease in the Zhuangzi* (Albany: State University of New York, 1998).

14. Thompson discusses this point in more detail in relation to the importance of fishing; see ibid., 16–19.

15. *Daodejing* 8. References to the *Daodejing* are to the Mawangdui version unless otherwise noted, as published in Liu Xiaogan 劉笑敢, *Laozi gujin* 老子古今 (Beijing: Zhongguo Shehui Kexue Chubanshe, 2006), cited by chapter number.

16. Ibid., 78.

17. Liu Zhao (2003), strip 42. For a translation of this text, see Robert G. Henricks, *Lao Tzu's Tao Te Ching: A Translation of the Startling New Documents Found at Guodian* (New York: Columbia University Press, 2000), 123–129.

18. *Mengzi* 6B11, 4B26, and 2A2, respectively. For an excellent examination of water metaphors in classical Chinese thought, see Sarah Allan, *The Way of Water and the Sprouts of Virtue* (Albany: State University of New York, 1997).

19. *Zhuangzi*, ch. 18; Mair, *Wandering on the Way*, 171–172.

20. David Wong nicely explains this function of appeals to nature in the *Zhuangzi* in David Wong, "Identifying with Nature in Early Daoism," *Journal of Chinese Philosophy* 36, no. 4 (2009): 68–84.

21. *Zhuangzi*, ch. 2; Mair, *Wandering on the Way*, 20–21.

22. There must be something natural about the connection between skepticism and the elevation of other animals. Sextus Empiricus gives an almost identical argument, first describing differences in taste between animals and then concluding that we cannot know which is correct, "[f]or we cannot ourselves judge between our own impressions and those of the other animals, since we ourselves are involved in the dispute and are, therefore, rather in need of a judge than competent to pass judgment ourselves." R. G. Bury, *Outlines of Pyrrhonian Skepticism* (Cambridge, MA: Harvard University Press, Loeb Library, 1993), book I, section 5. For a comparison between Zhuangzi and Sextus Empiricus, see Paul Kjellberg, "Sextus Empiricus, Zhuangzi, and Xunzi on 'Why Be Skeptical?'" in Paul Kjellberg and Philip J. Ivanhoe, eds., *Essays on Skepticism, Relativism, and Ethics in the* Zhuangzi (Albany: State University of New York, 1996). David Hume also emphasizes the similarity between human and animal reasoning in the chapter "Of the Reason of Animals" in *An Enquiry concerning Human Understanding*.

23. *Zhuangzi*, ch.1; Mair, *Wandering on the Way*, 3–4.

24. Brook Ziporyn (*Essential Writings*, 3) has a good discussion of the meanings of both names, bringing out the association of their phonetic elements with companionship: Kun 鲲 combines "fish" (*yu* 魚) and "older brother" (*kun* 昆); Peng 鵬 combines "bird" (*niao* 鳥) and "friend" (*peng* 朋).

25. *Zhuangzi*, ch. 6; Mair, *Wandering on the Way*, 53.

26. *Zhuangzi*, ch. 6; Mair, *Wandering on the Way*, 61.

27. *Daodejing*, 18. Here I have followed the Guodian version of the chapter in Liu Xiaogan, *Laozi gujin*.

28. *Zhuangzi*, ch. 23; Mair, *Wandering on the Way*, 226–227.

29. *Zhuangzi*, ch. 10; Mair, *Wandering on the Way*, 88–89. "Hard" and "white" and "same" and "different" were all common terms of dispute among philosophers and analysts of language. The first two words refer to the problem of the relationship between the hardness and the whiteness of a white stone.

30. *Zhuangzi*, ch. 10; Mair, *Wandering on the Way*, 89. Although the point of the passage is clear, the specific terms are difficult to work out. Compare the translations in Mair, *Wandering on the Way*, 88–89; Ziporyn, *Essential Writings*, 65–66, and Graham, *Inner Chapters*, 209–210.

31. *Daodejing* 3.

32. Chapters 8–10 of the *Zhuangzi* in particular seem to develop the philosophy of the *Daodejing* and are commonly labeled as the "primitivist" chapters following a suggestion by A. C. Graham.

33. *Zhuangzi*, ch. 26; Mair, *Wandering on the Way*, 274.

34. *Zhuangzi*, ch. 21; Mair, *Wandering on the Way*, 202.

35. Guo, *Zhuangzi jishi*, 715.

36. *Zhuangzi*, ch. 2; Mair, *Wandering on the Way*, 22.

37. Most commentators ignore this disanalogy. For example, Steve Coutinho relies on the analogy with animal tastes to argue for natural human standards. Steve Coutinho, *Zhuangzi and Early Chinese Philosophy: Vagueness, Transformation and Paradox* (Burlington, VT: Ashgate, 2004), 62–67. Thompson ("Failure or Success" 19) mentions fish only as a model for the sage. One exception is Lee Yearley ("Zhuangzi's Understanding of Skillfulness and the Ultimate Spiritual State," in Kjellberg and Ivanhoe [*Essays*], 155), who contrasts instinctive drives with "transcendent" drives: "unlike certain other Daoists (some of whose ideas appear in the *Zhuangzi*), Zhuangzi's spiritual fulfillment does not consist in the childlike gratification of 'natural' or instinctive dispositional drives. Rather he wants people to be animated by transcendent drives."

38. *Zhuangzi*, chaps. 5 and 6; Mair, *Wandering on the Way*, 43–44, 55.

39. *Zhuangzi*, ch. 18; Mair, *Wandering on the Way*, 172.

40. *Zhuangzi*, ch. 5; Mair, *Wandering on the Way*, 43.

41. *Zhuangzi*, ch. 2; Mair, *Wandering on the Way*, 14.

42. For the various senses of *cheng*, see the glossary in Ziporyn, *Essential Writings*, 213.

43. *Zhuangzi*, ch. 4; Mair, *Wandering on the Way*, 32. This concept is discussed further later on.

44. *Zhuangzi*, ch. 2; Mair, *Wandering on the Way*, 23.

45. *Zhuangzi*, ch. 17; Mair, *Wandering on the Way*, 164.

46. Thompson ("Failure or Success," 22) also emphasizes that Zhuangzi is in a pivotal position as "the halfway point between sagehood and nonsagehood."

47. *Zhuangzi*, ch. 26; Mair, *Wandering on the Way*, 270.

48. *Zhuangzi*, ch. 26; Mair, *Wandering on the Way*, 276–277.

49. *Zhuangzi*, ch. 21; Mair, *Wandering on the Way*, 205. The passage is extremely dense and difficult to translate, partly because *diao* 釣 can be the verb "to fish" or the noun "fishhook." I follow Mair in distinguishing the two meanings, but the original sounds more paradoxical and could be translated as "did not insist that his fishing have fishing." Graham (*Inner Chapters*, 140) translates it as follows: "he was not someone fishing-rod in hand fishing for something." In any case, the point is not so much about the hook but about not having any set goal.

50. *Zhuangzi*, ch. 17; Mair, *Wandering on the Way*, 165.

51. *Zhuangzi*, ch. 11; Mair, *Wandering on the Way*, 97.

52. The *Zhuangzi* contains many examples of *you* 游 (to swim) being used for wandering on land. The relationship between the two characters has been further blurred because the "simplified" writing system used now in mainland China has eliminated 遊, using only 游 for both characters.

53. Ames ("Knowing in the *Zhuangzi*: 'From Here, on the Bridge, of the River Hao,'" in Ames [*Wandering at Ease*], 220) takes the main point of the story as showing that "knowledge is always proximate, situational, participatory, and interpretative." Ames (ibid., 221) argues that because of their mutual interconnection, what is happy in the story is not so much the fish as the situation itself. (A new version of the original essay appears in this volume.)

54. *Zhuangzi*, ch. 19; Mair, *Wandering on the Way*, 182.

55. *Shijing*, Mao #184, translation modified from that of James Legge, trans., *The Chinese Classics, with a Translation, Critical and Exegetical Notes, Prolegomena, and*

Copious Indexes, 5 vols. (Hong Kong: Legge, 1861–1872), vol. 1. In contemporary Chinese, one still has the phrase "white heads growing older together" (*baitou xielao* 白頭偕老).

56. *Zhuangzi,* ch. 4; Mair, *Wandering on the Way,* 32.

57. Thus Ziporyn (*Essential Writings,* 26) translates it as follows: "The mind is halted at whatever verifies its preconceptions."

58. For opposition to the conception of human beings as outside of nature, see *Ethics,* part I, appendix. Part II describes adequate knowledge in propositions 38–47. Although Spinoza does not say *only* human beings have it, he does consistently say that such knowledge belongs specifically to human beings (for example, part II, proposition 38, corollary, "Hence it follows that there are certain ideas or notions *common to all human beings*"; emphasis added). Part IV, proposition 35 discusses living under the leadership of reason. Part V, proposition 23 says that the mind is not entirely destroyed with the body, but something of it is eternal. References to Spinoza are based on Carl Gebhardt, ed., *Spinoza Opera* (Heidelberg: Heidelberger Akademie der Wissenschaften, 1925).

59. Singer writes, "The point, of course, is that nonhuman animals are not capable of considering alternatives, or of reflecting morally on the rights and wrongs of killing for food; they just do it. . . . Every reader of this book, on the other hand, is capable of making a moral choice on this matter. We cannot evade our responsibility for our choice by imitating the actions of beings who are incapable of making this kind of choice." Peter Singer, *Animal Liberation: The Definitive Classic of the Animal Movement* (New York: Harper Perennial, 2009), 224–225.

60. *Mengzi* 6A7.

61. The status of the human is one of the key questions dividing commentators. For examples placing more emphasis on the human, see Philip J. Ivanhoe, "Was Zhuangzi a Relativist?" in Kjellberg and Ivanhoe (*Essays,* 196–214), and see Coutinho (*Vagueness*). The best representatives of readings more on the side of leaving the human are Robert Eno, "Cook Ding's Dao and the Limits of Philosophy," in Kjellberg and Ivanhoe (*Essays,* 127–151), and Yearley ("Perfected Person"). Yearley argues against taming the *Zhuangzi* into a "pragmatic approach" that would have us live fairly normal lives with just a bit more tolerance and skepticism, although he emphasizes that there are multiple voices in the *Zhuangzi.* My own interpretation is closest to that of Yearley.

62. *Zhuangzi,* ch. 5; Mair, *Wandering on the Way,* 49.

63. *Xunzi* 21.5.

64. In seeing the conflict between our labels and appreciating the world as it is, the *Zhuangzi* has some analogies with what Nietzsche says about morality: "For, facing morality (especially Christian, or unconditional, morality), life must constantly and inevitably be wrong because life is something essentially amoral; in the end, crushed under the heaviness of contempt and the eternal No, life feels unworthy of desire and in itself worthless." "Attempt at a Self-Criticism," section 5, in Nietzsche (*Werke in Drei Bänden,* vol. 1, 151).

65. *Zhuangzi,* ch. 18; Mair, *Wandering on the Way,* 169.

66. This essay benefited from discussions of earlier versions presented at the annual meeting of the International Association for Environmental Philosophy and at the inaugural Henan Daoist Salon. I am grateful to the participants and to Zhu Tieyu for sponsoring the latter conference. I am also grateful for suggestions from my colleague H. Peter Steeves and for the careful editing of Max Wong.

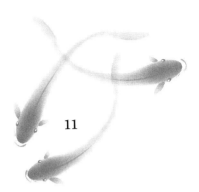

11

The Happy Fish of the Disputers

HAN Xiaoqiang

> Zhuangzi and Hui Shi were strolling on the bridge above the Hao river. Zhuangzi said, "Out swim the minnows so free and easy, this is the happiness of fish." Hui Shi said, "You are not a fish. Whence do you know the happiness of fish?" Zhuangzi said, "You are not me. Whence do you know I don't know the happiness of fish?" Hui Shi said, "Granted that I am not you, I don't know about you. Then granted that you are not a fish, the case for your not knowing the happiness of fish is complete." Zhuangzi said, "Let's trace back to the root of the issue. When you said, '*Whence* do you know the fish are happy?', you asked me already knowing I knew it. I knew it from up above the Hao."
> GRAHAM, *CHUANG-TZU: THE INNER CHAPTERS*

The conversation between Zhuangzi and Hui Shi in this intriguing story is so enigmatic that what it is meant to convey is often deemed curiously elusive. On the one hand, the story, as Chad Hansen characterizes it, "is one of a small cluster of examples of reasoning in ancient Chinese texts that Sinologists recognise as having a surface resemblance to Western philosophy more than to the manifest image of Chinese thought."[1] It has a "surface resemblance" because it appears to contain the use of reductio ad absurdum, generally considered a pattern of deductive reasoning familiar to the West but uncommon in the Chinese philosophical tradition.[2] On the other hand, this sense of resemblance quickly fades away as the

Originally published in *Asian Philosophy* 22, no. 3 (August 2012). Reprinted with permission.

debaters in the story do not seem to go where the perceived logic is supposed to lead, as one can expect in Plato's dialogues. In particular, they seem to proceed either by glaringly ignoring the contradiction exhibited by the reductio or by playing cheap sophistry to escape refutation. Because of this, the story serves to rather strengthen the manifest image of Chinese thought and has become, in the words of Peter Hoffmann, with a little exaggeration, "a symbol for the problems Westerners have with China or, in less self-critical instances, a symbol for the illogical queerness of Chinese thinking."[3] Although the charge of Chinese thinking being illogical may itself be part of the enduring China fantasy that is amusingly exemplified in Borges' description of the "Chinese encyclopaedia," the story does present some extraordinary difficulty that thwarts efforts to construe it in a logically coherent manner.[4]

Let's first read the story in a way that many may find largely unproblematic. Zhuangzi initiates the conversation by inviting Hui Shi to observe a scene of fish swimming around with great ease and playfulness and asserting, "This is the happiness of fish." Hui Shi's immediate response is a question that would naturally be construed as a demand for a justification for the truth of Zhuangzi's assertion, "You are not a fish. Whence do you know the happiness of fish?" Apparently Hui Shi is not satisfied with the reason Zhuangzi has already given; the latter derives his judgment about the happiness of fish from his observation of the way fish swim, which for Hui Shi is perhaps either insufficient or simply irrelevant. So he ignores it altogether and ask for a reason that appears to be based on the following unstated claim: you must be a fish in order to know the happiness of fish. So understood, Hui Shi's challenge sounds quite reasonable. The way fish swim, if it indicates anything unique to fish at all, is like linguistic expressions that can be understood only by those who master the language of which the expressions are a part.

Thus, it may well be the case, as many commentators have acknowledged, that Hui Shi is here talking about fish and human beings only as different species.[5] To say that Zhuangzi is not a fish is simply to say that he does not know the language of fish. However, Zhuangzi responds to Hui Shi's question with a question, "You are not me. Whence do you know I don't know the happiness of fish?" Zhuangzi's response seems to take it as an unstated assumption that for an individual to understand the mental state of another, the individual must become that other, an assumption that is made to look as if it is borrowed from Hui Shi, but it is not the one Hui Shi is understood to more likely to be making in his challenge. Interestingly, this logical leap is not rejected by Hui Shi, who detects no harm in accepting Zhuangzi's interpretation of his assumption and goes on to reiterate his initial challenge, "granted that you are not a fish, the case for your not knowing the happiness of fish is complete." What is so puzzling to many is that Hui Shi seems totally blind to the contradiction Zhuangzi has shown him. No less perplexing is the way Zhuangzi settles the debate; he seems to employ what many deem cheap sophistry: "Let's trace back to the root of the issue. When you said, '*Whence* do you know the fish are happy?' you asked me already knowing I knew it. I knew it from up above the Hao."[6]

THE FIRST CONTRADICTION

The story, according to many, contains the use(s) of reductio ad absurdum.[7] There does seem to be a reductio ad absurdum at least in Zhuangzi's response to Hui Shi's challenge. *Reductio ad absurdum* as standardly used is a method of proof that tries to establish a proposition by deriving a falsity or an absurdity from its denial. It can also refer to any form of refutation that shows that a certain proposition is false because it necessarily leads to contradictory or absurd consequences. Zhuangzi's response, "You are not me. Whence do you know I don't know the happiness of fish?" shows that Hui Shi's question, when understood as a refutation of Zhuangzi's claim that he knows the happiness of fish, necessarily leads to a contradiction. Now what exactly is the contradiction, and how does Hui Shi's refutation of Zhuangzi's claim result in it? Chad Hansen argues in his essay "The Relatively Happy Fish" that Hui Shi's skeptical challenge to Zhuangzi's initial claim implicitly commits him to there being a single correct *standard* for claiming knowledge of fish happiness—the self or subjective standard: in order to know the inner state of x, whether affective or cognitive, one must be x.[8] According to Hansen, it is precisely because of this commitment that Hui Shi is led by Zhuangzi into a reductio: Hui Shi both knows that Zhuangzi does not know the happiness of the fish and does not know whether Zhuangzi knows the happiness of the fish.[9] However, Hansen thinks that Hui Shi, in drawing the conclusion that he does not know whether Zhuangzi knows the happiness of fish, could have used his subjective standard in two ways: either in a direct or in an inferential way, although he chose the latter way. Using it in a direct way, Hui Shi knows directly that he does not know what Zhuangzi knows; using it in an indirect way, Hui Shi infers from the standard that he does not know Zhuangzi's knowing.[10] Now the problem is how Hui Shi can ever use the standard in a direct way. A standard is something that is used to judge the quality of something else (that is, being subjective in this case) and is therefore not identical to the latter. To know a standard is to know something general, and to use a standard is to apply a general statement to a particular thing or situation (or to judge whether a certain particular thing or situation conforms to a general characterization). Thus, to use a standard is necessarily to use it inferentially. Hui Shi may just know directly that he does not know what Zhuangzi knows, but that is not a consequence of his use of the standard in any way. Whenever he uses the standard, he is compelled to use it inferentially.

From the subjective standard, Hui Shi infers that Zhuangzi does not know the happiness of fish. According to Hansen, Hui Shi is led by Zhuangzi into a logical trap because he is committed to two different standards—knowing what it is like first person and knowing by inference. Hansen thinks that if Hui Shi takes the inner perspective as the only way of access to someone's inner state, he should stick to the subjective standard and should not also commit himself to the standard of knowing by inference. That is, he should abide by what Hansen calls the inner perspective principle since, as I have argued in the preceding, Hui Shi cannot use the subjective standard in a direct and noninferential way. It is not his commitment to these two standards but rather his commitment to the one single standard—the subjective standard and his inferences from it—necessitated by its being a standard that leads him into a contradiction. On the one hand, with regard to his own inner state, he *infers* from the standard that he does not know what Zhuangzi knows; on the other hand, with regard to Zhuangzi's inner state, he *infers* from the very same standard that he knows that Zhuangzi does not know the happiness of fish. His knowledge of the standard entails both his lack of the knowledge of Zhuangzi's inner state and his knowledge of Zhuangzi's inner state. Hansen suggests that if Hui Shi sticks to the subjective standard and is not at the same time implicitly committed to the standard of knowing by inference, he may well avoid the contradiction, and he can manage to abide by the inner perspective principle that the subjective standard expresses by simply keeping quiet:

He [Hui Shi] needs inference from the principle to justify his claim that Zhuangzi does not know, but his principle rules out knowledge by inference. His only escape is to say he does not know if Zhuangzi knows or not—and to withdraw his assertion. He may continue to believe that Zhuangzi does not know what he asserted, but Hui Shi, relying on the principle he does, should not comment on Zhuangzi's assertion. If Zhuangzi were committed to Hui Shi's principle, he would have asserted nothing as well. One consequence of Hui Shi's "way" of knowing is the familiar anti-language conclusion. Neither should have spoken.[11]

There is no doubt that if neither had said anything, no debate would have taken place. But that only avoids the contradiction being verbally expressed and does not avoid the contradiction itself, which will inevitably occur in thought whenever the principle is entertained as a belief. Hui Shi will not fall into the logical trap if and only if what he says, namely, that he does not know whether Zhuangzi knows or not, expresses merely a particular inner state that is not a result of applying the principle. That is, it is not the withdrawal of his assertion but rather his ignorance of the principle that can keep him away from the contradiction. Thus it makes no difference whether Hui Shi actually comments on Zhuangzi's assertion if he believes the principle. To refrain from publically articulating a private reasoning has nothing to do with the antilanguage position, which may be characterized by refraining from putting into words what resists linguistic expression. Private reasoning, albeit unspoken, is already linguistic or at least fully expressible linguistically. The principle commits Hui Shi to one single standard, the subjective standard, which is a contradiction. His reticence is no escape from it.

THE HAPPY FISH PARADOX

Although the subjective standard forces whoever adopts it to get bogged down in a contradiction, it in itself is not a contradiction. This may be better appreciated when it is formulated as containing a universal negative proposition: "one knows the inner state of oneself, and no one knows the inner state of another." This proposition, as it stands, does not by itself constitute a contradiction in much the same way the proposition "no one knows the pain of another" does not. A contradiction obtains when it is asserted by someone. In this respect, it is remarkably similar to Moore's

paradox: G. E. Moore noted that to say that "it's raining but I don't believe it's raining" is absurd.[12] There is nothing wrong with the proposition "it's raining but I don't believe it's raining," as it may well be true and
is certainly not self-contradictory, as both of its constituents, "it's raining" and "I don't believe it's raining," may well be true at the same time.
But one can contradict oneself by simply asserting the proposition. One
explanation, offered by Moore himself, relies on the following principle:
in making an assertion, one implies, in an everyday sense of "imply," that
one believes it. The contradiction obtains because what one says ("I don't
believe it's raining") contradicts what one implies ("I believe it's raining").
This explains why such absurdity does not arise from sentences in the
third-person or past-tense form, such as, "it's raining, but Moore doesn't
believe it," or "it was raining, but I didn't believe it." In the third-person
case, the first assertion is made by someone other than Moore, who makes
the second, whereas in the past-tense case the contradictory assertions are
made by the same person but at different times. Surely there is nothing
contradictory in "I believe it is raining, but Moore does not," or "I believe
it was raining, but at the time I did not."

The paradox in Zhuangzi's story, which I now call "the happy fish paradox," has similar features. Although there is nothing wrong in the proposition "no one knows the inner state of another," a sense of absurdity
emerges when it is asserted by someone. As in Moore's paradox, the speaker
in the happy fish paradox manages to contradict himself by simply uttering a sentence that nevertheless contains no contradiction. The absurdity
of asserting "it's raining but I don't believe it's raining" is explained by
appeal to the principle that in making an assertion, one implies that one
believes it (i.e., the "implied belief account"). The absurdity of asserting
"no one knows the inner state of another" may be explained by appeal to
the principle that in making an assertion, one implies that one knows it
(i.e., the "implied knowledge account").[13] For a speaker to assert that "no
one knows the inner state of another" is absurd because the speaker must
know what he or she is asserting, namely, that no one knows the inner
state of another. But if the speaker knows that no one knows the inner
state of another, then he or she does not know whether no one knows the
inner state of another, for that no one knows the inner state of another is
the inner state of others, which the speaker is not supposed to know.

Thus what differentiates the happy fish paradox from Moore's paradox
is that the sense of absurdity in the former is generated by the speaker

uttering the sentence alone and not uttering the sentence and saying at the same time that he does not believe it. In Moore's paradox, the speaker who asserts "it's raining" needs to make an additional assertion, "I don't believe it's raining," in order to contradict himself. In the happy fish paradox, however, the speaker needs no additional assertion to obtain a contradiction. The contradiction in the happy fish paradox is between "I know that no one knows the inner state of another" and "I don't know whether no one knows the inner state of another," both of which are what the speaker implies in making the assertion "no one knows the inner state of another": one is due to the principle that in making an assertion, one knows what one asserts, whereas the other is due to the semantic content of the assertion. Thus in contrast to the contradiction in Moore's paradox, which may be formalized as p & ~p (believing x and not believing x), the contradiction in the happy fish paradox is generated by p (knowing x) and hence, p ⊃ ~p (knowing x entails its negation, not knowing x).

In addition, p ⊃ ~p is the form shared by logical paradoxes such as the liar paradox and the barber paradox, which all involve self-reference. The resemblance to the liar paradox can be more readily perceived when the assertion made in the latter is formulated also as a universal negative, "No Cretan ever speaks truly." The problem with the liar paradox, which a Cretan, when saying this, speaks both truly and falsely, lies in the fact that the speaker is a member of the class "Cretans." If the speaker is not a Cretan, what he says will not result in a contradiction. Similarly, in saying "no one knows the inner state of another," the speaker will contradict himself if and only if he intends himself to be a member of the class "ones" (that is, "those who are able to know"), but he can avoid the contradiction by preventing what he says from being self-referential. For instance, by restricting the range of "ones" to the population of an island of which Hui Shi is not a member, he commits no self-contradiction when he says "no one knows the inner state of another," as what he is saying now simply means "no one on the island knows the inner state of another." That is, Hui Shi knows the inner state of these islanders, which is that they know nothing about each other's inner state.

Of course the self-reference involved in the liar paradox is of quite a different kind. It is not just the speaker that is a member of the class "Cretans." What the speaker says is also a member of what he says. The liar paradox is, according to Quine's classification of paradoxes, an example of what he calls "antinomies" and has the complete form (p ⊃ ~p) & (~p ⊃ p).

Its truth value cannot be determined, and the contradiction arising from it cannot be eliminated. The happy fish paradox, on the other hand, does not involve self-reference of this kind and is not an antinomy. What the subjective standard in the fish paradox says is "no one knows the inner state of another," not "no one knows the inner state of oneself," only the latter of which, when asserted by someone, constitutes an antinomy. The happy fish paradox, whose complete form is $(p \supset \sim p)$ & $(\sim p \not\supset p)$, may belong to the category of "veridical paradoxes" in Quine's classification.[14] Like other veridical paradoxes such as the barber paradox, its truth value can be determined: that no one knows the inner state of another is simply false.

Now if the subjective standard always results in a contradiction, why does Hui Shi introduce it in his challenge to Zhuangzi's initial assertion about the fish happiness in the first place? Perhaps Hui Shi is just careless and is unaware of the inherent paradox in the standard. But it is unbelievable that he remains totally blind to the problem even after it becomes so obvious when Zhuangzi responds to his question with a question and shows no sign of his detection of the paradox but only stubbornness. I think this is an unlikely image of Hui Shi, someone regarded as a skillful debater and Zhuangzi's philosophical partner. In portraying Hui Shi this way, one leaves out a great deal of what is going on in the debate, which, I believe, can be saved only by taking into account the ways of reasoning familiar to the ancient Chinese debaters.

CHINESE LOGIC

In a recently published paper titled "The Relatively Happy Fish Revisited," a critical response to Hansen's "The Relatively Happy Fish," Norman Teng rejects what he calls Hansen's inferential articulation of the dialogue, "particularly his portrayal of Hui Shi's logical maneuvering as an inept handling of philosophical dialectic and Zhuangzi's response to Hui Shi's question as a contrived, logical trap."[15] By "inferential articulation of the dialogue," Teng means presumably Hansen's interpretation of the dialogue as essentially involving deductive reasoning and in particular the use of reductio ad absurdum, which, according to Teng, are alien to ancient Chinese thinkers. Teng then proposes to apply the logic developed in the later Mohist text, the Lesser Pick, to an analysis of the dialogue. The conclusion he draws from his own analysis is that both Zhuangzi and Hui Shi, as excellent practitioners of the techniques prescribed in the Lesser Pick, are equal in the debating game, and there is no logical trap Zhuangzi sets for Hui Shi into which the latter falls, although Zhuangzi is able to stay focused on the point he initially makes, whereas Hui Shi is prone to a weakness for pointless argumentation. Teng contends that the intricate dialectic of the dialogue accords with the patterns of discourse as expounded in the Lesser Pick, namely, (1) "illustrating" (*bi* 辟, referring to other things in order to clarify one's case), (2) "parallelizing" (*mou* 侔, comparing propositions and letting all "proceed"), (3) "adducing" (*yuan* 援, if it is so in your case, why may it not be so in mine, too?), and (4) "inferring" (*tui* 推, using what is the same in that which he refuses to accept and that which he does accept in order to propose the former) (Graham, *Later Mohist Logic,* 483). Specifically, Zhuangzi's initial introduction of the fish topic is a use of illustrating that also completes in his final statement. To Hui Shi's remarks ("You are not a fish. Whence do you know the happiness of fish?"), Zhuangzi's response ("You are not me. Whence do you know I don't know the happiness of fish?") is a combined exercise of parallelizing and adducing rather than a contrived, logical trap. By establishing a parallel pattern in both questions, Zhuangzi shows Hui Shi that his question is as legitimate as his friend's. Given that the questions are rhetorical in nature, they are really assertions. Thus, what Hui Shi and Zhuangzi mean to say is this:

HUI SHI:"You [Zhuangzi] are not a fish, so you [Zhuangzi] don't know fish happiness." (A)
ZHUANGZI: "You [Hui Shi] are not me [Zhuangzi], so you [Hui Shi] don't know whether I [Zhuangzi] know the happiness of fish." (B)

Zhuangzi's response is therefore a deployment of the technique of adducing: if the opponent (Hui Shi) approves of his own case, he should approve of the arguer's (Zhuangzi's) case. All Zhuangzi tries to do is to force Hui Shi to approve B instead of setting a contrived, logical trap for Hui Shi. Hui Shi's next move is a combined exercise of parallelizing and inferring. That is, Hui Shi uses Zhuangzi's assertion (B) only to establish a parallel pattern in Zhuangzi's assertion and his own (A), on the basis of which Hui Shi forces Zhuangzi to approve what he has rejected (A) with the technique of inferring. Teng thinks that Zhuangzi's reasoning from A to B is a switch from the species-specific perspective to the first-person perspective. However, Hui Shi's use of B does not entail his endorsement of the subjective standard, which Teng finds lacks textual support. There-fore Hui Shi can reassert A without assuming the subjective standard and hence without committing a self-contradiction. According to Teng, to reassert A, Hui Shi also relies on an additional parallel pattern in his reasoning from B to A and Zhuangzi's reasoning from A to B: if Zhuang-zi's switch from the species-specific perspective to the first-person per-spective is approved of, so is his reverse switch, which seems to be another use of adducing, this time by Hui Shi. Finally, as Zhuangzi foresees the potentially indefinite application of the parallel patterns in the debate, he decides to end it by playing a verbal trick and "invites Hui Shi to go back to the root from which they have branched out into this situation."[16]

Although I welcome the proposal to construe the story in terms of Mo-hist logic, I have found Teng's Mohist reconstruction of the debate unsat-isfactory.[17] Hui Shi may escape the contradiction situation as described earlier through a Mohist interpretation, and in this sense his response to Zhuangzi's challenge may be said to be "elegant and powerful from an an-cient Chinese dialectical viewpoint."[18] However, Teng's Mohist reading leaves some crucial questions unanswered. I agree with Teng that some of the reasoning in the dialogue well accords with the four patterns of dis-course as expounded in the Lesser Pick. Zhuangzi's challenge (B), for in-stance, can be viewed as one that involves the use of both parallelizing and adducing. There is an unmistakable parallel between "You are not a fish. Whence do you know fish happiness?" (A) and "You are not me. Whence do you know I don't know the happiness of fish?" (B), as they are similar in phrasing, that is, similar both syntactically and semantically (similar in the kinds of things that are talked about). It is appropriate to characterize Zhuangzi's response as involving the use of adducing: since Hui Shi approves A, Zhuangzi is able to force Hui Shi to approve B, given the existence of the parallel pattern in both A and B. I can also agree with Teng's reading of Hui Shi's response as containing the use of inferring, which relies on both the parallel pattern in A and B and the parallel pat-tern in the reasoning from A to B and the reasoning from B to A: since Zhuangzi approves the reasoning from A to B, he should not reject the reasoning from B to A.

Now if what Zhuangzi tries to do is to force Hui Shi to approve B on the basis of the parallel pattern in what his opponent approves (A) and what he himself approves (B), why does he believe that his opponent would approve B at all, as there is no reason for Zhuangzi to expect, unrealistically, that his opponent, an able debater, would fail to notice the contradiction between A and B when asserted by him and the contradiction that results from his commitment to the subjective standard implied by B? On Teng's interpretation, since Hui Shi adroitly evades the contradictions by making a reverse switch, Teng needs to explain why Zhuangzi makes the first switch if he does not hold an unrealistic expectation of cornering Hui Shi in a contradiction.[19] Teng's solution is that in making the move from A to B, Zhuangzi, instead of aiming at setting a logical trap for Hui Shi, "is counting on Hui Shi's willingness to reorient himself with this shift in perspective by paralleling their respective questions."[20] But what is the point of debating with Hui Shi if all he can do is to invite his opponent to make a reverse switch, which he even foresees could lead to a deadlock or indefinite switches of perspective? A more serious question is this: why does Zhuangzi himself approve B to begin with, given that it implies the subjective standard, which always results in a contradiction? It seems that such a reading may render Hui Shi's handling of the dialectic adroitly, but at the expense of Zhuangzi, who now appears both strangely pointless and unbelievably innocent. Furthermore, can the elegance and power Hui Shi exhibits in his combined exercise of parallelizing and inferring spare him any contradiction generated from his exchange with Zhuangzi? Unless these questions are properly answered, I do not believe that the messages in the dialogue can be truly deciphered.

CONTRADICTIONS CIRCUMVENTED

Suppose that, in asserting B, Zhuangzi indeed makes a switch from the species-specific perspective to the first-person perspective. That is, Hui Shi does not assume the subjective standard in A, nor does Zhuangzi read it into A but only introduces it in B. Zhuangzi's reasoning is a switch in perspective that is nondeductive and is based solely on a parallel pattern in A and B.[21] In the absence of any other justification, the reasoning from A to B is not particularly strong, as Hui Shi can reject it by insisting that knowing the thoughts of a fellow human being is very different from knowing the mental state of a fish. Moreover, in introducing the subjective standard in B, Zhuangzi seems to put himself in a position of double self-contradiction. First, given the subjective standard (no one knows the inner state of another), Zhuangzi will contradict himself if he also claims that

Hui Shi does not know whether Zhuangzi knows fish happiness (B) because B implies that Zhuangzi knows B. Second, as discussed in the preceding, whoever subscribes to the standard contradicts himself anyway, that is, without even making any other claim. Interestingly, instead of pointing out that Zhuangzi's switch of perspectives is unwarranted or/and self-refuting, Hui Shi allows it.

Now we need to answer the following two questions: (1) Why does Zhuangzi volunteer a self-contradictory move? (2) Does Hui Shi have some good reason for allowing it? Zhuangzi's reasoning from A to B is a combined exercise of parallelizing and adducing. Adducing, as defined by the Lesser Pick, may be understood as a technique an arguer uses to force the opponent to approve what the arguer approves. An example can be found in Gongsun Long's defense of his thesis, "a white horse is not a horse." Gongsun Long argues that if one accepts Confucius' statement that a man of Chu is not a man, one should also accept that a white horse is not a horse.[22] But it should be noted that what is essential to the technique of adducing is that it is a response to the challenge posed by the opponent by arguing that some claim made by the opponent is subject to the same kind of challenge. As Dan Robins puts it, adducing "is an *ad hominem* argument that gains what[ever] force it has from facts about one's opponent. . . . Its conclusion is modest: the opponent is in no position to criticise the arguer."[23]

Since by inferring B from A to challenge Hui Shi to explain why B should not be approved, Zhuangzi does not have to approve A in the first place, and he is not guilty of self-contradiction. The burden of dealing with the self-contradiction shifts to Hui Shi, should he fail to block Zhuangzi's inference. For Hui Shi to accept the inference is to approve B on the grounds of A, whereas A and B, when asserted by Hui Shi, are again contradictory to each other. Moreover, B implies the subjective standard, which commits whoever endorses it to a contradiction. So Zhuangzi's argument is more likely a reductio ad absurdum, certainly not being strictly a form of deductive reasoning, but only in the sense that it is used to argue against a claim made by the opponent by showing that a contradiction follows from the opponent's claim, whether deductively or nondeductively (that is, analogically). Zhuangzi's use of adducing, as a reductio, aims to force Hui Shi to disapprove A by showing that B, which is inferable from A on the basis of a parallel pattern, either implies or results in a contradiction.[24]

I also agree that Hui Shi uses the technique of inferring in his response to Zhuangzi's challenge. Inferring involves using what is the same in that which the opponent refuses to accept and that which he does accept in order to propose the former. An example of inferring can be found in chapter 9 of Mozi's *Gongmeng* 公孟. *Gongmeng* says that "'the spirits do not exist, and also that the gentleman must learn to perform sacrifices,' which is like 'learning the etiquette for guests without having the guests, making a fishnet although there are no fish.'"[25] Hui Shi may be said to reason in accordance with this pattern: since Zhuangzi approves B, he should also approve A. Hui Shi's move from B to A, like Zhuangzi's from A to B, is a switch in perspective, but it is a reverse switch, one from the subjective perspective to species-specific perspective.

It should be noted that, contrary to the view of some commentators, the inferring Hui Shi uses here cannot be construed as involving a reductio ad absurdum even understood in a broad sense as described earlier because, in order to reason in the reductio pattern, Hui Shi should disapprove not-A (Zhuangzi knows fish happiness) on the ground that not-A implies a contradiction or not-A contradicts B, which derives from not-A.[26] This is not what Hui Shi is doing here. For one thing, it does not seem possible that B is derivable from not-A. One can hardly think even in terms of the Mohist logic (that is, parallelizing) that Hui Shi does not know whether Zhuangzi knows fish happiness just because Zhuangzi knows fish happiness. Unlike Zhuangzi's adducing, which tries to disapprove what his opponent approves (A) by showing that a logical consequence of it (B) contradicts it or implies a contradiction, Hui Shi's inferring aims at forcing his opponent to approve what the latter disapproves (A) by showing how what the latter approves supports it. In other words, reasoning in the pattern of inferring, Hui Shi is supposed to use B to support A and not to arrive at A, that is, disapprove not-A, through displaying a contradiction between not-A and B or one implied by not-A. Now, if this is correct, it seems that Hui Shi must first approve B, which is how his final utterances are commonly interpreted: "Granted that I am not you, I don't know about you. Then, granted that you are not a fish, the case for your not knowing the happiness of fish is complete."

Given that B implies the subjective standard, Hui Shi's approval of B commits him to a contradiction. A contradiction also obtains when A ("Zhuangzi does not know fish happiness") and B ("Hui Shi does not know whether Zhuangzi knows fish happiness") are asserted by Hui Shi because, given the norm of assertion that, in claiming something, one should know it, A implies "Hui Shi knows that Zhuangzi does not know fish happiness."[27] While neither of the contradictions has an effect on Zhuangzi's argument because his move from A to B is part of his reductio reasoning and a contradiction is precisely what Zhuangzi needs to reject A, it undermines Hui Shi's move from B to A, as his effort is to establish A or to force Zhuangzi to approve A. A contradiction is also inevitable for Zhuangzi, should he be persuaded by Hui Shi's reasoning from B to A. That is, if Zhuangzi approves A on the basis of the inferring, Zhuangzi has to either commit himself to the subjective standard or accept both A and B, which will now imply, respectively, that Zhuangzi knows that Hui Shi does not know whether Zhuangzi knows fish happiness and that Zhuangzi knows that Hui Shi knows that Zhuangzi does not know fish happiness. It is quite startling that Hui Shi notices no contradiction entailed by what he utters.

There may be some explanation for Hui Shi's adamant refusal to acknowledge the logical impasse he is getting into. One may argue that when Zhuangzi moves from A to B, his reasoning is based on the parallel pattern in A and B, that is, in "You [Zhuangzi] are not a fish. So you [Zhuangzi] don't know the happiness of fish" and "You [Hui Shi] are not me [Zhuangzi]. So you don't know whether I [Zhuangzi] know the happiness of fish," not between what they imply when they are asserted by Hui Shi or Zhuangzi, as there is no obvious parallel, for instance, between "I [Hui Shi] know that you [Zhuangzi] don't know fish happiness" and "I [Hui Shi] don't know whether you [Zhuangzi] know fish happiness."[28] If no contradiction exists between A and B considered in themselves, surely Hui Shi is able to escape the self-contradiction charge, as once again the parallel pattern on the basis of which Hui Shi makes his reverse switch of perspectives is in A and B, and not in what they imply. Zhuangzi should therefore be able to appreciate the reasonableness of Hui Shi's move from B to A and should find no incoherence in accepting both A and B. However, one can hardly ignore the fact that it is Hui Shi who presents the reasoning from B to A to Zhuangzi. Whereas there is nothing paradoxical about Hui Shi's being ignorant of Zhuangzi's ignorance, for Hui Shi to convey this message to Zhuangzi seems a logically impossible task. Neither Zhuangzi nor Hui Shi would deny that what the assertions imply is part of the reasoning itself, which is necessitated by the use of the pronouns "I" and "you"—Zhuangzi's use of adducing as a reductio is built precisely on the unavoidability of taking into account the implications of the assertions. However, to use the technique of parallelizing, one only needs to explore the linguistic similarities between what is actually asserted, not those that are implied by what is actually asserted.

Hui Shi may opt to withdraw his commitment to the norm of assertion and act as a third party who presents the reasoning to Zhuangzi but makes it unknown to Hui Shi.[29] This option, however, is not feasible, as Hui Shi assumes the norm when he challenges Zhuangzi's assertion about fish happiness and would be inexcusably inconsistent if he suddenly ceases to do so. The good news for Hui Shi is that the Lesser Pick allows inferring to be understood also as an ad hominem form of argument, which depends on the views the opponent happens to hold but which the arguer need not also hold.[30] To reason from B to A, Hui Shi does not have to approve B at all and is therefore not troubled by the contradiction entailed by the subjective standard in the first place or by the contradiction that resulted from a commitment to both A and B. Moreover, because the inference from B to A is a switch in perspective and Hui Shi does not have to approve the subjective standard implied by B, he does not need the subjective standard to arrive at A. That is, he does not reason in the following way: because no one knows the inner state of another, Zhuangzi does not know fish happiness. All he does is to point out that if Zhuangzi thinks that Hui Shi does not know whether Zhuangzi knows fish happiness, Zhuangzi should admit that he does not know fish happiness. Such a strategy is comparable to valid but unsound deductive reasoning, that is, reasoning with a false or an unacceptable premise that validly yields a true or an acceptable conclusion. For instance, one can reason from (1) "no white horses are horses" and (2) "all black donkeys are horses" to (3) "no white horses are black donkeys." Suppose that the opponent approves both (1) and (2) but does not approve (3). The arguer can force the opponent to approve (3) by showing that it follows from (1) and (2), which, however, the arguer does not approve.

However, for the comparability to hold, Hui Shi needs to establish that Zhuangzi indeed approves B, as Hui Shi's forcing his opponent to approve of A depends on the parallel pattern in A and B, as well as his opponent's approval of B.[31] Now, as I have argued in the preceding, B is not what Zhuangzi approves or would approve at all. His use of B serves only to disapprove A. To regard B as something Zhuangzi approves or would approve is to misrepresent Zhuangzi's position. In fact, there is no need for Hui Shi to play such a straw-man trick. The Lesser Pick defines inferring as using only what is the same in that which the opponent refuses to accept and that which the opponent does accept in order to propose the former. What the debaters approve and disapprove need not be any particular assertions; they can be the ways the debaters present their cases and in particular the ways they reason. Although Zhuangzi does not approve B, he certainly approves the move from A to B, which is part of the reductio he adopts. It is this move in Zhuangzi's reasoning that Hui Shi uses to support his own move from B to A. Notice that in addition to the parallel pattern in A and B, there is also the parallel pattern in A to B and B to A. Hui Shi's move, as Teng puts it, is that if the switch from the species-specific perspective to the first-person perspective is to be approved of, so is the reverse switch. In order to force the latter to approve A, Hui Shi does not have to approve B, nor does he need to establish that Zhuangzi approves B. So understood, Hui Shi's handling of the dialectic is indeed both elegant and powerful.

THE LAST CONTRADICTION

At this point, one might be inclined to think, with Teng, that there is potentially indefinite application of the parallel patterns in the debate that Zhuangzi foresees and decides to block by playing a verbal trick. The remarks Zhuangzi makes to conclude the dialogue do sound like a verbal trick, but the purpose of ending the debate, I believe, lies elsewhere. Notice that it is Zhuangzi who initiates the reasoning based on parallelizing. Because of this, he is in no position to dismiss Hui Shi's inferring, which is equally based on parallelizing. On the other hand, it is quite remarkable that instead of rejecting Zhuangzi's switch of perspectives to block his argument by adducing, Hui Shi allows Zhuangzi's move from A to B. As we have seen, the allowance enables Hui Shi to make a reverse switch, thereby forcing Zhuangzi to approve A. If Hui Shi approves Zhuangzi's move from A to B and shows no objection to the latter's argument by adducing, he should approve not-A even though he does not approve B. However, his own argument by inferring is supported precisely by exhibiting the parallel pattern in his move from B to A and Zhuangzi's move from A to B. Now both Zhuangzi and Hui Shi have to deal with the fact that they arrive at their conclusion by appealing to their opponent's reasoning, which yields a conclusion contradictory to their own.

The existence of the contradiction (A and not-A) makes it impossible to justify the view that the debate would end in a deadlock or go on indefinitely, a situation in which neither Zhuangzi's argument nor Hui Shi's refutes and is refuted by the other's argument unless, of course, such a contradiction is tolerated. It would be exceedingly fanciful and indeed preposterous to suppose that the debaters' logic and Chinese thinking in general do not recognize contradiction as a major logical blunder.[32] The idea of contradiction as a fault in reasoning is discussed or mentioned in nearly all the pieces attributed to the sophist Gongsun Long, a contemporary of Zhuangzi and Hui Shi, where the author often tries to refute his opponent's view by showing a self-contradiction, referred to as *bei* (誖 "self-contradictory" or "self-falsifying"), his opponent commits. The same term, *bei*, also frequently appears in the Mohist Canons.[33] It is precisely this *bei* that is used in the canons to characterize what is taken to be an impediment to rational speech, which a paradox under discussion constitutes, one that bears a striking resemblances to the liar paradox: "To claim that all saying contradicts itself is self-contradictory [*bei*]. Explained by: what he says himself."[34] Given this background, it is inconceivable that Hui Shi, a skilful debater, could just turn a blind eye on the contradiction between A and not-A.[35]

The case of Zhuangzi is more complicated. There is some truth to what Hansen describes as the dominant image of Zhuangzi, the mystic (as opposed to that of Hui Shi, the logician), if by a mystic one understands someone who allows his nonempirically and nonlogically based knowledge claims to sometimes violate the law of noncontradiction. Apart from those apparent contradictory utterances in the *Zhuangzi*, especially the "Qiwulun" 齊物論 or "Seeing Things as Equal," which can be explained away by subjecting them to a relativist or perspectivist interpretation, other utterances may plausibly be construed as containing real contradictions.[36] The question is, rather, whether Zhuangzi would allow a real contradiction between A and not-A even if he does allow such contradictions in other circumstances. My judgment is that he would not, as the whole point he intends to make is that he knows fish happiness (not-A), and it doesn't seem probable that something revealing or interesting will emerge from a contradiction between A and not-A.

If neither Zhuangzi nor Hui Shi tolerates the contradiction that obtains in their reasoning, the debate cannot simply end in a deadlock or go on indefinitely. Neither Zhuangzi nor Hui Shi can hold on to their own positions, as they both are in a situation of self-refuting. Moreover, one can hardly overlook the fact that the problem lies squarely in the uses of parallelizing, based on which Zhuangzi and Hui Shi advance their arguments. Parallelizing, as a reasoning pattern that appears to have no direct counterpart in other logical traditions, was much cherished by debaters in ancient China, including most notably the sophists of the School of Names (Mingjia 名家), to which Hui Shi belonged.[37] The notoriety of many of the sophists was a result of their willingness and even enthusiasm to engage in disputations whose sole aim was to win contests of wits or to defend sophistries. Because parallelizing can appeal to similarities between the assertions made by the arguer and those by the opponent at different linguistic and structural levels, which may or may not be relevant in preserving truth or warranting acceptance, the sophists were able to build fallacious arguments on some very neat parallelizing patterns. This is presumably what prompted the Mohists' effort to expose in the Lesser Pick how unreliable parallelizing often is. The Mohists thus insist on the need to distinguish among inferences by parallelizing those that are valid or admissible (that is, "this/so" *shi* 是/*ran* 然) and those that are invalid or inadmissible (e.g., "this/not so" *shi* 是/*buran* 不然).[38] The Lesser Pick provides ample examples of both valid or admissible and invalid or inadmissible uses of parallelizing.[39] For instance, the inference from "This horse's eyes are blind" to "This horse is blind" is valid or admissible, whereas the one from "This horse's eyes are big" to "This horse is big" is invalid or inadmissible despite the fact that both are of the same parallel pattern.[40]

There is no doubt that Zhuangzi philosophized within the intellectual milieu of the disputers. His "Qiwulun" can be seen as a reaction to *bian* (辨 disputation/distinguishing), which disputers of various schools, particularly the sophists, were freely drawn to.[41] As an astute observer of the many inherent flaws involved in the disputes, he was fundamentally dismissive of the reasoning techniques favored by the disputers. Graham, who is largely responsible for fashioning the dominant image of Zhuangzi and Hui Shi, the mystic vs. the logician, suggests that the fish dialogue is intended to be a parody of sophists' logical debates, a parody that presents Zhuangzi as a playful interlocutor who ridicules logic. But it is a mistake to portray the dialogue as a miscommunication between a logician and an antirationalist mystic. Even though Hui Shi is certainly an expert on reasoning and disputation, Zhuangzi is no enemy of rationality even though he sometimes embraces real contradictions. The target of his attack is actually the logic of the disputers, that is, the formulation of the ways of reasoning and disputation, particularly parallelizing, which were widely employed by his contemporaries and which were, as the Mohists later argued, unreliable. Perhaps Zhuangzi distrusts any logic, as any formulation of inferences for him is unable to distinguish adequately between what is valid or admissible and what is invalid or inadmissible. Such skepticism would later be testified by the Mohists' failure to explain how parallelizing can go wrong and hence their failure to provide useful guidance for correct reasoning.[42] On the other hand, Zhuangzi is not the more skilful dialectician leading Hui Shi into a logical trap, as Hansen claims he is. For one thing, the earlier reading of the dialogue in terms of the reasoning patterns as expounded by the Lesser Pick illustrates that Zhuangzi sets no logical trap for Hui Shi. For another, like Hui Shi, Zhuangzi, too, cannot avoid a contradiction resulting from his reasoning based on parallelizing.

With all this critical analysis in place, I believe we are now in a better position to speculate about the real purpose of the happy fish story. Hui Shi's challenge to Zhuangzi's initial assertion about fish happiness may prompt Zhuangzi's decision to engage his sophist friend in a game of parodying the sophists' logical debates. What Zhuangzi intends to do is to exhibit how the disputers' logic, reasoning based on parallelizing in particular, warrants no truth or acceptability and in this case leads to an absurd consequence: contradiction. Zhuangzi initiates the reasoning by parallelizing and in doing so invites Hui Shi to respond in kind by parallelizing. The dialogue between the two accords neatly with the well-received reasoning patterns. Neither appears to abuse or misuse the disputers' logic, and neither, from the disputers' "logical point of view," gains an upper hand. Zhuangzi's verbal trick marks the end of his excursion into a logic exercise and is greeted with no protest by Hui Shi, a sign of the latter's realization of Zhuangzi's true intent and perhaps also of his regret for allowing himself to be lured by Zhuangzi's switch of perspectives. After all, Hui Shi's remarks ("You are not a fish. Whence do you know the happiness of fish?") can be interpreted or reinterpreted as demanding that Zhuangzi explain how he knows fish happiness, presupposing that he knows it, rather than challenging his knowledge claim, when we consider a scenario where Zhuangzi does not make a move to lure Hui Shi into a debate.

NOTES

1. Chad Hansen, "The Relatively Happy Fish," *Asian Philosophy* 13 (2003): 149.

2. It is often claimed that the ancient Chinese focused primarily on analogical reasoning and paid little attention to developing deductive inference. See Zhang Dongsun 張東蓀, *Knowledge and Culture* 知識與文化 (Shanghai: Shanghai Commercial Press, 1946), 190; A. K. Volkov, "Analogical Reasoning in Ancient China: Some Examples," *Extrême-Orient, Extrême-Occident* 14 (1992): 15–48; and J. P. Reding, *Comparative Essays in Early Greek and Chinese Rational Thinking* (Burlington: Ashgate, 2004), 31–32. Christoph Harbsmeier, among those who try to demonstrate that there was room in ancient Chinese culture for deductively valid logical reasoning, recognizes that "the ancient Chinese were more inclined to argue 'analogically,' by analogy or comparison, rather than logically by demonstration or proof." See Harbsmeier, *Language and Logic in Traditional China,* vol. 7, part I of *Science and Civilisation in China* (Cambridge: Cambridge University Press, 1998), 264.

3. Peter Hoffmann, *Die Welt als Wendung: Zu einer literarischen Lektüre des Wahren Buches vom südlichen Blütenland* (Wiesbaden: Harrassowitz, 2001), 297.

4. Some scholars take seriously the view that the Chinese mind is illogical in itself. See A. Forke, "The Chinese Sophists," *Journal of the North China Branch of the Royal Asiatic Society* 34 (1901): 5, and M. Granet, *La pensée chinoise* (Paris: Albin Michel, 1934), 37. One should take notice of the fact that these claims range from very strong (the Chinese mind is simply irrational) to quite mild (the Chinese mind, which is rational, reasons in ways that cannot be captured by the existing Western logical systems, such as the Aristotelian syllogism).

5. See Hansen, "Relatively Happy Fish," 152; Hoffman, *Die Welt als Wendung,* 301; Norman Y. Teng, "The Relatively Happy Fish Revisited," *Asian Philosophy* 16 (2006): 43.

6. Much of the discussion on the happy fish episode in Taiwan has been centered on the question of who, Zhuangzi or Hui Shi, wins the debate. For instance, Boshi Pan 潘柏世, "Zhuangzi and Hui Shi: The Debate on the Fish Happiness 莊子與惠子: '魚樂' 之辯," *Ehu* 鵝湖月刊 27 (1977): 50–51, and " 'The Debate on the Fish Happiness' Revisited 再談 '魚樂之辯'," *Ehu*鵝湖月刊 31 (1978): 34–35, holds that Hui Shi is the loser, whereas Guimiao Chen 陳癸淼, "Hui Shi, The Scholar 惠施之學術生涯," *Ehu* 鵝湖月刊 27 (1977): 17–24, decides that Hui Shi wins the debate, although Zhuangzi is on the right side for his conclusion.

7. Apart from Hansen, however, Guimiao Chen and Yicheng Cen (岑溢成, "The Debate on Fish Happiness: Knowing and Being Happy 魚樂之辯: 知與樂," *Ehu* 鵝湖月刊 29 [1977]: 2–12) also take Zhuangzi's reasoning as a reductio ad absurdum. Unlike Hansen, however, they maintain that reductio ad absurdum is also used by Hui Shi in his counterattack on Zhuangzi's argument.

8. Hansen, "Relatively Happy Fish," 150. For Zhuangzi's argument to work, it is crucial that both being happy and knowing be treated as internal and subjective, though one is cognitive and the other affective. See ibid., 152.

9. Ibid., 153.

10. Ibid., 153–154.

11. Ibid., 154.

12. G. E. Moore, "Moore's Paradox," in Thomas Baldwin, ed., *G. E. Moore: Selected Writings* (London: Routledge, 1993), 207.

13. Although the implied belief account is sufficient to explain the absurdity in Moore's paradox, it may not, as many have argued, be sufficient as an account for assertions or what Timothy Williamson calls "the norm of assertion," which requires the implied knowledge account. See O. R. Jones, "Moore's Paradox, Assertion and Knowledge," *Analysis* 51 (1991): 183–186, and T. Williamson, "Knowing and Asserting," *Philosophical Review* 105 (1996): 489–523. In any event, the implied belief account is not sufficient to explain the absurdity in the happy fish paradox. On the implied belief account, "no one knows the inner state of another" implies: (1) "I believe that no one knows the inner state of another" and (2) "I believe that I don't know if no one knows the inner state of another," which are clearly not contradictory to each other.

14. W. V. Quine, *The Ways of Paradox and Other Essays* (New York: Randon House, 1966), 5.

15. Teng, "Relatively Happy Fish Revisited," 41.

16. Ibid., 43.

17. Norman Y. Teng is not the first scholar who urges us to read the story in light of the Mohist logic. Guimiao Chen ("Hui Shi, The Scholar," 20) argues that both Zhuangzi and Hui Shi use the Mohist logical technique of adducing. However, he believes both uses involve reductio ad absurdum. That is, in the first round of the debate, Zhuangzi forces Hui Shi to accept what Hu Shi has denied, namely B, by granting the truth of A. In the second round, Hui Shi forces Zhuangzi to accept what Zhuangzi has denied, namely A, by granting the truth of B.

18. Teng, "Relatively Happy Fish Revisited," 43.

19. A slightly different question should also worry Hansen—different because on his inferential reading of the dialogue, what happens is exactly what Zhuangzi expects, that is, Hui Shi takes the bait: why is Hui Shi so clueless about the consequence of allowing A to be interpreted as presupposing the subjective standard?

20. Teng, "Relatively Happy Fish Revisited," 43.

21. Hansen also recognizes that Hui Shi only presupposes the "being the same species" standard when he challenges Zhuangzi's initial assetion about the fish happiness. However, Hansen contends that Zhuangzi's move is warranted by the fact that Hui Shi's standard can be legitimately treated as a grammatically ambiguous standard, "one must be X to know X's F"—where F can be replaced by either *le* (happiness) or *zhi* (knowledge). For Cen, however, the switch that Zhuangzi makes is from knowing something about another individual (presumably including but not limited to being a member of a species) to knowing the subjective mental state of another individual, a switch which Cen believes is not warranted. Cen's criticism of Zhuangzi is based on Guo Xiang's commentary, which, however, does not do justice to Zhuangzi's reasoning. See Cen, "Debate on Fish Happiness," 9, and Guo Qingfan, 郭慶藩, *Commentary on* Zhuangzi 莊子集釋 (Beijing: Zhonghua Shuju, 1997), 607–608.

22. C. Harbsmeier, "Marginalia Sino-logica," in R. E. Allinson, ed., *Understanding the Chinese Mind* (New York: Oxford University Press, 1989), 125–166.

23. Dan Robins, "The Later Mohists and Logic," *History and Philosophy of Logic* 31 (2011): 247–285.

24. At this point, there is no way one can read Zhuangzi's reasoning as purely analogical without involving any deductive elements because B, as an application of the subjective standard, is a universal instantiation, and the move from the universal assertion expressing the subjective standard (i.e., that no one knows the inner state of

another) to its instantiation (i.e., that Hui Shi does not know whether Zhuangzi knows fish happiness) is a deductive move in reasoning.

25. A. C. Graham, *Later Mohist Logic, Ethics and Science* (Hong Kong: Chinese University Press, 1978), 14.

26. See Cen, "Debate on Fish Happiness," 2–12, and Chen, "Hui Shi, The Scholar," 17–24.

27. The norm of assertion, which Hansen invokes in his paper, is due to Williamson.

28. The Mohist Canons, for instance, do not contain examples in which a parallelizing pattern exists in a positive statement and a negative one.

29. This in itself is not entirely impossible. In fact, the norm of assertion is not universally accepted. Matthew Weiner, "Must We Know What We Say?" *Philosophical Review* 114 (2005): 227–251, and David Sosa, "Dubious Assertions," *Philosophical Studies* 146 (2009): 269–272, among others, challenge the knowledge account of assertion (one must know p in order to assert p).

30. Robins 262, notes, "Nothing in the Mohists' gloss implies that pushing [inferring] must appeal to views that the arguer also holds, though the Mohists may have been taking this for granted."

31. Teng, "Relatively Happy Fish Revisited," 42.

32. Granet (*La pensée chinoise,* 271) goes so far as to claim that the classical Chinese, being figurative or poetic, is ill equipped for analytic thinking and that, thinking in this language, the ancient Chinese cannot express the idea of causality and cannot even have the concept of the law of noncontradiction.

33. See Graham, *Later Mohist Logic,* 199–200, and Reding, *Comparative Essays.*

34. Mohist Canons, B 71, 540, translated in Graham, *Later Mohist Logic,* 445. Chris Fraser, "Mohist Canons," *Stanford Encyclopedia of Philosophy* (Summer 2009 ed.), http://plato.stanford.edu/archives/sum2009/entries/mohist-canons/, observes that although the Mohists' logical investigations tend to treat all argumentation as fundamentally analogical in nature and neither investigate formal logic or deductive inference nor formulate an explicit notion of logical consequence, they do apply versions of the laws of excluded middle and noncontradiction, along with concepts of logical "admissibility" (可) and "perversity" (悖), which are intertwined with a rough notion of logical consistency.

35. Hui Shi's ten theses listed in the *Zhuangzi* are often called paradoxes. But none of these can be justifiably interpreted as containing a real contradiction. See Y. M. Fung, "The School of Names," in Bo Mou, ed., *Routledge History of Chinese Philosophy* (New York: Routledge, 2009), 166–188, and C. Liu, "Ming-Jia (the Logicians) and Zeno: A Comparative Study," in Bo Mou, ed., *Comparative Approaches to Chinese Philosophy* (Burlington, VT: Ashgate, 2003), 297–305.

36. The following quote from "Qiwulun" is taken by Graham Priest as a good example of real contradiction or *dialetheia*: "That which makes things has no boundaries with things, but for things to have boundaries is what we mean by saying 'the boundaries between things.' The boundaryless boundary is the boundary without a boundary." See Priest, "Dialetheism," *Stanford Encyclopedia of Philosophy* (Summer 2010 ed.), http://plato.stanford.edu/archives/sum2010/entries/dialetheism/.

37. See Fraser, "Mohist Canons."

38. See Graham, *Later Mohist Logic,* 485.

39. The reason the Mohist Canons are long on examples of parallelizing and short on ones of other patterns, especially adducing and inferring, is that the success or failure of the latter by and large depends on the degree of similarity between the cases compared, which is in some way a matter of parallelizing.

40. Graham, *Later Mohist Logic,* 492.

41. Graham holds that the main targets of Zhuangzi's attack in "Qiwulun" are his contemporaries, the sophists Hui Shi and Gongsun Long (ibid., 138).

42. See Fraser, "Mohist Canons," and Robins, "Later Mohists."

12

Fact and Experience

A Look at the Root of Philosophy from the Happy Fish Debate

PENG Feng

1

The history of philosophy has been ambitious. It has taken getting to the bottom of things as its task and is happy to proclaim that it has discovered the root of the universe and of life. However, there is no consensus among philosophers in their answers about roots and origins, leaving us perplexed. Just what is the root and origin of the universe and of life? After arduously researching and comparing different philosophies, it still seems that a satisfactory answer to these questions is nowhere in sight. Indeed, this failure may evoke new and even more subversive questions such as these: Is there really any root to the universe and to life? Are such questions real questions? What is the meaning of contemplating such questions?

Let us for now suspend our evaluation of weighty philosophical doctrines to look at a debate that took place long ago between Zhuangzi and his philosophical rival, Huizi:

> Zhuangzi and Huizi were walking on the bridge over the Hao River when the former said, "These fishes come out and play about at their ease—that is the enjoyment of fishes." The other said, "You are not a fish; how do you know what constitutes the enjoyment of fishes?" Zhuangzi rejoined, "You are not I. How do you know that I do not know what constitutes the enjoyment of

fishes?" Huizi said, "I am not you, and though indeed I do not fully know you, you certainly are not a fish, and [the argument] is complete against your knowing what constitutes the enjoyment of fishes." Zhuangzi replied, "Let us keep to your original question. You said to me, 'How do you know what constitutes the enjoyment of fishes?' You knew that I knew this, and yet you put your question to me—well, I know this [from our enjoying ourselves together] over the Hao River." (*Zhuangzi,* chapter 17 "The Flood of Autumn"[1])

This debate between Zhuangzi and Huizi has its highs and lows. Of course Zhuangzi won the debate in the end. But Huizi can go into the history books with an equally glorious defeat because his ability in debate was fully exhibited, so much so that some people even think that Zhuangzi won the debate only by sophistry and that the true winner is Huizi.[2]

However, most people still believe that Zhuangzi won the debate. According to Sham Yat Shing's analysis, Huizi and Zhuangzi's happy fish debate had from beginning to end utilized the method of reductio ad absurdum. "Reductio" is a method of defeating an opponent's claim by starting with an intentional acceptance of all the premises raised by the opponent and then by using legitimate and logical reasoning, arriving at a conclusion that contradicts those premises, thus overturning the opponent's argument. From what Huizi said ("You are not a fish; how do you know what constitutes the enjoyment of fishes?"), Zhuangzi arrives at "You are not I. How do you know that I do not know what constitutes the enjoyment of fishes?" And Huizi, then basing his reply on Zhuangzi's "You are not I. How do you know that I do not know what constitutes the enjoyment of fishes?" arrives at "You are not a fish; how do you know what constitutes the enjoyment of fishes?" At this point, it could be said that Huizi won the debate. But Zhuangzi turns back and, basing his reply on Huizi's "You are not a fish; how do you know what constitutes the enjoyment of fishes?" arrives at "When you say 'You are not a fish; how do you know what constitutes the enjoyment of fishes?' it shows that 'You knew that I knew this, and yet you put your question to me.' Therefore, I tell you that I know that the fish are enjoying themselves by standing over the river Hao."[3] The key here is how Zhuangzi—basing his argument on Huizi's statement "You are not a fish; how do you know what constitutes the enjoyment of fishes?"— proved that he already knew the fish were enjoying themselves.

I summarize Guo Xiang's commentary as follows. What Huizi intended to say was that without being a fish, one cannot know whether the fish are enjoying themselves. Now you (Huizi) ask me (Zhuangzi) how I know the fish are enjoying themselves (implying that I could not possibly know the fish are enjoying themselves), showing you know that I am not a fish. If you know that I am not a fish, this shows that "knowing" can exist in the form of being one and knowing the other. Therefore I do not have to become a fish to know the fish are enjoying themselves (which is being one and knowing the same). In other words, though you are not me, you can still know that I am not a fish, which shows that I even though I am not a fish, I can still know that the fish are enjoying themselves. With your words "How do you know what constitutes the enjoyment of fishes?" you reveal that you already knew that I know something about the happiness of fish, and nevertheless you still ask me. Therefore, I tell you that I know the fish are enjoying themselves as I stand over the Hao River, and there is no need for me to jump in the water to become a fish to know the fish are enjoying themselves.[4]

Clearly, the first half of Guo Xiang's commentary goes beyond Zhuangzi's original text. Zhuangzi did not infer that "Your saying I don't know that the fish are enjoying themselves shows that you know I am not a fish (and thus do not know the fish are enjoying themselves); though you are not me, you are able to know that I am not a fish. Then, even if I am not a fish, I am able to know the fish are enjoying themselves." Actually, it is difficult for such an inference to be tenable. "You are not me, but you know I am not a fish" and "I am not a fish, yet I know the fish are enjoying themselves" are two very different types of "knowing." First, knowing that something is not something is different from knowing that something is something. Knowing that something is not, is not the same as knowing something to be what it is. This means that knowing Zhuangzi is not a fish is different from knowing Zhuangzi is Zhuangzi.[5] Second, knowing what something is is different from knowing what goes on in that something's mind. Knowing the fish is a fish is different from knowing the fish is enjoying itself. (More important, if "happy" involves a value judgment, the situation is even more complex. But we will not go into this here.) Third, that Huizi knew that Zhuangzi knows is different from Zhuangzi knowing the fish. That Huizi knows Zhuangzi is a knowing between the same species—they are both human. However, that Zhuangzi knows the fish is a knowing between different species because they are human and fish, respectively. That Huizi knows Zhuangzi is a knowing between the same species, and that Zhuangzi knows the fish is a knowing between different species. A knowing between different species cannot be deduced from a knowing between the same species. Therefore, there are still many gaps to be filled from "Huizi knows Zhuangzi is not a fish" to "Zhuangzi knows the fish are enjoying themselves." Zhuangzi cannot deduce that he knows the fish are enjoying themselves directly from "Huizi knows that he, Zhuangzi, is not a fish." This part of Guo Xiang's commentary is not something Zhuangzi had intended to say, and therefore we have no reason to go into it any further.

The second half of Guo Xiang's commentary is consistent with what Zhuangzi wanted to say and is by itself tenable. Let's go over it again. Your question "How do you know what constitutes the enjoyment of fishes?" shows that you already knew something about me knowing the fish are enjoying themselves, and yet you ask me that very question, and therefore I say I know the fish are enjoying themselves from here on the bridge over the Hao River. I do not have to become a fish to know that the fish are enjoying themselves. This involves different interpretations of the expression "How can you know?" (especially the words "how can"). What Huizi intended to ask was "How can you possibly know?" but Zhuangzi interprets the question as "How did you know?" "How can you possibly know?" implies that it is impossible to know, whereas "How did you know?" implies "You already know. I just want to know through what method you were able to know." Zhuangzi interprets "How can you know?" as "How did you know?" which includes the premise that Huizi already knew that Zhuangzi knows that the fish are enjoying themselves, and therefore Zhuangzi says that he knows the fish are enjoying themselves on the bridge. If Zhuangzi were to win the debate in such a way, one could assert that he resorted to sophistry, when in actuality he did not win the debate.

Zhuangzi did not need to rely on the sophistry of "How can you know?" to win. In other words, even if in compliance with what Huizi intended to ask ("You are not a fish, so how can you possibly know that the fish are enjoying themselves?"), we can also conclude that Zhuangzi knew that the fish are enjoying themselves. To every question there is a "what is asked" and a "why it is asked." "What is asked" carries with it the anticipated answer of the person asking. "Why it is asked" means that there is always a reason the question is asked, with the person asking the question basing it upon his preunderstanding. Huizi asks Zhuangzi, "How do you know what constitutes the enjoyment of fishes?" From the point of view of "what is asked," even though Huizi's anticipated answer was "I don't," at least the possibility that "I know" still exists. From the point of view of "why it is asked," the question shows that Huizi knew beforehand something about Zhuangzi knowing that the fish are enjoying themselves and is merely asking this question because he had a doubt about Zhuangzi's claim to know.[6] If Huizi knew nothing of Zhuangzi knowing that the fish are enjoying themselves, he would not have asked such a question. Zhuangzi could prove he knew that the fish are enjoying themselves from the "why it is asked" point of view, thus winning the debate in the end. Actually, in the conventional reading, this is how it is understood that Zhuangzi won the debate.

But did Zhuangzi win? Zhuangzi's winning argument was based upon "You knew that I knew it, and yet you put your question to me," with the conclusion being "I know it (from our enjoying ourselves together) over the Hao River." My question is this: even if Huizi accepted Zhuangzi's premise, it still does not mean Zhuangzi won. Huizi could have asked, "I know you know the fish are enjoying themselves, but this does not necessarily mean that the fish are enjoying themselves. You may have been tricked into believing that the fish are enjoying themselves—it is just your imagination, and it has nothing to do with the fish actually being happy."[7]

To summarize, to make the transition from knowing that the fish are enjoying themselves to the fish are enjoying themselves, there needs to be more evidence. According to Zhuangzi's original words, "These fishes come out and play about at their ease—that is the enjoyment of fishes," it is clear that he said "the enjoyment of fishes" and not that he "knows what constitutes the enjoyment of fishes." Therefore, Huizi could have asked Zhuangzi to "keep to the original question" and pointed out to Zhuangzi that he did not prove that the fish are enjoying themselves but only that he "knows that the fish are enjoying themselves." Unfortunately, Huizi did not continue on this path.

Allow me to use two different expressions to summarize "the fish are enjoying themselves" and "knows the fish are enjoying themselves." "The fish are enjoying themselves" is a fact, but "knows what constitutes the enjoyment of fishes" is an experience. In this debate, it seems that only the experience of "Zhuangzi knows the fish are enjoying themselves" can be proven, and he was not able to prove the fact that the "fish are enjoying themselves."[8]

If this were the case, then Zhuangzi really did lose the debate. But Zhuangzi's disciples did not seem to think so, or else they would not have recorded this debate. As we read this text, we would think that Zhuangzi won the debate. Why? The premise of Zhuangzi losing the debate is that when he said, "These fishes come out and play about at their ease—that is the enjoyment of fishes," this sentence was interpreted as a fact, not as an experience. In fact, this is where many have misinterpreted Zhuangzi. This sentence can only be a description of an experience, not a statement of fact, because there is no such thing as fish enjoying themselves. What we consider to be a fact—that "fish are enjoying themselves"—is merely an experience of us "knowing the fish are enjoying themselves." To take this one step further, "the fish are enjoying themselves" is meaningless to Zhuangzi, and it is impossible for Zhuangzi to say something that is absolutely meaningless and irrelevant to him. What is meaningful to Zhuangzi is his experience of "knowing the fish are enjoying themselves," which is why when he said, "These fishes come out and play about at their ease—that is the enjoyment of fishes," his statement could be related only to the experience of "knowing the fish are enjoying themselves" and is not a statement of fact, that is, that the "fish are enjoying themselves." The winner of this debate is Zhuangzi.

2

Through analysis, we can say with confidence that Zhuangzi won the debate. But what is the relationship between these kinds of analysis and philosophy, especially the nature of philosophy? If the nature of philosophy is analysis, then what follows is a waste of time, for we have already clarified the debate between Zhuangzi and Huizi. But analysis is merely a technique of philosophy, and not the nature and purpose of philosophy itself, and that is my subject.

Let's start where the analysis left off.

Through analysis, we understand the difference between fact and experience. We have pointed out that experience can be easily explained and that fact is difficult to prove. From the happy fish debate, we have learned that we come into contact with experience before we come into contact with fact (there might not even be such thing as a fact). We take part in and remember experience clearly, but we cannot say we are able to grasp fact every time without failure. Experience is directly given to us; fact can be proven only later, and even then such proof might still be faulty. If philosophy demands that we start at places where we can be certain, then we should begin with experience rather than fact. However, traditional philosophy has refused to accept that what we are experiencing is real and beyond doubt but instead relies on suspicious fact to be the foundation and origin of philosophy. How has this come about? Fact is thought to be permanently real, whereas experience is only temporarily realistic. When experience that is temporarily realistic is placed beside and contradicts the permanently real fact, then the former is be considered to be unrealistic.

Fact as the basis of traditional philosophy is being questioned and deconstructed by contemporary philosophers on a wide scale. Whether or not to accept fact as its root or origin seems to have become the great divide between traditional and contemporary philosophy. More and more of contemporary philosophy tends to claim that there is nothing which is not a product of interpretation.[9] Such a tendency in contemporary philosophy has reached its peak in deconstructionism. Contemporary philosophy's deconstruction of permanently real fact did not lead to its acceptance of real experience in the present; instead, it has led to another extreme—a place of differences that has total disregard for what is real. This is especially apparent in Derrida's works.

Derrida criticizes metaphysics in the Western tradition as "the metaphysics of presence," a type of metaphysics he denounces as assuming there exists a world of the absolutely real, which makes it the ultimate subject matter in philosophical description. Being factually present is the subject matter of linguistic description; linguistics is the subject matter of the description of words. Therefore, in the pyramid of Western metaphysics, being factually present is placed at the top, and words are placed at an unimportant, even marginal level. Derrida fundamentally opposes this tendency of giving priority to being present. His reasoning is that there is no way we can attain independent and pure fact. Indeed, what we have is merely a play on differences. According to Derrida's concept of *différance,* anything that is, is fundamentally an intersection of differences with other things. The nature of anything is created by differences between itself and other things from which it is different. Without differences from other things, a thing cannot be what it is, or it cannot stand out as what it is. Hence, nothing can ever appear as itself completely or simply be formed by itself.[10]

Derrida's opposition to the notion of the metaphysics of presence shows that his stance in philosophy does not begin with present fact but instead with language and even written symbols that are not present. However, I need to point out that the present fact to which Derrida is opposed is actually not present in the way that is similar to the notion of "fish enjoying themselves" in the debate between Zhuangzi and Huizi. "Fish enjoying themselves" is often mistaken as a present fact, when actually it is not present; what is really present is the experience of "knowing the fish are enjoying themselves."

As a fact, "fish enjoying themselves" is not present, but this does not mean philosophy can retreat into symbols and language games, for after all, there is still the experience of "knowing the fish are enjoying themselves" that is present, and in philosophy, one can not completely overlook this experience. From the happy fish debate, we can see that, regardless of whether we find the root or origin of philosophy in "fish enjoying themselves" or in language games, it could only lead to the conclusion that Huizi won the debate. Only when we find the root or origin of philosophy in the experience of "knowing the fish are enjoying themselves" can we conclude that Zhuangzi was the winner of the debate.

Our question now is, why does philosophy tend to rely less upon experience, which is present, and more upon fact and linguistic discourse, which are not present? The reason for this is probably because philosophers, who are used to abstract thinking and formal observations, find it difficult to understand the factuality of being present. To many philosophers, things that are not realistically factual are not facts, and thus one can play language games with them without limitation. Zhuangzi did not think the same way. He believed that between a fact, which is absolutely real, and discourse, which is totally lacking in reality, there still exists at least the reality of experience. The reality of the experience is neither permanently and absolutely true nor permanently and absolutely untrue, whereas the reality of being present is ostensibly factual and is something that philosophy can rely upon.

Now we have three different concepts of the root or origin of philosophy: (1) fact, which is permanently factual, (2) language games, which have a total disregard for what is factual, and (3) experience, which is presently factual (or momentarily factual). The first concept is the general consensus among traditional Western philosophers; the second is the consensus among contemporary Western philosophers following the linguistic turn; and the third is the basic stance of Eastern philosophy, with Zhuangzi as one of its representatives. We need further explanation to clarify Zhuangzi and his philosophical position.

Clearly Zhuangzi, who openly detests the linguistic, the verbal, and even the writing games played, is not a supporter of the language games in contemporary philosophy.[11] His essay "On Leveling All Things" in certain ways is an effort to be rid of the differences generated by the signifier and to emphasize the consistency of presence. To rephrase this using terms with which I am familiar, it means to be rid of differences of representation and to emphasize the consistency in the appearance of things. By "appearance" I mean things as they exist in their own way. By "representation" I mean a description of things as they exist in their own way, whether through language or other descriptive methods.

Zhuangzi believed that even the number "1," when described through language, becomes "3."[12] Linguistic representation is the source of the multiple appearances of things. This is a similarity in thought shared by Zhuangzi and other contemporary philosophers of language. Where they differ is this: contemporary philosophers of language recognize this variety in the appearance of language, whereas Zhuangzi did not. Not only did Zhuangzi oppose the idea of the representation of things through linguistic means, but he was also opposed to the notion of representation based upon causal relationships. The appearance is always in the "here" and "now," but people are used to explaining the "now" through "the past" and "the future" and explaining the "here" through the "there." Thus, the appearance of "now" and "here" is always represented and therefore veiled by "the past," "the future," and the "there" (as well as language and other writing methods). In light of this, there can be no true appearance, and the result is a total failure to reach a true "one."

Zhuangzi does not propose that "1" is a permanently real fact but instead treats it as a collection of many experiences that are present and realistic. Zhuangzi's "On Leveling All Things" is not an attempt to make everything the same but rather to make everything equally different.[13] Dao can be the root of the universe, but as the root to the universe, it does not have any meaning. In this sense, "dao" is often interpreted as "nothing" or "absence." Dao as the most primal nature of nothing or absence is to set no limitations and to allow all things to exist the way that they are, to allow all things in the universe to fully become what they are. This is the concept of the so-called Heavenly Ways.[14]

The "here and now" existence of things, for example, "1," is at one with itself. Any linguistic representation will, through the notion of "many," result in the veiling of "1." There exists for all things the "here and now" existence of "1," as well as the "there and then" existence of "1." On a more extreme level, the existence of the same thing in a different time and a different place can be interpreted as a totally different thing. Zhuang Zhou as a butterfly in his dreams is different from Zhuang Zhou as himself in person in the daytime. These are two different forms of being at different times, and they can be even more extremely interpreted as a totally unrelated butterfly and Zhuang Zhou the person (or two Zhuang Zhous who are totally unrelated to each other).[15] To take this one step further, life and death can be interpreted as two different forms of being in one's life, or it can be understood as two totally different "lives."[16] This does not mean that there is a one and only, permanently real Zhuang Zhou, nor is there a totally unreal Zhuang Zhou. What we have is a Zhuang Zhou who is realistically present in different experiences.

Through this analysis, we can easily understand the so-called reality in experience. "The fish are enjoying themselves" is real in the experience only when Zhuangzi was present at the bridge over the Hao River; it is not universally true, nor is it a completely fictional linguistic game.

3

Different concepts of the root or origin of philosophy will generate different kinds of philosophy. In summary, to base this root upon permanently real facts or upon linguistic games with total disregard of what is real will result in the interpretation of philosophy as merely a form of discourse, whereas basing philosophy upon realistic and present experience will result in the interpretation of philosophy as a way of life. "The fish are enjoying themselves" as a fact or as words relating to "the fish are enjoying themselves" are both unrelated to our lives (at least not closely related); only "knowing the fish are enjoying themselves" is related to our lives. When we read the debate between Zhuangzi and Huizi, we often have the impression that Zhuangzi won the debate. But when we pause and look at things again, we are convinced that Huizi won the debate. The reason for this is that, under normal circumstances, we are used to perceiving words through experience in life, and only in special circumstances—for example, in philosophical debates—do we perceive experience in life through words. Philosophy detached from presence is in fact detached from life.

After the "linguistic turn" in contemporary philosophy, only a few people still remain who believe that philosophy is intimately attached to life. Contemporary philosophy has become more and more detached from the notion of presence. Pressure from professional competition and the enjoyment of the freedom from being present to being detached has produced philosophy that is immersed in the game of redescription. Richard Rorty states frankly that, through using and redescribing, one can achieve the goal of self-enrichment and self-creativity.[17] Stanley Cavell points out that the practices in philosophy are mere practices in linguistics, with reading and writing as its basic form.[18] Philosophy is becoming more and more remote from the lives of people and even from philosophers themselves. This, in fact, is the reason behind the increasingly distant, abstract, and impoverished nature of philosophy.[19]

However, there is evidence showing that philosophy was once practiced as a way of life in both the Western and the Eastern histories of philosophy.[20] In the history of Chinese philosophy, philosophy was chosen and practiced as a way of life. In the "Tianxia" chapter of the *Zhuangzi,* the different schools of philosophy are described as different ways of living.[21] Those whom we refer to today as the pre-Qin philosophers were merely people who led different ways of lives. To accept a certain school of thought, one must first accept and practice its way of life. The profound wisdom of Zhuangzi's philosophy, which has long been forgotten and can easily be misinterpreted, is that identifying the root or origin of philosophy in the experience of life allows us to live meaningful lives in the present. Allow me to add some closing commentary.

To seek the root or origin of philosophy in realistic experience is to better understand the present once again. People are used to measuring the present through the past and future and are reluctant to understand the present by existing in the present. Also, once we focus on the present, the present seems to fade from existence. Especially as a result of modern technology, our time has been dissected into small segments. Though we exist in the present, we can never experience the present. The present has been segmented into slivers of a second, which are impossible to experience and are located within the swift transitioning from the past into the future. The loss of the present is the loss of the meaning of our life. Seeking the root or origin of philosophy in realistic experience means that the present that we live in cannot be infinitely segmented. We can indeed feel the present, and the present in which we live can be big or small; it can span a great deal of time, and it can span a shorter period of time. The present that we live in is not a point in time that can be infinitely divided but rather the entirety of an occurrence that we experience. In other words, we experience and calculate the present by the occurrences that we experience, not by the clock.

To return to the present does not mean that we revoke the past and the future. Indeed, to return to the present, one must sever the causal association between the present and the past and future and allow the existence of the present to make its meaning fully apparent. This does not mean that the present does not have its time dimensions in terms of the past and the future or a spatial dimension in terms of here and there. To return to the existence of the present, one need only to state that its association with the past, the future, and the "there" is based upon the existence of the present. The past, the future, and the "there" are extensions of the existence of the present, and not the opposite, where the past, the future, and the "there" determine the existence of the present.

Returning to the present does not mean hedonism. Hedonism is often denounced for its excessive consumption of the present. In the criticisms of hedonism, we seem to have unconsciously assumed that the existence of the present has been split into two aspects: one is the existence of the present, the other is the enjoyment and consumption of the existing present. The philosophy of returning to the present—far from accepting this division—rejects both it and the separation between the means and the objective. To allow the full appearance of the meaning of the existing present is to enjoy the existing present. However, this enjoyment is not an enjoyment or a consumption of "the present" but rather an enjoyment of "being in the present." This enjoyment of "being in the present" does not come at the price of the consumption of one's existence; it can even bring out the inert drive and passions of being in existence. In fact, returning to the present requires on certain levels qualities of ascetic practices, for one needs to abstain from the desires arising from the past, the future, and the "there." It is not easy—it takes arduous work to learn to direct one's existence to the here and now.

The philosophy of returning to the present is both theory and practice. It demands not only that philosophy provide an explanation of and guidance on the art of living but also that philosophers become exemplary models in the art of living for others to imitate. Philosophers cannot merely provide people with the art of living through words that are impossible to put into practice but must use their own lives as an experiment, as a prototype in the art of living. This demands that philosophers be equipped with not only knowledge of the world of living but also the courage to delve into life practices to find the wisdom to solve the specific issues of the day.

NOTES

Translated by Tu Qiang.

1. James Legge's translation: http://nothingistic.org/library/chuangtzu/chuang49 .html. Modified by the translator.

2. Scholars who share this view are not among the minority. For example, acclaimed Chinese philosophy historian Zhang Dainian openly stated that when he studied this debate in his twenties and thirties, he thought that what Huizi said ("You are not a fish; how do you know what constitutes the enjoyment of fishes?") was philosophically profound and that what Zhuangzi said ("that is the enjoyment of fishes") was merely his subjective assumption. See Zhang Dainian, "The Happy Fish Debate" 庄惠濠梁之辩, in *The Complete Works of Zhang Dainian* 张岱年全集, vol. 8 (Shijiazhuang: Hebei Renmin Press, 1996), 398. Chen Guimiao believed that Zhuangzi had shifted the focus of the debate by misinterpreting "how can" as "how did you know" rather than "how can you know." Thus, Zhuangzi was able to tell Huizi that he "knew it on the bridge over the Hao River" and was able to quickly and easily conclude the debate. "Therefore Zhuangzi did not really win the debate, even in the last round" (Chen Guimiao, "Huishi's Academic Life" 惠施之学术生涯, *Ehu Monthly* 鹅湖月刊 3, no. 27 [1977], 17–24.

3. For details, see Cen Yicheng, "On Knowing and Happiness in the Happy Fish Debate" 鱼乐之辩之知与乐, *Ehu Monthly* 鹅湖月刊 3, no. 27 (1977), 2–12.

4. Guo Xiang comments: "According to Huizi's original meaning: You are not a fish and therefore cannot know about the fish. You are not I. And today, you ask me how I can know the fish are enjoying themselves. This shows that you know that I am not a fish. Your asking me such shows that knowing can exist between different beings; therefore I don't have to be a fish to know about the fish. Though you already knew the answer to your question, yet you still ask me; therefore, I tell you I knew it while standing here upon the bridge over the Hao River, and there is no need for me to jump into the water!" (《庄子注》卷六："寻惠子之本言云：非鱼则无缘相知耳。今子非我也，而云汝安知鱼乐者，是知我之非鱼也。苟知我之非鱼，则凡相知者果可以此知彼，不待是鱼然后知鱼也。故循子安知之云，已知吾之所知矣，而方复问我，我正知之于濠上耳，岂待入水哉！").

5. This criticism is applicable to Feng Youlan's equation of positive method and negative method, which were formulated by Feng Youlan as the basic methods of philosophy. Feng Youlan said: "There are two methods in real metaphysics: one is Positive Method, the other is Negative Method. Positive Method is to analyze metaphysics through logic. Negative Method shows what is unspeakable in metaphysics. To show what is unspeakable in metaphysics is also a method to discuss metaphysics" (in *Sansongtang Quanji* 三松堂全集, vol. 5 [Zhengzhou: Henan Renmin Press, 1986], 173). Feng Youlan believes that the negative method articulates what metaphysics is not, "but once we know what it is not, we know something about what it is" (in *A Short History of*

Chinese Philosophy 中国哲学簡史 [Beijing: Peking University Press, 1985], 393). But knowing what it is does not appear directly from knowing what it is not. Instead, knowing what it is comes from another introspection or awareness; it requires a leap or transition. For details, see Peng Feng, "The Aesthetic Dimension in Feng Youlan's Theory of Life States" 冯友兰人生境界理论的美学维度, *Journal of Peking University* 北京大学学报, 34, no. 1 (1997), 57–62.

6. Lin Xiyi had subtly expressed this point in his commentaries: "Going back to your original question, when you asked me, 'You are not a fish, how is it that you know the enjoyment of the fishes?' it shows that you knew about me, therefore you were able to ask me this question. Since you knew this about me, my reply to you is that I knew it on this river. The two men knew each other best, and looking back on their conversation, one can see that they understood each other" (循其本者，请反其初也。言汝当初问 '我非鱼安知鱼之乐'，是汝知我之意，方有此问。汝既如此知我，则我于濠上亦如此知鱼也。二人最为相知，想当时对语亦自可观。" 见庄子口义卷六。).

7. Historically, many commentators have noticed this point. For example, Yidu's commentary reads: "From my reasoning as I was enjoying myself upon the bridge over the Hao River, I knew of the fish's enjoyment." Bixu's commentary: "As I was taking a stroll and so I saw the fish's state of being" （疑独注："以我在濠上之乐推之，则知鱼之乐矣。" 碧虚注："在我逍遥，则见鱼之容与。" 均见褚伯秀《南华真经义海纂微》卷五十五。).

8. The Song dynasty scholar Li Shibiao noticed this point, and he believed that this debate was not intended to clarify the fact that "these fishes come out and play about at their ease—that is the enjoyment of fishes" (李士表："夫出而扬游而泳，无网罟之患，无濡沫之思，从容乎一水之间者，将以是为鱼乐乎？以是为鱼乐，又奚待南华而后知？" 见褚伯秀《南华真经义海纂微》卷五十五。). He believed that the meaning of this commentary is to show the following: Can we indeed perceive the fishes playing about at their ease as the happiness of the fishes? If we do perceive it as the happiness of the fish, then why do we have to wait for Zhuangzi to know this? In other words, if the happiness of fish is an objectively existing fact, then every person is capable of knowing it, and there would be no need for Zhuangzi's confirmation of knowing this fact. This commentary implies that the "happiness of the fishes" is not an objectively existent fact.

9. As Friedrich Nietzsche remarked, "Facts are precisely what there is not, only interpretations," in *The Will to Power* (New York: Vintage, 1968), para. 481.

10. As Derrida says, "The play of differences supposes . . . syntheses and referrals which forbid at any moment, or in any sense, that a simple element be *present* in and of itself, referring only to itself . . . , no element can function . . . without referring to another element which itself is not simply present. This interweaving results in each 'element' . . . being constituted on the basis of the trace within it of the other elements of the chain or system . . . Nothing, neither among the elements nor within the system, is anywhere ever simply present or absent. There are only, everywhere, differences and traces of traces." See Jacques Derrida, *Positions* (London: Athlone, 1981), 26.

11. There are examples in which Zhuangzi openly denounces the overuse of words: "What the world thinks the most valuable about *dao* is to be found in books. But books are only a collection of words. Words have what is valuable in them—what is valuable in words is the ideas they convey. But those ideas are a sequence of something else—and what that something else is cannot be conveyed by words. When the world, because of the value that it attaches to words, commits them to books, that for which it so values them may not deserve to be valued—because that which it values is not what

is really valuable" (《庄子·天道》:"世之所贵道者，书也。书不过语，语有贵也。语之所贵者，意也，意有所随。意之所随者，不可以言传也。而世因贵言传书，世虽贵之，我犹不足贵也，为其贵非其贵也。"). "Fish traps are employed to catch fish, but when the fish are caught, the people forget the traps. Snares are employed to catch hares, but when the hares are caught, people forget the snares. Words are employed to convey ideas, but when the ideas are apprehended, people forget the words. I would like to have a word with such a person who has forgotten the words!" (《庄子·外物》:"筌者所以在鱼，得鱼而忘筌；蹄者所以在兔，得兔而忘蹄；言者所以在意，得意而忘言。吾安得夫忘言之人而与之言哉！"). "When we toil our spirits and intelligence obstinately determined (to establish our own views) and do not know the agreement (that underlies them and the views of others), then we have what is called 'Three in the morning.' What is meant by 'Three in the morning'? A keeper of monkeys, in giving them their acorns, (once) said, 'In the morning I will give you three (measures) and in the evening four.' This made them all angry, and he said, 'Very well. In the morning I will give you four and in the evening three.' His two proposals were substantially the same, but the result of the one was to make the creatures angry and of the other to make them pleased—an illustration of the point I am insisting on" (《庄子·齐物论》:"劳神明为一而不知其同也，谓之朝三。何谓朝三？狙公赋芧 曰：'朝三而暮四'。众狙皆怒。曰：'然则朝四而暮三'。众狙皆悦。名实未亏而喜怒为用，亦因是也。"). The difference between "Three in the morning and four in the evening" and "Four in the morning and three in the evening" exists only at the level of significance and not at the level of presence.

12. "Heaven, Earth, and I were produced together, and all things and I are one. Since they are one, can there be speech about them? But since they are spoken of as one, must there not be room for speech? One and speech are two; two and one are three. Going on from this (in our enumeration), the most skillful reckoner cannot reach (the end of the necessary numbers), and how much less can ordinary people do so! Therefore from nothing we proceed to something until we arrive at three; proceeding from something to something, how many will we reach? Let us abjure such a procedure and simply rest here" (《庄子·齐物论》:"天地与我并生，而万物与我为一。既已为一矣，且得有言乎？既已谓之一矣，且得无言乎？一与言为二，二与一为三。自此以往，巧历不能得，而况其凡乎！故自无适有以至于三，而况自有适有乎！无适焉，因是已。").

13. Zhuangzi said, "Everything has its inherent character and its proper capability. There is nothing that does not have these. Therefore, this being so, if we take a stalk of grain and a (large) pillar, a loathsome (leper), and (a beauty like) Xi Shi, things large and things insecure, things crafty and things strange; they may in the light of the *dao* all be reduced to the same category (of opinion about them)" (《庄子·齐物论》:"物故有所然，物固有所可。[郭注：各然其所然，各可其所可。]无物不然，无物不可。故为是举莛与楹，厉与西施，恢恑憰怪，道通为一。[郭注：夫莛横而楹纵，厉丑而西施好，所谓齐者，岂必齐形状同规矩哉？故举纵横好丑，恢恑憰怪，各然其所然，各可其所可，则形虽万殊而性同得，故曰道通于一也。]"). So we see that what Zhuangzi means by "leveling all things" (another translation for "the adjustment of controversies") is not the similarity shared by all things in terms of shapes and sizes but rather the "inherent character and proper capability" of all things. As long as all things become themselves and do not come into comparison and competition, though they are massively different, they can exist equally in independence.

14. The interpretation of "Heavenly Ways" in *Zhuangzi: Adjustment of Controversies* is as follows: "When the wind blows, the sounds from the myriad apertures are different, and its cessation makes them stop of themselves. Both of these things arise

from the wind and the apertures themselves—should there be any other agency that excites them?" (《庄子·齐物论》:"夫吹万不同,而使其自己也。咸其自取,怒者其谁也哉。"). Guo Xiang's commentary states the following: "These are the sounds of heaven. Could they be described as anything else? Heavenly sounds are the combined sounds of earthly sounds that come from the various caves, human sounds from things such as bamboo flutes, and together with all other life forms, they become what is called the heavenly sounds (or heaven-made sounds). Nothing that is nothing is incapable of bringing something into being; since something has not yet come into being, it is incapable of bringing all things into being. If this is the case, what then has brought all things into being? All things have come into being without knowing how. They come into being by themselves, and not through me. Since all things did not come through me, and I did not come through all things, I came into being through myself. Since I have come into being through myself, it can be said that I am self-made (or heaven-made). Heaven-made means not to be contrived and therefore is best described as what is heavenly. To describe something as heavenly is to clarify that all things are self-made (or heaven-made) and not that the heavens are not simply the heavens. There are those who believe that heaven is something that all things must fall subject to. Since heaven does not possess itself, how can it be in possession of all things? Heaven is the generic name of all things. Since nothing is on a par with heaven, who or what is able to dominate all things? Therefore, all things come into being by themselves and not through other things—this is the way of heaven. All things come into being through themselves and are in control of their own selves. Who else can make them become what they are? This sheds further light on the notion of heaven–made" (郭象注:"此天籁也。夫天籁者,岂复别有一物哉?即众窍比竹之属,接乎有生之类,而共成一天耳。无既无矣,则不能生有。有之未生,又不能为生。然则生生者谁哉?块然而自生耳。自生耳,非我生也。我既不能生物,物亦不能生我,则我自然耳。自己而然,则谓之天然。天然耳,非为也,故以天言之。以天言之,所以明其自然也,岂苍苍之谓哉?而或者谓天籁役物使从已也,夫天且不能自有,况能有物哉?故天也者,万物之总名也。莫适为天,谁主役物乎?故物各自生而无所出焉,此天道也。物皆自得之耳。谁主怒之使然哉?此重明天籁也。").

15. What follows is *Zhuangzi: The Adjustment of Controversies*, in which we hear the story of the "Dream of the Butterfly" and Guo Xiang's interlinear commentary, which can best support this argument: "Formerly, I, Zhuang Zhou, dreamt that I was a butterfly, a butterfly flying about, feeling that it was enjoying itself. (Guo: Acting happy with himself and with wishes gladly fulfilled.) I did not know that it was Zhou. (Guo: This 'not knowing about a Zhou' while 'Zhuang Zhou fell into a dream and then there was a butterfly' is not different from the case of being dead. Since in its own place everything is completely in accord with its intentions, the one that is alive belongs to life just as the one that is dead belongs to death. From that we see what a mistake it is to worry about death while one is alive.) Suddenly I awoke and was myself again, the veritable Zhou. (Guo: Since this is said from the perspective of Zhuang Zhou, there is talk of 'awakening.' This does not necessarily falsify the dream.) I did not know whether it had formerly been Zhou dreaming that he was a butterfly, or whether it was now a butterfly dreaming that it was Zhou. (Guo: The not-knowing about a butterfly at this moment is not different from the not-knowing about a Zhuang Zhou during the time of the dream. Because at its own time everything is completely in accord with its intentions. Therefore it cannot be proven that there was not earlier a butterfly dreaming, so there is a Zhou there now. Insofar as it is possible in a dream to live through a whole century during a noontime nap, it cannot be proven that our present century is not a

dream during a noontime nap.) But between Zhou and a butterfly there must be a difference. (Guo: The distinction between waking and dreaming is not different from the separation between life and death. The reason it is possible to be self-content in accord with one's intentions is that these distinctions are firmly established and not that there are no distinctions.) This is a case of what is called the 'Transformation of Things.' (Guo: Well, the passage of time does not stop for a moment, and today does not persist in what follows. Thus yesterday's dream changes into one today. How could it be different with the change between life and death? Why should one let one's heart be made heavy by being moved back and forth between them? Being one, there is no knowledge of the other. Being a butterfly when dreaming is genuine. Relating this to human beings: When alive, one does not know whether one later may actually have beautiful concubines. Only the stupid think they really know that life is something delightful and death is something to be sad about. That is what is called 'never having heard of the changing of things.')" (《庄子·齐物论》："昔者庄周梦为蝴蝶，栩栩然蝴蝶也。(郭注：自喻适志与。自快得意悦愉而行。) 不知周也。(郭注：方其梦为蝴蝶而不知周，则与殊死不异也。然所在无不适志，则当生而系生者，必当死而恋死矣。由此观之，知夫在生而哀死者，误也。) 俄然觉，则蘧蘧然周也。(郭注：自周而言故称觉耳，未必非梦也。) 不知周之梦为蝴蝶，与蝴蝶之梦为周与？(郭注：今之不知蝴蝶，无异于梦之不知周也。而各适一时之志，则无以明蝴蝶之不梦为周矣。世有假寐而梦经百年者，则无以明今之百年非假寐之梦者也。) 周与蝴蝶则必有分矣。(郭注：夫觉梦之分，无异于死生之辩也。今所以自喻适志，由其分定，非由无分也。) 此之谓物化。(郭注：夫时不暂掉，而今不遂存。故昨日之梦，于今化矣。死生之变，岂异于此而劳心于其间哉？方为此，则不知彼梦为蝴蝶是也。取之于人，则一生之中，今不知后丽姬是也。而愚者窃窃然自以为知生之可乐死之可苦。未闻物化之谓也。)"). For analysis of this excerpt in detail, see Hans-Goreg Moeller, "Zhuangzi's 'Dream of the Butterfly': A Daoist Interpretation," *Philosophy East and West* 49, no. 4 (October 1999), 439–450.

16. Just before the "Dream of the Butterfly," Zhuangzi told another story to clarify the differences between life and death: "Li Ji was a daughter of the border Warden of Ai. When (the ruler of) the state of Jin first got possession of her, she wept till the tears wetted all the front of her dress. But when she came to the place of the king, shared with him his luxurious couch, and ate his grain-and-grass-fed meat, then she regretted that she had wept. How do I know that the dead do not repent of their former craving for life?" (《庄子·齐物论》："丽之姬，艾封人之子也晋国之始得之也，涕泣沾襟，及其至于王所，与王同筐床，食刍豢，而后悔其泣也。予恶乎知夫死者不悔其始之蕲生乎！").

17. Richard Rorty, *Contingency, Irony, and Solidarity* (Cambridge: Cambridge University Press, 1989), 24, 73–80.

18. Stanley Cavell, *In Quest of the Ordinary: Lines of Skepticism and Romanticism* (Chicago: University of Chicago Press, 1988), 10, 18, and *Conditions Handsome and Unhandsome: The Constitution of Emersonian Perfectionism* (Chicago: University of Chicago Press, 1990), 42.

19. For criticism, see Richard Shusterman, *Practicing Philosophy: Pragmatism and the Philosophical Life* (New York: Routledge, 1997).

20. After completing his in-depth study of ancient philosophy, the French historian of philosophy Pierre Hadot stated that "In ancient times, the essential characteristics of the phenomenon of 'philosophy' was that: at that time, philosophers were at foremost, people who lived by philosophy. In other words, philosophers were people who lived their lives by the rational guidance of their doctrines in which they believed. They were the practitioners of virtues—in its original meaning, philosophy is a choice of life,

and philosophical discussion can provide life with equality and theoretical foundation. But philosophical discussions were different from philosophy. . . . these discussions are not the essence of philosophy, also, only when it establishes a relationship with life can it have any meaning. As one of Epicurus's mottos tries to express: 'philosophers' discussions are pointless unless it [*sic*] can heal the souls in pain.'" (See Pierre Hadot, *Philosophy as a Way of Life: Spiritual Exercises from Socrates to Foucault,* (Oxford: Blackwell Publishing, 1995), 281–282.) Because philosophy is foremost a way of life and subsequently a form of discourse, in ancient philosophical times not only people such as Epicurus, who raised philosophical questions, were considered philosophers but also anyone who lived by the rules of Epicurus was also regarded as a philosopher. Cato the politician of Utica was also widely regarded as a philosopher, even a saint, though he did not raise thought-provoking matters, nor did he teach, but simply because he led a life according to the doctrines of the Stoics. Hadot includes many excellent examples of where philosophical life was highly regarded and philosophical debate was belittled. (See ibid., 272–275.)

21. Consider, for example, Zhuangzi's commentaries on Mozi: "To leave no example of extravagance to future generations; to show no wastefulness in the use of anything; to make no display in the degree of their (ceremonial) observances; to keep themselves (in their expenditure) under the restraint of strict and exact rule, so as to be prepared for occurring emergencies. . . . But now Mozi alone would have no singing during life and no wearing of mourning after death. As the rule for all, he would have a coffin of elaeococca wood three inches thick and without any enclosing shell. . . . The effect of this is that in this later time most of the Mohists wore skins and dolychos cloth, with shoes of wood or twisted hemp, not stopping day or night, but considering such toiling on their part as their highest achievement. They say that he who cannot do this is acting contrary to the way of Yu and not fit to be a Mohist" (《庄子·天下》："不侈于后世，不靡于万物，不晖于数度，以绳墨自矫，而备世之急。⋯⋯独生不歌，死不服，桐棺三寸而无椁，以为法式。⋯⋯使后世之墨者，多以裘褐为衣，以屐蹻为服，日夜不休，以自苦为极，曰：'不能如此，非禹之道也，不足谓墨。'"). Zhuangzi's commentaries on Song Xing and Yin Wen are as follows: "To keep from being entangled by prevailing customs; to shun all ornamental attractions in one's self; not to be reckless in his conduct to others; not to set himself stubbornly against a multitude; to desire the peace and repose of the world in order to preserve the lives of the people; and to cease his action when enough had been obtained for the nourishment of others and himself, showing that this was the aim of his mind. . . . They made the Huashan cap, and wore it as their distinguishing badge. In their intercourse with others, whatever their differences might be, they began by being indulgent to them. Their name for 'the Forbearance of the Mind' was 'the Action of the Mind.' By the warmth of affection they sought the harmony of joy, and to blend together all within the four seas; and their wish was to plant this everywhere as the chief thing to be pursued. They endured insult without feeling it a disgrace; they sought to save the people from fighting; they forbade aggression and sought to hush the weapons of strife, to save their age from war. In this way they went everywhere, counseling the high and instructing the low. Though the world might not receive them, they only insisted on their object the more strongly, and would not abandon it" (《庄子·天下》："不累于俗，不饰于物，不苟于人，不忮于众，愿天下之安宁以活民命，人我之养，毕足而止，以此白心。⋯作为华山之冠以自表，接万物以别宥为始。语心之容，命之曰心之行'。以聏合欢，以调海内。请欲置之以为主。见侮不辱，救民之斗，禁攻寝兵，救世之战。以此周行天下，上说下教。虽天下不取，强聒而不舍者也。"）.

His commentaries on Peng Meng, Tian Pian, and Shen Dao are as follows: "Public-spirited, and with nothing of the partisan; easy and compliant, without any selfish partialities; capable of being led, without any positive tendencies; following in the wake of others, without any double mind; not looking around because of anxious thoughts; not scheming in the exercise of their wisdom; not choosing between parties, but going along with all" (《庄子·天下》:"公而不党，易而无私，决然无主，趣物而不两，不顾于虑，不谋于知，于物无择，与之俱往。").

13

Rambling without Destination

On Daoist "You-ing" in the World

Hans-Georg MOELLER

1

A. C. Graham translates the title of the first chapter of the *Zhuangzi*, "Xiaoyaoyou 逍遙遊" in Chinese, as "going rambling without a destination."[1] The crucial word in this expression is *you* 遊, which, on its own, Graham often renders as "roaming." The addition to *you* in the chapter title, "Xiaoyao 逍遙," means "carefree" and serves to underline what one may call the happy-go-lucky character of this specific mode of moving around. *You* in the sense of "roaming" (or "rambling," but I return to this slightly alternative translation only at the end of this essay) is without doubt a very important term in the *Zhuangzi*. It occurs not only in the title of the first chapter but altogether ninety-five times in the whole text and, if one also adds the ten occurrences of the practically synonymous character *you* 游, written with the "water" radical, even more than one hundred times. There are only very few philosophically significant terms that are used with such frequency in this core Daoist text.

One of the most famous passages about *you* in the *Zhuangzi* is the "happy fish" dialogue between Zhuangzi and his philosopher friend Hui Shi. In English it goes like this:

Zhuangzi and Hui Shi were roaming around (*you* 遊) and got to a bridge above the Hao River. "The minnows swim around (*you* 遊) so free and easy," said Zhuangzi, "that's how the fish are happy." Hui Shi said: "You are not a fish, whence do you know that the fish are happy?" Zhuangzi replied: "You aren't me, whence do you know that I don't know the fish are happy?" Hui Shi said: We'll grant that not being you I don't know about you. You'll grant that you are not a fish, and that completes the case that you don't know the fish are happy." Zhuangzi said: "Let's go back to where we started. When you said '*whence* do you know that the fish are happy?' you asked me the question already knowing that I knew. I knew it from up above the Hao.[2]

This dialogue can be interpreted as a playful philosophical dispute between Hui Shi, the epistemological skeptic, and Zhuangzi, the Daoist. Rather than giving in to Hui Shi's reasoning, Zhuangzi finally "wins" by turning Hui Shi's own words against him in a pun. When Hui Shi asked "whence" or "where from" he, Zhuangzi, knew about the happiness of the fish, he implicitly admitted that Zhuangzi already knew about their happiness. If one takes into account the second pun in the story as well, namely the parallel use of the term *you* for both Zhuangzi's and Hui Shi's way of moving around and the motion of the fish, it can further be said that despite the species difference between Zhuangzi and the fish, which confines one of them to a life on land and the other to a life in water, they still share a common "mode of moving around in the world," namely *you*, and thus are capable of sharing their happiness.

For now, however, I intend to leave the philosophical meaning of the dialogue behind and, so to speak, move away from the bridge over the Hao and take a closer look at the term *you* and its meanings in the *Zhuangzi* and, by extension, in Daoism. I will, however, return to the bridge towards the end of this essay.

2

You in the sense of "roaming" is, right at the beginning of the text, associated with the movements of fish and birds. The "Xiaoyaoyou chapter" and thus the book itself begin with the depiction of a mythical fish named Kun, who transforms (note the notion of change, which is so important in the *Zhuangzi* and in Daoism) into a mythical bird named Peng, traversing the world. I think it is highly significant that this Daoist type of moving around is exemplified by the motion of animals and, as has been pointed out by Graham Parkes,[3] that these animals are quite removed from the human species by not being mammals. Graham's translation of *you* as "roaming" is therefore, I think, very appropriate. As opposed to terms referring to human movement such as "traveling," "journeying," or "going," "roaming" designates an *aimless* wandering that is not focused on getting from a starting point A to a final destination B. It is neither spatially nor temporally framed by an intentional beginning and end. It rather is a mode of motion one can be in or not and one that fish, birds, or, for that matter, Daoist sages may enter. In this sense, it may well be comparable to being asleep, a mode of consciousness that one also cannot consciously get into or out of and that does not lead from a purposeful start to a finish.

My closest personal experiences with this kind of movement, at least as far as I can remember, date back to my childhood. Having been lucky enough to grow up in the countryside and at a time when children were often simply outside in the company of other children who happened to be around, I spent quite a few days, or at least mornings or afternoons, in such aimless drifting. Of course, this aimlessness did not mean that we were not frequently looking for something, though usually not really knowing exactly for what, or that we did not have any practical concerns at all. Roaming animals will be constantly *aware* of their surroundings, having great sensitivity for food or water that may be close by, or for an enemy who is approaching. While roaming, children and animals will switch to a gathering, hunting, or fleeing mode from time to time, but again, this does not lead them from a specific point A to another specific point B.

I am afraid I increasingly lost the capacity for such roaming in the countryside as I grew older. (On the other hand, perhaps as a toddler I may have been capable of such "endless" roaming simply in my bedroom.) Today, even when hiking for pleasure, I usually rely on a map and have a certain goal or at least a path fixed before venturing out. And while on the move, I am anxiously making sure not to "get lost." There is hope, though. Once, during a class on Daoism in the United States, I talked about that apparent inability of human adults to experience *you* in their own everyday activities. I was, however, contradicted by some of the participants. Several "mature" female students assured me quite convincingly that they would regularly enter into an at least somewhat comparable state of "*you*-ing," namely, when shopping. It was soothing to come to know that such ancient Daoist forms of motion can be pursued even right at the heart of contemporary capitalism.

In sum, the term *you* in the *Zhuangzi* can refer to an itinerant form of life and inhabiting the world, which is common to animals such as fish and birds. This very form of life is shared by the Daoist sage, who, to refer to the *Zhuangzi* again, "has abodes for no longer than a morning."[4] *You* refers to a mobile form of dwelling within one's surroundings, subject to constant change and without orientation toward a final goal. This "non-teleological" or "carefree" type of, so to speak, "being on the way" is at the same time one of heightened awareness. It is not a dumb or an inattentive state of mere vegetation but rather open and sensitive to all kinds of stimuli and environmental triggers. Thus, while lacking any utilitarian focus on final outcomes or "net results," it is both a pragmatically efficient and aesthetically pleasurable form of existence (again: think of shopping).

3

When we look at the numerous occurrences of *you* in the *Zhuangzi,* it becomes clear, however, that this "profane" use of *you,* indicating an itinerant, aimless, and attentive way of moving around in the world concretely practiced by animals and sages, is complemented by a more poetic use of the term illustrating a more elevated form of existence.

A sage may "roam in the wilderness where no humans are" (*you yu wurenzhiye* 遊於無人之野) as a recluse outside of society.[5] Such an existence outside the human sphere can be extended beyond all confines, and in these instances the *Zhuangzi* speaks about "roaming the limitless" (*you wuqiong* 遊無窮)[6] or "roaming the realm of Nothingwhatever" (*you wuheyouzhixiang* 遊無何有之鄉)[7] or of "the one who roams in nonpresence" (*you yu wuyouzhe* 遊於無有者).[8] Similarly, a sage may "roam the land without borders (*you wujizhiye* 遊無極之野)[9] or "roam the boundless" (*you wuduan* 遊無端).[10] One passage in chapter 11 of the *Zhuangzi* depicts a dialogue between a Daoist sage and an obviously yet unenlightened questioner. Describing his state of being, the sage says: "Floatingly I roam not knowing what I am getting at, and wildly crazy not knowing where I go to" (*fuyou buzhi suoqiu, changkuang buzhi suowang* 浮遊不知所求，猖狂不知所往).[11]

In these instances, the sages or mythic figures who engage in *you*-ing are not simply strolling around but have entered some extraordinary state of, for lack of a better word, trance. Perhaps more reminiscent of the appearance of shamans than children, these figures are somewhat aloof, difficult to talk to, seemingly erratic and detached. The language in which they talk or with which they are described is much bolder and lyrical and much less plain than that used, for instance, in the dialogues between Zhuangzi and Hui Shi. If one would still be allowed to make such a distinction, one could say that the quite striking linguistic differences between some more prosaic passages in the *Zhuangzi,* on the one hand, and some quite mannerist passages, on the other, mirror a difference between the philosophical and religious dimensions of this text.[12] Be that as it may, the roaming ones in these poetic passages are often, but not always, single, in every case, though, probably male, accomplished Daoist sages, dwelling wonderfully and strangely in some other dimension, altogether different from those, if there are any, they encounter.

The profound difference between these sages and others is explicitly stressed in some passages: they roam (*you,* of course) in different realms.[13] These sages are *outside* of or *beyond* some confined sphere, whereas the others are *inside* this space. Actually, these different spheres of roaming are used to indicate the—not so much essential as existential—differences between Daoists and Confucians. In a passage in chapter 6 of the *Zhuangzi,* Confucius, as always concerned with mourning rituals, had sent one of his disciples, Zigong, to take part in the funeral of a Daoist sage. When Zigong arrives, he sees the two Daoist sage-companions of the deceased happily celebrating the death of their friend.[14] When Zigong reports his encounter to Confucius, the Master explains to him what sort of people these men are:

> "They are the sort that roam beyond the guidelines," said Confucius, "I am the sort that roams within the guidelines. Beyond and within have nothing in common, and to send you to mourn was stupid on my part. They are at the stage of being fellow man with the maker of things, and go roaming in the single breath that breathes through heaven and earth. . . . Heedlessly they go roving beyond the dust and grime, go rambling through the lore in which

there's nothing to *do*. How could they be finicky about the rites of common custom, on watch for the inquisitive eyes and ears of the vulgar?[15]

No longer concerned with the shift from life to death, a Daoist sage is capable, as the text says about those three companions, of "climbing the sky, roaming the mists, and go whirling into the infinite."[16] They do not swim in water like fish or walk on the earth like Hui Shi and Zhuang Zhou but have propelled themselves to loftier grounds and are, somewhat bird-like, as it is famously said of the elusive Daoist master Liezi, "riding the wind."[17] This is, apparently, "how they *roam*."

4

In the *Zhuangzi,* the term *you* also appears several times along with the term *xin* 心 or "heartmind." Here it is used verbally in a "causative" fash-ion (following Graham's translation) so that the expression *youxin* 遊心 means "to let the heartmind roam." In certain cases this phrase is used parallel to *you* on its own. Just as, as mentioned earlier, we find the expression "roaming the limitless" (*you wuqiong* 遊無窮),[18] we also find "letting the heartmind roam in the limitless" (*youxin yu wuqiong* 遊心於無窮).[19] Obviously, both expressions are quite similar. However, *youxin* adds a more specific sense to the notion of "*you*-ing" that is worth explor-ing a little further.

The expression *youxin* indicates that the *you*-ing of the sages is some-thing their heartmind does. While, on the one hand, it is their general mode of existence, it is also the way their *xin* operates. Three occurrences in the Inner Chapters shed more light on what this entails. A passage in chapter 4 states the following: "To let the heart-mind roam with other things as its chariot, and by trusting to the inevitable nurture the centre of *you*, is the farthest one can go."[20] Another passage in chapter 5 depicts yet one more Daoist sage, who says, "Such a man cannot even tell apart the function of eyes and ears, and lets the heart-mind go roaming in har-mony with efficacy (*de* 德)."[21] Acknowledging the difficulty of interpret-ing these once more rather "poetic" proclamations, *youxin* still seems to refer to a state of intensified bodily *and* mental awareness and capacity as an effect of Daoist cultivation. This is confirmed by the third occurrence of *youxin* in the Inner Chapters. In chapter 7, an obscure "man without a name" instructs an equally obscure figure who apparently intends to become a sage-ruler by pointing out the following:

> Let your heart-mind roam in the flavourless, blend your Qi 氣 with the featureless, follow the self-so of things, leave no room for what is selfish, and the empire will be in order.[22]

Here, by being directly aligned with the cultivation of Qi energy, being in accord with the self-so (*ziran* 自然) of nature, and the elimination of a peculiar self, the roaming heartmind is clearly meant to indicate a perfected state of body and mind as an effect of Daoist "nurture." This "physiological" dimension of the practice *of youxin* is all the more evident in the following (abridged) fictitious dialog between a flabbergasted Confucius and an enlightened Laozi, occurring in chapter 21 of the *Zhuangzi* and reminiscent of the famous opening scene of chapter 2, introducing Master Nanguo Ziqi, who just "lost his self" (*sangwo* 喪我):

> Confucius visited Old Dan [Laozi]. Old Dan, fresh from a bath, was drying out, hair hanging down his back, so still that he seemed other than human. Confucius . . . said: " . . . Just now, sir, your body was as motionless as withered wood, as though you had left everything behind and parted from humankind, to take your stand in the unique." " Laozi said: "I was letting the heart-mind roam at the beginning of things. . . . The heart-mind is straitened by it and incapable of knowing, the mouth gapes at it and is unable to speak. . . . The utmost Yin is sombre, the utmost Yang is radiant, the sombre goes on emerging from the sky and the radiant goes on issuing from the earth; the two pervade each other, and by their perfected harmony things are generated . . . ." Confucius said: "Let me ask about your roaming in this." Laozi replied: "To grasp it is utmost beauty, utmost joy. One who grasps utmost beauty and roams in utmost joy is called the 'utmost human.'"[23]

This text, regarding both its content and its language, strongly resembles later Daoist writings on cultivation of the body and the heartmind, which have been previously referred to as texts of the Daoist religion (*daojiao* 道教) and may now perhaps be better classified as texts on "Daoist practice."[24] In this context, "letting the heart-mind roam" is an expression for exercising Daoist "utmost humanity" (*zhi ren* 至人).

It is interesting to note that just as different ways of roaming distinguish Daoist sages from Confucians (as outlined earlier), different ways of letting the heartmind roam distinguish Daoists from Mohists and other heretical "disputers of the Dao." The latter, as chapter 8 of the *Zhuangzi* says, "let their heart-minds roam among questions about 'the hard and the white,' 'the same and the different,' and fatuously admire useless propositions."[25] Apparently, how one roams indicates quite precisely who one is.

5

After these excursions, I would like to return to the bridge across the Hao River. It now seems that there are at least two ways of reading that short dialogue. They are not mutually opposed or directly contradictory but still quite different.

In light of the just presented more poetic, more practical, and more "religious" occurrences of *you* in the *Zhuangzi,* which seem to somewhat overshadow the more prosaic and profane usages of this term, we might simply say that Zhuangzi is a Daoist sage and thus fully capable of *you*-ing in its highest form and that therefore Hui Shi is no match for him. Hui Shi only "roams" within those boundaries that Zhuangzi has long crossed and annihilated. Poor Hui Shi, just like those Mohists and others, lets his heartmind stray and deal with pointless questions and language games. He seems to be confined to whatever "the inquisitive eyes and ears of the vulgar" supply him with. Only Zhuangzi's way of roaming allows him to experience this "utmost joy" described by "Old Dan." This kind of joy transcends the narrow boundaries of his self and enables the Daoist sage to share it with the fish—or his natural environment in general. The existential mode of *you*-ing in the world makes the sage "part from humankind" and "roam the limitless."

Another reading can be based on the more mundane, profane, and concrete meaning of *you* as "rambling without destination." This reading can point to the fact that, in the story, Hui Shi and Zhuangzi are, after all, *you*-ing *together* and strolling around in this earthly sense of *you*. They are simply walking side by side and do not seem as existentially apart as the obscure sages and their unsophisticated questioners in so many other passages in the *Zhuangzi.* The story does not really fit this narrative pattern, and it is also markedly different in style. Zhuangzi uses no lofty vocabulary here; he does not point to anything limitless or "beyond" the common. Both Zhuangzi and Hui Shi, like the fish, move around leisurely and aimlessly, and perhaps they also *talk* in this very way to one another. Perhaps the short dialogue only presents a concrete example of the "useless" pleasure of *philosophical rambling,* and perhaps this is what Daoist *you-*ing means here. Perhaps the happy fish story illustrates this intellectual but also social and physical engagement in a simultaneously playful and challenging, foolish and witty, and humorous and ironic form of communication that does not lead to any end or conclusion but is enjoyable and meaningful as such.

6

From a strictly historical perspective, the first and more "elevated" reading is probably more convincing. As scholars such as Harold D. Roth have shown, pre-Qin Daoism was already very much concerned with cultivation practices aiming at reaching a sagelike form of extraordinary existence.[26] With the development of a well-documented "proper" Daoist religion in all its varieties, such practices became all the more important and central. There is nothing that prevents one from interpreting the happy fish story, and particularly the notion of "*you*-ing" in the larger context of such efforts to "let the heart-mind roam."

Philosophically speaking, however, I prefer the second reading. It is questionable, of course, as to how far philosophical musings are scholarly acceptable. Scholars of Daoism, for instance, in departments of sinology, are expected to analyze texts and traditions on the basis of historical and philological evidence and to remain as "neutral" with respect to the sources as possible. In my view, too, historical and philological accuracy is not only important but crucial. If dealing philosophically with Daoist texts, though, one may want to add something to historical and philological analyses and attempt to make the texts one deals with relevant within a philosophical discourse. Examples of this method exist. Confucian texts, for instance, have been made philosophically relevant by authors such as Roger Ames and Henry Rosemont, who have both historically identified an ancient Chinese role ethics *and* recommended that it be taken seriously as a source for a contemporary role ethics as a valid alternative to other current forms of ethics stemming from Western traditions.

There is no lack of similar attempts with respect to Daoist sources. Personally, I am afraid, though, they have often been less successful than their Confucian counterparts. "Mystical" appropriations of Daoist sources have sometimes led to associations with New Age or "spiritual" literature of our times. I think that texts like the *Zhuangzi* deserve better, and it is probably in order for interpreters of Daoism who have jobs as philosophers that they come up with some other ways of making these sources interesting.

If, as I think it is both philologically and historically possible, one interprets the happy fish story and the Daoist notion of "*you*-ing in the world" as referring to a mode of mundane conversation rather than of existential elevation, one may conceive of it as a specific way of philosophizing. I assume that this type of—if one can forget about the negative connotations of the word in this usage for a while—"rambling" has been a method of philosophy throughout its history in both East and West. Philosophers sometimes realize that their actual philosophical practice does not, as envisioned by authors like Descartes or Spinoza, consist in developing in a "geometrical" fashion a set of propositions into a proven system of certainties. What they do is rather a form of *intellectual and linguistic "rambling" that, instead of leading to certain ends, establishes a form of communicatively productive discourse* that they can enjoy or make their profession—and in some cases even both of these at the same time.

One of the major philosophers of the twentieth century, Ludwig Wittgenstein, experienced a shift in attitude toward philosophy that led him from his early attempts to philosophize in a strictly systematic fashion to the insight that, at least for him, doing philosophy meant to ramble in this sense. He says as much in the preface to his *Philosophical Investigations:*

> It was my intention at first to bring all this together in a book whose form I pictured differently at different times. But the essential thing was that the things should proceed from one subject to another in a natural order and without breaks. After several unsuccessful attempts to weld my results together into such a whole, I realized that I should never succeed. The best that I could write would never be more than philosophical remarks; my thoughts were soon crippled if I tried to force them on in any single direction against their natural inclination.—And this was, of course, connected with the very nature of the investigation. For this compels us to travel over a wide field of thoughts, criss-cross in every direction.—The philosophical remarks in this book are, as it were, a number of sketches of landscapes which

were made in the course of these long and involved journeys. The same or almost the same points were always being approached afresh from different directions, and new sketches made. Very many of these were badly drawn or uncharacteristic, marked by all the defects of a weak draughtsman. And when they were rejected a number of tolerable ones were left, which now had to be arranged and sometimes cut down, so that if you looked at them you could get a picture of the landscape. Thus this book is really an album.[27]

Perhaps most philosophical books, if not all of them, are such albums, including, by the way, not the least, the *Zhuangzi*. This is of course not to say that the *Zhuangzi* and the *Philosophical Investigations* are similar in content or that they were written in a similar way—they were not—but it is to say that it is a widespread illusion that philosophical writings are, or even are capable of, "proceeding from one subject to another in a natural order and without breaks." In "real life" we may like to fool ourselves into believing that our motions in this world, where we go and what we say, follow such a "necessary" development and that we pursue goals and "get things done."[28] Similarly, philosophers sometimes like to fool themselves that they reach conclusions and that they get to results. Empirically speaking, our motions in life may consist of individual passages from point A to point B, and our individual philosophical essays, like the present one, may set out from somewhere and lead to certain points. In the larger context, though, it turns out we are rambling in a highly contingent fashion.

Contingency, of course, does not mean "anything goes." Communication in general and philosophical communication in particular are contingent upon its previous path and can continue only if future contingencies are open. One can "ramble on" only from *whence* one has arrived at. It is this "whence" that is at the center of contingency. It is not a larger "rationally determined" or ultimately "necessary" scheme that guides our communicational motions; we rather operate in a highly complex environment. My philosophy teacher back in Germany, Josef Simon, used to say that the books one *happened to read,* the ones one encountered or stumbled upon in one's life, are the formative elements for the books one is later to write.

All communication and philosophical activity emerges within the context of such complex ramblings, and both that and how Zhuangzi and Hui Shi discuss the happiness of the fish have much less to do with a coherent approach to any truth of the matter than with the contingent paths of their ramblings: their biographical rambling through life, their "carefree" rambling together on that day along the river Hao that day, and their previous intellectual ramblings, which enabled them to talk in the way they do. And this, and not any "actual" happiness of the fish, is what allows them to construct such a thing as the happiness of fish to begin with. That philosophers can make up topics such as the "happiness of fish" is a result of their ramblings, and these very ramblings constitute, so to speak, the happiness of philosophers. This is from *whence* they can observe it.

NOTES

1. A. C. Graham, *Chuang-Tzu: The Inner Chapters* (Indianapolis: Hackett, 2001).

2. Ibid., 123; cited with a few changes. Unlike elsewhere, Graham translates *you* here not as "roaming" but first as "strolling" and then as "swimming."

3. Graham Parkes, "Nietzsche und Zhuangzi: Ein Zwischenspiel," in Rolf Elberfeld, Johann Kreuzer, John Minford, and Günter Wohlfart, eds., *Komparative Philosophie: Begegnungen zwischen östlichen und westlichen Denkwegen* (Munich: Wilhelm-Fink-Verlag, 1998), 212–222, 216.

4. Graham, *Inner Chapters,* 90; *Zhuanzi yinde,* Harvard–Yenching Institute Sinological Index Series, suppl. 20 (Peking: Harvard–Yenching Institute, 1947), 18/6/79.

5. *Zhuangzi yinde* 52/20/14.

6. Ibid., 2/1/21.

7. Ibid., 20/7/9. See Graham, *Inner Chapters,* 95.

8. *Zhuangzi yinde* 20/7/15.

9. Ibid., 27/11/42.

10. Ibid., 28/11/65.

11. Ibid., 27/11/49.

12. This linguistic difference reminds me of perhaps somewhat similar differences in the works of Nietzsche, as exemplified in, for instance, the mannerist *Thus Spoke Zarathustra* on the one hand and the comparatively prosaic *Gay Science* on the other.

13. In addition to the passage discussed here (*Zhuangzi yinde* 18/6/61–71), see *Zhuangzi yinde* 66/24/29–30.

14. Graham, *Inner Chapters,* 89.

15. Ibid., 89–90.

16. Ibid., 89.

17. See *Zhuangzi yinde* 2/1/19. Also see Graham, *Inner Chapters,* 44.

18. *Zhuangzi yinde* 2/1/21.

19. *Zhuangzi yinde* 70/25/29. See Graham, *Inner Chapters,* 154.

20. Graham, *Inner Chapters,* 71 (translation modified); *Zhuangzi yinde* 10/4/53.

21. Graham, *Inner Chapters,* 77 (translation modified); *Zhuangzi yinde* 12/5/8.

22. Graham, *Inner Chapters,* 95 (translation modified); *Zhuangzi yinde* 20/7/10–11.

23. Graham, *Inner Chapters,* 130 (translation modified); *Zhuangzi yinde* 55/21/24–30.

24. See *Zhuangzi yinde* 75/26/40 for a similar passage.

25. Graham, *Inner Chapters,* 200 (translation modified); *Zhuangzi yinde* 21/8/6–7.

26. See, for instance, his book *Original Tao* (New York: Columbia University Press, 1995).

27. Ludwig Wittgenstein, *Philosophical Investigations,* trans. G. E. M. Anscombe (Oxford: Basil Blackwell, 1953), vii.

28. On such necessity in the Hegelian sense and its Luhmannian counterpart "contingency" see chapter 4 in my book *The Radical Luhmann* (New York: Columbia University Press, 2011), 32–50.

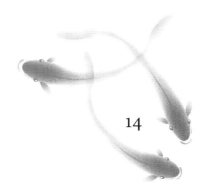

14

"Knowing" as the "Realizing of Happiness" Here, on the Bridge, over the River Hao

Roger T. AMES

WHAT IS AN INTERPRETIVE CONTEXT?

One assumption we might all agree upon is that as a first step in making sense of the *Zhuangzi*—a philosophical text that is decidedly distant from us in time and place—we must try with imagination to locate it within its own interpretive context. In this essay I begin by making just this argument: to the extent possible, we must strive to read and to understand any text within the parameters of its own historical and intellectual circumstances. Although we can be quite certain that the *Zhuangzi* is a composite text and thus the product of many hands and compiled over several centuries, this fact does not absolve us of the imperative of establishing an interpretive context that would enable us with all of its complexity to take it on its own terms. Having made this argument, I sketch out what might be taken to be some pervasive assumptions that ground a general Daoist cosmology, beginning from what I call a commitment to process and a radical contextuality. I then try to locate the example of the *Zhuangzi*'s "happy fish" story within this cosmology to determine what if any difference this effort to find context might make for the substance of our own interpretation.

An earlier version of this essay was published in Spanish in Paulina Rivero Weber, ed., *Daoísmo: Interpretaciones contemporáneas* (Mexico City: UNAM, Facultad de Filosofía y Letras).

In taking account of the diverse historical and intellectual milieu of this formative period in Chinese philosophy, we need not only to accommodate the broad, prevailing cosmology of pre-Qin China but, more specifically, also to register the Mohist challenges to the mainstream worldview that animated debate throughout these centuries. Zhuangzi's own premise in this debate is that proximate context is integral to what it means to know—that is, that the *how, what, who,* and *whence* of knowing are conterminous and mutually entailing. I would argue that if this is so, then the Zhuangzi-Huizi philosophical engagement might serve us as an object lesson in the sense that the quality of our interpretation will not only depend on the degree to which we are able to locate the text within its own interpretive context but also alert us to the uncommon assumptions that we bring with us in the interrogation.

It was precisely this struggle to read a classical Chinese text on its own terms—not the *Zhuangzi* but the *Mencius* in his case—that inspired the Cambridge rhetorician I. A. Richards to write his *Mencius on the Mind:*

> Can we in attempting to understand and translate a work which belongs to a very different tradition from our own do more than read our own conceptions into it? Can we make it more than a mirror of our minds, or are we inevitably in this undertaking trying to be on both sides of the looking-glass at once? To understand Mencius, for example, must we efface our whole tradition of thinking and learn another; and when we have done this, if it be possible, will we be any nearer being able to translate the one set of mental operations into the other?[1]

Richards insists that we first be critically aware of the philosophical presuppositions that we willy-nilly bring with us when we with our own common sense try to read a classical Chinese text—a vocabulary that for Richards is strongly indebted to Platonism and is largely constituted by the persistent assumptions of Plato's metaphysical realism:[2]

> Our Western tradition provides us with an elaborate apparatus of universals, particulars, substances, attributes, abstracts, concretes, generality, specificities, properties, qualities, relations, complexes, accidents, essences, organic wholes, sums, classes, individuals, concrete universals, objects, events, forms, contents, etc. Mencius . . . gets along without any of this and with nothing at all definite to take its place. Apart entirely from the meta-

physics that we are only too likely to bring in with this machinery, the practical difficulty arises that by applying it we deform his thinking. . . . The danger to be guarded against is our tendency to force a structure, which our special kind of Western training (idealist, realist, positivist, Marxist, etc.) makes easiest for us to work with, upon modes of thinking which may very well not have any such structure at all—and which may not be capable of being analysed by means of this kind of logical machinery.[3]

The only exception I would take with Richards here is with regard to his suggestion that "Mencius . . . gets along without any of this *and with nothing at all definite to take its place* [my italics]." As Richards indicates, while standing on our own side of the looking-glass, we can at least appeal to our logic and deploy our own methods of analysis to guide us in identifying and avoiding those philosophical assumptions that might dispose us inadvertently to reduce the *Zhuangzi* to our own cultural importances. It is finding our way to the other side of the looking-glass in order to discover what in fact does "take its place" that is the more elusive challenge.[4] Indeed, as Alice soon learns, the other side of the looking-glass is not secured by her own familiar assumptions, and hence her once reassuring patterns of reasoning quickly give way to a more fluid world that is confoundingly fanciful if not fantastical and, at times, even bizarre. To follow Alice through this other portal requires that we strive to understand the historical and the intellectual conditions under which the *Zhuangzi* itself was compiled and then, to the extent possible, to recover the questions that the authors of the text were trying to address and to anticipate the competencies of the audiences who were being challenged by these same questions. At the end of the day, it will be our success in accessing this other side of the looking-glass in our reading of the *Zhuangzi* that will allow for the entertainment of sometimes profoundly new ideas and for the recognition of the important differences in living and thinking that separate us from this early culture. After all, it is the perspective from the other side of the looking-glass that properly motivates comparative studies in the first place and that will ultimately reward our best efforts at cultural translation.

AN INTERPRETIVE CONTEXT FOR READING
THE *ZHUANGZI:* THE PRIMACY OF PROCESS
AND RADICAL CONTEXTUALITY

The earliest reference to "Daoism" as a philosophical tradition occurs in Sima Tan's essay "On the Essential Thought of the Six Lineages" (論六家要指), which provides a retrospective description of six "schools" of thought during the pre-Qin period and the early Han dynasty. In this reference, the term that is translated as "Daoism" is not the now-familiar *daojia* 道家 but is rather the expression *daodejia* 道德家, underscoring the correlative relationship that obtains between the dyadic term, *daode* 道德. The importance of this binomial is reinforced by the fact that the title *Daodejing* (or alternatively *Dedaojing*) is now attested by the text recovered in an archaeological find at Mawangdui (168 BCE), which is composed of the combined "*dao* classic" and the "*de* classic." A starting point, then, for establishing an interpretive context for the early Daoist texts might be to explore the relationship that obtains between these two interdependent and inseparable terms as they have emerged in the tradition to designate this specific philosophical lineage.

Fig. 1

Fig. 2

For the classical cosmology broadly, it is significant that the character for *dao* on the bronzes and in the recently recovered bamboo strips (figures 1 and 2, respectively) is not simply a road—"the Way," as it is conventionally translated—but includes within it a graphic representation of human beings and, in the earliest occurrences, with eyes and feet, which makes it specifically a journey along "our" way.[5] Simply put, *dao* references the human sojourn through the life experience and might alternatively be translated as "world-making" with the understanding that the etymology of the term "world" is literally "the age of man."[6]

And there is graphic resonace between the character *dao,* as this resolutely and specifically human project of forging our way in the world, and its correlate, *de* 德, conventionally rendered nominally as "virtue" or "excellence"—that is, "excelling" in those relationships that constitute each of us, thereby enabling us to thrive as we make our "way" in the world around us. On the oracle bones, similar to the graph for *dao* that designates a specifically human way, *de* appears as in figure 3, again depicting persons walking on a road with eyes focused on moving straight ahead.[7] This clear complementarity and interpenetration of *dao* and *de* reinforces the assumption that early Chinese cosmology is an account of the spe-

Fig. 3

cifically human attempt to optimize our experience in the world. The characters themselves reflect what the *Zhuangzi* means when it insists that "the way is made in the walking" (道行之而成), reflecting the collaborative nature of our shared narratives as they unfold on a path that we forge together. The metaphors of "walking the human way" (*dao* 道) and "moving straight ahead" or "excelling" (*de* 德), which are expressed by this *daode* binomial, have both physical and normative connotations. Indeed, on the bronzes, the heartmind (*xin* 心) signific is added as an additional element in the character *de* (figure 4), underscoring the intellectual, the affective, and the irreducibly social dimensions of our search for an optimal propriety in our relations as we move forward together to shape our pathway.[8]

Fig. 4

Assumptions about the processive nature and the radical contextuality of the human experience is made evident in the way in which *xin* 心, conventionally translated as "heartmind," is understood within the early cosmology. First, and most obviously, the heartmind does the work of both cognizing and feeling—there is no dichotomous relationship between thinking and living, between intellection and sensation, between body and mind. Second, taking our cue from Chinese medicine, we have to give primacy to physiology over anatomy. The term *zhenmai* 診脈, for example, does not refer simply to the anatomical project of locating and examining a blood vessel or an artery. Rather, it is certainly "taking a pulse," but, more important, it is using one's tactile sensitivity to feel and interpret the visceral dynamics of the living body holistically and, as such, has synoptic reference not only to the organism but also to the organic relationship this organism has with its environment. Life is a holographic focus of activity within a domain that reaches to the farthest limits of the cosmos. We might use the language of focus and field to describe *xin* as, first and foremost, the dynamic focus of a specific systemic center of thinking and feeling that extends both psychologically and physiologically to an unbounded cosmos as its contextualizing field. Indeed, *xin* is only derivatively and abstractly the physical organ that has become metonymic in its reference to this holistic function. The opening chapter of the *Huainanzi* provides an image of the physical, intellectual, and moral compass of the heartmind as it functions in the world and the world in it:

> The heartmind is the lord of the five viscera. It is responsible for regulating and engaging the four limbs, circulating the blood and *qi*, galloping about in the realm of approving and disapproving, and going in and out of the

gateway whence the various affairs of the world issue forth. Hence for persons to have the aspiration to manage the world while not finding the world in their own heartmind is like someone without ears wanting to tune the bells and drums, or like someone without eyes wanting to take delight in color and design. They are sure to be unequal to the task.[9]

There is another resonant passage in the *Zhuangzi* that correlates the capacity to be "penetrating" in the ways in which the heartmind engages the world, functioning wisely, and in so doing, realizing a productive virtuosity:

It is the penetrating eye that is clarity of vision, the penetrating ear that is acuity in hearing, the penetrating nose that is a heightened sense of smell, the penetrating mouth that is a discriminating palate, the penetrating heartmind that is able to realize things, and it is this penetrating realization that is virtuosity.[10]

This Daoist language of *daode*—the field of experience (*dao*) and the myriad insistent particulars (*de*) that constitute it—references a focus-field relationship between the unique particular and the totality as construed from its own perspective, which is analogous to this holographic *xin*. It is a way of expressing the inseparability and ontological parity of the one and the many that within the *Zhuangzi* text has inspired a whole chapter as a "discourse on the parity among things" (*qiwulun* 齊物論) and the recognition in this same chapter that "the world and I being born together, I am continuous with all things" (天地與我並生，萬物與我為一).

WHITEHEAD'S LOGICAL AND AESTHETIC ORDER

In this processive worldview, the embedded particular and its context are at once continuous and distinct. The radical contextuality of particulars expressed by *daode* references the flourishing of the insistent particular, which is "radical" in the sense that it is firmly rooted in its context and presences as both the unique product and the producer of the flourishing relationships that constitute it. The ontological parity between the one and the many means there is no privileged and foundational order in this cosmology that we might associate with familiar classical Greek assumptions such as *logos, kosmos, eidos* that would serve as ground for a singled-ordered *uni*-verse. Indeed, this dominant Daoist understanding of the order of things advertises an important ambiguity in the notion of "order" itself.

The most familiar "cosmic" understanding of order is associated with the reductionistic gathering of detail within a uniform, patterned regularity to constitute a cosmos. Alfred North Whitehead refers to this sense of order as "logical" or "rational" order and takes it to be an implication of those assumptions about the *logos* of a *kosmos* defined in terms of antecedent causal laws and formal patterns that come to *rationalize* the human experience in one way or another.

But there is a second sense of an unbounded, dynamic, and diverse order—what Whitehead calls an "aesthetic" order—a holistic order that promises continuing disclosure rather than a predetermined finality. An aesthetic order is constituted by the ongoing introduction of novel patterns from interpenetrating, concrete particularities or *kosmoi,* whose uniqueness is essential to the order itself and whose differences thus make a difference for each other. Said another way, aesthetic order is holistic in the sense that every detail is relevant to every other as constituting what it has come to be, just as every detail in a painting or a piece of music is relevant to and implicated in all the others. This aesthetic sense of order encompasses any and all ostensive rational orders, but with the difference that such rationalizations provide their coherence as relatively persistent structures that exist only provisionally within the transformative process itself. No final unity is possible in this view since, were it so, the order of the whole would dominate the order of the parts, thereby canceling the uniqueness of its constituent elements. Such a holistic "aesthetic" order is "*kosmoi*-tic" in the sense that a matrix of many, unsummed orders prevails but is ultimately acosmological (or "acosmotic") in the sense that no single order is privileged or dominates the others.[11] The order that we might call the *dao* 道 and that we might alternatively call the manifold of "the myriad things" (*wanwu* 萬物) is simply two nonanalytic ways of describing the same phenomenon, the former emphasizing the continuous and unbounded nature of our experience and the latter its complexity and multiplicity.

It can be argued that these understandings of logical and aesthetic order trace back to the earliest stages in the formative process of both Indo-European and Chinese cultures and that both have persisted as interpretive options within them. It so happens that in the course of their respective histories, however, the two cultural narratives have disposed themselves in distinctly different ways with respect to these variant senses of order, and this trajectory has led to the emergence of their different cultural dominants as grounds for the organizing of their personal, social, and cosmic environments.

As an illustration of the nonexclusivity of these two notions of order, we have all in our time witnessed a twentieth-century internal critique within the Western philosophical narrative that can be fairly read as a rejection of systematic philosophy, dominated as it has been by the logical sense of order—what Heidegger has called "onto-theological thinking," what Whitehead has called "misplaced concreteness," and what Dewey has called "*the* philosophical fallacy." And positively, this same internal critique can be understood as a concerted attempt on the part of Western philosophers to embrace variants of an open-ended aesthetic sense of order with a shared commitment to what it means to think "process," namely, hermeneutics, existentialism, poststructuralism, pragmatism, and so on.

The crucial difference between these two senses of order is that in the one case there is the presumption of an external, objective, and duplicable standard that one perforce must instantiate; in the other, there is no source of order other than the dynamic agency of those unique participants that compose an improvisational and always emergent order. Rational order seeks closure, depending as it does upon the assumption of a single-ordered world, a cosmos; aesthetic order, on the other hand, focuses on disclosure and speaks of the world in much less unitary terms. In the Western narrative, which traces back to early Greece, mathematical order has been thought the purest form of an eternal and unchanging order, and in a tradition of what Angus Graham has called "truth-seekers," mathematics has persistently served as an ideal model in the search for apodictic truth. By contrast, the early Chinese "way-seeking" thinkers worried that any notion of order that abstracts from the concrete details of this-worldly experience does so at the expense of a decreasing richness and relevance to what is actually happening and hence must seek its warrant by authenticating the theoretical in practice—that is, by assaying the practical effects of such speculations. This concern is captured in the ubiquitous appeal in the commentaries to the term "forming and functioning" (*tiyong* 體用) to explain the symbiotic, mutually shaping relationship between structure and content in Daoist cosmology.[12] In this cosmology, the "cosmos" is simply "everything present-to-hand" as it is entertained from one perspective or another with the understanding that philosophical thinking as *ars contextualis,* or "the art of contextualizing," allows for the things of nature to be ordered in any number of ways.

In his important work on Chinese philosophy of science, Nathan Sivin has observed that "man's prodigious creativity seems to be based on the permutations and recastings of a rather small stock of ideas."[13] Whitehead's contrast between these two senses of order—the logical and the aesthetic (or alternatively, the reductionistic and the holistic, respectively)—might qualify as an example of ideas that illustrate this claim. Indeed, John Dewey finds just such a distinction in his account of the liberation of late nineteenth- and twentieth-century Western epistemology from "the logic of the changeless," that is, the assumption that our knowledge of cosmic order is grounded in and guaranteed by a foundational and causal *eidos.* For Dewey:

> There are, indeed, but two alternative courses. We must either find the appropriate objects and organs of knowledge in the mutual interactions of changing things; or else, to escape the infection of change, we must seek them in some transcendent and supernal region. The human mind, deliberately as it were, exhausted the logic of the changeless, the final and the transcendent, before it essayed adventure on the pathless wastes of generation and transformation.[14]

In this Daoist "our way together" cosmology, "the objects and organs of knowledge" are not only to be discovered but also to be attended to and grown within "the mutual interactions of changing things." The process of personal "realization," which is the desired outcome of this "epistemology," is to be achieved in coordinating one's own unique narrative with the emergent cadence and regularity of the world that gives one context. Positively, such coordination requires unrelenting attention to bringing resolve—in contemporary parlance we might say achieving high pixel resolution—to one's focal relations, thereby making them optimally meaningful. And negatively, it involves the quelling of any inclinations that would foster a sense of a discrete and independent identity expressed as an isolating individualism and closed self-sufficiency. In the text that provides the "classic" statement of "*daode*"—the *Daodejing*—we read the following:

> Hence, because the sages do what they do authentically and noncoercively (*wuwei* 無為),

They do not ruin things,
And because they do not try to exercise control,
They do not lose them.[15]

Chris Jochim cautions us on how we are to understand this point about optimizing relations in the project of personal realization. Jochim insists it is important not to superordinate and thus naturalize an independent ego-self by making it something that we initially have and thus need to overcome.[16] Rather, we begin as a shallow "we"—a focus of inchoate, incipient relationships. Taking advantage of the opportunity to cultivate and extend these initial bonds, we can transform them into a robust, situated, and relationally constituted "self" that is inclusive of this unbounded field of vital, virtuosic relations.[17] To fail to grow ourselves is to live myopically as "frogs in the well" (*jingwa* 井蛙)—that is, as persons of limited perspective who are unresponsive to relations beyond the horizon of their own immediate interests.

A second caution concerning the Daoist notion of personal realization is that in understanding the familiar Zhuangzian exhortation, "I abandon myself" (*wusangwo* 吾喪我), we must not confuse the relinquishing of any undesirable sense of discreteness with self-sacrifice or self-abnegation.[18] On the contrary, it is the achievement of virtuosity in relations through becoming one with all things that is the source of and makes possible the realization of one's own proper uniqueness and distinctiveness. Persons— we might say human "becomings" rather than "beings"—emerge as a matrix of constitutive relations who are insistently unique, not exclusive of their bonds, but because of the quality of them, and who become distinctive and sometimes even distinguished by achieving a real virtuosity in these familial, communal, and ultimately cosmic relations.

THE INSEPARABILITY OF THE ONE AND THE MANY

The contemporary philosopher Tang Junyi 唐君毅 uses the proposition, "the inseparability of the one and the many" (*yiduo bufenguan* 一多不分觀)—or, stated more elaborately, "the inseparability of uniqueness and multivalence, of continuity and multiplicity, of integrity and integration"—as a way of characterizing this classical Chinese cosmology.[19] This notion of the inseparability of continuity and multiplicity is necessary to explain the claim we find throughout the early Daoist philosophical literature about the "oneness" of things, or of becoming "one" with all things cited earlier, which is often stated as a kind of personal achievement. What Tang Junyi means by this proposition is that if we begin our reflection on the emergence of cosmic order from the wholeness of lived experience, we can view our everyday experience in terms of both its dynamic continuities and its manifold multiplicity, as both one ceaseless flow and as a process constituted by many distinct, consummatory events. Simply put, the uniqueness of any one thing is a continuing expression of its many productive relations; it is what it is because of what it means for other things.

In the *Yijing,* this sense of the mutuality of oneness and manyness is captured in the image of the turning of the four seasons, wherein each day is at once profoundly distinct from every other[20] and yet is continuous with and implicated within each and every other day:

> In their flux (*bian* 變) and in their continuity (*tong* 通) the processes of nature are a counterpart to the four seasons.[21]

The inseparability of one and many is one more example of the mutual implication of binaries, which characterizes all phenomena in the natural world—in this case, particularity and the unsummed totality. This woman is uniquely who she is as distinct from anyone else, yet her magnitude and reach are such that in weighing up and taking the measure of the manifold of social, natural, and cultural relationships that constitute her to give a full accounting of her, we must exhaust the cosmic totality and ask in what degree her personal virtuosity is in these relations productive of cosmic meaning. Any particular phenomenon in our field of experience can be brought into focus in many different ways: On the one hand there is this unique and insistent particular—*this* woman, *this* American, *this* mother, *this* scholar—and on the other, since any particular is constituted by its boundless relationships, it has the entire cosmos and all that is happening implicated within its own particular pattern of relations.

We might cite a passage from William James' *A Pluralistic Universe* that resonates with this Daoist focus-field understanding in providing his own similar response to the relationship between the one and the many—for him, the relationship between the one unique focus (or "center" or "moment") of consciousness and its bottomless and unbounded field of our "full" selves:

In the pulse of inner life immediately present now in each of us is a little past, a little future, a little awareness of our own body, of each other's persons, of these sublimities we are trying to talk about, of the earth's geography and the direction of history, of truth and error, of good and bad, and of who knows how much more? Feeling, however dimly and subconsciously, all these things, your pulse of inner life is continuous with them, belongs to them and they to it. . . . The real units of our immediately felt life are unlike the units that intellectualist logic holds to and makes its calculations with. They are not separate from their own others, and you have to take them at widely sepa-rated dates to find any two of them that seem unblent . . . my present field of consciousness is a centre surrounded by a fringe that shades insensibly into a subconscious more . . . Which part of it properly is in my conscious-ness, which out? If I name what is out, it already has come in. The centre works in one way while the margins work in another, and presently overpower the centre and are central themselves. What we conceptually identify our-selves with and say we are thinking of at any time is the centre; but our *full* self is the whole field, with all those indefinitely radiating subconscious pos-sibilities of increase.[22]

RADICAL CONTEXTUALITY AND
THE CLASSICAL CHINESE LANGUAGE

We can further illustrate these cosmological notions of process and radi-cal contextuality by appealing to assumptions sedimented into the clas-sical Chinese language. Certain usually unannounced features of the clas-sical language are illustrative of a situational rather than an agency-centered conception of experience. To begin with, classical Chinese terms, much to the perplexity of the English translator, must often be read as being in-clusive of both the subject and the object of understanding. For example, *ming* 明 (bright) can refer derivatively either to the penetrating perspi-cacity of the subject (the enlightened ruler, *mingjun* 明君) or to the bril-liance of the object (brilliant advice, *mingjiao* 明教) but, more funda-mentally, to both at the same time, that is, to illuminated governance. Conversely, *bi* 蔽 can mean derivatively either obscured and distorted vision on the part of the subject or a blind that obstructs the object of the subject's vision but, more fundamentally, to both at the same time, that is, to an obscure situation. *De* 德 can refer derivatively to either the be-neficence of the ruler or to the gratitude of the people but, more fundamentally, to both at the same time, that is, to a thriving and well-ordered polity.[23] And *zhi* 知 can refer derivatively to either the knowing of the subject or to what is known but, more fundamentally, to both at the same time as a "knowing" situation. This situatedness is evident in the fact that "knowing" (*zhi* 知) and its cognates "knowing, managing, wise persons, and their wisdom" (*zhi* 智) are used interchangeably in the early texts, collapsing any severe distinction among who knows, what is known, and the use of what is known efficaciously in acting wisely. Unsurprisingly, in the grammar of the language that expresses this cosmology, such distinctions in meaning are determined by context—that is, the meaning of a term is parsed and brought into focus by what it means for the other terms.

A second revealing feature of the classical Chinese language that foregrounds both process and radical contextuality is paronomastic definition—that is, definition through association. When we consult the dictionaries and glosses that purport to explain the Chinese world, we discover that classical terms were often brought into focus paronomastically by semantic and phonetic correlations. "Exemplary persons" (*junzi* 君子), for example, are defined by the cognate and phonetically similar character, "gathering, assembling" (*qun* 群), on the assumption that "people gather around and defer to exemplary persons."[24] "Mirror" (*jing* 鏡) is defined as "bright" (*jing* 景) in that it provides a source of illumination. "Battle formation" (*zhen* 陣) is defined as "displaying" (*chen* 陳), where saber rattling serves as a deterrent to erstwhile enemies. "Consummate person" (*ren* 仁) is defined as "being slow to speak" (*ren* 訒), reflecting the careful attention to language that is characteristic of living deliberately. And "knowing" and "wisdom" (*zhi* 知 or 智) are defined as "recognizing, remembering, and expressing terms" (*shici* 識詞) in both the retrospective and the prospective sense of using language effectively. An intimate relationship is assumed between virtuosic communicating and living wisely, aligning "knowing" with wit and wisdom. This connection is captured in *Analects* 20.3: "Persons who do not know words have no way of knowing others" (不知言而無以知人) in the sense of becoming intimate friends (*zhiren* 知人) and "realizing" a robust relationship with them. And the Qing dynasty commentator Duan Yucai 段玉裁 explains the etymology of *zhi* 知 with "arrow" (*shi* 矢) and "mouth" (*kou* 口) as *shimin* 識敏: being sharp and quick-witted in speaking and making connections.

What is remarkable about this paronomastic production of meaning is that a term is defined nonreferentially by mining and mapping relevant and sometimes seemingly random associations implicated in the terms themselves. Further, erstwhile nominal expressions ("things") usually default to gerundive, processive expressions ("events")—for example, "exemplary person" to "gathering" and "wisdom" to the performative "recognizing and remembering of terms"—underscoring the primacy of vital relationality over form and emergent situation over agency as two grounding presuppositions in this cosmology.

RADICAL CONTEXTUALITY AND THE ELIDING OF EPISTEMOLOGY AND ETHICS

These notions of process and radical contextuality as cosmological assumptions can be reinforced by rehearsing what the twentieth-century comparative philosopher Zhang Dongsun 張東蓀 takes to be distinguishing characteristics of Chinese epistemology. According to Zhang, three conditions emerge when a relationship develops between knower and what is known:

1. Knower and known become intrinsically related such that each in the relationship influences the other, their relationship is intricate and complex, and each member of the relationship is different after the relationship has been established and changes together with it.
2. All such relationships are mediated by layer after layer of intervening experience rather than being unmediated and direct.
3. Knowing is always a kind of interpretation rather than a copy or representation.[25]

In reflecting on an important shift that occurs when moving between European sources and their Chinese counterpart that is relevant to Zhang's organic understanding of this situated and dynamic sense of knowing, An Yanming observes that there seems to be a "priority of ethics over epistemology." That is, epistemological concepts in their European form often become "a source of ethical standards rather than . . . a key to reality" when removed to China.[26] Applying this insight to Zhang Dongsun's characterization of Chinese epistemology, we would have to allow that Zhang is not only reflecting on epistemic assumptions characteristic of the Chinese tradition but, more fundamentally and importantly, on how personal, communal, and political relationships are formed in experience and how they are developed. The epistemic commitment lies in a practical "realizing" of a viable community rather than just a cognitive understanding of communal relations and in living wisely in the world rather than just "knowing" some truth about it.

JOINING THE GRAND THOROUGHFARE

The Daoist texts, like their Confucian counterparts, can be read as an exhortation to cultivate "virtuosity" (*de* 德) in one's relations as a condition for integrative, authentic conduct. That is, the Daoist tradition would not reject the primacy of vital relationality expressed in the Confucian project of personal "extension" through the development of consummate relations (*ren* 仁). But it would be critical of a perceived willingness on the part of the Confucians to deracinate this term from its unique and living circumstances, thereby making it into an abstract and impositional moral principle and then limiting what it means to become consummatory in one's relations to the human world alone. The Daoist aspires to respect the radical particularity of each situation and to make our sphere of concern as broad as possible as we "transform together with things" (*wuhua* 物化) by "acting authentically and without coercion" (*wuwei* 無為) in our relationship with all of them—human and nonhuman alike.

In a *Zhuangzian* parody of a conversation between Confucius and his favorite protégé, Confucius is humbled by Yan Hui, who has been able to overcome any sense of discreteness and human exceptionalism to join the "Grand Thoroughfare" (*datong* 大通), thereby becoming fully integrated in the ceaseless and boundless processes of transformation:

> Yan Hui said, "I have made progress."
> "How so?" inquired Confucius. . . .
> "I am sitting and forgetting" (*zuowang* 坐忘).
> Confucius, noticeably flustered, inquired: "What do you mean by 'sitting and forgetting'?"
> "My appendages and body have fallen away, I have gotten rid of my sight and my hearing, I have abandoned my physical form, have shucked off knowledge, and have joined the Grand Thoroughfare," said Yan Hui. "This is what I call 'sitting and forgetting.'"

Confucius replied: "In joining the Grand Thoroughfare you have become free of personal preferences and in your transformations you have become free of any constant horizons of value and relevance. In the end it is you who have become worthy and wise. Please allow me to be your follower."[27]

For Whitehead, the discrete individual that Yan Hui is challenging here is a prime and powerful example of what he calls the "fallacy of simple location," that is, the familiar and yet fallacious assumption that isolating, decontextualizing, and analyzing things as simple particulars is the best way to understand the content of our experience, including ourselves. The language of "Grand Thoroughfare" in this passage—literally, "grand penetrating and passing through"—has clear epistemic reference, with Yan Hui "shucking off knowledge" and cultivating a penetrating discernment of, and coalescence with, the world around him. In "forgetting" those isolating assumptions that inhibit his participation in the grand flow of experience—that is, abandoning the boundaries of his bodily form and the limiting senses that separate and distance him from what is putatively external to him—Yan Hui has come to appreciate the constitutive, interpenetrating, and holographic nature of those internal relations that embed him in the world and the world in him. In thus "sitting" in such a world, he is able to demonstrate his virtuosity by "doing things authentically and noncoercively" (*wuwei* 無為), thereby allowing this world to emerge spontaneously without intruding upon it with his own distorting individual preferences and prejudices.

Understanding this absence of severe boundaries among things is taken to be a mark of sagacity in the *Zhuangzi*:

With the ancients, understanding had gotten somewhere. Where was that? Its height—its extreme—that to which no more could be added was this: some of them thought that there had never begun to be things. The next lot thought that there are things but that there had never begun to be boundaries among them. And the next thought there are indeed boundaries but that there had never begun to be a distinction between a "this" and a "not-this."[28]

Peter Hershock offers a relatively uncontested account of the nature of such internal, constitutive relations assumed in these Daoist sources by first diagnosing the problem that we have when we continue to see the world as comprising discrete "things":

Autonomous subjects and objects are, finally, only artifacts of abstraction. . . .
What we refer to as "things"—whether mountains, human beings, or complex phenomena like histories—are simply the experienced results of having established relatively constant horizons of value or relevance ("things").
They are not, as common sense insists, natural occurring realities or [things].
Indeed, what we take to be *objects* existing independently of ourselves are,
in actuality, simply a function of habitual patterns of relationships.[29]

Hershock also offers us a Yan Hui cure that allows us to "forget" ourselves
by seeing "through the conceit that relations are second-order realities contingent upon pre-existing actors" and to "seat" ourselves fully in the transformations of experience by recognizing the fact that the nature of these
relations gives primacy to our interpenetration with other things rather
than to any ostensive boundaries among us:

This amounts to an ontological gestalt shift from taking independent and
dependent actors to be first order realities and relations among them as second order, to seeing relationality as first order (or ultimate) reality and all
individual actors as (conventionally) abstracted or derived from them.[30]

VIRTUOSITY (*DE*) SATISFIES THE TALLY

A helpful metaphor available in the Daoist texts to elucidate the notion
of a holographic "interpenetration" with all things that Yan Hui achieves
by "sitting and forgetting" and joining the "Grand Thoroughfare" is that
of the tally (*qi* 契 or *fu* 符)—yet another way perhaps of expressing what
it means to "do things authentically and noncoercively" (*wuwei* 無為). The
Daodejing states the following:

The sage, holding on to the left half of the tally
Does not demand payment from others;
The person of virtuosity (*de* 德) tends to the tally
While the person without virtuosity looks to collect on it.[31]

The meaning of this rather obscure passage is clarified in the fifth chapter of the *Zhuangzi*, the title of which is "Virtuosity (*de*) Satisfies the Tally"
(*dechongfu* 德充符). This chapter is a series of anecdotes about a motley
parade of mutilated cripples who, under normal circumstances and under

the sway of conventional values, would be ostracized by their communities. Their disfigured physical forms—often to be understood as the deliberate result of the customary amputation and branding punishments that would single out the criminal element for all to see and further humiliate these ne'er-do-wells before their ancestors—would be certain grounds for societal rejection. However, these maimed individuals have overcome such isolation by achieving a virtuosity (*de* 德) in their relations that enables them to contribute to and integrate themselves fully within their communities. In so doing, they have been able to "satisfy the tally" and thus not only are able to blend in harmoniously with their neighbors but also have further come to exercise considerable influence on the values and the aesthetic and moral order of their time and place.

In the Daoist tradition, the extension of one's virtuosity tends to be described not simply in social but also in cosmic terms. As in the Confucian tradition, such exceptional persons certainly become the embodiments and protectors of the human order, stylers of new culture, and sources of new meaning. But the Daoists take virtuosity beyond the anthropocentric and extend it into the natural world. The "authentic person" (*zhenren* 真人) is the Daoist variant of the Confucian consummate person (*renzhe* 仁者), whose virtuosity extends to and transforms the natural as well as the human environment. By becoming coextensive with the ox, for example, Cook Ding in butchering its carcass is able to penetrate and disassemble it at its natural lineaments smoothly and without impediment, and by demonstrating the efficacy of his world-making (*dao*) as a butcher is able to show Lord Wenhui how to nurture life;[32] by fasting and becoming coextensive with his wood, Cabinetmaker Qing is able to be responsive to the quality of his lumber and, in becoming efficacious as a craftsman, is able to show the Marquis of Lu what happens when his inspired virtuosity is able to collaborate seamlessly with the natural quality of his wood (以天合天).[33] These Daoist exemplars collaborate with the environing conditions that provide them with resources and enable their virtuosity. And they in turn contribute to their environments, interpreting and making the most of the creative possibilities provided by those things that constitute their world. What might be perceived as their interface with "other" is in fact a coincident virtuosity—a coalescence—that enables them to interpret and facilitate the natural expression of whatever it is that they encounter.

In the opening chapter of the *Huainanzi* we find an extended, hyperbolic account of the epistemic charioting of these authentic persons as they course through the cosmos:

> Hence these persons of great stature:
> Being placidly free of all worries
> And serenely without thoughts for the morrow,
> Have the heavens as their canopy
> And the earth as their box-frames,
> The four seasons as their horses
> And the *yin* and *yang* as their charioteers.
> They mount the clouds and climb beyond the skies
> To keep company with the demiurge of change.
> Doing as they please and free in their rhythm
> They gallop the great abode.
> They walk their horses when they should walk them
> And run them hard when they should run them.
> They get the god of rain to sprinkle their path
> And the god of wind to sweep away the dust.
> With lightning as their whip
> And thunder as their wheels,
> They ramble in the free and vaulting vastness above
> To emerge out of the gate of the boundless below.
> Having surveyed all around and illumined every cranny
> They return to guard what is within them to keep it whole.
> They manage the four corners of the world
> Yet always return to this pivot.[34]

The lives of these authentic persons are characterized by a coalescence with their environments in which the ever-present competing tensions are productive of a shared harmony. Unattached and unperturbed by the course that circumstances run, their activities are characterized by resonance and responsiveness, collaborating with the social and natural environments in mutual disclosure, and serving as a frictionless ground for the "self-so-ing" of the transformative processes. These genuine persons achieve a kind of immortality not by escaping change and ascending to some purer realm but by realizing themselves as integral to the concrete transformative processes of the here and now.

This Daoist cosmology has a fundamental commitment to optimizing the growth and transformation that attend all experience. A human being is not what one *is;* it is the compounding narrative of what one *does*—an always unique field of experiences, beliefs, and feelings—that contributes itself to the continuous patterns (*li* 理) that emerge and persist in the natural, social, and cultural flux and flow. These patterned regularities are not imposed upon the world by some external agency but rather presence within the world itself as the rhythm and cadence of a living stream, giving our experience coherence and making it sometimes more and sometimes less predictable. Such order is always reflexive, locating the agent within the activity itself. Agency and action, subject and object, person and context, far from being exclusive contraries, are interchangeable aspects of this single continuous category: one's experience (*daode*). And any particular human being is simply one impulse integral to this continually unfolding process.

These Daoist texts give us a situational rather than a causal cosmology, seeking to understand the whole range of relevant conditions and the relations that obtain among them as they come to sponsor any given occurrence. Instead of appealing to isolated causal agency, this "situationality" is captured in the notion of *shi* 勢, which, as an ongoing process that includes agency within it, means at once "situation," "configuration," "momentum," and "virtuosity." *Shi* includes all of the conditions that collaborate to produce a particular situation, including place, agency, and activity. Perceived regularities are always attended by change, making order dynamic, site specific, and provisional. Given that the patterned regularity is never decontextualized or detemporalized, the rhythm of life is indefatigable and irreversible, evident in the configuration of each snowflake, the striations of each piece of jade, the aura of each sunset, the complexity of each personality, as these always unique phenomena surface in the temporal flow only to recede into it again.

John Dewey, like his mentor, William James, provides us with language that captures the holographic and nondualistic nature of experience, in which the entire cosmos is implicated in every moment:

Thus an environment both extensive and enduring is immediately implicated in present behavior. Operatively speaking, the remote and the past are "in" behavior making it what it is. The action called "organic" is not just that of internal structures; it is an integration of organic-environmental connections.

ROGER T. AMES

It may be a mystery that there should be thinking but it is no mystery that if there is thinking it should contain in a "present" phase, affairs remote in space and in time, even to geologic ages, future eclipses and far away stellar systems. It is only a question of how far what is "in" its actual experience is extricated and becomes focal. . . . The thing essential to bear in mind is that living as an empirical affair is not something which goes on below the skin-surface of an organism: it is always an inclusive affair involving connection, interaction, of what is within the organic body and what lies outside in space and time, and with higher organisms far outside.[35]

THE HAPPY FISH DEBATE

Having argued for the importance of establishing an interpretive context in reading the classical texts and having sketched such a context for the Daoist canons specifically, I want to now turn to one popular anecdote that is recounted at the end of the "Autumn Floods (*qiushui* 秋水)" chapter of the *Zhuangzi*. On my reading, for Huizi at least, at one level this exchange is indeed a debate. But Zhuangzi by contrast takes a position familiar in Daoist cosmology and in the *Zhuangzi* itself: knowing is a "realizing" that is at once holistic and perspectival. In the event that is recounted in this passage, there is a shared virtuosity in which all of the elements of the experience interpenetrate to transform the bridge over the river Hao into the Grand Thoroughfare (*datong* 大通):

> 莊子與惠子遊於濠梁之上。莊子曰：「儵魚出遊從容，是魚樂也。」惠子曰：「子非魚，安知魚之樂？」莊子曰：「子非我，安知我不知魚之樂？」惠子曰：「我非子，固不知子矣；子固非魚也，子之不知魚之樂全矣。」莊子曰：「請循其本。子曰『汝安知魚樂』云者，既已知吾知之而問我，我知之濠上也。」

> Zhuangzi and Hui Shi in their carefree ramblings found themselves on the bridge over the river Hao.

> Zhuangzi observed, "The fish swim out and about and 'ramble' as carefree as they please—this is fish happiness."

> Huizi replied, "You're not a fish—how do you know fish happiness?"

> Zhuangzi returned, "You're not me—how do you know that I don't know fish happiness?"

> Huizi said, "I am not you and I certainly don't know what you know. But you are certainly not a fish. The argument that you do not know fish happiness is thus made QED."

Zhuangzi said, "Let's get back to your original question. When you said *'How (and whence)* do you know fish happiness?' you asked me because you already knew that I know fish happiness. I know it *here,* on the bridge, over the river Hao."[36]

Let's first consider a few textual points.

Perhaps an important key to understanding this anecdote, which is revealing of Zhuangzi's own position on what it means to know, is the curious use of the same character "ramble" (*you* 遊)—that is, "strolling, wandering at ease"—to describe the leisurely activity of both the philosophers *and* the fish. This character *you* is classified under the "walking" (*chuo* 辵) radical, indicating graphically that feet and ground are involved in this pleasant pastime, making it appropriate for Zhuangzi and Huizi but somewhat less so for the fish. In that the account introduces Zhuangzi and Huizi as *you*-ing together, it locates them in a shared experience.

That Zhuangzi would make his initial observation about the activity of the fish by appealing to this term is made particularly significant by the fact that the classical language has available to it (and the *Zhuangzi* frequently uses) an alternative cognate character that expresses the more appropriate version of "rambling," which is classified with the water radical and is specific to playing about in the water: "floating and swimming about" (*you* 游). It would seem that identifying the leisurely activity of the fish explicitly with that of the philosophers is an important enough factor in the story to deliberately elide this semantic distinction between "rambling" (*you* 遊) and "swimming about" (*you* 游). This claim is reinforced by the fact that when this passage is cited in the later encyclopedic texts—once in the *Yiwenleiju* 藝文類聚 and five times in the *Taipingyulan* 太平御覽—even though *you* 遊 appears in the *Yiwenleiju* and *you* 游 in all five of the *Taipingyulan* occurrences, in each instance the same character is used to describe the activity of both philosophers *and* fish.

As Hans-Georg Moeller has observed in his essay in this same volume, this term "rambling" (*you* 遊) occurs some ninety-five times in the *Zhuangzi*, with the "swimming about" (*you* 游) cognate term occurring an additional ten times. *You* occurring in both senses is clearly doing the work of a technical philosophical term that has important implications for the style of philosophy being advocated by the Daoists—what Moeller describes as a kind of a philosophical "musing"—that stands in rather stark contrast to the disciplined, theoretical analysis of the human experience that we usually associate with professional philosophy today.

One inference we might make from the fact that the same *you* is used for philosophers and fish is that the text is telling us that any assertion on the part of Zhuangzi about knowing the content of fish happiness would be limited to his ability to analogize either his and Huizi's own "rambling" (*you* 遊) on the bridge with what the fish are experiencing or perhaps to analogize the other way around in comparing their past experience as humans of "playing about in the water" (*you* 游) with what the fish are doing. At the very least, for Zhuangzi, the language itself used to express the event on the bridge is a basis for assuming that there is shared experience between the human beings themselves and with other sentient animals even as remote from us as fish. Zhuangzi, far from putting these two seemingly disparate things together, is registering the depth of their interrelatedness.

Another inference that could be made from the use of this *you* language might be that continuing the enjoyment first experienced both on and under the bridge over the river Hao is the ultimate purpose of this debate without any investment in who is actually to be declared the winner. Or said another way, while different commentators over the centuries—a representative cadre of them in this present volume—have expressed real rigor in their arguments about who wins the debate, the happy experience that continues to be a possibility for us latter-day philosophers who are still *you*-ing in this stimulating exchange between Zhuangzi and Huizi is both the meaning and the end of the debate itself. Indeed, scores of "happy fish bridges" (*leyuqiao* 樂魚橋) to be found in gardens in every corner of China and beyond are fair testimony to the rippling affect that this story continues to have on the *topos* of a living culture.

And focusing on the function of "place" in what it means to know more specifically, Angus Graham in interpreting this passage observes that Zhuangzi in picking up on the expression *anzhi* 安知 in the last lines of the exchange has an opportunity to show off his considerable debating skills:

> Chuang-tzu's [Zhuangzi's] own final stroke of wit is more than a mere trick with the idiom *An chih* [*anzhi*] "Whence do you know . . . ?," one of the standard ways of saying "How do you know . . . ?" What he is saying is: "Whatever you affirm is as relative to standpoint as how I see the fish while I stand up here on the bridge."[37]

The point is that the interrogative pronoun *an* in the expression *anzhi* is broad in meaning, asking not only how and from where do you know it but further who knows it and what is it that is known? And the passage does not at one time mean "*How* do you know . . . ?" and at another time "*Whence* (or *from where*) do you know . . . ?" but implies all of these meanings at the same time. Indeed in this debate, Zhuangzi presents the notion of "locus" or "place" or "situation"—in fact, the always particular and yet unbounded nature of experience—as being integral to how, what, and from where we know, and who we become by virtue of such knowing. In associating knowing with experience from a particular place, he distances his perspectivism from any possible claims about unconditioned, apodictic knowledge or exclusive, single, subjective knowers that might make such claims. And as Graham observes, Zhuangzi is not depending upon a linguistic ambiguity just to win a sophistical argument. Indeed, Zhuangzi has—dare we say—bigger philosophical fish to fry.

PROXIMATE CONTEXT AND KNOWING

One example of how the interpretive context of a text has changed the way in which we read the classical Chinese philosophical literature has been the recent recognition of the dialectical force that a specific kind of later Mohist realism had as the prevailing intellectual tide in the pre-Qin period, provoking a sharp response from both Daoist and Confucian rivals alike.[38] Huizi, in insisting that knowledge is the subjective entertainment of a world that can belong only to an independent, single knower, is arguing for the certainty of knowledge (Huizi can be certain that Zhuangzi does not know fish happiness), for the context-independent nature of knowledge (only Zhuangzi can know his own mind, and only fish can know fish happiness), and for the universalizability of such knowledge (all things, including philosophers and fish, have special privilege to the experience of their own minds).[39] The philosophical issues that Zhuangzi and Huizi are engaging at this level fit this dialectical framework as a debate over the Mohist claim for the possibility of certain, universal knowledge, which is unconditioned in the sense that it need not take account of context.

Zhuangzi's larger argument—the bigger fish to fry—is that, contra this narrow Mohist position on cognitive knowledge, knowing belongs to a world of shared experience, in which the knower and the known are both implicated. Knowing for Zhuangzi is collaborative and is always radically situated. Huizi on the bridge already knew that Zhuangzi knows happiness, just as Zhuangzi knows the fish are happy—with the fish and the bridge also being implicated in such knowing as it occurs—because being integral to this happy experience is itself what it means to know. The situated experience that is known has primacy—we might say "it" knows rather than "I" or "you" know.[40] And specific agency and the world as entertained are simply abstractions from this shared experience. Zhuangzi wants to challenge any notion of discrete agency as the site of knowing along with the possibility of the unconditioned nature of what is known— that is, any putative independence of the world known from those who know it. For Zhuangzi, knowing, rather than being a true idea in the mind of some isolated experiencer, is always proximate as the quality of a particular, situated experience.

Second, and corollary to this primacy of shared experience, for Zhuangzi, knowing is performative in the sense that it does and realizes something: knowing is the product of fruitful correlations among the various elements that collaborate in the experience. Thus, knowing is something *done*—an achievement that contributes to the quality of the experience not only for all of the sentient players in it but also for the venue of the experience itself. Just as the life of a cathedral achieves its spirituality, so, too, can a bridge find happiness. Knowing is an active tracing out and mapping of the patterns of the experiential environs (*li* 理) in such a manner that enables us to move about efficaciously and without obstruction within them— an activity that is captured in the expression in the vernacular language: "knowing by unraveling the patterns" (*lijie* 理解). Huizi, Zhuangzi, the fish, and the bridge are all complicit as collaborators in producing this welcome outcome, and their "knowing" of their situation is the "realizing" of it in the sense of "bringing it about" and "making it real." As Zhang Dongsun suggested earlier, one implication of such knowing—the growth of productive relations occurring on the bridge—would be that the epistemic and the ethical are continuous and that such "knowing" cannot be separated from the efficacious, practical wisdom of the friendship achieved in enjoying an afternoon of philosophical musing.

Knowing is thus also perlocutionary in the sense of setting the affective tone of the experience—in this case, the enjoyment that permeates this shared event above and below the river Hao. The knowers and the known, as well as the enjoyers and the enjoyment, are inseparable aspects of this same occasion. Agency cannot be isolated from action, and facticity cannot be separated from affect and modality. As Zhuangzi says elsewhere, "It is only when there are authentic persons (*zhenren* 真人) that there can be authentic knowing (*zhenzhi* 真知)."[41] Persons and their narrative postures and perspectives are thus integral to and constitutive of what is known and contribute immediately to the value and quality of the experience. Given this ubiquitous affective texture of experience, we might characterize this specifically Daoist "knowing" as more "knowing our free and easy rambling" (*zhiyou* 知遊) than "knowing our way" (*zhidao* 知道). *Where* we are, *what* we know, *how* we know it, and *who* we have become by virtue of knowing it are overlapping abstractions from the concreteness of the happy experience itself.

In summary, the point of this debate between Zhuangzi and Huizi in which Zhuangzi claims that he knows fish happiness *from here* on the bridge is that knowing is holistic—a focused event within an unbounded field of experience. Knowing is always proximate and situational (where and when), participatory, inclusive, transformative (who), and interpretive (how). The reflexivity of Zhuangzi means that he is not Zhuangzi exclusive of his relations—Huizi, fish, and bridge—but is rather Zhuangzi-in-context, where the relations that constitute Zhuangzi and his social and natural worlds are porous and fluid and intrinsic to the realization of the happy experience. It is the transactions of the narrative situation rather than some discrete agent that is properly described as happy, and this happy event is "realized" in their doing of it together.

Zhuangzi's experience with the fishes certainly reflects the resolute continuity between his world and the world of the fishes, and as such, his claim to knowledge is a claim to having been there. However, being continuous with the fishes and collaborating with them in the knowing experience does not deny the fishes their difference. The absence of a discrete and individuated self and the attachments that define it does not discount the importance given to the particular and to the uniqueness of their contribution. The happiness of the occasion would have been less so absent the ambiance of the darting about of the fish. In fact, it is only through Zhuangzi's deference to their difference—by allowing the fish to be what they are and do what they do—that the experience can be optimally fruitful and "enjoyable" for all concerned.

This is where Zhuangzi's analytic "sidekick," Hui Shi, comes in. His is a unique perspective that is illustrative of the importance of particularity in life's many collaborations. As we learn from Lisa Raphals, the portraits of the sometimes sophistical Hui Shi in the classical corpus are many and conflicted, and we do well to respect their disparities without overwriting them with an imposed uniformity.[42] Still, the Huizi remembered in the pages of the *Zhuangzi* is a relatively consistent figure. And there is no disputing the fact that Zhuangzi loved this man dearly and credited Huizi with providing those occasions on which Zhuangzi himself could rise philosophically to craft his very best ideas. The felt emptiness left by Huizi's passing is told with some poignancy after Zhuangzi's favorite interlocutor had left this life:

> Zhuangzi was in a burial procession when he passed by the tomb of Huizi. Turning around to address his followers, he said to them:
> "There was a man of Ying who, in finding a piece of mortar on the tip of his nose as delicate as a fly's wing, sent for Carpenter Rock to swipe it off with his blade. Carpenter Rock wielded his axe like the wind, and doing as he was asked, sliced the bit of mortar off cleanly without injury to the nose. And the whole time the man of Ying stood there without batting an eye."
> Lord Yuan of Song heard of this, and summoning Carpenter Rock to him, said, 'Try to do what you have done on me.'
> Carpenter Rock replied. 'As for me, I once was able to swipe the mortar off with my blade. But it has been some time now since my chopping block died.'
> Since Huizi died, I too have had no one as my chopping block—no one to really talk with!"[43]

Huizi, a philosopher of an analytical, positivistic bent—indeed, a logic chopper—appears in many anecdotes throughout the *Zhuangzi* as the rather straight and humorless target of Zhuangzi's many ripostes. In this particular reverie, Zhuangzi acknowledges that his own repartee—his ability to wield his wit like the wind—has been dependent upon his chopping block, Huizi, who could stand his impeccably logical ground without batting an eye. Death has made Huizi one of a kind because, in Huizi's absence, there is no one who can take his place. Zhuangzi cannot carry the conversation on alone, and the quality of his experience in the world is diminished with the demise of this cherished interlocutor. On this particular day although there was no *you*-ing and there were no fish, still Zhuangzi and his followers, too, were able to rekindle something of the happiness of that earlier shared experience not on the bridge, but *here,* in a funeral procession, by the tomb of Huizi.

NOTES

1. I. A. Richards, *Mencius on the Mind: Experiments in Multiple Definition* (London: Kegan Paul, Trench, Trubner, 1932), 86–87.

2. Although Richards does not specifically refer to metaphysical realism, this is the point that he seems to be making with his concern that our common sense is going to intrude on our reading of the *Mencius*.

3. Richards, *Mencius on the Mind*, 89, 91–92.

4. Peter Wong in his review of Richards' *Mencius on the Mind* in *China Review International* 5, no. 2 (1998), 340, suggests the magnitude of the challenge we face as we try to gain access to the worldview in which the text itself is located:

> Richards' mention of the looking glass may imply that he also has something else in mind—an allusion to Lewis Carroll's *Through the Looking-Glass: And What Alice Found There*. It appears that Richards is suggesting that . . . perhaps we could, like Alice, enter the world of the looking glass.

5. See Kwan Tze-wan's "Multi-Function Character Database" [西周晚期] CHANT: 4469 and 郭店簡老子甲 10).

6. Before 900; Middle English; Old English world, *weorold;* cognate with Dutch *wereld*, German Welt, Old Norse *verǫld*, all < Germanic *wer-ald—* literally, "age of man."

7. See Kwan Tze-wan's "Multi-Function Character Database" 殷墟文字甲編 CHANT: 2304.

8. See Kwan Tze-wan's "Multi-Function Character Database" [西周早期] CHANT: 2837. Reinforcing this understanding of *daode* is the fact that in several of the recently recovered archaeological texts, the character *de* 德 is written using an alternative graph, 悳, with a heartmind radical, *xin* 心, placed underneath the character *zhi* 直, which means "honestly, straight, true, upright, forthright" (figure 5). See Kwan Tze-wan's "Multi-Function Character Database" 郭店簡語叢三 CHANT: 54. There is clearly a cognate relationship between the two characters *de* 德 and *zhi* 直, and in the archaic language where the latter occasionally appears as a loan character for the former they are similar in pronunciation.

Fig. 5

9. D. C. Lau and Roger T. Ames, trans., Yuan Dao: *Tracing the Dao to Its Source* (New York: Ballantine, 1998), 123. 夫心者，五藏之主也，所以制使四支，流行血氣，馳騁於是非之境，而出入於百事之門戶者也。是故不得於心，而有經天下之氣，是猶無耳而欲調鐘鼓，無目而欲喜文章也。亦必不勝其任矣！

10. *Zhuangzi* 74/26/37. All references are to *Chuang Tzu* [*Zhuangzi*] (Peking: Harvard–Yenching Sinological Index Series, suppl. 20, 1947). 目徹為明，耳徹為聰，鼻徹為顫，口徹為甘，心徹為知，知徹為德。

11. A. N. Whitehead, *Modes of Thought* (New York: Macmillan Company, 1938), 55–63 develops this distinction between logical and aesthetic order.

12. This term, *tiyong* 體用, first appears in the Wang Bi commentary to *Laozi* 38.

13. Nathan Sivin, "Foreword" to Manfred Porkert, *The Theoretical Foundations of Chinese Medicine* (Cambridge: Massachusetts Institute of Technology Press, 1974), xi.

14. John Dewey, *The Essential Dewey*, Vol. 1, edited by Larry A. Hickman and Thomas M. Alexander (Bloomington: Indiana University Press, 1998), 41.

15. *Daodejing* 64: 是以聖人無為故無敗；無執故無失。

16. Chris Jochim, "Just Say No to 'No-Self' in *Zhuangzi*," in *Wandering at Ease in the Zhuangzi*, ed. Roger T. Ames (Albany: State University of New York Press, 1998), 34–75.

17. This notion of the extension of proximate knowledge is also found in the *Analects*. See 14/35: 子曰：... 下學而上達。 The Master said, "I study what is near at hand and aspire to what is lofty."

18. *Zhuangzi* 3/2/3; cf. A. C. Graham, trans., *Chuang-Tzu: The Inner Chapters* (London: Allen and Unwin, 1981), 48. All translations are my own; the A. C. Graham translation is for reference.

19. Tang Junyi, "Zhongguo zhexuezhong ziranyuzhouguan zhi tezhi" 中國哲學中自然宇宙觀之特質 (The Distinctive Features of Natural Cosmology in Chinese Philosophy), in *Zhongxi zhexue sixiang zhi bijiao lunwenji* 中西哲學思想之比較論文集 (Collected Essays on the Comparison between Chinese and Western Philosophical Thought) (Taipei: Xuesheng shuju, 1988), 16.

20. "This new day is too dear, with its hopes and invitations, to waste a moment on the yesterdays" (Ralph Waldo Emerson, *Collected Poems and Translations*).

21. *Great Commentary* A6.

22. William James, *A Pluralitic Universe* (Cambridge, Mass.: Harvard University Press, 1977) 282ff.

23. The passage in the *Analects* 14/34, echoing perhaps *Daodejing* 63, requires this understanding of the language to be intelligible: 或曰：以德報怨，何如？子曰：何以報德？以直報怨，以德報德。 Someone asked, "What do you think about the saying: 'Repay ill-will with beneficence.'" The Master replied, "Then how would one repay beneficence? Repay ill-will by remaining true. Repay beneficence with gratitude."

24. As it insists in the *Analects* 4/24: 德不孤，必有鄰。 "Excellent persons do not live alone; they are sure to have neighbors."

25. See Zhang Dongsun, *Zhishi yu wenhua: Zhang Dongsun wenhua lunzhu jiyao* 知識與文化： 張東蓀文化論著輯要, ed. Zhang Huinan (Beijing: Zhongguo Guangbo dianshi chubanshe, 1995), 172ff.

26. See An Yanming, "Liang Shuming and Henri Bergson on Intuition," in *Philosophy East and West* 47, no. 3 (1987): 337.

27. *Zhuangzi* 19/6/89; cf. Graham, *Inner Chapters*, 92. 顏回曰：「回益矣。」仲尼曰：「何謂也？」...曰：「回坐忘矣。」仲尼蹴然曰：「何謂坐忘?」顏回曰：「墮肢體，黜聰明，離形去知，同於大通，此謂坐忘。」仲尼曰：「同則無好也，化則無常也。而果其賢乎！丘也請從而後也。」

28. Zz 2 with commentary Zz23; compare Graham, *Inner Chapters,* 54 and 104, respectively. 古之人，其知有所至矣。惡乎至？有以為未始有物者，至矣盡矣，弗可以加矣。其次以為有物矣，而未始有封也。其次以為有封焉，而未始有是非也。

29. Peter D. Hershock, *Buddhism in the Public Sphere* (New York: Routledge, 2006), 140.

30. Ibid., 147.

31. *Daodejing* 79: 是以聖人執左契，而不責於人。有德司契，無德司徹。

32. *Zhuangzi* 7/3/2; cf. Graham, *Inner Chapters,* 63–64.

33. *Zhuangzi* 50/19/54; cf. Graham, *Inner Chapters,* 135.

34. Lau and Ames, *Tracing the Dao,* 69–70. 是故大丈夫恬然無思，澹然無慮，以天為蓋，以地為輿，四時為馬，陰陽為禦，乘雲陵霄，與造化者俱。縱志舒節，以馳大區。可以步而步，可以驟而驟。令雨師灑道，使風伯掃塵；電以為鞭策，雷以為車輪。上游於霄霓之野，下出於無垠之門，劉覽偏照，復行以全。經營四隅，還反於樞。

35. Dewey, *The Essential Dewy,* 146–147.

36. *Zhuangzi* 45/17/87; cf. Graham, *Inner Chapters,* 123.

37. Graham, *Inner Chapters,* 123.

38. See, for example, Chad Hansen, who claims the following:

> Later Mohists formulated a more "realistic" theory of what counts as the normatively correct way to use names. We should mark the distinctions that underlie names in ways that trace patterns of objective similarity and difference in things. This realism governs the correct ways both to use terms and to interpret them. ("Taoism," *Stanford Encyclopedia of Philosophy* (Winter 2012), ed. Edward N. Zalta, http://plato.stanford.edu/archives/win2012/entries/taoism/)

I have argued that the *Zhongyong* can best be interpreted as a Confucian argument against a possible Mohist reading of the relationship between *tian* and the human world. See "Reading of the *Zhongyong* 'Metaphysically,' " in *Conceptions of Reality in Chinese Metaphysics,* ed. Chenyang Li, Alan Chan, and Franklin Perkins (Cambridge: Cambridge University Press, forthcoming).

39. I would still argue—and I am not sure all would agree—that the external, objective standard of the Mohist as a publically determined and implemented objective norm, although certainly conservative and impositional, remains as one possible extreme within an assumed framework of a still correlative relationship between *tian* and the human world: that is, within "the continuity and inseparability of the human and the cosmic orders" (*tianrenheyi* 天人合一). As such, as a putatively objective standard it is of a quality of "objectivity" that is fundamentally different from that derived from the dualistic order that attends the conventional Abrahamic notion of the aseity (self-sufficiency) of an independent and transcendent God.

40. This definition of knowing as "shared experience" in the *Zhuangzi* has an analog in John Dewey, who says the following:

> Intelligence . . . is not ours originally or by production. "It thinks" is a truer psychological statement than "I think." Thoughts sprout and vegetate; ideas proliferate. They come from deep unconscious sources. "I think" is a statement about voluntary action. Some suggestion surges from the unknown. Our active body of habits appropriates it. The suggestion then becomes an assertion. . . . The stuff of belief and proposition is not originated by us. It comes to us from others, by education, tradition, and the suggestion of the environment. Our intelligence is bound up, as far as its materials are concerned, with the community life of which we are a part. We know what it communicates to us, and know according to the habits it forms in us. Science is an affair of civilization not of individual intellects.

See John Dewey, *The Philosophy of John Dewey,* ed. John J. McDermott (Chicago: University of Chicago Press, 1973), 713.

41. *Zhuangzi* 15/6/4; cf. Graham, *Inner Chapters,* 84. 且有真人，而後有真知。

42. Lisa Raphals, "On Hui Shi," in *Wandering at Ease,* 143–161.

43. *Zhuangzi* 66/24/48; Graham, *Inner Chapters,* 124. 莊子送葬，過惠子之墓，顧謂從者曰：「郢人堊慢其鼻端若蠅翼，使匠石斲之。匠石運斤成風，聽而斲之，盡堊而鼻不傷，郢人立不失容。宋元君聞之，召匠石曰：『嘗試為寡人為之。』匠石曰：『臣則嘗能斲之。雖然，臣之質死久矣。』自夫子之死也，吾無以為質矣，吾無與言之矣。」

Contributors

Roger T. AMES is professor of philosophy and editor of *Philosophy East and West*. His recent publications include translations of Chinese classics: *Sun-tzu: The Art of Warfare* (1993); *Sun Pin: The Art of Warfare* (1996) and *Tracing Dao to Its Source* (1997) (both with D. C. Lau); the *Analects of Confucius* (1998) and the *Chinese Classic of Family Reverence: A Philosophical Translation of the* Xiaojing (2009) (both with H. Rosemont); and *Focusing the Familiar: A Translation and Philosophical Interpretation of the* Zhongyong (2001) and *A Philosophical Translation of the* Daodejing: *Making This Life Significant* (2003) (both with D. L. Hall). He has also authored many interpretive studies of Chinese philosophy and culture: *Thinking Through Confucius* (1987), *Anticipating China: Thinking through the Narratives of Chinese and Western Culture* (1995), and *Thinking from the Han: Self, Truth, and Transcendence in Chinese and Western Culture* (1997) (all with D. L. Hall), and *Confucian Role Ethics: A Vocabulary* (2011). Almost all of his publications are now available in Chinese translation.

HAN Xiaoqiang received his BA from Beijing University, his MA from People's University of China and Memorial University of Newfoundland, and his PhD from Queen's University at Kingston. He previously taught at Queen's University, the University of Toronto, and St. Thomas University. He is currently teaching at Lakehead University. His interests are in metaphysics, epistemology, philosophy of language, Chinese philosophy, and comparative philosophy. Two of his recent publications are "A Butterfly Dream in a Brain in a Vat," *Philosophia* (2010) and "Feature-Placing Sentences and the Canonical Scheme," *Abstracta* (2009).

Chad HANSEN has lived in Hong Kong and worked for the University of Hong Kong for most of his professional life. Earlier he taught for twelve years at the University of Vermont and for seven years at the University of Pittsburgh. He has also had visiting professorships at international universities. His books include *Language and Logic in Ancient China, A Daoist Theory of Chinese Thought,* and *Laozi: Tao Te Ching on the Art of Harmony.* His main research has focused on the issues of philosophy of language as applied to and as found in Chinese philosophy. He studies Chinese semantic theory, logic, philosophy of mind, and metaethics and also explores the philosophy of language underpinnings of the thought of Mozi, the Later Mohists, and Zhuangzi-Laozi— the classical Daoists. He is presently honorary professor and chair professor of Chinese philosophy emeritus at the University of Hong Kong.

Hans Peter HOFFMANN studied Chinese studies and German literature at the University of Tübingen, Shifan daxue (Taipei) and Beijing University and pursues research on modern Chinese literature and classical Daoist philosophy, comparative literature, intercultural studies, and translation theory. He has published numerous monographs and translations of modern Chinese prose and poetry, some of the more recent of which are *Die Welt als Wendung: Zu einer literarischen Lektüre des* Wahren Buches vom Südlichen Blütenland (Zhuangzi) [The World as Turning Trope: Toward a Literary Reading of the *True Book of the Southern Land of Blooms* (Zhuangzi)] (2002); Shang Qin, *Traum oder Morgen: Texte des surrealistischen taiwanesischen Autors Shang Qin* [Dream or Morning: A Selection of Texts of the Taiwanese Writer Shang Qin] (2006); Chen Guidi, Wu Chuntao, *Zur Lage der chinesischen Bauern* [On the Situation of the Chinese Peasants] (translation) (2006); Liao Yiwu, *Fräulein Hallo und der Bauernkaiser* (translation) (2009); Liu Xiaobo, *Ich habe keine Feinde, ich kenne keinen Hass* (translation) (2011); Liao Yiwu, *Massaker: Frühe Gedichte* (2011); Yang Jisheng, *Grabstein: Die grosse chinesische Hungerkatastrophe 1958–1962* (translation) (2012).

KUWAKO Toshio (PhD 1994, University of Tokyo) is professor of philosophy at the Tokyo Institute of Technology. His publications include *Space and Body* (1998), *The Philosophy of Environment* (1999), *The Philosophy of Environment in Landscape* (2005), *The Historical Profile of Space* (2008), and *The Philosophy of Life and Landscape* (2013). He is now interested in philosophy and the practice of consensus building and project management within the parameters of the Japanese cultural tradition.

Hans-Georg MOELLER is senior lecturer in the Department of Philosophy at University College Cork in Ireland. His research focuses on Chinese and comparative philosophy and on the social theory of Niklas Luhmann. Among his book publications are *Daoism Explained: From the Dream of the Butterfly to the Fishnet Allegory* (2004), *The Philosophy of the Daodejing* (2006), *The Radical Luhmann* (2011), and a treatise in defense of amorality: *The Moral Fool: A Case for Amorality* (2009).

Eske Janus MØLLGAARD received his PhD in East Asian languages and civilizations from Harvard University. He is currently associate professor in the Department of Philosophy at the University of Rhode Island, where he teaches East Asian and contemporary European philosophy. He has published *An Introduction to Daoist Thought: Action, Language, and Ethics in Zhuangzi* (2007) and articles on Chinese and comparative philosophy. Among his recent articles are "Confucian Ritual and Modern Civility," *Journal of Global Ethics* (2012), "Confucianism as Anthropological Machine," *Asian Philosophy* (2010), and "Slavoj Žižek's Critique of Western Buddhism," *Contemporary Buddhism: An Interdisciplinary Journal* (2008).

Takahiro NAKAJIMA is associate professor of Chinese philosophy (Institute for Advanced Studies on Asia). His publications include *The Philosophy of Evil: Imaginations in Chinese Philosophy* (2012), *Practicing Philosophy between China and Japan* (2011), *Praxis of Co-Existence: State and Religion* (2011), *Deconstruction and Reconstruction: The Possibilities of Chinese Philosophy* (2010), *The Zhuangzi* (2009), *Philosophy in Humanities* (2009), *The Reverberation of Chinese Philosophy: Language and Politics* (2007), and *The Chinese Turn in Philosophy* (2007). He is now interested in the phenomenon of Confucian revival in China and Japan.

PENG Feng, who received his PhD from Peking University, is professor of aesthetics and art criticism at Peking University. He is also a playwright, freelance art critic, and curator of exhibitions at the international level. He has published eleven academic books, including *Pervasion: China Pavilion at the Fifty-Fourth International Art Exhibition of La Biennale di Venezia* (2012), *Introduction to Aesthetics* (2011), *The Return of Beauty: Eleven Issues of Contemporary Aesthetics* (2009), *The Western Aesthetics in China* (2006), *Perfect Nature: Intercultural Aesthetics of Environment* (2005), *Arts and Aesthetics in the West* (2005), *Principles of Aesthetics* (2004), and *Uplifting: An Aesthetic Interpretation of Traditional Chinese Religion, Ethics, Philosophy, and Arts* (2003); eight translations, including Nelson Goodman, *Languages of Art* (2013); Peter Kivy, ed., *Blackwell Guide to Aesthetics* (2010), and Richard Shusterman, *Pragmatist Aesthetics* (2000); and 150 papers in philosophy, aesthetics, art theory, and criticism.

Franklin PERKINS is professor of philosophy at DePaul University. His main interests are in intercultural philosophy, with particular interests in early modern European philosophy and classical Chinese philosophy. He is the author of *Leibniz and China: A Commerce of Light* (2004), *Leibniz: A Guide for the Perplexed* (2007), and *Heaven and Earth Are Not Humane: The Problem of Evil in Early Chinese Philosophy* (forthcoming). He is coeditor with Chung-ying Cheng of *Chinese Philosophy in Early Excavated Bamboo Texts* (*Journal of Chinese Philosophy* suppl. 2010).

SHAM Yat Shing received his PhD in Chinese literature from New Asia College of the Chinese University of Hong Kong in 1984 and is professor in the Department of Chinese Literature at National Central University in Taiwan. For more than thirty-five years he has been a frequent contributor to *Ehu Monthly Journal* on topics in Chinese philosophical literature, philosophical pedagogy, and contemporary Western philosophy, collaborating with distinguished scholars such as Ian Bunting.

Norman Y. TENG is research fellow at the Institute of European and American Studies, Academia Sinica, Taiwan. Teng is best known for his work in metaphor and has also made contributions to philosophy of mind, philosophy of cognitive science, and philosophy of language. Recently he began developing a version of Confucianism that (1) meets the joint demands of democracy and science, (2) prioritizes humanitarian governance and public discourse, (3) incorporates fundamental ideas of political liberalism, (4) pays careful attention to the asymmetrical power relation between a strong authoritarian regime and a small democracy, and (5) makes use of findings from cognitive science and metaphor research to develop a discourse methodology suitable for this project.

Hideki YUKAWA (1907–1981) was a Japanese theoretical physicist who won the 1949 Nobel Prize in physics for a theory he published in 1935. Yukawa was the first Japanese to receive a Nobel Prize. Yukawa taught at Kyoto Imperial University and at Osaka University, where he earned his doctorate in physics in 1938. In 1939 he became professor of physics at Kyoto Imperial University. In 1935, a few months after announcing his theory, Yukawa published his paper "On the Interaction of Elementary Particles." His paper contained a series of equations that predicted the existence of a new basic particle of subatomic matter, which became known as the meson. This work brought Yukawa to the attention of physicists internationally. The Royal Swedish Academy awarded Yukawa the Nobel Prize in physics in 1949 "for his prediction of the existence of mesons on the basis of theoretical work on nuclear forces." He served as director of the Research Institute for Fundamental Physics, now the Yukawa Institute for Fundamental Physics, at Kyoto University from 1953 to 1970. In 1955 Yukawa became one of eleven eminent scientists who put their names on a document that came to be called the Russell-Einstein manifesto. It was written by American scientist Albert Einstein and British philosopher and mathematician Bertrand Russell. The Russell-Einstein manifesto called upon the scientists of the world, no matter what their political persuasion, to meet and discuss the threat to civilization posed by nuclear weapons. Kyoto University established the Research Institute for Fundamental Physics, now the Yukawa Institute for Fundamental Physics, as mentioned before, to commemorate Yukawa's receipt of the Nobel Prize. Yukawa wrote *Introduction to Quantum Mechanics* (1946) and *Introduction to the Theory of Elementary Particles* (1948), both in Japanese. In 1946 he founded the journal *Progress of Theoretical Physics,* written in English, which he also edited. Besides his scientific writings, he also published his reflections on philosophy in *Creativity and Intuition: A Physicist Looks at East and West* (1973). He studied the works of Asian philosophers such as Taoist philosophers Laozi and Zhuangzi. Yukawa died in 1981 in Kyoto.

ZHANG Longxi holds an MA in English from Peking University and a PhD in comparative literature from Harvard University. He has taught at Peking, Harvard, and the University of California at Riverside and is currently chair professor of comparative literature and translation at the City University of Hong Kong. He is an elected foreign member of the Royal Swedish Academy of Letters and of Academia Europaea, and an advisory editor of *New Literary History.* He has published many books and articles in both English and Chinese, and his books in English include *The Tao and the Logos: Literary Hermeneutics, East and West* (1992); *Mighty Opposites: From Dichotomies to Differences in the Comparative Study of China* (1998); *Allegoresis: Reading Canonical Literature East and West* (2005); *Unexpected Affinities: Reading across Cultures* (2007); an edited volume, *The Concept of Humanity in an Age of Globalization* (2012), and *From Comparison to World Literature* (forthcoming 2015).

Index